Minor Railways
of France

by

W. J. K. DAVIES

PLATEWAY PRESS

ISBN 1 871980 45 3

ISBN 1 871980 45 3

PLATEWAY PRESS

Taverner House, Harling Road, East Harling, Norfolk NR16 2QR

Printed in England by POSTPRINT
Taverner House, Harling Road, East Harling, Norfolk NR16 2QR

FRONT COVER ILLUSTRATION:
The CFD Réseau du Vivarais was using steam traction on goods work well into the 1960s.
Here SLM Mallet 403 leaves St Jean de Muzols on the regular Tuesday morning goods to Tournon.
(Author)

BACK COVER ILLUSTRATION:
The End: In 2000, the Tramway du Mont Blanc still terminated abruptly in front of an uncompleted culvert
where work stoped in 1914; a stub of track on the grade emerging from a tunnel;
a ticket hut and a "temporary" restaurant.
(Author)

TITLE PAGE:
A train of the SE's Seine-et-Marne system with a cab-first Cail 0-6-2T.
(Author's Collection)

Dedication

To Jean Arrivetz, whose "Les Tramways Français"
first inspired me to write about France
(and who is certainly a godfather of the French preservation movement)

and to the memory of the late Maitre Henri Domengie
who faithfully chronicled the light railways of France
for over 50 years and to who we all owe much of our information

this book is respectfully dedicated.

Author's Notes and Acknowledgements

In the thirty-five-odd years since the writer first tried to picture the general history of French minor railways for English enthusiasts, much has happened. Then, apart from Jean Arrivetz' seminal work "Les Tramways Français", there was very little published information save for the journal of the, fairly new, Federation des Amis des Chemins de Fer Secondaires and for occasional notes and articles in La Vie du Rail or modelling journals such as Loco Revue. On the other hand there was still a substantial, though steadily declining, band of living railways to visit and study. Now there is a plethora of detailed studies (some contradictory as is the nature of these things) but only a very few railways are still running in public service. So how can one convey the essence of over three hundred lines and systems - some of them up to a dozen branches long - with all the combinations of motive power and scenery under the sun and without simply replicating what has gone before...and why do it in any case?

Strangely, there is still no real general history of French minor railways, either in French or English. This book tries to close that gap, concentrating mainly on the overall story, with what might be called historical gazetteers of the regional scenes but not going into detail: if it inspires readers to explore further, then Domengie and Banaudo's massive five volume study is probably the place to start since (even given the problems of thirty years' gestation) it honourably covers individual systems in more than outline. As to the technical side a general survey is all one can realistically provide here.

Even so, what does one include and what leave out? Technically speaking, both urban tramways and funicular railways have been classed as Railways of Intérêt Local....but....but. In the end I have compromised, listing the major tramway systems in the appropriate places and providing some basic information about funiculars in an appendix. As to industrial railways, they have their own chroniclers and are mentioned only if they provided a public service in addition to their real task. As to photographs, there is no possibility of anything like complete coverage in one medium-sized volume; illustrations have therefore had to be selected to show the variety of railways and their scenery rather than trying to illustrate every one.

Acknowledgements

My own acknowledgements must be first to Jean and Denise Arrivetz, friends from over thirty years back, to the late Jacques Pradayrol of APPEVA and to Jean Delmotte of Nangis. I am always indebted to the many fellow members of FACS who have answered queries and gave permission for use of photographs in particular M. Geiger and the late J. Chapuis. I am grateful, also, to all the companies and their personnel who have patiently answered queries over the years - to CFD, SE, BA, Corsica, Provence, Est de Lyon, Bouches du Rhône and others.... In England there are all the enthusiasts of long standing, in particular Graham Hoare, Lance King, John Morley, Fred Pugh, D. Trevor Rowe, John Snell, C. Walker...If anyone feels omitted I apologise.

As to published sources no one wishing to investigate the history of minor railways in France can ignore the massive contribution of the late Maitre Henri Domengie and his collaborators, in particular José Banaudo who so ably completed Domengie's regional history. For individual lines, the selective bibliography will show how munch information there now is for those who want to explore in depth.

Contents

PART 1

General History

PART 2

Gazetteer by Regions

PART 3

Technical History

PART 4

Regional Atlas of Minor Railways

PART 5

Appendices

MAPS AND DIAGRAMS IN THE TEXT

Part 3: Technical history

Chaper 13

Chapter 14

Chapter 15

Part 4: Regional Atlas of Minor Railways

Part 5: Appendices

Appendix 1

Appendix 2

Preview

Eighty years ago, if one had crossed the Channel and ventured onto French soil there would have been over 20,000km of local railways to explore if anyone had been interested....Even when I first wrote about French minor railways only thirty five years back, there must have been some 1200km or so still open to passengers and many more still in use for freight...but then, of course, thirty-five years ago, only a small band of British enthusiasts were interested in minor railways "abroad" and the diversity of those in France was still largely unknown despite Bryan Morgan's delightful book The End of the Line. The writer himself was brought up on the myth, as an ideal, of the "British Light Railway", that quaint standard gauge device worked by elderly wheezing steam locomotives and cast-off mainline stock, with its stations only vaguely in the neighbourhood of the places they purported to serve, and tentative suggestions that there might be something more interesting elsewhere tended just to bring the retort.."Can't see why, if you want scenery and efficiency you've still got the Festiniog/ Vale of Rheidol/ remains of the Lynton & Barnstaple....What more do you want?"

What with that and the only serious works of reference being Lartilleux' "Geographie des Chemins de Fer", and Jean Arrivetz' pioneering work "Les Tramways Français", it took almost too long for the realisation to dawn that British lines were largely untypical and that, "abroad", secondary railways of character had once netted the land, running actually through the villages on their station names, and that even diesel and electric railcars could have a charm of their own, especially when combined with scenery the like of which was not common in these islands. As always in such cases, the lines which one missed seem in retrospect so much more intriguing than the few that remain. When one thinks that, in the early 1950s, even just getting to Calais Ville would have opened the gate to several rambling and ccentric networks stretching across Pas de Calais and down into Somme.....

So what was there..? Many of my own most vivid memories are of railways that have not survived so let us start with a few small vignettes of what has gone. I remember particularly one baking-hot Whitsun on

A baking hot day on the Cambrésis – and the bright green Piguet 2-6-0T and its train doze in the sun at Denain (Cambrésis) with not a crew member in sight. (AUTHOR)

On the CFD du Tarn, an elderly Verney railbus, converted to parcels use, also dozes; at least we know where the crew are – in the nearby cafe/bar. (AUTHOR)

the Cambrésis and the thrill of what must have been even then the last metre-gauge steam train in regular daily passenger service in all France. We stood on the swaying balcony of the front coach and watched the Flaman recorder on the bucking Piguet 2-6-0T in front flicker up to and over the 45km/h mark. The dust was thick, the sun was hot and at each stop, as we all jumped down to record the event a sea of workmen's faces appeared at the windows and shouted remarks. "Cheering us on", remarked one member of the party hopefully; "More likely cursing us" opined another and probably he was right, for at one halt the whole train population, includng the crew, made a dive for the nearest bar. We had committed the heinous crime of shortening the - apparently quite regular – Sunday beer stop. The rest of the journey was much more convivial and even the rows of decaying stock in the decaying station at Caudry did little to lower one's liking for the line; and in any case a railway which has to take the last resort of asking passengers not to urinate on the coach balconies must have a character. Only just round the corner fron Denain (Cambrésis) was something so diferent it might have been in another world. The French Coal Board line from Somain to Peruwelz was standard gauge, very substantial and with, as it transpired, a fascinating history. Even then its long, frequent trains of immaculate green bogie coaches headed by an elegant 2-6-0 tender locomotive or a chunky 0-8-0T were far removed from the conventional idea of a minor railway and its smoky yards were crammed with fascinating oddities.... and around Valenciennes it paralleled an interurban tram with a gangling charm of its own - and international termini on the Belgian border.

Another day, another part of France. "Scenery and diesels. That's all there is on the Tarn and I wouldn't go to see a diesel for any scenery". That's what one friend said but he missed a great deal. The CFD du Tarn, 80km of rejuvenated metre gauge track climbing eastward from the sleepy old city of Castres down in the south-west, was a lovely line and its diesels - a fascinating collection bought from all over the place – an appropriate symbol for its energetic management. There was plenty of quiet charm too. The drivers acted as guards, conductors, ticket collectors, parcels agents, the lot, and their little Billards roared away at a very brisk speed, positively leaping round the curves, scudding over liaducts and diving through tunnels; if you sat in a front seat you really had to ride those cars...and by contrast old men played endless slow games of Boules in the yards at Brassac, and in the quiet tree-shaded station of Vabre one might encounter an elderly converted railbus loading parcels traffic – or rather waiting placidly to do so since the crew had gone off to watch the Olympics on television in the station bar.

Some of the standard gauge lines were quite impresive. A handsome 2-6-0 of the French Coal Board's standard gauge line from Somain on passenger duty. (AUTHOR)

Too often, though, one came too late: the stock of the Tramways de la Corrèze rots in its sidings at St Bonnet Avalouze. (AUTHOR)

Sometimes of course, you came just too late. I did to the Tramways de la Corrèze, to find the lifting so recently finished that the wrecking train was still as it had been left on the last day of work, the little Piguet tank engine coupled to a selection of flat wagons, water in its tanks, coal piled in the bunker and a flat plate atop the chimney to stop water dripping in, just as though it was going to be used again. The tramway sidings were full of neat four-wheeled wagons and rusty, disused coaches. Some of them had been there a long time too, for bushes were growing out of the control desks in the ancient brown-and-white railcars and glassless windows gaped along their sides. I felt much the same on the Somme when, commenting on the sad line of derelict steam locomotives, I was told casually "Oh yes, we sent the last four serviceable ones away for scrap last month..." or in the overgrown yards of Coucy le Château where the 60cm gauge relics of a recently-closed sugar-beet line were rusting gently in the rain.

Yet there are still wonderful things to be seen, even if mainly with diesel or electric traction; the sweeping vistas of Corsica, the deep gorges of the Alpes and the Pyrenées with their tunnels and viaducts are still accessible publicly by the narrow gauge, while several portions of former lines in gentler country have been preserved in a fair approximation of their original state. And of course, the joy for the true enthusiast is that, all across the land, you can still stumble over lasting remains, for many of the old départemental companies built so substantially that their buildings have survived as private houses, cafés or industrial sites. They are easily recognisable on the whole, for standard patterns existed on many lines and only the building material varied. At most stations of importance a tall, two-storey station house, often stuccoed, dominated the scene and attached to it was a matching goods shed with characteristic loading bank, while a smooth ornamental plaque on each wall bore the name - painted, enamelled or incised - and these plaques alone are enough to give away the former purpose of many a private house today. Smaller lines and stations made do with a similar one-storey building and these often survive as sheds or shacks in the midst of a field. It is one of the minor pleasures when travelling through France to 'spot the station' and one comes upon them in the most unexpected places. Once, climbing in a car the steep Col de l'Escrinet in the Cevennes we ground through a cutting, rounded a corner and there, perched incredibly on the edge of the hill was the crumbling embankment and small stone hut that marked the path of the former Tramways de l'Ardèche. In the tree-shaded squares of towns like Vernoux or Gourin you can still see the old stations of local companies lost in wastes of asphalt; and university students now eat their meals under the monumental former train shed at St. Brieuc.

Whether much of that romance will survive the prosaic details of a general history is uncertain and this is a general history which will hopefully fill a gap. More and more British enthusiasts are travelling the lines that remain, helped by package tours which were not available in the early days, and the ever increasing bands of French enthusiasts are digging deeper and deeper into local archives to chronical individual systems but, oddly there is no overall picture in either French or English. To take an analogy, plenty of individual trees in the French light railway forest have been catalogued in detail and the monumental five volume work of Henri Domengie and José Banaudo has given us a pretty good idea of the content at, shall we say, coppice level but no one since Arrivetz has described the wood as a whole. If this book helps to fill that gap I hope it will prove worthwhile.

W J K Davies
Wheathampstead, 2000

PART 1
A General History
French minor railways from birth to the present

CHAPTER 1
Inception and Early Development 1860-1900

The beginnings of secondary railways in France: early narrow gauge experiments: Mondalazac; Trebiau; Rochebelle

The early history of minor railways in France to some extent parallels that of British ones in that the first true secondary, or "feeder" railways other than branches of the main line companies were basically industrial lines, and on rather odd gauges. The most notable one was probably a subsidiary of the main-line Chemin de Fer de Paris à Orléans (PO), being a mineral line from a junction at Salles-la-Source in the Aveyron département to their mines at Mondalazac some 7km away. It was constructed in 1861 on the gauge of 1.10 metres and was steam-worked from 1864 until its closure in the early 1880s. This was not the only narrow gauge industrial line to be built during the 1860s – there were steam-worked mines railways of 80cm (nominal) gauge in the Gard département from 1866-on at Trebiau and by 1872 at Rochebelle – but just as Vignes had to come to Britain when considering the very narrow gauges, so French proponents of the narrow gauge had to look elsewhere, to Greece, Algeria, Sardinia, for all but the shortest lines. In France, the Modalazac one was that most often cited probably because it was promoted by a main line company.

Its importance for us lies in the fact that it was the subject of comparisons with a number of light standard gauge branch lines which had been built around Strasbourg by the equally big CF de l'Est (the French had no more imagination than the British when it came to naming their main line companies). As usual with gauge controversies, "conclusive" points were scored by both sides. The standard gauge supporters instanced the difficulties of lack of power on steep gradients and the problems of transhipment; the

EUGENIE-les-BAINS (Landes). — La Gare.

L. phot. (Déposé). - Delhoste éditeur

In the beginning there was always the construction train – here on the Twys à Vapeur de la Chalosse et du Béarn, down in the south-west. (FACS)

1

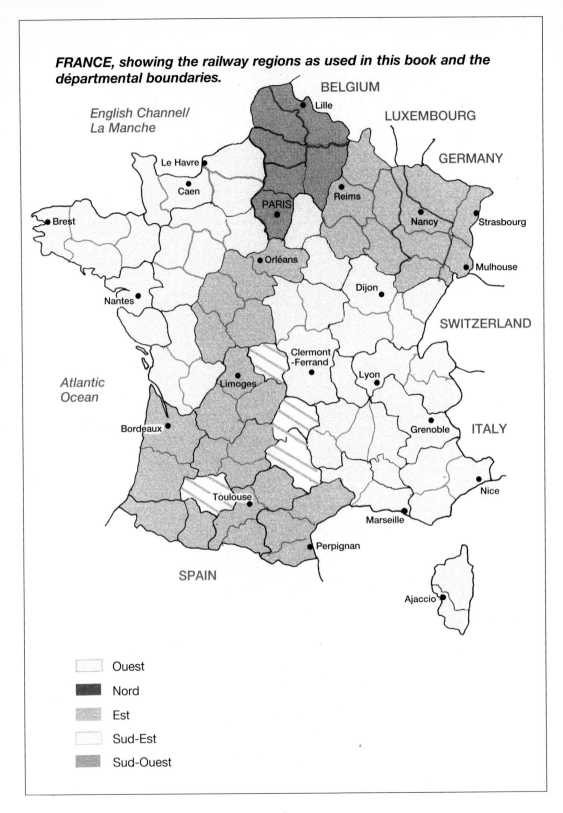

FRANCE, showing the railway regions as used in this book and the départmental boundaries.

BELGIUM

LUXEMBOURG

English Channel/
La Manche

GERMANY

Lille

Le Havre

Caen

PARIS

Reims

Nancy

Strasbourg

Brest

Mulhouse

Orléans

Dijon

Nantes

SWITZERLAND

Clermont
-Ferrand

Atlantic
Ocean

Limoges

Lyon

Bordeaux

Grenoble

ITALY

Toulouse

Nice

Marseille

Perpignan

SPAIN

Ajaccio

Ouest

Nord

Est

Sud-Est

Sud-Ouest

proponents of the narrow gauge retorted that to construct a standard gauge line in such an isolated spot, with the larger infrastructure and heavier track that would have been needed, would have cost far too much. Point, set and match to both sides at once! It is, however, noteworthy that an 1865 project for passenger traffic on the Mondalazac line allowed for an increase in gauge – to 1.20 metres of all things – to allow of increased power, and the first national law authorising secondary railways envisaged their construction on the standard gauge only.

The Loi Migneret and its provisions; classifications of Intérêt Général and Intérêt Local; the concessionary principle.

This was the Loi Migneret of 12 July 1865 which for the first time established the definitions of Intérêt Général and Intérêt Local which were to govern future light railway construction. The essential difference between them was that lines of Intérêt Général were considered sufficiently extensive or important to be a charge upon the state which, therefore, granted concessions and provided financial help where necessary; they included not only lines with heavy traffic but those where strategic military considerations were paramount especially after the disastrous Franco-Prussian war of 1870. Lines of Intérêt Local were to be entirely the responsibility of individual départements (roughly the equivalents of English counties), which were authorised to construct and work branch railway lines either by their own labours or by granting concessions to private companies; the state might provide a portion of the cost but not a great proportion. Most urban or suburban tramways systems also came under this heading as did various privately promoted industrial railways which decided to add some element of public service.

It should perhaps be explained at this point that a concession, in legal railway terminology, is simply an agreement between two parties whereby one undertakes the construction and/or management of a railway on behalf of the other, usually for a fixed period of time. So far as French light railways were concerned there were two basic types: concessionaire, where the concessionary company took on all or part of the financial risk; and fermière where it simply worked the line on behalf of the département or other authority for an agreed recompense, the process of granting such management concessions being termed affermage. Construction was in any case regulated by the elaborate preliminaries analagous to those which beset British minor companies before the 1896 Light Railways Act. For French entrepreneurs these included first a decision as to whether the State should be the conceding authority, using national funding in which case it was Intérêt Général, or the départements using mainly local money; then a careful examination by civil servants of any proposals leading, if successful, to a declaration that the line was "of public utility"; and the drawing up and approval by both local and national administrators of a detailed Cahier des Charges containing and defining all technical data and service requirements of the project in minute detail.

Early developments; the Bas-Rhin experiments; the first narrow gauge public carriers.

The Loi Migneret suffered to some extent from its antecedents. M Migneret was a professional politician, successively prefect (effectively civil governor) of the Sarthe, Haute-Vienne, Haute-Garonne and Bas-Rhin départements; it was for the latter that he wished to provide a network of rural communications and he hit on the plan of using money allocated by a law of 1836 for the construction of local roadways (chemins vicinaux). These roads might be constructed henceforward in such a way that they could be easily converted to light branch railways and, in Bas-Rhin indeed, this was actually carried out to some extent. The politics were fierce, the CF de l'Est ending up as operator rather than local companies, as noted above, and the programme was not fully implemented but lines were built in 1864 from Strasbourg to Wasselonne and Barr; from Schlesstadt to Ste.Marie-aux-Mines and from Haguenau to Niederbronn. The results of all the deliberations and experiments were encapsulated in the 1865 law.

The Loi Migneret did not really succeed in its aims partly because a further measure, in 1871, allowed neighbouring départements to combine in interdépartemental ventures – which in turn encouraged entrepreneurs in the belief that they might be able to develop major empires. Hence some effort was diverted into large standard gauge systems, particularly in Charentes and Vendée, which tried to compete with the main line companies. A number of smaller standard gauge lines was built, including such well

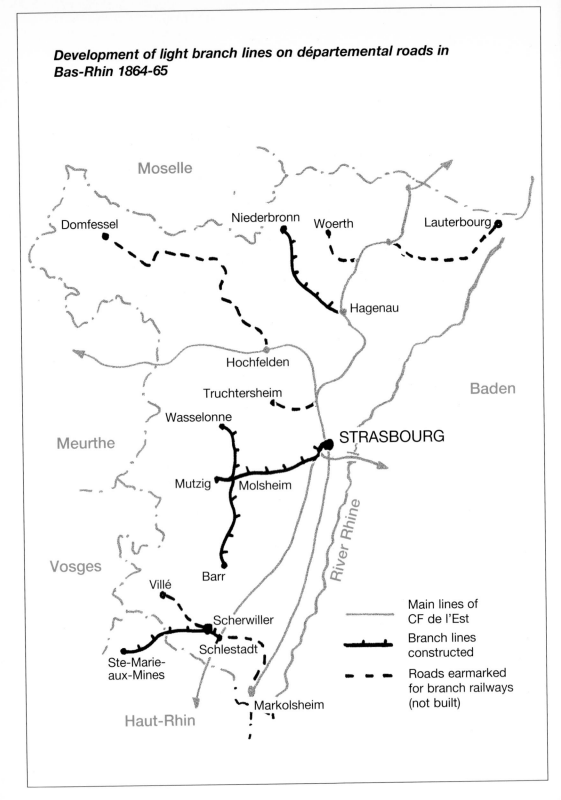

Development of light branch lines on départemental roads in Bas-Rhin 1864-65

Moselle

Domfessel

Niederbronn   Woerth   Lauterbourg

Hagenau

Baden

Hochfelden

Truchtersheim

Wasselonne

Meurthe

STRASBOURG

Mutzig   Molsheim

River Rhine

Vosges

Barr

Villé

Scherwiller

Schlestadt

Ste-Marie-
aux-Mines

Markolsheim

Haut-Rhin

—————— Main lines of
         CF de l'Est

———•——— Branch lines
         constructed

– – – – Roads earmarked
         for branch railways
         (not built)

4

known ones as the Chemins de Fer de Mamers à St Calais, de St Quentin-Guise, de Caen à la Mer, de Vertaizon à Billom (Puy-de-Dôme) together with the first parts of big systems in Gironde and Hérault; alas, the financial and technical problems of building standard gauge lines, which in any case would often have been too large for the traffic offered, prevented much expansion and by the end of 1880 only 2,189km of lines had been built. The narrow gauge was not favoured initially and the few early narrow gauge lines that did come into existence were mainly initiated as mineral railways and then upgraded. This was the case, for instance, on the very early line from Lagny to Mortcerf, in Seine-et-Marne, which started in 1865 as a mineral railway from Lagny to Villeneuve le Comte and acquired a passenger service in 1872 when its usefulness was recognised. Even so it was not financially successful and its example may have discouraged others, particularly since politics led to major complications with who conceded it to whom (and who was to pay for it). Originally built under purely local agreements, the proposed extension to Mortcerf brought it to the notice of the State which then declared it to be of Intérêt Général and, when the operating company failed, took it over en régie (under administration). It remained of Intérêt Général until it proved financially embarrassing, when it was mysteriously discovered that it should have been Intérêt Local all the time....

The Plan Freyciney and the 1880 Law; tramways as a category; authorised gauges and their results; financing arrangements

By the late 1870s, however, the need for improved rural communications in the wide countryside of France was becoming urgent and, having regard to the slow rate of construction under the Loi Migneret, another Act was passed on 11 June 1880. This embodied the so-called Plan Freyciney of 1878-79 which had tried to draw up a logical network of railways, both Intérêt Général and Intérêt Local, and was specifically intended to hasten development of secondary railways. In addition to railways of Intérêt Local on their own rights of way, the Act envisaged a third category (also legally of Intérêt Local) identified as tramways, or

PRÉFAILLES (Loire-Inf.) — Arrivée du Train

When the first train reached its goal, there was always a crowd to greet it, all in their sunday best – This is just titled "arrival of a train" but there must have been something special happening down at Préfailles on the CF du Morbihan.

(AUTHOR'S COLLECTION)

CHARTRES. — Arrivée du Tramway.

Even when things had settled down there was always a certain social atmosphere when the tramway came to town
– as here at Chartres on the Tramways de Eure-et-Loir.   (FACS)

more specifically, tramways pour voyageurs et marchandises (as opposed to tramways urbains et suburbains
which were for passengers and light luggage only). The main difference between the third category and
railways of Intérêt Local was that, to save infrastructure costs, the lines were to run mainly along the verges
of roads already owned by the départements, thus simplifying routeing and land purchase; a proportion of
over 70% of roadside running classified a line as a tramway. The advantages were that infrastructure and
legal costs were much reduced and that lighter track and equipment could be used; the corresponding
disadvantage, which became more important as road transport developed, was that routes were often
circuitous and not designed for speed. In addition the loading gauge, in particular width, was necessarily
restricted – usually to a maximum of 2100mm or even 2 metres, whereas lines on their own right of way
often had widths of up to 2400mm.

The Law also provided for standard cahiers des charges for standard and narrow gauge lines to speed up
the legislative processes. Three gauges were initially authorised, being standard (1435mm); metre; and
750mm, the use of narrow gauge being encouraged especially for roadside lines where space was at a
premium and sharp curves were likely to occur. Indeed the normal specification in the Cahier for such lines
limited dimensions so drastically that standard gauge would have been of little advantage; overall width
rarely exceeded 2.200 metres for example, as noted above, and many lines were initially controlled by a
formula known as the 'three 15s' – 15-tonne locomotives running at 15 km/h on rail weighing only 15kg
per metre.

In the event only one line, the CF Economiques Forestiers des Landes, from Roquefort to Lencouacq-
Jourets in the south west, was built to the 750mm gauge although the Calvados département was seriously
considering it when, in 1888, a ministerial decree forbade the construction of any more 750mm gauge lines,
on the grounds that standardisation was necessary for military purposes. The place of the 750mm gauge was
only partly taken by the 60cm gauge following the success of a demonstration line, promoted by the firm
of Decauville Aîné, at the 1889 Paris Exhibition. This gauge was then perceived also to have military

applications and, after experiments and applications by Decauville between 1889 and 1891, was authorised for those concerns which wished a narrower track than metre. Details of the results will be found below.

Perhaps the most important part of the Act, however, was that concerning the financing of light railways. In order to attract private capital for the construction of lines which might prove unrenumerative, a scheme was worked out whereby the concessionaire provided the capital, built and equipped the line(s) for a fixed price and then operated the lines, the state and the département(s) concerned guaranteeing a fixed rate of interest on the capital involved, together with a fixed sum per annum and a proportion of the gross receipts, made up to an agreed minimum if receipts fell below a certain level. The basic arrangement was widely adopted in Europe but here the sting was in the tail - the sliding subsidy. Since the operating company was guaranteed both interest on its capital and a minimum receipt it had no real interest in developing the traffic; indeed such development was undesireable since it only increased working expenses. To make matters worse, the initial estimates of cost and earnings had to be based on what experience there was of secondary railways and, since the existing ones were almost all of standard gauge, these estimates were often unduly high where narrow gauge lines were concerned; even worse still, the State carefully limited its share to a very small proportion of the whole so that most of the extra money had to be found by the départements.

Results of the 1880 Act; entrpreneurs and their financial groupings

Unfortunately, although it certainly stimulated the building of light railways in districts which would not otherwise have possessed them, this scheme, as might have been expected, proved financially embarrassing for the local authorities. The outcry from ratepayers was so great that within ten years the scheme had to be dropped but not before a number of enterprising concerns had obtained long-term and fairly lucrative concessions. They included some small, and no doubt genuine, companies such as the CF du Cambrésis but also provided the genesis of the two largest private empires, those of the Societé Générale des Chemins de Fer Economiques (SE) and the Compagnie des Chemins de Fer Départementaux (CFD). They also gave initial opportunities to a number of, perhaps less known but still very substantial, entrepreneurs who, on the strength of their first efforts, subsequently built up consderable collections of railways, either locally based or widely scattered. They included amongst others the following major groupings:

- *Baert-et-Verney*, at some time controlling such systems as the Ardennes, VFE du Poitou; Tramways de la Vienne and a whole cluster of concerns in the north west where they began. They also later had an interest in the SCF Verney equipment firm, specialising in railcar production. M.Baert was originally in partnership with a M.Beldant but, after linking with M.Verney, the groupe was usually referred to as Verney.

- *Carel et Fouché*, who were also rolling stock manufacturers and later built many railbus bodies for De Dion Bouton. Based in the west, their empire was wholly regional, comprising at some time the main systems in Ille-et-Vilaine, Loir-et-Cher, Orne and Sarthe.

- *Empain*, under the control of the Baron Empain, which also had considerable assets in the developing Belgian market, both in operating companies and in stock manufacturing. Its substantial holdings eventually covered much of the eastern edge of France, plus the ex-Decauville concession in Calvados and several others down in the south west; the Cie des Chemins de Fer Economiques du Nord de la France (CEN) was their main, but by no means their only, vehicle.

- *Jeancard*: most well-known for its operation of the CF Economiques des Charentes - a particularly glaring case of non-viable concession - this group also at times ran systems in Ain, Morbihan, and various départements in the South-West.

- *Jourdain*: Another purely regional group, this was really two family concerns run by father and son, had both standard and metre gauge holdings in the north of France and was instrumental, later on, in forming the Cie des Chemins de Fer Secondaires du Nord-Est (NE) which was prominent in the 1920s and 1930s.

- *Laborie:* M Laborie was, first and foremost an entrepreneur with an enthusiasm for light railways; "his" systems included spells in control of such systems as the CF du Doubs (on which he experimented with light, fast rubber-tyred railbuses); the CF de Normandie; and the Cormeilles à Glos Montfort system in Eure.

- *Ortal:* The Entreprises Ortal, basically contractors, stayed down in the south west, with a selection of standard and narrow gauge, mainly isolated lines, of which they maintained one, the standard gauge line from la Testé to Cazaux, until quite recently.

- *Tartary:* M. Tartary was another ingenious entrepreneur with départemental tramway systems scattered across the middle of France which he later blessed with a series of early railbuses of his own devising. His base was the Tramways des Deux Sevres, whose Parthenay works fabricated the railbuses.

There were also several other groups initially of lesser importance, among them the loosely associated collections of lines in the north east ammassed (nominally individually) by Messrs, Dequeker, Lambert and Level who came together after the 1914-18 war as a consolidated whole, forming the Cie Générale des Voies Ferrées d'Intérêt Local (CGL, or VFIL). The involvement of the railway construction firm of Decauville Aîné is well known but it is not such common knowledge that several other material manufacturers got into the act at one time or another – Cail, Fives-Lille and Batignolles from France; the Société Suisse (otherwise Schweizer Lokomotiv und Maschinenenfabrik – SLM) and, in Alsace Lorraine, the German firm of Krauss all tried their hands – usually unsuccessfully – at building and operating secondary railways. Independently, again, several lesser known figures took a considerable part: François Mercier, for instance, was a prominent figure among railway builders although he appears largely to have steered clear of operation; Messrs Giros and Loucheur had specialised interests in many of the bigger electrified light railways, forming what became the Voies Ferrées Départementales du Midi (VFDM) with the backing of the main line Midi company. In addition, many of the entrepreneurs cited above had financial interests in apparently independent concerns and were often involved, separately or in combination, in the formation

And people seem happy to have been photographed en-route – on the CFIL du Sud-Ouest near Toulouse; "types meridionales" indeed!
(FACS)

11 – La Ferté-sous-Jouarre (S.-et-M.) - La Gare

B. F., PARIS

The early lines of Intérêt Local might come in one in one of two formats: common was a train with a conventional 0-6-0T or 0-6-2T, as seen here on the CFD's Montmirail branch in Seine-et-Marne.   (FACS)

of such organisations as the Cie Française des Voies Ferrées Economiques (CFVE), the Compangnie Générale des Chemins de Fer et Tramways (CCFT), or the Compagnie Générale des Transports Départementaux (SGTD) which, if they had been really successful, might have rivalled the CFD and SE. In practice most of them diversified into urban tramways or, later, into road transport operation. Perhaps some French historian will chart their convoluted histories.

Light railway nomenclature and its confusions

Since the system names adopted by entrepreneurs in many cases paralleled those of the SE and CFD, it may be advisable at this point to sort out another problem of nomenclature. Besides the classifications of Intérêt Général and Intérêt Local, lines specifically of Intérêt Local were often loosely termed chemins de fer départementaux (because they were) or chemins de fer économiques - the latter being the only term really translating as 'light railways' in the true sense of the term. It was, therefore, desirable to distinguish the two big private concerns which had, so to speak, trademarked the names. They were normally, therefore, referred to as 'CFD (SE) Réseau de...' while an independent company would style itself CFD du.. or CF Economiques de.. or CF d'Intérêt Local de.. followed in each case by the name of the département or area concerned. If classified as such, many systems styled themselves Tramways (à vapeur, or électriques) de.., thus allowing some confusion between rural roadside lines and town trams (Tramways urbains ou suburbains). In either case a number of urban tramway companies also had long, semi-rural branches which had many of the features of light railways and might even haul goods on occasion. An additional, though not obvious complication was the French habit of having a single, central holding company which formed a series of (usually) locally-based operating companies to run the concessions obtained by the Group (for example, the Cie Centrale des Chemins de Fer et Tramways (CCFT) formed the Cie des Chemins de Fer des Côtes du Nord specifically to run that concession). Since many lines of all types had more than one concessionaire during their lives, confusion was never far away.

9

Intérêt Général classification: reasons and results

The confusion was, to some extent at least, exacerbated by the use of the Intérêt Général classification for some important – and usually interdépartemental – secondary railways. Some, such as the CFD's Réseaux du Vivarais and Corsica were funded by the state because they were perceived as having more than local value and because the costs involved would have been beyond the capacities of individual départements. Others were classified as IG because they were, rather vaguely, considered to have a strategic value in time of war. Being classified as Intérêt Général for the latter reason had two main consequences: the concession was expected to be taken up by a main line railway company which operated neighbouring routes; and there was a vague intention for them to be built on the standard gauge for obvious reasons of connectivity (for example where a system such as the le Blanc - Argent (p.11) linked across a number of east-west transversals). The trouble was that most of these lines were unlikely to be very profitable and the main line companies were not enthusiastic about taking up the concessions on offer. A very few – notably the Réseau des Alpes of the big Sud-France company and some lines in the North East where invasion might be a reality – were built to standard gauge or, in the case of the Sud-France, had mixed gauge installed initially over a substantial part of their route. The Sud-France even had fortified tunnels and blockhouses, together with a standing plan for mobilisation of the complete railway in the event of possible war. Most, however, were not going to be built at all until the authorities, reluctantly, allowed development on the metre gauge with the proviso that major infrastucture features had to allow for conversion to standard gauge if necessary. That grudging permission having been given, the PO and the Etat in particular did accept concessions, build and equip various systems, notably the Réseau Breton, le Blanc - Argent, and PO lignes de Corrèze. All, however, hastily sub-let operation to private concerns such as the SE, although they were always careful to put their own markings on locomotives and stock – interestingly, many locomotives carried their Etat/PO plates right up to closure, alongside the SNCF and operator logos.

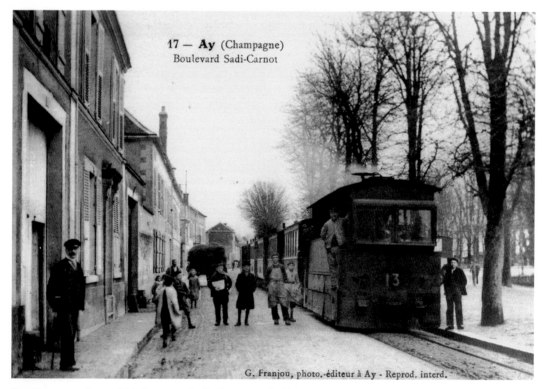

17 — **Ay** (Champagne)
Boulevard Sadi-Carnot

G. Franjou, photo.-éditeur à Ay - Reprod. interd.

Equally common for roadside lines was the "train-tramway" with its enclosed bicabine and (at least at first) protective skirts. No. 13 of the CF de la Banlieue de Reims poses at the tiny halt in Ay. (FACS)

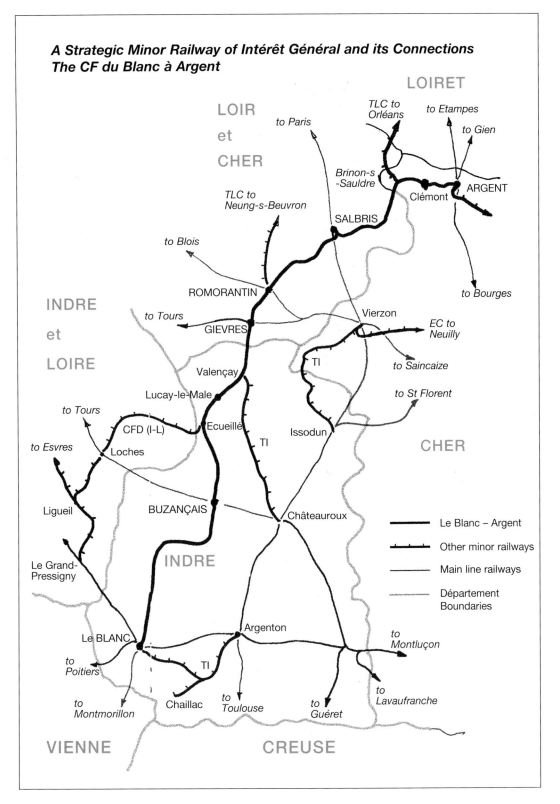

A Strategic Minor Railway of Intérêt Général and its Connections
The CF du Blanc à Argent

LOIRET

LOIR et CHER

INDRE et LOIRE

CHER

INDRE

VIENNE

CREUSE

TLC to Orléans
to Etampes
to Gien
to Paris
Brinon-s -Sauldre
ARGENT
Clémont
TLC to Neung-s-Beuvron
SALBRIS
to Blois
to Bourges
ROMORANTIN
to Tours
Vierzon
GIEVRES
EC to Neuilly
TI
Valençay
to Saincaize
Lucay-le-Male
to St Florent
Ecueillé
CFD (I-L)
Issodun
TI
to Tours
Loches
to Esvres
Ligueil
BUZANÇAIS
Châteauroux
Le Grand-Pressigny
Argenton
to Montluçon
Le BLANC
to Poitiers
TI
to Lavaufranche
to Montmorillon
Chaillac
to Toulouse
to Guéret

Le Blanc – Argent
Other minor railways
Main line railways
Département Boundaries

Of course the systems of Intérêt Général were often more imposing and powerful. Here one of the original 0-4-4-0T Mallets of the Réseau Breton prepares to take a long mixed train out of Carhaix.
(FACS/CHAPUIS COLLECTION)

Replacement schemes of development and their effects; the gauge problem again.

For Intérêt Local systems, two alternative schemes eventually took the place of the unsuccessful one established by the 1880 law. In one, the département built and equipped its lines itself, leasing them out to an operating company. This, it may be said, is the explanation of various references in manufacturers' records where locomotive and stock are recorded as having been sold to companies which apparently never existed. For example, several locomotives were sold to the 'CF de la Loire Inférieure' which was the département's purchasing authority, but were then leased to, and run under the name of, the Cie Française des Chemins de Fer à Voie Etroite; as another example, the Aisne département bought both its standard and narrow gauge locomotives and placarded them conspicuously with AISNE No XX, whatever concessionary company they were allocated to.

The other scheme differed in that the département subsidized an independent company to build and run the lines it required on terns that encouraged economical working and efficient development. These concessions, in contrast to earlier ones, were usually short-term, of fifteen to twenty-five years, thus enabling reconsideration of the lines' futures at regular intervals. This was a protection for the département in the case of an inefficient concessionaire since it could repurchase or repossess the line and either lease it to another company or run it itself. The former solution was adopted in the majority of such cases, the alternative of direct operation being unpopular, for obvious reasons. Nevertheless, in later years, it was forced on many départements leading, as we shall see, to the formation of Régies Départementales or compagnies fermières set up by a département to operate its own internal transport services.

In the end these schemes of finance seem to have been almost as hard on the départements as was the original one, since they still had to subsidize losses which, especially after the 1914-18 war, increased alarmingly; yet in the short term they enabled even poor districts to obtain large grants or loans of public money for the establishment of local railways and a surge of building resulted, mainly on the narrow gauge.

And the 60cm gauge...ah... A Mallet-hauled train on the CF du Calvados pauses in the street of Lion-s-Mer to pick up passengers – who are clearly in too much of a hurry for the photographer. (AUTHOR'S COLLECTION)

13

Small and large systems on the 60cm gauge

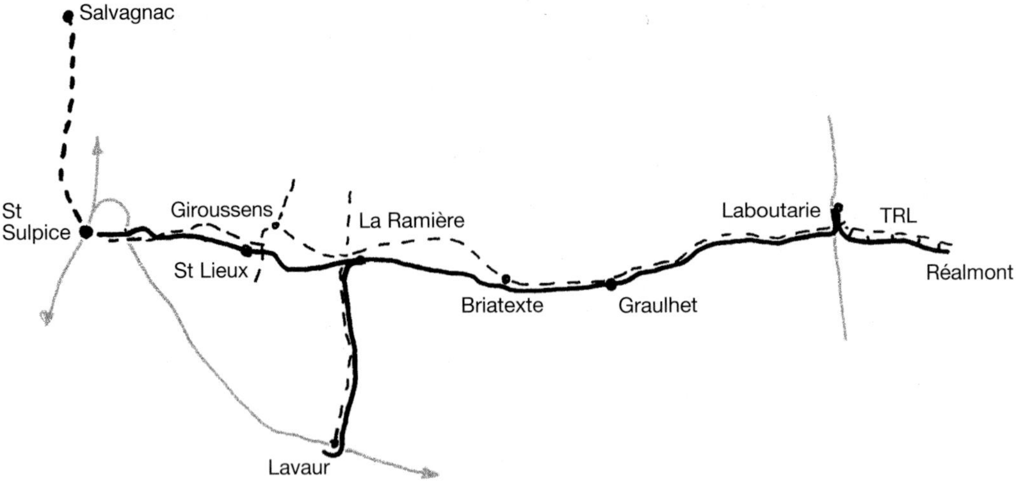

1. Tramways à Vapeur du Tarn

2. CF du Calvados

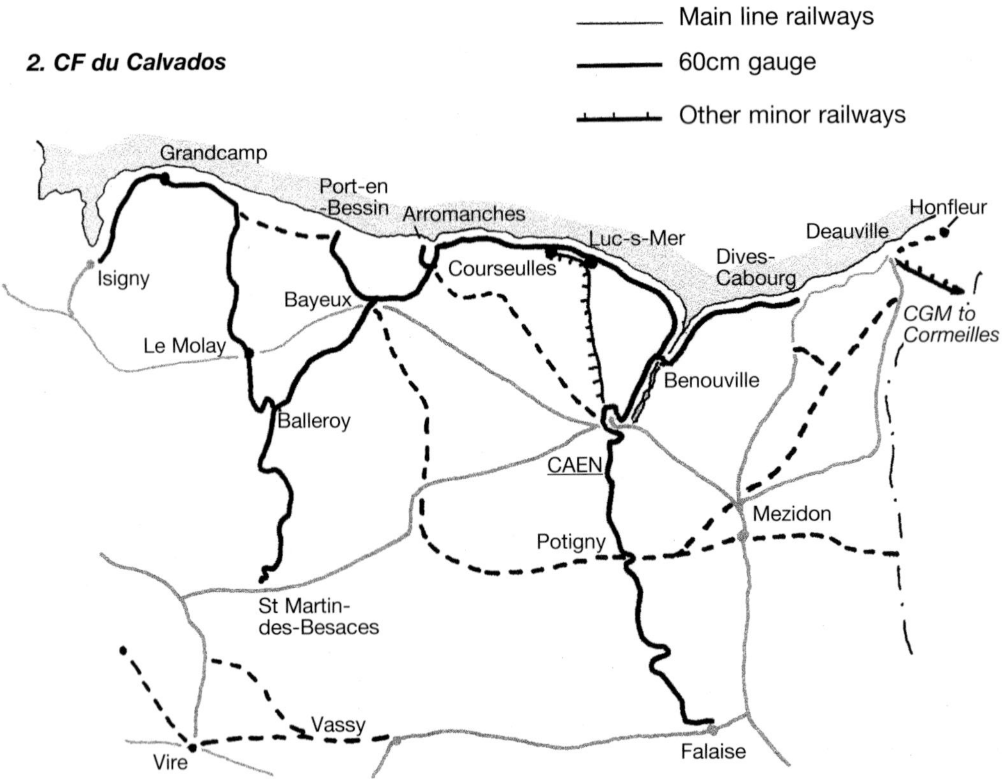

Main line railways
60cm gauge
Other minor railways

The peak was between 1900 and 1914, in which period the railways and tramways of Intérêt Local, in the sense indicated by the 1880 law, more than doubled their length from 11,046km to 22,364km. Only the outbreak of the 1914-18 war prevented a considerable expansion of this kilometrage, much of which, unfortunately, was not really viable even when it first opened. The actual results of all this expansion are discussed in chapter 2.

In retrospect, there were two main reasons for this rather surprising lack of viability and both had their origins in late 19th century legislation. Firstly there was no real alternative to the rather expensive, and in many cases overlarge, metre gauge for the smaller companies. The usefulness of the 750mm gauge as an intermediate width had not really been shown by the 1880s – the colonial experts such as E R Calthrop were only developing their theories. Additionally the military, with colonial wars and servicing of fortifications in mind, were very enamoured of the 60cm gauge as being portable and flexible both in construction and operation. As noted above, therefore, they virtually suppressed further development of the wider gauge, aided by the big manufacturers. Unfortunately, the 60cm gauge was, as the legislators had originally realised, not very suitable for the uses to which it was to be put. Indeed it was only owing to considerable pressure from the big manufacturer, Decauville Aîné, whose speciality it was, that its use was authorised at all; the legislators may well have been impressed by the very efficient 1889 Paris exhibition line which carried over 6 million passengers but in reality this was only 3km long, in an ideal "people-mover" situation, and did not carry freight.

Results of the 60cm gauge experiment

The military accepted the 60cm gauge with enthusiasm and developed what became known generally as the "Systéme Péchot" after its originator. It is best known for the double-ended Fairlie analogues which comprised much of the motive power but the system in fact embraced design of rolling stock, trackwork and operation and a number of quite extensive permanent networks were laid down, particularly in the fortified areas in eastern France. In public service, the 60cm gauge was used for a number of local systems but it is interesting to note that the Decauville company signally failed to make a success of the three branches it laid down as demonstration lines, having to surrender its concessions prematurely; and that only two were eventually of significant size. It is also fair to add that part of Decauville's problems concerned financial machinations within the company and that the stem lines of two systems were also the last 60cm gauge branches in France to retain a public passenger service, that from Caen to Luc sur Mer being the one branch of the big 234km CF du Calvados to survive into the second world war; while the other, the main line of the Tramway de Pithiviers à Toury, retained its passenger service until 1952 and survived for freight – mainly sugar beet – until 1964. Looked at more closely, however, the Calvados system was very uneven; its later extensions, which were typcal rural light railways, had almost all closed by the early 1930s and it was only the stem (a people-mover for holidaymakers) which continued its seasonal task. The TPT probably was suited to its task since it needed to lay light branches all over the countryside to cope with seasonal bulk beet traffic.

It was in fact for military and semi-industrial use, in particular carriage of sugar beet, that the 60cm gauge proved valuable and several extensive, though not public, systems of this type had respectably long lives in northern France. The ex-military ones did perform one valuable service in the aftermath of World War 1 when most of northern France was lying in ruins; an extensive connected series of ex military lines, extended as required, was taken over by the Ministry of Liberated Regions (Regions Libérées) and ran both passenger and freight services for several years in the 1920s. The 60cm gauge lines in general, however, were particularly vulnerable. They were almost invariably roadside, and the slow speed and lack of comfort inseperable from such a narrow gauge in the European context made them an easy prey to road transport. Indeed the later concessionaires of the Calvados system, who were admittedly metre gauge men, did point out that the lines could have been built to the wider gauge for much the same cost – in actual dimensions and infrastructure they differed surprisingly little from a metre gauge tramway. The table overleaf shows the extent of publicly authorised railways on the 60cm gauge.

km	name	dates	dept	ident
1007	Ministère des Regions Libérées	1919-1927	Region nord	MRL
0234	Calvados, CF du	1891-1944	Calvados	CFC
0046	Tarn, CFVE et Twys à Vapeur du	1895-1937	Tarn	STT
0043	Royan, Twys de	1890-1945	Charente-Inferieure	TR
0033	Pithiviers à Toury, Twy de	1892-1965	Loiret	TPT
0031	Savoie, Twys de	1892-1932	Savoie	TS
0021	la Trinité à Etel, Twy de	1901-1934	Morbihan	TTE
0013	Quend et Fort Mahon Twy de	1899-1931	Somme	TM
0005	Laboutarié à Réalmont, Twy de	1905-1933	Tarn	LR
0004	Rotheneuf, Twy de	1896-1914	Ille-et-Vilaine	TR
0004	Paris-Plage - Casino Golf, Twy de	1910-1925	Pas-de-Calais	TPC
0003	Plage de Ste Cecile, Sté de la	1898-1914	Pas-de-Calais	TsC
0002	Rouen-Trianon à La Forêt-de-Rouvray	1906-1908	Seine-Inferieure	TRL
0002	La Baule, Twy de	1887-1914	Loire-Inferieure	TlB
0002	Aigue-Vives, (station - ville) Twy	1892-1901	Gard	TAI

That said, by the end of the 19th century, rural France was in a fair way to being covered by a network of rural railways opening up previously undeveloped areas. Too many of them were of the most basic and vulnerable tramway variety but then hindsight is one of the easiest sources of criticism; at a time when road motor transport was hardly envisaged, even a 12-15 km/hr steam tram was an unimaginable advance on the creaking horse-drawn cart or lengthy trudge to the nearest town.

CHAPTER 2
The Golden Age – Expansion to 1914

Solid Gold or thin veneer?

Was there ever a golden age of secondary railways in France and, if so, what were its main features? Certainly at the end of the 19th century, there was a great pressure to develop communications in even the remotest districts – after all other people had them, why not département X? Equally at that period, road communication was hardly a viable option; most local (ie départemental) roads were often little more than tracks, unpaved except perhaps for a top-dressing of crushed stone that could easily deteriorate under heavy weather. Horse or mule transport was so slow and cumbersome that even a roadside steam tramway seemed a wonder of the age..... and, given the restricted finances of rural départements in particular, that was what most of them got. Using the verges of public roads saved the expense and negotiation required in setting up proper rights of way and enabled lines to go right into and through settlements. The downside, as we have seen, was that such plans often meant a too-narrow loading gauge; a very restricted speed and axleload which were disastrous as soon as reliable road motors appeared; an often winding route which may have served the smallest village but led to protracted journeys especially as mixed trains were the norm. Even foreigners realised the dangers this posed. There is a splendid letter from Mr Warburton, British consul at La Rochelle, in response to queries from drafters of the British 1896 Light Railways Act; it sets out quite cogently and clearly what not to do as evidenced by the then new, CF Economiques des Charentes (Appendix 2). Perhaps the sad thing was that, once the problems were realised, too few attempts were made to build really useful systems with sensible axleloads, loading gauges and equipment. Those which did get built were usually interdépartemental lines considered to have strategic value in time of war and thus of Intérêt Général and mostly conceded to major main-line railway companies – who usually sub-let operation to smaller concerns but did build solid systems often with an infrastructure that could be converted to standard gauge if needed.

Developments that deviated from the norm: use of electricity; racks and gripper wheels

There was also another explosion of development at this time. Widespread use of electricity both as power for traction and power for domestic purposes was very much the coming thing and "progressive" départements perceived (or, alas, were sometimes conned by entrepreneurs into thinking) that this clean, speedy method of transport would meet their requirements excellently – and they could have the power station supplying light and power to their communities as well. Certainly there were occasions when it was sensible - in mountainous country where steam traction would be much less practicable or where the rural lines linked up with existing urban and suburban electric tramways and a fairly intensive service was envisaged. Most rural systems such as the extensive network of Loir-et-Cher or the smaller Tramways du Libournais, with the more common two or four trains daily, did not really justify the expense or running costs. Even in the mountains they were, more often than not, systems like the two-branch Voies Ferrées des Pyrénées (alias the Tramways de la Bigorre [Map p.50]) which were deficitary from the start and just hung on grimly until their equipment wore out or the creditors foreclosed.

Lastly, although they were never so prevalent as in truly alpine countries such as Switzerland, there grew up a scattering of lines using various forms of rack or other types of assistance. Most of these were conventional mountain cogwheel railways employing Riggenbach, Abt or Strub racks as their designers chose and mostly serving largely seasonal tourist populations in the Alpes and Pyrenées; they included, or so the French claim, the first rack line in the world to use electrically propelled railcars – the CF du Salève. Two, at Langres and Laon in the flattish north, might have set a fashion since they successfully linked hilltop cities to their rail stations on the plain below but the idea never caught on. The other main form of assistance was the raised centre rail with gripper wheels – either the basic Fell system or its French variant

J. J. 8455 Aix-les-Bains — Sommet du Mont-Revard (alt. 1560 m)
Départ d'un train
Jullien frères, Phot.-Editeurs, Genève

Rack lines had a brief heyday in the early years of the century. Here a conventional Abt train departs from the summit of Mont Révard, over in Savoie. (Author's Collection)

L'AUVERGNE
817. - Le PUY-de-DOME. - Le Chemin de fer au sommet du Puy de Dôme

So did other forms of assistance: This is the highly unusual centre-rail railway (Fell or Hanscotte as you wish) from Clermont Ferrand to the summit of Puy-de-Dôme. (Author's Collection)

the Systeme Hanscotte. Three only of these were built although they did include the epic, if short-lived line over the Mont Cenis pass to Italy. The others were a PLM (now SNCF) line near Mont Blanc which still survives though bereft of its centre rail, and a delightful but short-lived tourist line up the conical Puy de Dôme. For reference they are listed below.

km	name	gauge	dates	dept	rack	ident
Centre rail:						
0078	Mont Cenis Rly Co	1067mm	1868-1871	Savoie	Fell	MC
0034	St Gervais-Vallorcine	metre	1901-now	Haute-Savoie	Fell	PLM
0015	Puy-de-Dôme, CF du	metre	1907-1926	Puy-de-Dôme	Hans.	CPD
Rack & pinion						
0012	Mont-Blanc, Twy du	metre	1909-now	Haute-Savoie	Strub	TMB
0010	Munster – la Schlucht	metre	1907-1914	Haut-Rhin	Strub	MLS
0009	Aix-les-Bains – Mont-Revard	metre	1892-1936	Savoie	Abt	AMR
0009	Salève, CF du	metre	1892-1937	Haute-Savoie	Abt	CFS
0005	Luchon – Superbagnères	metre	1912-1966	Haute-Garonne	Strub	LS
0005	Chamonix au Montenvers	metre	1906-now	Haute-Savoie	Strub	CM
0004	St Ignace – la Rhûne	metre	1924-now	Basses-Pyrénées	Strub	VFDM
0003	Monte-Carlo à la Turbie	metre	1894-1932	Alpes-Maritimes	Rigb.	MCT
0002	Laon, CF de	metre	1899-1971y	Aisne	Abt	CFL
0001	Langres, Régie municipale	metre	1887-1971	Haute-Marne	Rigb.	CL
0001	Riviera-Palace, Twy du	metre	1903-1903*	Alpes-Maritimes	Strub	*
0001	Lyon St.Just – St.Jean	metre	1901-1955x	Rhône	Abt	LS

*   ephemeral. 623m long electric line partly in commom with la Turbie one.

y   replaced by POMA2000 guided light transit system

x   originally a funicular; from 1958 a funicular again

When all is said and done, however, there was still an enormous blossoming of rural, and especially départemental, railways in the first decade of the 20th century and, but for the war, an even greater length of line would have come into service. In general, expectations were very high and by 1914 many départements had planned, and even built, two or more réseaux in succession, sometimes with a third one being projected. Some were not even deterred by the war and continued development thereafter but that is another story. In the meanwhile, the situation can perhaps best be visualised by looking in detail at some typical examples of the main types of réseaux. Inevitably most examples are narrow gauge but one standard gauge one has been included as fairly typical of the short standard gauge branches; Apart from their gauge, the larger standard gauge ones had most of the characteristics of any départemental network fulfilling a similar function.

Some typical systems: Tramways à Vapeur du Tarn; Tramways du Loiret; CF d'Etival à Senones; Tramways de l'Ardèche; CF de Cormeilles à Glos Montfort; CF des Côtes du Nord; Tramways Electriques de Loir-et-Cher; SE Réseau du Centre (IG); P.O Lignes de Corrèze

Let us start with the 60cm gauge. There were not enough systems for any one to be really "typical" but what might have been envisaged more widely if it had succeeded can be seen in the **Tramways à Vapeur du Tarn,** a three-branch, 46km system in relatively easy country in the west of that département. (Map p.14). Quite why the département allowed it to be built is uncertain but it seems to have been swayed by Paul Decauville's success at the Paris Exhibition. Certainly the Decauville company built it and supplied the rolling stock – Weidknecht 0-6-2Ts plus their standard bogie coaches and various forms of goods stock, later augmented by 4-6-0Ts when those had proved their worth in Calvados; after the 1914-18 war it even acquired a bogie railcar. The two main branches were built between 1895 and 1903 and a third, even longer one, was approved in 1913 just before the war intervened; part of this line, between La Ramière and St Sulpice, was eventually opened in 1925 and the rest is said to have been almost ready for traffic but never put into public service (another source says that it never approached completion!). Alas, it was all too late. Road competition was too strong, passenger traffic was withdrawn in the early 1930s and total closure followed in 1937. Its infrastructure could easily have suited a light metre gauge line since the steepest gradients were only 25mm/m, the sharpest curve radius was 50m and the rail was Vignoles flat-bottomed of 15kg/m weight. Perhaps significantly, the département specified metre gauge for its later lines.

For a typical unecomonic metre gauge system of the simplest type, take the **Tramways du Loiret,** a rural département south-west of Paris. This département, partly seduced by its experiment with the Tramway de Pithiviers à Toury, intended originally to opt for 60cm gauge but was persuaded instead to go for a light metre gauge network because it might link with neighbouring systems. It had grandiose plans but what actually got built was a collection of roadside tramways on the "three 15s" principle and consisting of two lines radiating from the prefecture at Orléans, with a branch off one, and an isolated line some distance away. It certainly did link to other systems Orléans PO station was reached via a section of an existing Tramways à Vapeur de Loir-et-Cher (TLC) branch from Oucques while the TL itself entered Loir-et-Cher to link up with the TLC again at Neung-s-Beuvron. That line also connected at Cléry with the Tramways Electriques de Loir-et-Cher and the other route from Orléans crossed into Cher to meet the CF du Blanc à Argent at Brinon-s-Sauldre. The whole system, opened between 1905 and 1909, was of the lightest type, almost entirely roadside with curves down to 40m radius, gradients of up to 35mm/m and a loading gauge width of only 2m. Stations were largely simple, one-storey structures, timber framed with brick infilling and the twelve locomotives were light Corpet Louvet 0-6-0Ts weighing only 12.5t tare – and thus neatly slipping under the 15t limit when in working order. Rolling stock was all four-wheeled, a few coaches having radial axles (the poor tramway's alternative to bogies). After experiencing a Purrey steam car for Orléans suburban services prior to 1914, and an early Tartary railbus in the 1920s, it settled for three conventional De Dion cars but they did not last long. The Département rashly reclaimed the TLC branch in 1931 and this so inflated the deficit that the whole system was hurriedly turned over to buses three years later. (Map p.21)

Fairly typical of the shorter standard gauge lines was the **CF d'Etival à Senones** down in Vosges near the eastern frontier. This was opened in 1885 mainly to serve industrial settlements in the valley of the Rabodeau and was a simple, 9km long branch connecting to the CF de l'Est at Etival. It started from the station square there and ran on its own right of way, with a single intermediate station at Moyemoutier where it served its major industrial customer, the local granite quarries; En route and nearer Senones, were various private sidings for a variety of small industries and at Senones it actually connected to another private line, from Senones to Moussey - many standard gauge routes had rail links of some kind at both ends. The track was reasonably substantial, with 30kg/m Vignoles rail, maximum gradients of 20mm/m and a minimum curve radius of 250m; a small workshop was established at Senones. Like many lines in the north-east it suffered in both wars, being partly destroyed in World War 1 and only restored in 1919, and again being damaged and losing stock in the 1944 fighting. Like most small companies (ie those not taken over by a big Grouping) it remained faithful to steam traction apart from a sngle Billard railcar between 1934 and 1946; the loss of this by fire led to closure to passengers in 1948 but goods traffic continued until 1975 when its major customer withdrew; a tourist operation ran fitfully over part of the line for a few more years but that is outside this study. Equipment consisted of various light tank locomotives both new and secondhand, with four-wheeled coaches from various sources. In general goods traffic was carried in main line vehicles but up to twenty-five wagons of its own were kept for local traffic.

Moving up a grade, there were the metre gauge **Tramways de l'Ardèche** (Map p.21), traversing a very hilly region in south east France on the west bank of the river Rhône. What was really needed in such territory was a well-funded, substantial system of Intérêt Général as was evidenced by the CFD's Vivarais system a little to the north. Southern Ardèche, however, had nothing of strategic importance, just a string

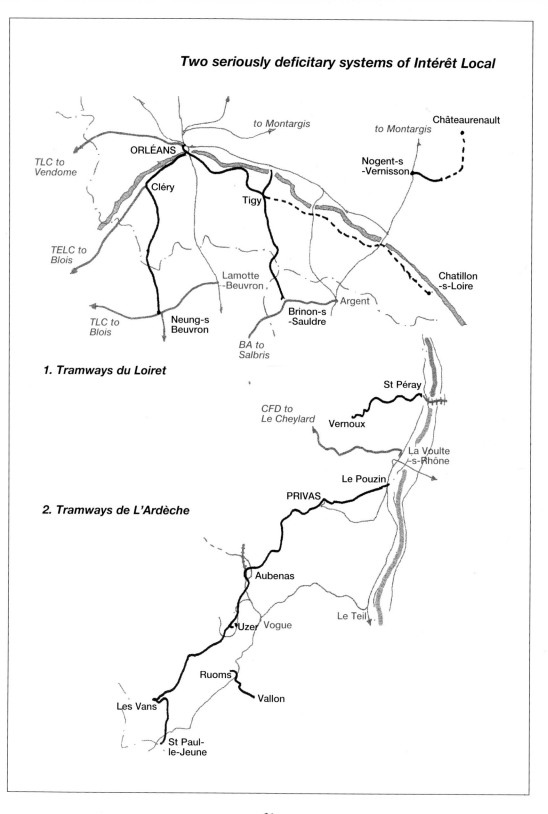

Two seriously deficitary systems of Intérêt Local

1. Tramways du Loiret

2. Tramways de L'Ardèche

More conventional lines flourished too: The small but substantial CF de Cormeilles à Glos Montfort in Eure runs into the village station at Drucourt (FACS)

of small towns and administrative centres reaching back into rugged country but it still wanted transport – at as cheap a price as possible. It started late and what transpired, between 1910 and the war, was a single "main" line of 104km together with one branch and two separate short lines joining towns of administrative importance. Where possible it kept beside the very inadequate départemental roads, with minimum engineering work, curves of down to 40m radius and gradients of up to 60mm/m with the odd reversal thrown in. Buildings were kept to the minimum, most stations being little more than single-storey shacks. To operate this lightly engineered line, the best it could get were 22.5 tonne Piguet 2-6-0Ts, handsome locomotives and certainly capable of handling the "typical" départemental loads but quite outclassed by what they had to face. The traffic was minimal and the concessionaire quickly went bankrupt. The stock in general was insufficient, wore quickly and by 1914, when war broke out, was already "au bout d'usure" even though building works were still going on. Traffic was so light, with only one through train a day on the main line taking some eight hours, that services were largely suspended and in 1917 the military had little compunction in lifting all but one branch for war service. It was only in 1921 that, incredibly and after much argument, part of the main line, from Aubenas to St Paul, was restored to use and, with the still existing Vernoux branch, ceded to the CFD. Old friends the SGTD took over the southern line in 1928 and, true to their principles, lost little time in converting the service to road transport; the CFD promptly followed suit with the Vernoux branch and both lines were declassified in 1930.

For a more substantial, but still small company of Intérêt Local let us consider the **CF de Cormeilles à Glos Montfort et Extensions** (Map p.25) – very important that extensions bit since it indicated you were thinking progressively which, indeed, was what the company did. The original concessionaire was part of the Laborie group, receiving its concession from the Eure Département in 1900 direct to the Laborie brothers who then formed the Compagnie du Chemin de Fer de Cormeilles à Glos-Montfort et Extensions to build and operate it. Cormeilles was a pleasant market town situated neatly within a rectangle of standard gauge lines and the stem route, out to Glos Montfort on a Rouen – Epernay link, was completed in 1902. Almost immediately the first "extension", northwest from Cormeilles to another standard gauge junction at

22

More substantial (and often with bags of swank) were the big réseaux like the CF des Côtes-du-Nord, here seen loading a holiday train at its monumental St Brieuc station. (FACS)

Nonetheless trouble, in the shape of road motors was on the way (this is a bit of a cheat since the Cormeilles line train has actually paused to let a road race through but it makes the point). (FACS)

Pont l'Eveque, was put in train, opening in 1904; oddly enough it was officially a tramway, possibly because it ran mainly through the neighbouring département of Calvados which favoured tramways. Perhaps for the same reason, Laborie seems to have contracted to build it on his own account and then passed it over to the CGM in 1905. Lastly a third branch was built south east to Bernay, on yet another standard gauge route, opening in 1905 though not getting a goods interchange until four years later. So that was the CGM, a sensible three pointed star totalling some 75km and opening up a fertile region which duly benefitted. A fourth branch to Pont Audemer was projected but the war came first. The aftermath of the war, alas, also brought a rapidly rising deficit since the country was almost ideal for development of road transport and, in spite of the introduction of railcars, Calvados foreclosed on the Pont l'Eveque line in 1933. Most of the Bernay route was turned over to roadbuses the following year, except for about 7km retained for the lucrative cider traffic. The original stem survived the second war, providing valuable services thoughout. Regrettably a bridge got blown in the fighting, the services were truncated and traffic fell off so the stub closed finally in 1946.

As for track and equipment, the CGM was fairly typical of its type. The original line was a proper railway, mainly on its own right of way, with curves not reducing below 100m radius, gradients of no more than 30mm/m, and 20kg/m flatbottom rail on a substantial roadbed. The other two lines were mainly roadside, but with the same quality of track while station buildings were mostly substantial two storey structures with attached goods sheds; an adequate central workshop and running sheds were provided at Cormeilles. Equipment comprised three 19,5 tonne 0-6-0Ts by Buffaud et Robatel, three slightly lighter Corpet 2-6-0Ts for the tramway lines and, in 1926, two Corpet,Louvet 0-8-0Ts for the heavy goods traffic. With the exception of two bogie composites, all passenger stock was four-wheeled, of end-balcony, saloon type and provided two classes of accommodation with separate luggage vans. Goods stock was conventional for the period though, unusually, the Cormeilles cider works briefly used some private owner wagons ex the British War Department lines. Following World War 1, M. Laborie used the line for his first railcar experiments, starting with three converted draisines and proceeding to AM 41, a not particularly successful

133   *SAINT-BRIEUC. — Pont de la Rue du Gouëdic.*

Some acquired quite elaborate structures, even for minor works – A simple road overbridge as interpreted by Harel de la Nôe became almost a work of art.   (AUTHOR'S COLLECTION)

24

Small and large two-stage systems of Intérêt Local

1. CF de Cormeilles à Glos-Montfort et Extensions

2. CF des Côtes du Nord

Key:

first stage built	——
second stage built	—·—·—
second stage not built	———
other minor railways	—+—+—
CF de l'Ouest/État	——

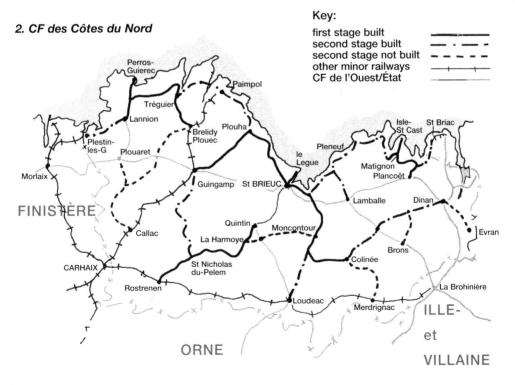

25

single-ended machine resembling a coach conversion. After that the company sensibly bought three standard De Dion JM railbuses which lasted to the end.

For a large départemental network which developed over a period of time and went through all the stages of modernisation, the extensive system of the **CF des Côtes du Nord** (Map p.25) is fairly typical. Sprawling all through the département it was actally built in two stages or réseaux. The first set of four lines, some 211km with branches, was conceded in 1900 as a system of Intérêt Local to one of the big groupings (Cie Centrale des Chemins de Fer et Tramways) who formed the CF des Côtes du Nord as an operating company. It was distinguished from other systems mainly because of the ingenuity and skill of its first Engineer, Harel de la Nöe, who was a pioneer in the use of reinforced concrete; this was used widely for the many viaducts and bridges necessitated by the broken country through which the lines passed and also for some of the buildings.

The réseau proved successful and even profitable, encouraging the département, in 1912, to bid for and plan a second set of lines totalling 357km. As with many other systems the war prevented these from coming to fruition immediately but in 1921 the département took over its lines 'en régie' and proceeded partially with the plan. 246km were opened between 1922 and 1932 but included lines with very low traffic and brought the whole system into deficit. This again was typical of those départements who continued to build rambling local lines into the 1920s ignoring the rise of road competition. Despite considerable investment in railcars, the deficit increased, leading to closure and lifting of over 240km from inland lines by 1939. As usual, too, the remaining routes proved very useful during the war but were quickly closed thereafter save for the long coastal line from St Brieuc. This had a heavy holiday traffic in summer and survived until 1956.

The lines in both réseaux were mainly on their own right of way, using comparatively heavy 23kg/m rail on the first system and the standard 20kg/m rail on the second; curves rarely fell below 100m radius except in stations but gradients often exceeded 30mm/m owing to the difficult terrain. The engineering works were often very elaborate and in the distinctive style of de la Nöe, and stations, with the exception of a monumental HQ at St Brieuc, varied from substantial houses to mere shelters. To run its original services the company had a standard series of heavy 0-6-0Ts by Tubize/Blanc Misseron, later reinforced for the second Réseau mainly by a set of Corpet, Louvet 0-6-0T with distinctive full cabs. Coaching stock comprised a mix of bogie vehicles and long-wheelbase radial-axled four-wheelers. The Régie was also an enthusiastic user of motor rail vehicles, favouring initially the products of De Dion Bouton. It began with no less than eleven J series railbuses, later complenented by three of the six-wheeled, full-cab, KG model and, in 1937, two streamlined, double-ended bogie cars of series OC1. Meanwhile Renault delivered a single massive bogie car, flippantly named "Mamm-Goz" (grandma) by the staff. After the war six Brissoneau-et-Lotz diesel-electric cars were bought second hand for the surviving lines and the following year were complemented by three modern Renault ABH6 cars analagous to those being built for Provence and Corsica. This habit of buying modern cars and then closing soon after was by no means confined to the CdN and was usually due to changes in composition of the départemental councils! The big Renaults went to Spain on closure while the Réseau Breton took the two OC1s.

A typical "loser" among the electrified systems might well be the **Tramways Electriques de Loir-et-Cher** (TELC) (Map p.50). The Département had already, from 1888 on, built an eight branch system of roadside steam tramways conceded to a filiale of the Carel-et-Fouché group and built in three stages. Still not satisfied it proposed a fourth system in 1910 (mainly it appears on the principle of keeping up with the Joneses) and was seduced by the claims of one M. Lefebvre that he could kill two birds with one stone – provide a modern (definitely upmarket) electric system while bringing the benefits of electricity to the villages it ran through. Having got the concession he promptly split it into two companies, the TELC to build and run the railways and the Cie Electrique du Loir-et-Cher to provide and sell the power; the result was that the tramways, alas, were continually bedevilled by the high price of their power supply. Nonetheless the réseau, three lines based on Blois and a single one up in the north from Châteaudun, was built although the final portions were not completed until after the 1914-18 war. At a number of places, they linked with but did not seriously interwork with, the steam tramways, each system having its own station at junction points which was slightly stupid but a consequence of having different concessionaires.

Some, like the Tramways de l'Ardèche, hardly had a chance from the beginning. Here one of their neat Piguet 2-6-0Ts ambles into a wayside station, with milk apparently the main cargo to be loaded.   (AUTHOR'S COLLECTION)

Lines were almost entirely roadside, with the usual 20kg/m rail except when actually in the streets when 38kg/m Broca tramway rail was used. Curves at some points were down to 50m radius and gradients exceeeded 30mm/m but that was one of the reasons put forward for electric traction. Power was supplied at 6000V AC 25 cycles and fed through overhead catenary and pantographs, the original bow collectors proving unsuitable. Initially the coal-fired power station was sited at Montils, a few kilometres outside Blois, along with the workshops and main depot. It was later moved to Blois and later still, power was taken from a regional hydro-electric station. Buildings, except for a highly ornamental station at Blois Electrique, were single storey, tramway pattern, with attached goods sheds or loading docks and the catenary poles were either concrete or steel. The main motive power was provided by a series of heavy-duty bogie tramcars able to pull several matching trailers or a gaggle of four-wheeled wagons as required. Initially an average of four trains daily on each line was agreed, but this reduced to two after 1918. Clearly the advantages of electric power for flexibility and frequency of service were not required and the lines closed in 1934.

So much for modern power. What, then of the Intérêt Général lines? Several of the larger ones have survived into our times and have been extensively chronicled but there were a number of lesser examples – usually single lines linking two places of strategic importance but sometimes fairly substantial systems – which tend to get forgotten. Perhaps typical of these was the **SE's Réseau d'Intérêt Général de Cher et Allier** (Map p.28). It was composed of two linked lines, one mainly in Allier from Lapeyrouse to Sançoins and one in Cher from Chateumeillant via Sançoins to la Guerche. Between them they ensured the link between the SE's two départemental systems of Intérêt Local and in most ways were assimilated into them. Both were opened in 1890-91 and survived, fairly uneventfully, until 1951 when their adjoining réseaux closed also. As an indcation of their "strategic" origin, their three main termini were within the appropriate PO main line stations although the lines were conceded directly to the SE. Stock was theoretically separately allocated although it consisted mainly of the 2-4-0T and 0-6-2T common on the other lines, together with the standard SE patterns of bogie passenger and four-wheeled goods stock, and was

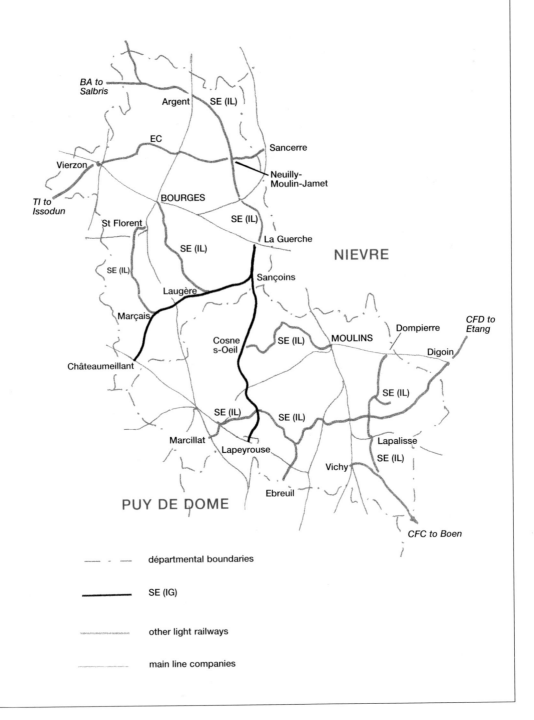

A medium-sized system of Intérêt Général and its connections
SE Reseau d'Intérêt Général de Cher et Allier

BA to Salbris

Argent SE (IL)

EC

Sancerre

Vierzon

Neuilly-Moulin-Jamet

TI to Issodun

BOURGES

SE (IL)

St Florent

SE (IL)

La Guerche

NIEVRE

SE (IL)

Sançoins

Laugère

Marçais

CFD to Etang

Cosne s-Oeil   SE (IL)   MOULINS

Dompierre

Digoin

Châteaumeillant

SE (IL)

SE (IL)   SE (IL)

Marcillat

Lapalisse

Lapeyrouse

SE (IL)

Vichy

Ebreuil

PUY DE DOME

CFC to Boen

- - - départmental boundaries

━━━ SE (IG)

········ other light railways

──── main line companies

numbered in the general SE series. Permanent way was also of standard pattern although gradients rarely exceeded 20mm/m. Buildings were substantial, with two-storey stations of standard SE design and in general the system was somewhat analagous to the much more famous PO Lignes de Corrèze; it just did not last long enough to be known!

The **PO Corrèze** itself (Map p.319) may well serve as a final illustration of major secondary systems which were officially conceded to a main line company that did not really want them - and hence often had a very convoluted career. The Corrèze département, which appears to have considered itself the crossroads of France, had been agitating for railway communication since 1841 but with only partial success. Several standard gauge routes crossed it but the rural areas north and south of the important town of Tulle were virtually untouched even by the mid-1880s. No main line concern appeared anxious to take up the various strategic suggestions in the Plan Freyciney even when an agreement of 1887 allowed nominally strategic lines to be built on the metre gauge. It was not until 1893 or thereabouts that the PO grudgingly agreed an overall concession for lines entitled the PO Lignes de Corrèze from a main line junction at Uzerche down via Seilhac to Tulle (east-west standard gauge connection), with a short branch from Seilhac to Treignac, and on from Tulle to Argentat near the Cantal border. Even then the actual construction and operation was sub-leased to the private Societé des Constructions Battignoles who, in turn, formed a Societé d'Exploitation de Chemins de Fer en Corrèze (SECC) to carry out the work. The system opened in 1904 after a last minute panic as to what rolling stock should be provided; the PO, in the manner of big companies, took the line of least resistance, ordering stock "as running on the le Blanc-Argent" from Blanc Misseron and letting Battignoles themselves supply the four 0-4-4-OT Mallets for heavy work and ten light 2-4-0T for lighter trains. Hence what was a fairly substantial railway had to put up for most of its life with very traditional four-wheelers rather than the bogie coaches of most Intérêt Général systems. Apart from that flaw, the lines were well-engineered with minimum curve radii of 100m and gradients no steeper than 30mm/m, while the rail, originally on metal sleepers, was 25kg/m giving an axleload of 10 Tonnes. The stations, too, were substantial two-storey structures with goods facilities and adequate siding space.

Like several others, the system eventually had a connection to a départemental line of Intérêt Local (the Ussel – St Bonnet Avalouze line of the Tramways de la Corrèze); it was slightly unusual in that the SECC took on operation of the TC and the latter's trains worked right into Tulle over a substantial stretch of the PO Corrèze. The Sté Battignoles had hoped for much larger developments and was much disappointed. It effectively gave up and when its concession ran out in 1933, operation was handed to a PO subsidiary, the Societé des Transports Auxiliaires du PO (STAPO) which, to complicate matters, retained the SECC as operating company while turning most of the tramway lines over to road transport. Little attempt was made to modernise passenger services with railcars. In 1938 overall control passed to the SNCF and in 1949 one of its subsidiaries, the Societé de Controle et d'Exploitation des Transports Auxiliaires (SCETA), successor to STAPO, took direct charge of operation. Modern railcars improved services considerably but even so the last TC line closed in 1959 and the POC seemed set to follow. In 1962, however, the big Societé Générale des Chemins de Fer Economiques (SE, which became CFTA in 1966) took on an eight year operating concession and introduced two diesel locomotives for the goods traffic. The SNCF, regrettably, was not fond of its narrow gauge lines and, traffic continuing to decrease while the deficit rose, closed the system in 1970.

The overall picture to 1914

It was, in a sense, the defects described in the examples above which were the main handicap of many even of the later metre gauge lines. Some were doomed from the start by a lack of potential traffic but the départements usually accepted this and the associated subsidies in order to open up their country areas. The major fault seems to have been that light-railway builders did not move with the times. By about 1910, the threat of road transport was already becoming a reality, yet this was also the peak period for the construction of roadside tramways employing principles laid down thirty years previously and no longer valid. These lines took little or no account of technical advances. Their routes and stock virtually prohibited any real increase in journey speeds; their locomotives were still of a, by now traditional, design of small-

La Corrèze Illustrée
BEAULIEU – La Gare du Tramway
Juillet 1914

Even sadder were the Tramways de la Corrèze, whose Beaulieu terminus was returning to nature only a few years after it opened
(FACS)

wheeled 0-6-0T, 0-6-2T or 2-6-0T, trailing uncomfortable four wheeled coaches with wooden seating in the third class. Furthermore their services, for reasons of economy, were largely based on a sparse service of mixed trains which shunted interminably at each station whereas, on the road, passenger and freight services were separated and therefore quicker. These latecomers often had a very short life; The Tramways de la Corrèze mentioned above, for example, cut short only by the war with 179.5km of of lines in operation and further extensions planned, had closed all but one branch by 1934, only twenty years after. Even in their heyday, traffic on most of its routes was negligible and there exists a most pathetic view of the little terminus at Beaulieu, only a year or so after it opened, with weeds sprouting between the tracks and a general air of poverty about it. Similar sad, or amusing, stories can be told of many little companies. There was, for instance, the poverty-stricken CF de la Vallée de Celles which, when it was more than usually penurious, used to resort to borrowing a wagon of coal from a nearby factory to keep the trains running.....

If there was a golden age, then, it was short-lived and was drawing rapidly to a close by the time the First World War broke out in 1914. The, almost unrestrained, expansion of local tramways and railways could not realisically continue to be funded, particularly as road transport was even then becoming a competitor for short-distance traffic. In addition the major railway companies were beginning to get seriously concerned about the way in which these lines were affecting their local traffics and branches. The dual concerns were recognised by a new law of 31 July 1913, which sharply reduced State subventions and guarantees. Almost incidentally it clarified nomenclature, lines of Intérêt Local officially becoming chemins de fer (carrying all types of traffic) or tramways urbains (carrying only passengers and small-goods) – it's a pity that in English there seems no useful compendium word equivalent to the French "messageries" which covers so much more than "parcels". So there may have been, in development terms, a golden age but it was gold that quickly turned to dross and it was (as always) the inhabitants of the départements concerned who had to pay heavily over the years through extra taxes.

CHAPTER 3
The 1914-18 war and its aftermath

The opening moves and their effects on minor railways (Map p.324)

The outbreak of the Great War brought considerable problems to all the communication systems of France and secondary railways had their own particular difficulties. The hardest hit were those in north-east and northern France, many of which were in the actual battle area. Following the predetermined Schlieffen plan the German armies thrust rapidly toward the French/Belgian border and then turned southwest towards Paris. Although temporarily checked by the Belgian army and a hastily landed British Expeditionary Force, they had reached the River Marne, on the southern flank of the French line, by the autumn of 1914. There they were held by desperate measures, among them the now-famous device of rushing forward reserves in commandeered taxicabs. Both sides rapidy extended their flanks (the so-called rush to the sea) and by the end of 1914 the front had stabilised along a line of some 115 miles, from the Swiss border to the Channel coast. There were changes from time to time but in general the British, with the remaining Belgians strengthened by a French corps, held the northern sector and the French stretched east and south to the anchor points in their fortified zones round Toul and Verdun. Despite massive offensive efforts on both sides, this line remained largely unaltered for the next three years as both sides first dug themselves in and then started a war of attrition punctuated by sporadic violent attacks which gained little of value although they cost millions of lives.

The full story of French standard and metre gauge light railways in the 1914-18 war is too complex to be recorded fully here; some highlights are noted below and in the appropriate regional chapters on the Nord and Est regions. Suffice to say that, in the main, they were used simply as lines of communication, though the British in particular found the metre gauge ones inconvenient since they were not light enough to penetrate far into the forward area and so two transhipments were needed: use of standard gauge and road,

2751. JUNIVILLE. - La Gare

Lines destroyed: Neither side liked the 800mm gauge of the CFD des Ardennes, so scenes like these disappeared quickly as the fighting rolled past them.   (FACS)

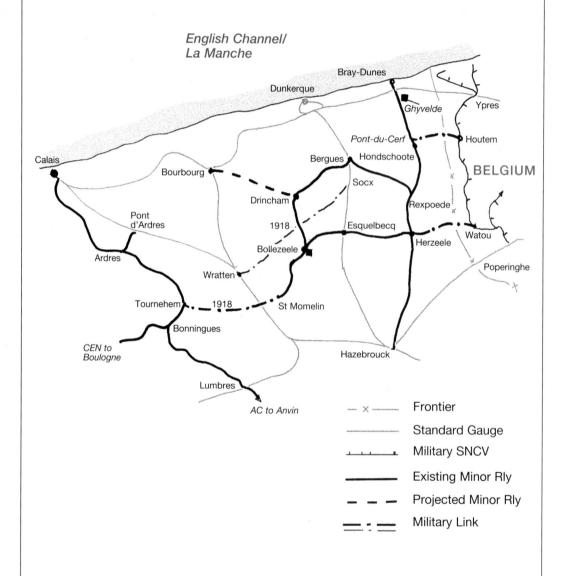

Metre Gauge Railways and Military Links in Flanders, 1915-18

English Channel/
La Manche

Bray-Dunes

Dunkerque

Ghyvelde

Ypres

Pont-du-Cerf

Houtem

Bergues

Hondschoote

Calais

Bourbourg

Socx

BELGIUM

Drincham

Rexpoede

Pont
d'Ardres

1918

Esquelbecq

Watou

Ardres

Bollezeele

Herzeele

Wratten

Poperinghe

Tournehem

1918

St Momelin

Bonningues

CEN to
Boulogne

Hazebrouck

Lumbres

AC to Anvin

— ×——	Frontier
————	Standard Gauge
┴┴┴┴┴	Military SNCV
━━━━	Existing Minor Rly
━ ━ ━	Projected Minor Rly
═ · ═	Military Link

or 60cm gauge, involved only one. The French military had their own problems too, although they had had the foresight to build and stockpile a large reserve of field railway equipment using the 60cm gauge. Yet one of the biggest problems concerned gauge and was of their own making. Alone of all French narrow gauge systems, the group of lines in the south of the Ardennes département had been built at the insistence of the military to the sub-metric gauge of 800mm, with the express intention of denying their speedy use to an advancing enemy. The theory was that in an emergency all stock would be quickly destroyed and an enemy would find it difficult to collect more material of such an odd gauge. Ironically, when war came, it was the French themselves who needed the system and it had to be hurriedly converted to metre gauge because of the shortage of stock! Where the Germans encountered it they simply replaced it by standard 60cm gauge Feldbahnen and were grateful for the ready-made infrastructure.

Secondary railways in the war zone: early years

At the end of 1914 the position of the secondary railways was as follows. In the north a small portion of the Belgian SNCV metre gauge system around Ypres (Ieper), Furnes (Veurne) and la Panne (De Panne) was still within Allied lines and a considerable amount of SNCV stock had been evacuated onto it; it was in the hands of a military section composed largely of staff from SNCV concessionary companies (the Section Vicinale de Chemins de Fer) and was organised as an army support system. Behind it the French local railways around Hazebrouck and further back in the Pas-de-Calais were also available for allied use if required. These included the north-south lines of the CF des Flandres between Hazebrouck and Hondschoote with, to the west, the SE's Groupe Nord in the Nord département. Both were used extensively to help resupply the allied forces and the ex CFIL du Nord de la France line from Hondschoote on to Bray-Dunes on the coast was actually operated first by the French 5th railway Battalion and then by the 10th Section of the French Field Engineers which made a speciality of minor railways. The Engineers lost no time in building a link forward from Pont-aux-Cerfs to Houtem on the remaining SNCV trackage, which was opened in June 1915, and subsequently the British army also worked traffic over much of this network, having a big depot at Ghyvelde near the coast. Another link, from Herzeele where the CFF joined the SE, to Watou, was opened in October 1915 and the two were used extensively throughout the war. The military authorities were always conscious of the possibilities of a German breakthrough and, besides duplicating some standard gauge routes, also built a metre gauge link west from the SE at St.Momelin to Tournehem on the CF d'Anvin – Calais. This was not complete until May 1918 by which time it was not really needed and it appears to have been lifted very soon after the armistice. The apparently desirable links between French and Belgian lines also proved awkward in practice since it was found that very little French stock would work over Belgian metals. Indeed in 1916 it was calculated that there were only about 500 suitable wagons in the whole of France and their use would entail stripping whole systems in central and western France of much of their equipment; the Charentes lines in particular were affected by this. To help remedy this situation, the British produced, in rather leisurely fashion, fifty 0-6-0 Tram locomotives of SNCV pattern (but to imperial measurements) and some 1200 wagons; the last of these were not delivered until 1917. In general, however, especially after the War Department Light Railways Directorate was formed in late 1916, the British preferred to lift the, usually battered, metre gauge lines in their area and replace them with standard or 60cm gauge railways as appropriate, using the old formations wherever possible. Among the lines affected in this way were the Oise département system around Noyon, exploited by a company with the resounding title of CF de Milly à Formerie et de Noyon à Guiscard et Lassigny, and much of the SE's Albert group, especially the line from Doullens. The standard gauge lines were largely retained as such unless they ran too near the front line, although many, in particular those around the Cambrai area, suffered badly from both sides. Some, like the Achiet-Bapaume branch, were useful enough not only to be rebuilt but to acquire new links to nearby systems (links which, in digression, were later something of a problem to the authorities since they had never gone through proper legal processing). Equally, the German authorities tended to scrap and relay to 60cm gauge the many lines they overran, particularly in the Département du Nord.

In this general area, the front line cut right through the sprawling systems of the Somme département, especially those centred on Albert and operated by the SE; some branches were in Allied hands, some in

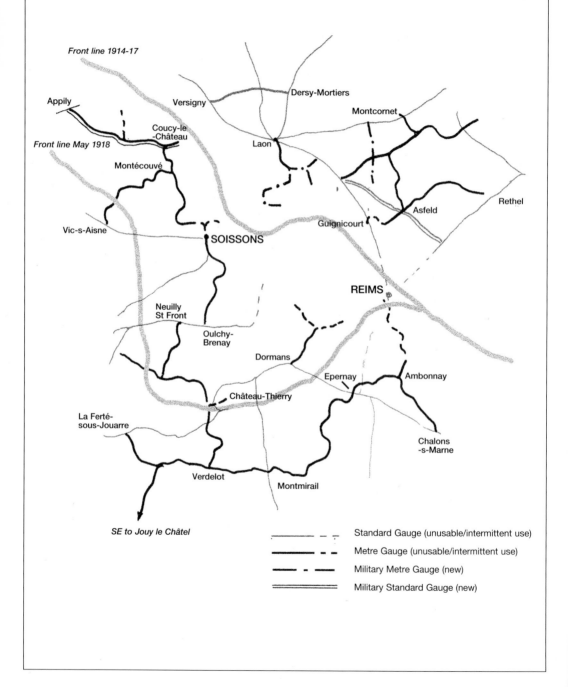

Military use of minor railways on the Aisne/Marne front (Chemins des Dames) 1914-18

Front line 1914-17

Appily

Versigny

Dersy-Mortiers

Montcornet

Coucy-le
-Château

Front line May 1918

Laon

Montécouvé

Rethel

Asfeld

Vic-s-Aisne

Guignicourt

SOISSONS

REIMS

Neuilly
St Front

Oulchy-
Brenay

Dormans

Epernay

Ambonnay

Château-Thierry

La Ferté-
sous-Jouarre

Chalons
-s-Marne

Verdelot

Montmirail

SE to Jouy le Châtel

Standard Gauge (unusable/intermittent use)

Metre Gauge (unusable/intermittent use)

Military Metre Gauge (new)

Military Standard Gauge (new)

Lines quickly modified: The antiquated stock of the Cie Meusienne, seen here just prior to 1914, did not amuse the military very much, either.

(FACS)

German hands and some other railways – for example the unfortunate Tramways de l'Artois, a steam-worked system from Bethune – were in the middle. All this sector was finally held by the British but, except for lines in the actual front areas (the Albert group and bits around Bethune and Lens), they were worked by the French authorities – the Commissions de Réseau for the regions covered by the Nord and Est railway companies. The metre gauge played a small role only in this area, the military engineers, as already noted, preferring to replace them either with standard or, from about 1916, with 60cm gauge lines to reduce transhipment problems.

The front then swung south-eastward across the bottom end of the Nord and Aisne départements, once more dividing the straggling light railways of the Cambrésis and Soissonais districts, crossed the southern part of the Ardennes and entered the département of the Meuse. Apart from the disastrous French offensive on the Chemin des Dames – in and around the Aisne valley – this front was fairly static until the German advances of March 1918 and substantial transport links were organised by both sides. The metre gauge networks between Soissons and Reims were largely in the battle zone and thus unusable but the Germans did make use of parts of the CFD des Ardennes and of the CF de la Banlieue de Reims around the centres of Montcornet, Rethel and Asfeld, together with the CFD de l'Aisne line from Laon to Nouvion-le-Vineux; this latter was greatly extended, with several new branches to serve the central portion of the front. On the French side, most of the remaining metre gauge branches - notably the CF du Sud de l'Aisne – were operated by the military as lines of communication, much traffic being passed forward from the SE's Réseau de Seine et Marne over its link with the CFD line from La Ferté-sous-Jouarre to Montmirail. This linked with the CF du Sud de l'Aisne at Verdelot, whence traffic could reach almost to Château Thierry, and with the CF du Banlieue de Reims (CBR) at Montmirail. They were, however, too far back to be of much tactical use and the 60cm gauge was used in the forward areas instead. One semi-strategic metre gauge line, mainly using ex-Ardennes material, is noted as having been built down into the Aisne valley west of Reims to serve as a temporary feeder until standard gauge could be restored when the "great advance of 1917" took place. Since the latter never happened, it was not, apparently, of much value and its course is not clear.

Some metre gauge railways were quite heavily used as lines of communication well behind the front lines: This is the SE's line that ran westward from Amiens.

(C. WALKER'S COLLECTION)

This is the important junction betwen the CFD La Ferté – Montmirail branch which fed the Aisne front, and the neighbouring SE system that brought stores up from the rear areas.

(FACS)

Light railways and the Verdun campaign

It was to the east of this vicinity, in the département of Meuse, that the most interesting use of metre gauge railways for military purposes took place, around the French stronghold of Verdun. Two companies served this area; one was the Compagnie Meusienne, running a network of mainly roadside metre gauge lines around Verdun itself, with charming but rather old-fashioned stock notable features of which were the named locomotives and the standard gauge pattern of coupling which involved double buffers instead of the, more usual, central type. The other was the SE which had opened its 126km SE Réseau de la Woevre in the east of the département only just prior to the outbreak of war. This connected with the Meusienne at Verdun, whence it ran branches north to Montmédy and south east to Commercy. In contrast to the Meusienne it had modern stock with central buffing gear so that interchange of vehicles between the two was not possible even though they had a common station at Verdun.

The reason why these systems became so important was a historical one. The great fortress of Verdun, in reality an overlapping series of connected forts and fortifications, was the hub of the French defence system. At the same time it had acquired an almost mystical fame by surviving a Prussian seige in the war of 1870 and therefore held a special quality for the French people. The German commander-in-chief, Von Falkenhayn, decided to take advantage of these two facts and early in 1916 launched an all-out attack on Verdun. He hoped to capture it but calculated that, even if he did not, the French would be so anxious to prevent its fall that he might well destroy the flower of their armies and make Verdun a vast suppurating wound into which their valuable reserves of men and materiel might be poured and thus destroyed. In consequence a concentrated and determined attack was launched in February 1916 and pressed forward with no consideration for the losses incurred. Outlying forts fell and the main complex of fortifications was soon closely besieged, the sole channels of communications left to the French being an inadequate départemental road - and the equally inadequate Meusienne roadside branch from Bar-le-Duc and Revigny. By a fantastic feat of industry, the French army kept the unmacadamed road usable and a constant stream of supply vehicles passing to and fro along it; it is this route, the Voie Sacrée, which therefore receives most of the credit for the retention of Verdun. Most modern historians merely comment, in pitying tones, that there was a narrow gauge railway nearby and then do not mention it again.

A fairly rare view of the standard gauge in military use – The Avricourt – Blamont – Cirey taken over by the German army for ambulance purposes.

(FACS)

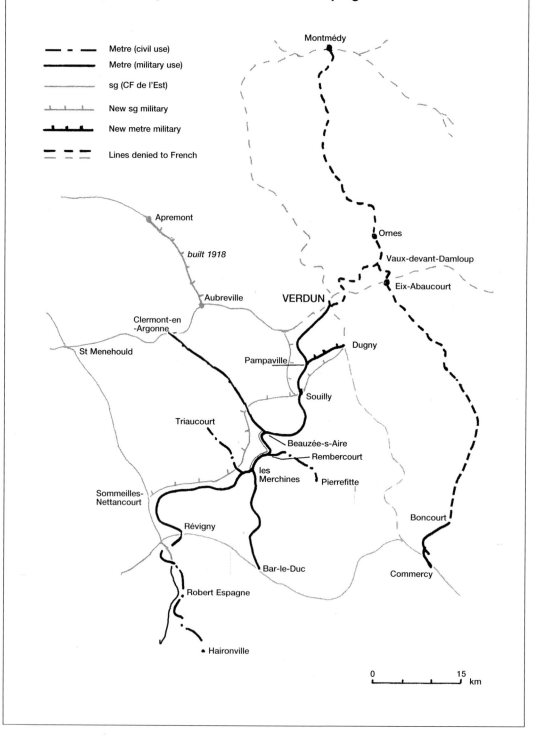

Secondary Railways in the 1916 Verdun Campaign

Legend:
- — ·— ·— Metre (civil use)
- ———— Metre (military use)
- ———— sg (CF de l'Est)
- —┴—┴— New sg military
- ▬▬▬▬ New metre military
- – – – Lines denied to French

Montmédy

Apremont

built 1918

Ornes

Vaux-devant-Damloup

Aubreville

VERDUN

Eix-Abaucourt

Clermont-en-Argonne

St Menehould

Pampaville

Dugny

Souilly

Triaucourt

Beauzée-s-Aire

Rembercourt

les Merchines

Pierrefitte

Sommeilles-Nettancourt

Boncourt

Révigny

Bar-le-Duc

Commercy

Robert Espagne

Haironville

0   15 km

This, however, gives a false picture for the Meusienne did play a considerable part in the victualling of Verdun, particularly at the beginning of the attack. The line itself was not quite as hopeless as is sometimes made out. The importance of Verdun was recognised and the main route, from the standard gauge junctions of Bar-le-Duc and Revigny to Verdun itself, had been taken over by the military engineers earlier in the war. By February 1916, when the real battle started, much of the track had been upgraded, one vital portion doubled, and proper transfer points established at a number of stations while a new branch was built east to Dugny on the former CF de l'Est line into Verdun from the south. Verdun itself could be attained only at night and with some danger so this transhipment point was important. A network of military 60cm gauge lines did carry on from these forward transfer points but the Verdun military system had never been dense and most branches were to the north and east of the city where they were interdicted by the enemy.

The metre gauge was of particular use for bringing up supplies such as rations and munitions which were not easy to carry by road, together with quantities of roadstone for repairing the Voie Sacrée, but also handled personnel in bulk; two special ambulance trains were even created to evacuate wounded. A traffic amounting at its peak to about 34 trains each way daily was organised over the single line between a new transhipment yard at Revigny and the supply points for Verdun fortress. To give some indication of its usefulness, in the month of June 1916 it carried no less than 69,000 tonnes of supplies and 73,000 men and, even after the completion in that month of a military standard gauge line roughly paralleling part of its course, from Sommeilles-Nettancourt to Dugny, it was still intensively worked. Locomotives and rolling stock from all over France were collected to supplement the inadequate Compagnie Meusienne material, no less than eighteen French systems contributing locomotives. It should be emphasised that these results were only achieved under formidable difficulties which may be appreciated when it is realised that, between them, the locomotives and stock used mustered no less than four largely incompatible buffing/coupling systems. The French lack of insistence upon true standardisation in earlier years proved particularly embarrassing when exposed to this sort of situation.

The SE Réseau de la Woevre was not so fortunate. Once the front had stabilised late in 1914, the northern section to Montmédy was divided by the front line and the St.Mihiel salient effectively precluded use of much of the Commercy branch. In the north, the Germans made intensive use of the line south from Montmédy, upgrading and laying new track and bringing in equipment from various sources – particularly the SNCV and the CF des Ardennes which had similar coupling arangements, and from various German secondary railways: Mallet locomotives from these were particularly in demand for the heavier trains. The French army did work, briefly, a short stub from Commercy north to Boncourt but eventually withdrew the stock onto the Meusienne at Bar-le-Duc. They were more successful initially with the common stem from Verdun out to Vaux-devant-Lamloup and thence north to Ornes and south to about Eix-Abaucourt, although the latter line ran very close to the front line and was difficult to operate. When the German attack began these lines became untenable and the equipment, including the contents of the main workshop at Verdun, was evacuated onto the Meusienne where it remained for the rest of the war.

Once the war settled down, the remainder of the front line, running mainly north-south across the eastern end of Vosges and along the 1871 Alsace-Lorraine frontier, was largely static until French advances in mid-1918. Light railways were, in any case, not numerous in this area and those around Gerardmer and Belfort particularly were in part taken over to serve as lines of supply to the French front positions. There was not much significant alteration; the Gerardmer – Le Schlucht was eventually linked to its German counterpart (a link dismantled after the war since they belonged to different départements!) and the CFIL du Territoire de Belfort had a feeder branch added at the western end and were extended east over the border to Sentheim – again a short lived connection; the Belfort system is interesting in that it did use a series of Baldwin 0-6-2T to supplement its electric stock and kept some of them post-war.

Effects of the war on light railways away from the battle zone

The lines already mentioned were not by any means the only ones to serve the allied (or in places the German) front lines but they will serve to illustrate one of the railways' two main wartime problems. The other one, already touched on above, was that facing the many lines operating elsewhere in France on their

Most common, however, were the specialist military 60cm gauge lines; their mainstay was the Pêchot-Bourdon double locomotive, seen here in American hands.   (AUTHOR'S COLLECTION)

normal business. The war was curiously localised so far as most of the country was concerned and railways 50 miles or more behind the main battle area could go about their everyday work almost as though nothing was happening. (indeed even the Meusienne worked one branch, from Revigny south to Haironville, throughout the 1916 campaign). But ...and it was a big but... they had to deal with constant demands from the military for equipment to use on lines actively engaged in supplying the war zone. Although big concerns like the Sud-France or the CFD could face this with a certain equanimity, transferring stock between their systems to help those which were hard-pressed, small départemental companies like the Tramways de Tarn-et-Garonne were seriously depleted of equipment with which to run their services. Their plight was made worse by the fact that, owing to the pressure of military production, even the proper maintenance of what they did retain was often difficult and spare parts were hard to come by. Some small lines, like the 60cm gauge Tramway de Trinité-sur-Mer à Etel in the Morbihan even found their complete property, both stock and track, requisitioned and taken off for war service, thus putting an end to their operations. It was all very well, as that company later bitterly pointed out, for the military later to return the stock (in a rather well-used condition) if the company no longer had any track to run it on.

After the war: the aftermath and its effects on minor railways; the return of Alsace-Lorraine; reconstruction of the devestated areas in the war zone.

Inevitably the war also had a considerable effect on the light railways further south, around the disputed provinces of Alsace-Lorraine. Most of these were in German hands at its beginning, as Elsass-Lothringen, and their light railways were very much on the German model. When the war ended, the territories west of the Rhine reverted to France and the "new" départements of Moselle, Haut-Rhin and Bas-Rhin had to pick up the pieces, somewhat aided (or hampered?) by retrospective legislation in 1923 which brought former German lines under French regulations. Somewhat naturally there were no suitable concessionaires already in place and the authorities were reduced to sequestering the existing railways and offering them around. Some were taken on by the newly formed main line company (CF d'Alsace-Lorraine or AL) and run directly by it, survivors duly passing to the SNCF in 1938. Some were taken on fairly fleetingly by local companies or régies municipales - the station-to-town lines in particular. The big SE took most of the rest but in general they did not last long.

Elsewhere more pressing problems arose. The preceding years had been bad enough but In 1918 the static war had been replaced by one of movement, first by the massive German advances of March and April and then, from August on, by the equally massive allied counter advances. Hence the devasated area was drastically enlarged and the job of restoring some semblance of normal life to communities which had, quite literally, been razed to the ground, was immense.

So far as the départemental authorities were concerned, the problem, over-simplified, fell into two parts. They had, theoretically, networks of existing secondary railways which, in practice, were often no longer there. They had either been destroyed during the fighting or their trackbeds had been utilised by the armies of both sides for their own purposes – 60cm gauge lines had replaced former standard or metre gauge ones where this was expedient but, equally, some standard gauge branches had been built new, or over former metre gauge routes and these were often not really adapted to serve civilian and community needs. It was incumbent on the départements to restore already authorised lines to their former use and status but the old concessionaires were often reluctant to reclaim "their" properties... after all, many had been of dubious viability even before the war, now the material was dispersed and the physical infrastructure needed complete rebuilding. Why go to all that trouble just for certain arguments with the département over levels of subsidy and funding? The problem was only partly solved by new commercial groupings such as the CFS du Nord Est (NE) and by the formation of Régies Départementales to reconstruct and operate lines directly; a few départements gave short-term concessions to groups such as the SE specifically to rebuild lines and return them to operating condition before offering them for tender once more.

After the war, the 60cm gauge agricultural lines reaped a rich harvest: an ex WD Baldwin 4-6-0T on the Vis-en-Artois System.   (D. Trevor Rowe's Collection)

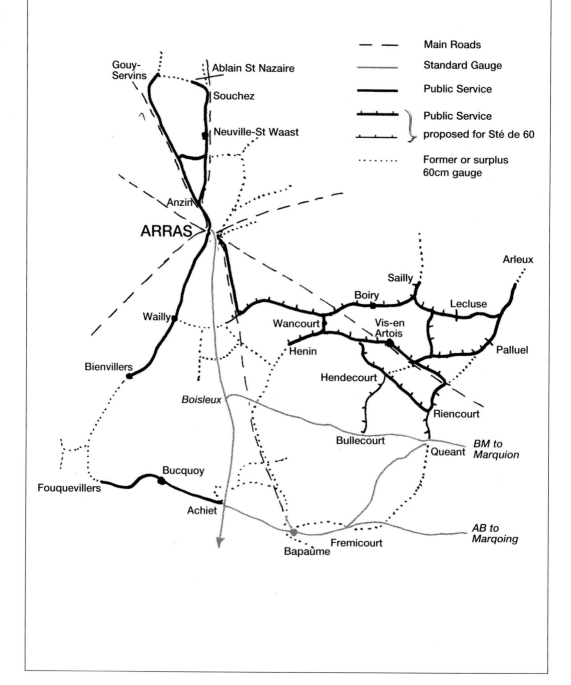

Ministère des Régions Libérées: past and current 60cm gauge lines around Arras, showing sections later sold to Sté de Voie de 60 (Vis-en-Artois system). Year 1923.

Main Roads

Standard Gauge

Public Service

Public Service proposed for Sté de 60

Former or surplus 60cm gauge

Gouy-Servins

Ablain St Nazaire

Souchez

Neuville-St Waast

Anzin

ARRAS

Wailly

Bienvillers

Boisleux

Fouquevillers

Bucquoy

Achiet

Bapaume

Fremicourt

Henin

Wancourt

Boiry

Sailly

Vis-en-Artois

Lecluse

Arleux

Palluel

Hendecourt

Bullecourt

Riencourt

Queant

BM to Marquion

AB to Marqoing

Light railways & their role in rebuilding the devestated areas

Added to this problem was another: in the war zone many towns and villages were partly or wholly flattened and their surrounding countryside was what one might describe as war-weary: riddled with trenches and dugouts; covered with grotesque tangles of barbed wire; pitted with the remains of exploded and unexploded munitions; criss-crossed by what had been already inadequate roads even before the military got at them. These had to be revived wholesale and to do so, the government formed a national department, the Ministère des Regions Libérées to organise and oversee the whole business.

It was just in time. As the previous inhabitants returned and camped out in their ruins, they naturally wanted to get rid of all traces of the past years as rapidly as possible. The MRL, however, realised quickly that it was sitting on one massive asset – the systematic networks of 60cm gauge field railways which had been built up right across the region by all the participating armies. The MRL promptly froze all plans to rip these up and started instead to consider how they might be used. Those in the former French sector – Ardennes, Marne, Aisne, parts of Somme – were largely ex-French Army in any case so could just be taken over; former German systems were prizes of war so they were all right. The MRL had, however, to negotiate with the British and, to a lesser extent, the Americans, and to buy-in such of their existing lines and plant as were likely to be needed – for example it bought "all lines east of the Paris-Dunkerque road" and the main British maintenance base at Beaurainville lock, stock and...rails, including a vast store of some 100 steam locomotives, 250 tractors, over 5000 wagons, 47000 tonnes of rail and sleepers, plus a range of spares. An even greater prize was the former German army works at Haubourdin in the Département du Nord, a typically Teutonic major workshop capable of the heaviest repairs.

Between 1919 and 1926 the networks provided a service of inestimable value in clearing up the mess and were directly accountable to the Ministry; as an example those in Pas de Calais alone shifted over 11 million tonne/kms of freight during 1920, most of which was war clearance activity. In some places, particularly the Département du Nord which was mainly behind the ex-German lines, they were used for nothing else but in other départements - Pas-de-Calais; Aisne; Oise; Marne; Ardennes – they were also organised to provide public passenger and goods service in place of destroyed systems. Around Arras especially, there was a

And some had very long lives; these ex-German 0-8-0Ts (plus a Decauville) rotting at Coucy le Château lasted in service until about 1960. (AUTHOR'S COLLECTION)

network of public services ranging from one train on Saturdays only to four trains daily and these continued into the mid 1920s. In spite of charging custormers for the public goods and passenger services they provided, all were very much in overt deficit; the comparison may be a little unfair since no account appears to have been taken of the "unpaid" services such as shifting the huge piles of rubble and debris of war but by 1924 most of this had apparently been done. The Ministry therefore sought ways of offloading the cost of surviving lines onto départements, who, in turn, ran selected survivors "en régie" or offered short operating concessions to private individuals or groups.

The whole operation had, in any case, been considered as a short-term expedient and so it was not surprising that operating kilometrage plummeted during 1925 and 1926. A very few lines retained public service into the 1930s – the CFS du Nord Est worked a couple of branches – and industrial concerns like the Dompierre sugar refinery in Somme bought short sections but the only long term survivor on a large scale was the network of lines east of Arras, around Vis-en-Artois in Pas-de-Calais. There were undoubtedly political implications in this one, a M. Bellenger forming a rather shadowy "Sté du Voie de 60" in 1924 and continuing to run both passenger and goods services for a couple of years. Behind it all, however, were the big sugar refineries at Cambrai and Vis who were busily dividing up the territory between them. In 1925 they took advantage of a government decision to sell off surviving systems rather than offering them as concessions. There was a bit of a blip since they wanted to get the 1925 beetroot season out of the way under existing rulings but in January 1926 the "Societé Anonyme des Chemins de Fer à Voie de 0.60 du Pas de Calais" was formed, buying the maintenance equipment, 105km of track, 30 locomotives and 700 wagons; headquarters and central workshops were transferred to Vis and the system returned to purely industrial use. It survived until 1957.

As to the rest, most of the destroyed metre gauge lines were painfully rebuilt, and the standard gauge ones either reconditioned or relaid if their trackbeds had been used for field railways. Nobody seemed to know just what to do about the additional branches, both metre and standard gauge, that had been built for supply purposes; some were scrapped because they belonged to no-one – the Flanders links were of that type. Some, mainly standard gauge, were assimilated by nearby systems but often without any formal authorisation which caused trouble later. "Borrowed" stock was officially reconditioned and restored to its previous owners. Life went on.

CHAPTER 4
Between The Wars: The autorail era.

Postwar Consolidation: The new Light Railway Empires & Régies Départementales

One of the main effects of the war was political. In the north-east, especially, concessionaires coming back to pick up the pieces found that there were very few left to pick up. In an atmosphere of financial uncertainty and with the rapid development of road transport, many decided to surrender their concessions rather than face the task of laboriously rebuilding lines that might be liabilities – thus the CF de la Banlieue de Reims (CBR) gave up entirely and its various properties were dispersed to others. Départements, therefore, were themselves compelled to reconstruct systems they felt were still necessary and either run them directly (en régie) or look for new concessionaires. This need brought forth a new breed of entrepreneurs who saw a future in combining large empires cheaply and often on advantageous terms – so arose the big new groupings such as the Compagnie Générale des Voies Ferrées d'Intérêt Local (CGL, or VFIL) based on the old fiefdoms of Messrs Level, Dequeker and Lambert or the CFS du Nord Est which developed from combining the St Quentin – Guise and the other Jourdain family lines in Aisne.

These empires were usually based on an existing system from which they consolidated. Thus the CGL started by combining the CF d'Anvin – Calais with its neighbours the Aire – Rimeux – Berck and the Tramway d'Ardres – Pont d'Ardres. From there it was able to pick up the remains of the Oise system from Noyon and its associated line from Milly to Formerie. Standard gauge too was acceptable to it; the smashed lines around Bapaume, Boisleux, Marquion and Cambrai made a nice little cluster and the CGL was well known in the Département of Pas-de-Calais so it got preference.

This delightful vignette will have to commemmorate all the little seaside tramways – or were they partly light railways? A train of the Beziers tramways system has reached its seaside destination at Valras Plage but surely it is mainly locals who patronise it. (FACS)

Needless to say old groupings such as the SE, the CFD and the CFS made sure that they were not left out. Did a département find itself with a system on its hands? well, here was an excellent company, very experienced in running other peoples' railways and with all the organisation needed. Even well away from the battlefronts, départements such as Dordogne, with two ailing companies to support, saw a lot of sense in reclaiming them and handing the whole lot over to the CFD; others turned to the SE. Commercial groupings, then, were one answer to the post-war crisis; the other was a proliferation of Régies Départementales, direct operation by a unit of the département, especially where that département had initially built and equipped the lines. Many were really holding operations but some were very progressive. For example the Département de l'Ain found itself with a collection of scattered and generally helpless concessionaires and, as discussed below, turned it into a genuine département-wide transport system. One should say that there was method behind all this. The new groupes and régies had to be among the most progressive operators even if only because what they took over was generally in a very rocky state financially; they had every incentive to get costs down and improve services if they were to survive at all.

New developments: tactical links; completions of previous systems

So, despite all this devastation and consolidation, light-railway development was by no means dead. New lines, indeed, were being built right up to about 1930, although it was noticeable that these were almost entirely on their own right of way. Even the remotest départements had realized the folly of constructing any further roadside lines, when motor road transport was developing so fast. Such new lines as there were fell into three main categories. There were the important but short 'link lines' constructed by the new light-railway empires to join up previously independent and separate portions of their systems; there were the second and third réseaux that had been under consideration by some big départements when war broke out, and a few of which were optimistically completed; and there were a few genuine new branches, once again usually built by the big private companies.

Early attempts at i/c electric drive were never very successful, although the crew seem quite proud of this Crochat car on the Tramways de l'Ouest du Dauphiné   (AUTHOR'S COLLECTION)

The link lines were built more for operating convenience than to open up fresh country. They enabled economies to be made in locomotives and stock, since these could be easily transferred from one section to another and heavy repairs could be concentrated on one or two depots instead of the four or five that had been needed by the original small companies now taken over. Sometimes they brought into being connected systems of quite impressive size, as in the case of the Tramways de l'Ain, already mentioned, to the north and east of Lyon. The Ain Département had originally leased its lines to no less than seven separate companies, all of which were taken over en régie from 1921. To join up the old lines, various small links were constructed, especially in the major towns of Villefranche and Bourg; a central depot was built at the latter town; and a new crosscountry link with the SNCF's Besançon branch was opened as late as 1934, the whole giving a connected length of some 441 km. Furthermore a sizable chunk was electrified with modern bogie stock.

The genuinely new branches, on the other hand, did serve hitherto untapped districts, although the reasons for building them were more varied. Thus the CF des Côtes du Nord simply wished to complete the system which had been in course of construction before 1914, and did so in 1923; political reasons undoubtedly had a hand in bringing forth the Etat's Réseau Breton extension line from Châteaulin out to Camaret on the western coast of the Brittany peninsula; while the VFDM (it said) had strictly commercial reasons for the creation of its superb 75km electric route from Toulouse eastward to the important market city of Castres. Yet, whether soundly conceived or built rashly for an already diminishing traffic, these lines marked only an Indian summer of the light-railway era. Unfortunately, too, the technology rarely met the needs of its proponents. Most small companies which had survived the war, and a good many of the larger ones too, were urgently seeking ways of economizing on those railways that they already ran, and this desire ushered in what might fitly be called the autorail era but its results were very patchy.

Dead-ends in motive power development: Steam railmotors; failure of the electric power option

Autorails, or railcars, were no new thing to French minor railway companies. Some of the more penurious among them had experimented with steam-cars from their early days. That these, mainly on the

i/c mechanical drive won the battle. A De Dion JM-series car and trailer van (an old luggage van by the look of it) constitute a typical train on the Cormeilles – Glos-Montfort in Eure.   (FACS)

CAMPAN (H.-P.) — Station du Tramway

One of the smaller rural electrified systems – the ill-fated Tramways de la Bigorre pauses en-route; the state of the country road shows why the "tram" existed at all. (FACS)

LE LIMOUSIN PITTORESQUE
2355 ROCHECHOUART — Le Tram

Quite different were the substantial lines and power cars of the CFD de la Haute Vienne. (AUTHOR'S COLLECTION)

Of course, soon people started modifying things in "artisanale" fashion. A standard De Dion ML car and what is probably a locally rebodied JM on the CF du Blanc a Argent.   (FACS/CHAPUIS)

Purrey, Serpollet or Rowan patents, had not been very successful was due to the disadvantage common to most steam-cars; the limited space allowed only a small boiler and engine, which were easily strained and could not cope with peak traffic periods. Moreover, when they broke down, the carriage part was naturally immobilized as well, and for a poor company this could be a considerable embarrassment. Early experiments with petrol-electric drive, mainly on the Pieper and Westinghouse systems, had not been much more successful.

Neither, alas, had overhead electrification had the success which its protagonists forecast before 1914. Most of the shorter electric lines that had been built were little more than country versions of contemporary urban tramways, electrified on the classic tramway pattern of 550 or 600 volts DC and stocked with near relatives of the typical urban tramcar equipped with conventional coupling gear to haul light freight. This was especially so in the Ouest, Nord and Est regions where routes were not particularly difficult to build and operate. Even in the south-east, the majority were former German-designed town to station tramways or short suburban lines. Extensive départemental systems such as the Tramways des Alpes Maritimes were only built where steam would have failed and, even so, usually had short lives; the odd exceptions, such as the CFIL du Territoire de Belfort and the CF de la Camargue only pointed the moral. Only in the south west were serious attempts made at full-scale départemental networks employing alternating current at industrial frequencies and with purpose designed four-wheeled or bogie power cars and stock and it is notable that hardly anything major was produced after the mid 1920s - a time when Belgium, for example, was rapidly extending its electrified secondary system. Traffic on the one completely new line that was built, the very high quality VFDM route from Toulouse to Castres, really did not justify its existence and it was that, as much as politics which caused its closure only ten years after opening. The total list, overleaf, shows how little development really took place. Note that the opening date given is that at which electrification was implemented which was sometimes many years after an original opening with steam traction.

Small and large electrified railways of Intérêt Local

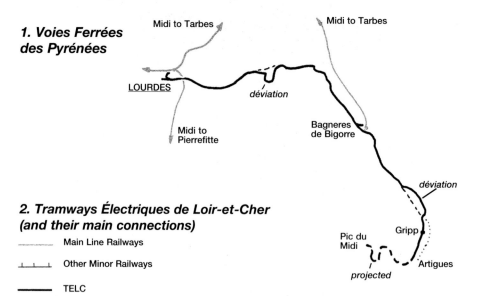

1. Voies Ferrées des Pyrénées

Midi to Tarbes

Midi to Tarbes

LOURDES

déviation

Midi to Pierrefitte

Bagneres de Bigorre

déviation

Gripp

Pic du Midi

Artigues

projected

2. Tramways Électriques de Loir-et-Cher (and their main connections)

············ Main Line Railways

ⴴⴴⴴⴴ Other Minor Railways

▬▬▬ TELC

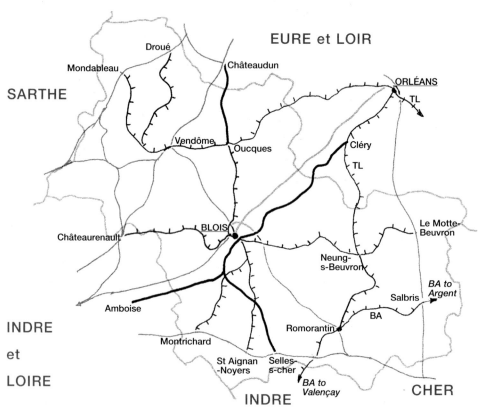

EURE et LOIR

Droué

Mondableau

Châteaudun

ORLÉANS
TL

SARTHE

Vendôme

Oucques

Cléry

TL

Le Motte-Beuvron

Châteaurenault

BLOIS

Neung-s-Beuvron

BA to Argent

Salbris

Amboise

BA

Romorantin

INDRE et LOIRE

Montrichard

St Aignan -Noyers

Selles-s-cher

BA to Valençay

INDRE

CHER

opened	line	gauge	current	close	group
Region Ouest					
1903	Finistère, Twys electriques du	metre	DC 550	1932	
1907	Avranches (Ouest-Ville) Twy de	metre	DC 550	1914	Manche CF
1911	Querqueville – Urville, ligne de	metre	DC 550	1944	Cherbourg Twys
1923	Bretons, Twys	metre	DC 550	1949	Régie
Region Nord					
1881	Valenciennes à Anzin et exts, Twys	metre	DC 600	1966	CEN
1899	CEN Réseau du Nord (extension lines)	metre	DC 600	1966	CEN
1899	Laon, CF de	metre	DC 600	1971	régie 1947
1900	Cassel, Twy de	metre	DC 600	1934	
1900	Etaples à Paris Plage, Twy de	metre	DC 600	1940	
1900	le Portel – Boulogne Gare	metre	DC 600	1940	CEN/TEB
1910	Tergnier – St Gobain et Anizy, Twy	metre	DC 600	1940	
1915	Villers-le-Bel et Exts, CF de	metre	DC 600	1949	
1935	Carvin, Mines de	sg	AC 700	1940	***

*** really a mines branch with public service.

opened	line	gauge	current	close	group
Region Est					
1904	Gerardmer, Twys de	metre	DC 600	1939	
1907	Munster – la Schlucht (rack rly)	metre	DC 750	1914	*
1910	Dornach – Morschwiller-le-bas, Twy	sg	DC 800	1917	
1910	St Avold (Gare-Ville)	metre	DC 850	1944	*
1910	Territoire de Belfort, CFIL du	metre	AC 6600/25	1940	
1912	Hagondage – Mezières-les-Metz, Twy	sg	DC 1000	1964	*
1912	Novéant – Gorze, Twy de	sg	DC 750	1933	*
1913	Beaucourt (Gare-Ville) Twy de	metre	DC 550	1944	
1919	Strasbourg Twys (suburban lines)	metre	DC 800	1957	*
1923	Turckhein – Trois Epis, Twy de	metre	DC 600	1933	*
1929	Mulhouse, Twys de	metre	DC 600	1957	*
1930	Strasbourg – Ottrot, ligne de	metre	DC 800	1955	CTS
1935	Colmar-Wintzenheim, ligne de	metre	DC 600	1960	*
1935	Langres, Régie municipale du CF de	metre	DC 600	1971	Régie

* former German operations

opened	line	gauge	current	close	group
Region Sud-Est					
1907	Nice et du Littoral, Twys de	metre	DC 600	1947	deptl lines
1889	Fourvière et de l'Ouest Lyonnais	metre	AC 550	1954	OTL 1911
1889	Viricelles à St Symphorien Twy de	metre	DC 550	1933	
1892	Saleve CF du (3rd rail, rack)	metre	DC 700	1937	
1898	Aubenas – Vals-les-Bains, Twy de	metre	DC 550	1950	
1899	Grenoble à Chapareillan, Twy de	metre	DC 600	1947	
1899	Moutiers – Bride-les-bains Twy de	metre	DC 500	1930	
1901	St Gervais – Vallorcine, ligne de	metre	DC 600/800		PLM/SNCF
1902	Grenoble – Veurey, ligne de	metre	DC 600	1954	SGTE
1902	VFD lignes du (3 lines in Isère)	metre	DC 600	1951	VFD
1903	Aix-en-Provence – Marseille, Twy de	metre	DC 600	1948	BdR
1903	St George de Commiers à la Mure..	metre	DC 1200\2400		
1907	Lyon – la Balme, ligne de (rural)	sg	AC 6000/16	1937	OTL

opened	line	gauge	current	close	group
1907	Lyon – la Balme, ligne de (urban)	sg	DC 600	1952	OTL
1909	Alpes-Maritimes, Twys des	metre	AC 6600/25	1932	Sud France
1909	Dijon – Gevrey Chambertin, Twy de	metre	DC 600	1953	Dijon Twys
1911	Grenoble à Villard de Lans, Twy de	metre	DC 800	1951	SGTE
1912	Bellegarde à Chezery, CFIL de	metre	DC 600	1937	
1920	Camargue, CF de la	metre	AC 6600/25	1951	
1921	Morez - la Cure, ligne de	metre	DC 2200	1958	NStCM
1925	la Ciotat (Gare-Ville) ligne de	sg	DC 600	1955	BdR
1927	Valence-St Peray, Twy de	metre	DC 600	1950	TA
1928	Vicinaux CF (Champagnole lines)	metre	DC 1500	1950	CFV
1929	Ain, régie des Twys de (5 lines)	metre	AC 10000/25	1954	RDTA
1932	Annemasse - Sixt, ligne de	metre	DC 1500	1954	CEN
1932	Lyon à Neuville, Twy de	metre	DC 600	1957	OTL
1954	Chamonix au Montenvers, CF de	metre	AC 11000/50		
1957	Mont Blanc, Twy du	metre	AC 11000/50	1957	TMB

Region Sud-ouest
opened	line	gauge	current	close	group
1888	Bayonne-Lycée-Biarritz, Twys de	metre	DC 650	1948	POM
1897	Pierrefitte, Cauterets, Luz, CF de	metre	DC 600	1970	
1908	Bordeaux à Beychac et Cailleau, Twy	sg	AC 600	1949	TEOB**
1908	Bordeaux à Camarsac, Twy de	sg	DC 600	1949	TEOB**
1908	Limoges - Aix-s-Vienne ligne de	metre	AC 10000/50	1949	CHDV 1912
1910	Cerdagne, ligne de	metre	DC 850		MIDI/SNCF
1911	Ariége, Twys electriques de l'	metre	DC 750	1937	
1912	Haute-Vienne, CFD de la	metre	AC 10000/50	1949	Giros
1912	Luchon - Superbagneres, ligne de	metre	AC 3000/50	1966	
1913	Libournais, Twys electriques du	metre	AC 6600/16	1949	Ortal
1913	Loir-et-Cher, Twys electriques de	metre	AC 6000/25	1933	
1913	Pyrenées Orientales CF des	metre	AC 6000/25	1927	
1914	Bigorre, Twys electriques de la	metre	AC 6000/25	1934	
1914	Marignac au Val d'Aran, Twy de	metre	DC 650	1954	
1918	Réseau Basque, VFDM	metre	DC 650	1948	VFDM
1922	Bayonne-Anglet-Biarritz, CF	metre	DC 650	1952	
1924	St Ignace - la Rhûne, ligne de	metre	AC 3000/25		VFDM
1930	Toulouse à Castres et Revel, CF de	metre	DC 1500	1939	VFDM

+   at time of electrification

*   formerly German

Successful substitution: The rise of the internal combustion engine

So for most concerns, steam or electricity was not really a modern option. By the 1920s, however, the internal-combustion engine was giving promise of economy coupled with sufficient power, and experiments were started with petrol-engined cars. The earliest ones were, as might have been expected, buses-on-rails - or, rather, converted ambulances on rails. Some of the other early experiments were even more original in conception, involving more often than not the attachment of a motor to a wagon or coach underframe. It may be thought that this would be a very inefficient way of producing a railcar but this was apparently not so. It is true that the Tramways de Tarn-et-Garonne, in the first few months after receiving their Horme-et-Buire cars, had more breakdowns than successful runs but, as the operating superintendent pointed out:

Finally one got efficient vehicles: the common Billard A80D, running "bunker first" (if that is the correct term) with a purpose-built luggage trailer at Le Cheylard. (AUTHOR)

53

'The delays are due not so much to motor failure as to the fact that the driver, though willing and brave, does not yet understand his gears.'

Once he became experienced, the line seems to have been satisfied, as for instance were the Chemins de Fer du Rhône, Saône-et-Loire, which in 1923 got Berliet of Lyon to convert a four-wheeled passenger coach to a single-ended petrol-mechanical railcar. They grumbled a bit because it could not pull a trailer but 'it served well until the line closed' some eleven years later. As well as these oddities, some conventional petrol-mechanical cars were produced, mainly by Renault-Scemia who turned out some very tram-like vehicles, copying electric tramway practice even to the elaborate lining-out on the paintwork. The main utility, however, came first from buses-on-rails and then from specialised bogie vehicles.

The technical development of the railmotor is covered in more detail in Chapter 14. From the historical point of view their importance lies in the improved services and lesser costs they provided. Yes the early railbuses were rattly, noisy and gave a bone-shaking ride if the track was bad - but then so did elderly four-wheeled conventional railway coaches or the same buses jarring along the, largely unmacadamed, byroads of the period; it was only later, when roads were much improved, that passengers began being really rude about the ageing "sauterelles" as they came to be known. The later, purpose designed, bogie cars must have been comparative bliss. Most importantly, of course, they speeded up the passenger services since they enabled these to be separated from the old mixed-train concept with its interminable shunting; parcels and small-goods traffic also benefited and some systems even developed, or converted, special parcels railcars or trailers.

If these early cars caused something of a revolution at a time when secondary lines in Britain were still wedded to steam, then those developed during the mid-1930s were a genuine advance in both economy and comfort. There certainly were dead-ends – the Crochat petrol-electric system was one and battery electrics were another – but the potential market was big enough for some very substantial development to take place. By the mid 1930s, four firms were really specializing in light-railway railcars and all had developed efficient machines. De Dion Bouton built mainly for the narrow gauge, developing their railbuses from the very bus-like JM3 and 4, to the more sophisticated M and N series of six-wheelers which hid their bus origins under a sophisticated body and then on to the 'O' series of genuine bogie railcars; their main characteristic was lightness of construction. Renault, with the exception of the successful ABH series for the metre gauge, concentrated on the standard gauge and, with the receipt of big main-line and overseas orders, largely retired from the light-railway market; while SCF Verney and Billard of Tours steadily developed railbuses and double-ended railcars for both standard and narrow gauges. Verney was the more conservative firm, clinging for a long time to single-ended cars and bodies of a very square-built pattern, while Billard, in conjunction with the CFD, made the most notable advance of the period. This happened in 1937 when the CFD, which had previously experimented with various types of railbus, took the courageous step of ordering large numbers of double-ended diesel railcars of a completely new design to re-equip its major railway systems.

To meet the requirement, Billard produced not one design but a range from 80hp. to 210hp. All were double-ended, incorporated a large luggage compartment for parcels traffic, and were built with a low centre of gravity to enable advantage to be taken of the higher speeds made possible by advances in design. Moreover, they were designed from the start to tow trailers, and matching goods and passenger trailers were produced for them. No less than 55 cars were built for metre-gauge lines before the 1939-45 war stopped production, and some of these are still in service today, together with one or two built after the war. They were so successful that if a branch closed they found a ready sale elsewhere.

Lines in decline: early closures and attempts at retention

In spite of the prospective economies which railcars offered, however, they wwere not a panacea. A considerable number of light railways closed down in the face of road competition during the 1930s. These were mainly lines of the tramway type which had often not been able to support more than two trains daily each way, even at their inauguration. A typical example was our old friend the Tramways de la Corrèze which, after passing from concessionaire to concessionaire, was finally bought back by the département, all

Edit. Biez

MONTSOLS (Rhône) La Gare

Despite all the modernisation plans, many rural systems simply collapsed and closed; typical is the three-branch CF du Beaujolais, here seen in its early pride but swept away by 1939.

except one line being replaced by road services between 1932 and 1934. This, it will be noted, was a system initiated only twenty years previously and other lines and systems fared yet worse. Even the expedient of trying to interest the big private concerns such as the CFD eventually met with only partial success, for these 'empires' promptly closed any lines which they could not make viable, or else took short-term concessions which they did not renew. The following list, by no means complete, gives an idea of the variety of lines which were forced to close:

List of total closures during 1930's

Line or system	Number of lines	Length (km.)	Dates opened	Final closure
Tramways de l'Ardèche	4	138	1910-11	1930
Tramways de l'Aude	12	336	1901-08	1932
CF du Beaujolais	3	94	1901-02	1938
Tramways de l'Indre	4	182	1902-05	1939
Tramways de Loir-et-Cher	19	285	1888-1908	1934
Tramways du Loiret	4	135	1905-17	1933-34
CF de Rhône, Saône-et-Loire	2	63	1911-13	1934
Tramway de la Trinité à Etel(mg)	1	19.9	1922	1935
SE Réseau de la Woevre	2	123	1914	1938
CVFE de l'Orne	3	89	1913	1937
Tramways de Eure-et-Loir	6	215	1899	1936
VF Economiques du Poitou	3	164	1914	1934
Tramways de Tarn-et-Garonne	6	182	1913	1933
Tramways de Lot-et-Garonne	3	130	1911	1933

Yet many more railways survived. Particularly where the roads were bad – and this meant most country districts – the départements often bought back individual lines, either when their concessions ran out or when they would otherwise have closed, and amalgamated them into directly operated Régies as mentioned earlier; the Régies shut down the most uneconomic branches, replacing them with bus services, and modernized the rest. This modernization was sometimes on a large scale, including in some cases extensive electrification and the private companies were not left out. Thus the CF Economiques du Nord electrified its 43 km. long line from Annemasse to Samoens in the French Alps, extending it 6km to Sixt and rebuilding it on a better alignment between 1930 and 1932. In the north, the CGL kept virtually all its empire in being by constructing a whole fleet of diesel railcars and, later, diesel locomotives in its own works for use by its constituent companies. In this way a considerable mileage remained in operation, although increasingly in the hands of big companies and régies départementales; many lines might have had a reasonable future in front of them if they had not suddenly been faced with another setback, the so-called "co-ordination scheme" of 1938.

CHAPTER 5
Co-ordination and after

The 1938 co-ordination scheme and its effects

The national 'co-ordination scheme' of 1938 arose out of a laudable desire to organize and improve French transport, both national and local. On the national side, it consisted largely of amalgamation of all the major railway companies into the Societé Nationale de Chemins de Fer (SNCF), virtually a compagnie fermière subsidized by the exchequer and entrusted with the running of the nation's railways for a normal concession period - in this case initially up to 1976. On the local side, it took the form of demanding planned transport, on the very plausible theory that rationalization would help to reduce the considerable losses that were being made, especially where different forms of transport competed with each other.

The départements, particularly, were very concerned since they had to meet the losses of their concessionary companies; therefore each département had to submit to central authority a "plan de transport", the chief feature of which was the elimination of parallel services. So far this appears reasonable, but in practice it was spoiled by the extremely restrictive nature of the regulations which extended even to the number of services to be authorized on any one route. Furthermore, the execution of the plan, so far as light railways were concerned, was disastrous. Over a third of the existing mileage was declared redundant and closed, along with many SNCF branch lines. In most cases the services were nominally replaced by buses and lorries, often run by the old concessionaires or by extensions of existing parallel services.

Since the overall system of Intérêt Local dropped from a peak of over 20,000km in 1928 to some 12,000km in 1939, there is no doubt that much of this pruning was desirable and already taking place with or without legislation. Many systems, like the CF de l'Yonne, had outlived their usefulness and could

1722. SAINT-JEAN-d'ASSÉ (Sarthe) — La Gare

The war, and road transport, finally saw off the few surviving steam tramways such as the Tramways de la Sarthe, which closed its final branch in 1947.

(FACS)

Examples of three major affermages, showing SNCF connections

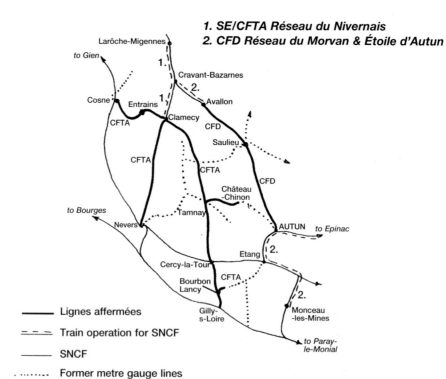

1. SE/CFTA Réseau du Nivernais
2. CFD Réseau du Morvan & Étoile d'Autun

Larôche-Migennes
to Gien
1.
Cravant-Bazarnes
2.
Cosne
1
Avallon
Entrains
Clamecy
CFTA
CFD
Saulieu
CFTA
CFTA
CFD
Château
-Chinon
to Bourges
Tamnay
Nevers
AUTUN   to Epinac
Etang   2.
Cercy-la-Tour
Bourbon   CFTA
Lancy
2.
Monceau
-les-Mines
Gilly-
s-Loire
to Paray-
le-Monial

——— Lignes affermées

= = = Train operation for SNCF

——— SNCF

· · · · · · · Former metre gauge lines

to Paris   Révigny
to
Strasbourg
Mont-s-
Meurthe
Rambervillers
to Paris
Doulevant
-le-C
Bruyères
Troyes   to   to St Die
Epinal
Chaumont
Langres
Châtillon
-s-Seine   Culmont   to
-Chalindrey   Belfort
Poinson
Beneuvre   Vesoul
Is-s-Tille   GRAY
to Dijon
Essertene-Cecey

3. SE/CFTA Reséau de Franche Comté

hardly have been made viable even with extensive modernization; others, particularly concerns with long stretches of roadside track, could be more conveniently replaced by buses running on the improved roads which the départements were having to provide in any case. There were, however, many seemingly 'political' closures, where road transport interests with influence on départemental councils promised what often turned out to be illusory savings; secondary lines of Intérêt Général which came under the State, or major inter-départemental links, were almost certain to be closed if there was a competing SNCF service, even if substantial and carrying good traffic. A typical and much publicised example was the Toulouse – Castres line of the VFDM already cited, opened only ten years before with modern equipment but closed (at least officially) because it, very roughly, paralleled a more roundabout SNCF branch; the latter had to be retained since it provided 'essential connections' with other lines but whether the electric line would actually have kept enough traffic to survive in any case was problematic. Nonetheless it was one of the local scandals of the era. For the railway enthusiast the whole gloomy picture was only slightly brightened by the fact that some of the lignes co-ordonnées were acquired by private interests, such as sugar refineries, for their own purposes.

A gesture of help; the lignes affermées

As briefly mentioned elsewhere, the big private companies in particular suffered when whole départemental systems under their control were ruthlessly closed. In order to lessen the blow, and provide some relief for otherwise redundant staff, the new SNCF was charged with conceding operation of certain secondary lines in the most threatened areas to large private concerns – notably the SE, CFD and CFS; presumably the SNCF staff thus displaced were redeployed elsewhere. This venture, known as "affermage", had actually started back in 1934 when the, then, CF de l'Est passed over a set of lines in Franche-Comté to the SE, partly replacing the latter's metre gauge holdings there. This Réseau de Franche Comté, based on the old regional depot and workshops at Gray, originally comprised:

Gray – Is-s-Tille (46km)
Is-s-Tille – Chatillon-s-Seine via Poinson-Beneuvre (73km)
Gray – Culmont-Chalindrey (45km)

Two 4-wheeled cars of the CFD at Monceau les Mines SNCF, on the Morvan affermage. (AUTHOR)

From 1939, the Chatillon line affermage was extended to Troyes (67km) and a cross-country branch from Langres to Poinson-Beneuvre (47km) was added. Later the CFTA took over train operation, but not the infrastructure, on the routes from Chatillon to Chaumont and from Langres to Vesoul via Culmont-Chalindrey. From 1963 onwards (closure of Langres – Poinson) there was a steady decline in rail operation on these lines, most passenger services being turned over to road by 1970; on the other hand in 1973 outlying lines from Wassy and Bruyères were assimilated into the system and traction was largely dieselised while Gray workshops capitalised on their knowledge of antique steam locomotives to offer repair facilities for preserved railways!

As noted briefly in Chapter 10, the CFTA also acquired a substantial group of lines on the borders of Nievre (Réseau du Nivernais) centred on Clamecy and running south west to Nevers and south-east via Tamnay-Chatillon to Cercy-la-Tour with a branch from Tamnay to Château-Chinon, and from Cercy on to Gilly-s-Loire via Bourbon Lancy; this last section lost its central portion, from Cercy to just north of Bourbon Lancy, in 1954. On the other hand a part of the line from Clamecy to Cosne-sur-Loire, cut back to Entrains, was acquired as late as 1977 and the system also took over some services between Clamecy and Laroche-Migennes. It was this system which acquired the remaining stub of the CFD's Saône-et-Loire lines at Bourbon Lancy, when the latter company withdrew. The other major affermage was also in this area, just to the east, and was the CFD's Réseau du Morvan. In essence this comprised the long north-south line from Avallon to Autun, which still runs for freight and actually extends for operational purposes to a link with the CFTA at Cravant-Bazarnes, north of Clamecy. For many years, the CFD, on behalf of the SNCF, also ran some services from Autun, in particular to Etang and Monceau-les-Mines.

These were by no means the only lignes affermées but most of the others were single routes ranging from the short CFD operations in Indre-et-Loire to the quite long CFS-operated branch in Marne from Longueville to Provins and Esternay; part of the latter, from Provins to Longueville, has now been reassimilated into the SNCF but that is the only real long-term success story. The others lasted longer than they might otherwise have done but the surviving stretches have been freight-only for some time.

In general the CFD mainly used its own locotractors and railcars, leasing SNCF material only when needed, while the SE used SNCF stock almost exclusively except for some ex-Gironde and Hérault diesel locomotives and railcars when it finally disposed of steam traction in the 1970s. The CFS had a mixture that included a variety of SNCF stock but also a couple of handsome Billard railcars and a few CFD diesel locomotives as well as some of their own steam tank engines.

The Second World War and its effects

Ironically enough, it was the next setback which, at least temporarily, saved some of the lines that were threatened, or which had already been condemned. Many branches had only just been closed when the Second World War broke out in 1939 and, after a period of idleness, they were put back into service as petrol became short and the replacement road services were, perforce, withdrawn; indeed rails were even relaid on a number of totally defunct branches. To provide retrospective cover, a law enacted on 4th March 1942 specifically provided that lines officially declassified – which was normally done after closure – could have their closure and declassification postponed until the Authorities decreed. As the war progressed, and especially after the occupation of France, the secondary lines recovered a great deal of their former importance, coming into their own once more as virtually the only real means of rural communications. They worked under considerable difficulties. Fuel and material for repairs were hard to come by. Petrol and diesel were almost unobtainable, so that the few railcars remaining in service trundled along with bulging gasbags on their roofs or in small trailers tagging behind to provide fuel for gasogenes. There was considerable and constant interference from the Occupying Power. They were bombed, shot at and blown up by both friend and foe – the RAF, and later the USAF, tended to strafe anything that moved under a cloud of steam, while the maquis were certainly not loath to put out of action any line providing, even unwillingly, a transport service of use to the Germans.

Whole systems disappeared in this manner. The Calvados réseau, for example, reduced by 1944 to the single branch from Caen to Luc-s-Mer, finally succumbed on D-Day to the onslaught of tanks and other

Even those temporarily reprieved just struggled on, often sustained by bulk farm traffic: The last line of the SE de Seine-et-Marne lasted into the 1960s but only because the local sugar refinery used it to collect beets and it actually had sidings into the farms. (AUTHOR)

vehicles trampling over its roadside track (as incidentally, did the equally antiquated, but standard gauge CF de Caen à la Mer, but nobody mentions that!). One of the most pathetic sights of that day, to one railway enthusiast, was the morning train on the Calvados system, marooned and derelict in the deserted station at Luc. Many lines felt some smaller losses. In sheds and stations up and down the country there are memorial plaques to railwaymen killed at their posts. On the Houillères Nationales line from Somain to Peruwelz, the writer well remembers even a cabside plaque on one 0-8-0T, commemorating a former driver killed on the footplate during an air raid.

Nevertheless, somehow the majority kept going. Some, like the CF du Blanc à Argent, found themselves stuck between occupied and unoccupied zones, rather after the manner of Irish cross-border lines, and occasionally helped the allied war effort with a bit of judicious smuggling. Others, farther from the war areas, provided much-needed transport at the weekends for strained townsfolk going to the country for at least a little relaxation. These trains on lines like the Voies Ferrées du Dauphiné, in the Alpes of Savoie, or the CF du Sud-Ouest, radiating from Toulouse, must, even in the circumstances, have had a certain charm about them and have left some vivid impressions – 15 or more coaches, packed to the rooftops with temporarily cheerful humanity and its clutter of belongings, dragging along for miles behind an old Pinguely or Corpet-Louvet. There are several amateur films of the time, some available on video, which still conjure up the atmosphere.

The majority of lines just performed their day-to-day tasks with undermaintained and overworked equipment so that, when the end of the war came, many railways, particularly the narrow gauge ones which had had to rely on their own resources, were in a very serious condition; one or two might even have had cause to be aggrieved at being caught out just when they should have been safe – like the Tramways de Royan, which saw its depot and stock destroyed by a full scale bombing raid as late as January 1945. Certainly the German army was still holding out locally but its surrender was only a matter of time and there was no real need to flatten the whole town.

The post-war period: closures and the Plan Monnet

After the war, faced with the need for expensive reconstruction of their systems and the rapidly returning competition of road transport, even the big private companies were hesitant about finding the large amounts of money required to rebuild and modernize départemental systems of doubtful validity. Moreover, bridges and viaducts are inevitably major targets for advancing and retreating armies since their destruction offers a convenient way of cutting communications; thus even some flourishing systems of Intérêt Général found themselves in difficulties. These included, for example, the CF de Provence, whose long line from Nice to Meyrargues was cut not once but in half a dozen places, and the Corsican system which had effectively lost the whole of its east coast line. Few of these viaducts were ever repaired; by the time it could be done the traffic had been lost for good.

There was one hopeful prospect for the secondary railways. In 1947, as part of the 'Monnet Plan'- a post-war reconstruction scheme by the then finance minister – selected light railways were to receive financial aid. About 6,000 kilometres, almost half the existing trackage, were to be modernized, the remainder being left to die a lingering death in their own good time. In the event very little came of the plan, its only real (indirect) results being the purchase by the SNCF of some railcars for its narrow gauge lines; the extension of leasing-out of parts of the national standard-gauge system to private operators; and the purchase by the 'Union des Voies Ferrées' of ten 600hp diesel locomotives in 1951, for distribution to some of its more deserving members. Light railways continued to diminish in number, the operative length having decreased to some 3,700km by 1954 and even further to about 2,800km ten years later.

Naturally some systems did attempt to modernize themselves from their own resources or the départemental coffers but they all found the menace of road transport was much fiercer than before the war. Thus in Ille-et-Vilaine, the local tramways company, still exploiting some 274 km. of metre-gauge track, was quite prepared to continue running all but the most uneconomic sections. It drew up several alternative plans for dieselization and even persuaded the département to purchase new railcars to supplement the existing fleet, one of which had been destroyed in the war. Yet the following year, in 1948, road transport interests on the council were able to reverse the whole plan so that most branches were closed at very short notice, and the whole system had gone by 1950.

This was by no means an isolated closure. To the uninitiated, it comes as a surprise to find how much light-railway trackage in France was still being worked in 1947. Large portions of such systems as the CFD Réseau des Charentes (290km., last closure 1951), CF du Morbihan (534km., closed by 1948), Sarthe (440km., closed 1947), and Vendée (342km., closed by the end of 1949) survived the Second World War, but had all disappeared by 1951. The SE's huge metre-gauge 'Réseau du Centre', 493 km sprawling through the départements of Cher and Allier and which had come through the war almost intact, vanished completely in three years between 1949 and 1951. Besides these, of course, many small concerns closed entirely or discontinued their passenger traffic, becoming little more than rail outlets for industrial firms. The one slight consolation was that modern equipment from these lines was freed for purchase by or transfer to the survivors, thus bettering their chances of survival.

The struggle for survival: 1950s

If the 1948-51 period saw the most wholesale closure of many great systems, the next few years were not without their share of tragedies. Those last strongholds of connected lines, the metre-gauge CF des Côtes du Nord in Brittany, and the standard and narrow-gauge VFIL groupings in north-east France, had disappeared by 1956. The latter were almost intact in 1954, operating ingenious, though somewhat thin, schedules over vast tracts of Flanders, Pas de Calais, Aisne, Somme and Oise, often with modern material recently purchased from less fortunate concerns or built in their own workshops. Two years later, only a few isolated lines survived. The VFIL line from St.Just-en-Chaussée to Froissy and Crèvecœur-le-Grand, in Oise will serve as an example of how such railways struggled and finally had to concede victory to the road – and particularly to the private car. Originally a connected route from Estrées-St.Denis through St.Just to Crèvecœur, it lost its link to Estrées in 1948 and, in 1953, the Froissy – Crèvecœur stretch was truncated to Francastel and made freight only; a belated once a week bus was not much substitute. By then

The surviving passenger lines kept going for a while (just) on holiday traffic – railcar trains of the CF des Côtes du Nord just before it closed in 1956. (FACS/CHAPUIS)

Some even had a continuing market day role: here a Billard of the CFD's Vivarais system loads to capacity after Lamastre market even in 1961. (AUTHOR)

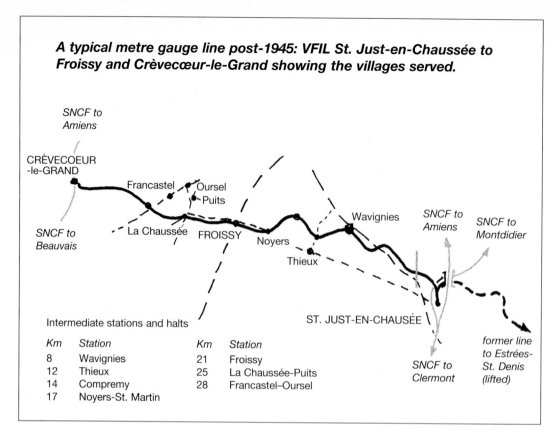

A typical metre gauge line post-1945: VFIL St. Just-en-Chaussée to Froissy and Crèvecœur-le-Grand showing the villages served.

SNCF to Amiens

CRÈVECOEUR -le-GRAND

Francastel   Oursel
              Puits

Wavignies

SNCF to Amiens

SNCF to Montdidier

SNCF to Beauvais

La Chaussée   FROISSY

Noyers

Thieux

SNCF to Clermont

ST. JUST-EN-CHAUSÉE

former line to Estrées-St. Denis (lifted)

Intermediate stations and halts

Km	Station	Km	Station
8	Wavignies	21	Froissy
12	Thieux	25	La Chaussée-Puits
14	Compremy	28	Francastel–Oursel
17	Noyers-St. Martin		

the passenger service was in any case very thin as the appended timetables show and it got steadily worse until complete closure in 1961; surviving traffic by that time was mainly freight and still worked by a motley collection of steam locomotives while two ageing railcars (when serviceable) carried the passengers – who, in default, often had to go by bus anyway.

Against this gloomy picture, in 1947 and again in 1954, there were examples of what could be done by enterprising managements. In the former year the standard-gauge CF de Mamers à St Calais, operated en régie by the département of Sarthe, was transformed from a moribund and ramshackle system into a thriving concern by judicious modernization and the expenditure of some money. In the latter case, a small private operating company took over the VFDM's failing metre-gauge line from Castres, near Toulouse, to Murat and Brassac. With the help of the Département of Tarn and its own energy, the company made the line an example to all secondary railways, relaying the track to high standards, purchasing and rebuilding railcars from closed lines, and running a quick and convenient service. And while these transformations were taking place, the CF du Blanc à Argent was quietly extorting railcars from its ground landlord the SNCF, building up diesel locomotives in its own shops and devising economic ways of carrying grain in bulk. Nothing spectacular, you understand, but it all added up to a most efficient railway.

The trouble was that these were exceptions and other managements seemingly made little attempt to emulate them. The CFD frankly lost heart. The SE hung on to its railways but in a rather negative manner. Great gaps appeared in two of the surviving standard-gauge systems, the SE's Réseau de la Gironde and Réseau de l'Hérault. In fact after September 1956, when the last red train of the Côtes du Nord ran into the impressive private station at St Brieuc, there were so few railways left that each individual closure assumed an almost tragic importance.

All the surviving lines seemed efficient, but one by one they fell. The electrified CF de la Camargue, for example, lost its lucrative chemical traffic to water following wartime destruction of a bridge over the

CFIL d'Estrées-St. Denis a Froissy et Crèvecœur-le-Grand   (operated by CGL/VFIL from 1920)
Specimen timetables for pre-1914 and the final years

Timetable for January 1913 (at greatest extent)

Km.	place	all daily					
	Estrées-St. Denis	06.29			12.15		18.15
	St Just-en-Chaussée (arr)	07.23			14.18		19.13
	St Just-en-Chaussée (dep)			08.48	15.32		19.53
21	Froissy			09.53	16.18		20.39
33	Crèvecœur-le-Grand			10.19	16.42		21.03

Km.	place	all daily					
0	Crèvecœur-le-Grand	06.18			12.40		17.55
12	Froissy	06.43			13.13		18.20
33	St Just-en-Chaussée (arr)	07.28			14.23		19.05
0	St Just-en-Chaussée (dep)			08.53		15.27	
	Estrées-St. Denis			10.23		16.36	

CFIL d'Estrées-St. Denis a Froissy et Crèvecœur-le-Grand   (expl: CGL des VFIL)

Timetable from October 1954

Km.	place	Mons & Sats	Suns & hols.	Tues	Suns & hols.	M. Tu. Th. Sat
0	St. Just-en-Chaussée	09.00	10.25	12.15	19.14	19.55
21	Froissy	09.55	11.20	13.10	20.05	20.26
33	Crèvecœur-le-Grand			freight only		

Km.	place	M. Th. Sat. Sun.	Tues	M. Tu Sat. Sun. hols.	
0	Crèvecœur-le-Grand		freight only		
12	Froissy	06.30	07.26	16.58	
33	St. Just-en-Chaussée	07.23	08.24	17.53	

Final timetable, summer 1960

Km.	place	Th. Sat.	Sun. & hols	Thurs bus	daily	Sun & hols	Mon. Sat.
0	St-Just	09.00	10.25		12.18	19.14	20.02
21	Froissy	09.55	11.20	13.30	13.11	20.05	20.53
33	Crèvecœur			13.35			

Km.	place	Mon.	daily hols	Sat. & Sun.	Thurs bus	
0	Crèvecœur				16.55	
12	Froissy	06.30	07.44	16.58	17.22	
33	St-Just	07.21	08.40	17.53	18.05	

Note: St Just – Estrées-St. Denis one bus each way Weds & Sat, not holidays

A few combined the roles and modernised. This diesel-hauled train on the SE's Somme system took the holidaymakers to le Crotoy but it also brought the folks back from shopping.

(AUTHOR)

Those in remote places just did not have the traffic and their overheads were high…as evidenced by this railcar train in the wilds of Lozère. (AUTHOR)

Rhône, and its last branch closed in 1958. The following year saw three deaths: the CEN's metre gauge electric line from Annemasse to Sixt in Savoie, thought to have a considerable traffic potential, closed at short notice though not without a struggle to save it by a preservation group – pressure from road transport interests was widely rumoured. The CFD's Seine-et-Marne line from Montèreau to Egreville closed to all traffic, with its freight-only branch to Château-Landon; the line had never really recovered from the war and its stock and track had just been run-down until they wore out. The last line of the Tramways de la Corrèze, struggling into the hills south-east of Tulle, gave up too, its track in such a state that complete relaying would have been necessary if services were to continue. The stock, on the other hand, was in good condition and rotted away in open store for several more years in the vain hope of finding a buyer, before being broken up for scrap.

So the sad story went on. A full list would get tedious. Suffice to note the end of the last exclusively steam-worked metre-gauge line, the CF du Cambrésis, in October 1960; the surprising closure of the rejuvenated CFD du Tarn (Castres-Murat-Brassac) in 1962, a victim of road-mindedness on a newly elected départemental council; the dieselization, industrialization and consequent closure to passenger traffic of the French Coal Board's quite fascinating standard-gauge line from Somain to Peruwelz, up in the north-east (as the chef said, the passenger trains were a ****ing nuisance to the coal traffic, anyway); the closure in 1962 also of the old VFIL (in recent years Régie du Pas de Calais) branch from Cambrai to Boisleux; and the total closure of the freight-only metre-gauge roadside trwnway from Nangis to Jouy le Châtel, in Seine-et-Marne, at the end of 1964. This last, incidentally, was important as showing the probable fate for those odd sections of former light railways still utilized in the beet season by, or on behalf of, sugar refineries. They were approaching the stage where renewals would be uneconomic and their gradual replacement by road transport was not long delayed. The 1964 season was the last one for the Tramway de Pithiviers à Toury and the final fragment of the old CFD des Ardennes, abandoned by the sugar refinery at Montcornet. Add to all this the facts that some of the few surviving lines were in a very unhealthy condition, and that the

Even the big systems of Intérêt Général were not immune; The Réseau Breton had modernised its passenger services except for the odd steam-worked substitute but that did not save it. (AUTHOR)

govermnent had already, in 1959, made one unsuccessful attempt to close the remaining light-railway systems of Intérêt Général, and it must be confessed that the future for minor railways in France was by no means bright.

An optimistic digression

Oddly enough, however, in 1952 there also appeared the first sign of a railway revival – of a sort. A M. Milet suddenly decided that what he wanted to do was to build a railway and, in the good old tradition of seaside tramways, settled on a spot on the west coast which actually needed seasonal tramsport. On the Arcachon peninsula, the tourist developments were on the east, or sheltered, side; the dunes and beaches were on the west... So, braving all the rigmarole of official procedures, he eventually laid down the 60cm gauge Tramway de Cap Ferret – heir to a whole network of forestry lines in the area but a railway in its own right. He found some diesel tractors (and converted them roughly to steam outline), built some baladeuses and set up in business....and the line still runs in summer. His example, or similar enthusiasms, provoked the other "godfather" of French preservation schemes, Jean Arrivetz, and some Lyonnais colleagues to build a similar operation far to the east, near a country leisure park at Meyzieu in 1962. It, too, had a new route, in this case from a main road to a bathing lake, but had a difference in that it used both steam and diesel stock collected from closing lines and restored passenger vehicles to match. The CF Touristique de Méyzieu, alas, had later to close because of urban development along its route but it set a fashion, besides inspiring the first serious preservation scheme, on the CFD du Vivarais (see chapter 6) which was operated by the same company, reintitled Chemins de Fer Touristiques et de Montagne to use up the same initials. From the orginal initiatives have sprung a number of others, such as the Tramway de St.Trojan, on the Ile d'Oléron.

There are also a number of similar initiatives which would not lay any real claim to be genuine puublic transport, such as the CF de la Vallée de l'Ouche on an old trackbed near Dijon and the CF du Parc des Chanteraines. One, on a former German World War 1 route, has established itself firmly as the Petit Train

The PO Corrèze was using steam for mixed trains into the 1960s; even total dieselisation did not save it.

(AUTHOR)

de l'Haute Somme (Froissy – Cappy – Dompierre) and the Meyzieu line itself has recently been reborn at a new country park near Sault Brenaz as the CF de l'Haut Rhône while part of the route of the old Tramways à Vapeur du Tarn has been reused on a narrower gauge as the CF Touristique du Tarn but in general they are constrained by availability of equipment and enthusiast support.

The final decline: 1965 – the present day

Meanwhile commercial light railways continued to decline. That certainly was the position prophesied in 1965 when the writer's first attempt to chronicle French minor railways appeared. Alas, the prophecy was all too true. With the Intérêt Local systems reduced to virtually nothing, the big narrow gauge réseaux came under attack. The mighty Réseau Breton was the first to go, being closed outright in 1967 save for the existing standard gauge section to Paimpol and the Guingamp-Carhaix branch which was standard-gauged as a token gesture – its infrastructure had been built to standard gauge dimensions in any case. In 1968 the CFD's associated systems of Vivarais and Lozère followed and in 1970 the PO Corrèze, reduced for several years to a goods-only line, was closed as well, while the le Blanc-Argent was steadily cut back from both ends, although its stem line still fulfils its public transport function in 2000. The last "real" Intérêt Local line of the CFTA's Réseau de la Somme closed in 1972 but was rescued by a preservation group as related in chapter 6; the same thing happened to other closed lines such as the Mamers – St Calais and parts of the Vivarais but those are now tourist railways and no longer local transport systems. What remain from the private sector, apart from one or two long-serving survivors of Intérêt Général, are chiefly specialist railways that also depend largely on tourists – the two SNCF electric mountain lines, various rack railways – or else stubs of former standard gauge lines used mostly as industrial sidings.

What hope there is for the commercial sector, lies mainly in the CFTA, the Cie Générale des Chemins de Fer et des Transports Automobiles, both of whose components, the SE and the Cie des Chemins de Fer Secondaires et de Transport Automobiles (CFSTA), had a reputation for hanging on to their railways although even CFTA is now only part of the huge VIVENDI conglomerate formed from Compagnie des Eaux; in the more progressive Regions Autonomes such as Corsica which have grouped neghbouring départements together and had their secondary railways made over to them by the State; in the SNCF itself which has modernised its two electric systems, in Cerdagne and around Chamonix; and in the privately worked Le Blanc-Argent. The Cie des Transports de l'Indre has leased the line since 1975 and. as we have seen above, its forward-looking management has somehow organised its survival. There is also one final hope. Just as in Britain, as the number of commercial lines decline, so the interest in them grows. The French were fairly late into serious standard and metre gauge preservation, the first two schemes on former light railways not starting until 1965 (Tramway de Pithiviers à Toury) and 1968-69 (eastern end of the CFD Réseau du Vivarais). Indeed given the spreadout nature of the land and the restricted number of active enthusiasts with financial backing, it is not surprising that development was so slow or that only a few more lasting schemes have followed - the most notable are those on the CFTA's old Somme system (1972) and the western end of the Vivarais. As in Britain this trend has also led to a number of small, enthusiast-run standard gauge concerns based either on ex-SNCF lines or "new" trackbeds, living precariously on tourist traffic but trying to recapture some of the atmosphere of the old tortillards. There are also several collections of preserved vehicles.

And so we have arrived, by devious routes, at the present day; and there remains the problem of presenting a clear and useful picture of the survivors, a problem intensified by the widely differing degrees of interest they afford and the shaky position of some of them. I have thought it best to take them by categories – commercial and enthusiast – for easy reference. The most interesting ones are dealt with at length, those which may close and those which are now only of academic interest are listed more briefly.

CHAPTER 6
The Current Scene

The general position at 2000

Is it worth it, one may well ask, to delineate the current scene or will it change as it did soon after previous attempts at chronicling French secondary railways? The answer, in all probability is yes and yes (but only round the edges). The surviving systems of any worth are probably now all safe for the next ten years or so, given changing views on public transport. Most have been either made over to the Régions Autonomes or are still in the hands of the SNCF. The same probably applies also to those substantial portions of former minor railways "preserved" as tourist railways and increasingly recognised as part of the "patrimoine nationale" or common heritage - individual buildings and items of rolling stock are even able to be classed as national monuments which brings both funding (small) and some measure of security against destruction. On the other hand lttle groups, largely of the "playing at trains" variety, rise and fall almost every year; usually based on disused sections of SNCF branches, they tend to acquire a railcar, a coach or two, perhaps a couple of diesels or an industrial steam locomotive, running one or two trains at summer weekends until the enthusiasm dies away or their sponsors grow disillusioned. This is not to denigrate them. They provide interest to their supporters, a minor enhancement to the local economy and a pleasant experience for tourists passing by but, in the old Michelin adage, they are not "worth a detour" and may not be there in years to come. The one aspect of this sector worth mentioning is the very French idea of the "Vélorail". Descendants of the old track gang's scooter, these are basicaly two or four seat light quadricycles which can be hired to traverse scenic bits of former line where the rails still exist. They may have a future: they are cheap to provide, they do not put any strain on slowly decaying track or structures, they are flexible in operation (if you meet another, one is just lifted off the track – and, yes, there are usually rules about this!). Enquire at your local syndicat d'initiative and you may be in for a pleasant surprise. A variant is the use of light draisines but one feels those operations are very much "faute de mieux".

What there is left to see: commercial lines

So, apart from these, what is there left to see? On standard gauge very little: Basically there are the two **Réseau Breton** lines which carry both passenger and goods traffic at the time of writing and are likely to continue to do so; with an eye on the tourist market, the CFTA which still runs them has even introduced steam tourist trains at the Paimpol end albeit with a former main line locomotive. Although standard gauged, the branches still have something of their former character. One or two preservation operations run over substantial kilometrages of SNCF track but few appear really secure.

Of the rest, while the **Régie des Bouches du Rhône** and others may officially still exist, they are basically long industrial sidings with few of their more interesting characteristics surviving. Even the lignes affermées in Franche Comté and Morvan have largely been given over to goods or lost their identifying characteristics; indeed success does not always help; Provins – Longueville is now just another SNCF suburban branch.

On the metre gauge, the position is rather better, although it must be remembered that France is a big country and distances between survivors are vast. No less than six lines or clusters of lines are still in commercial operation, three in the south east, two in the south west and one in the centre.

The central one is that romantically named **CF du Blanc à Argent**, (from the white to the silver) or what remains of it, since it was of such importance and complexity that it is still, in part, with us though now reduced to a shadow of its former self. This (Map on p.11) was originally projected as a strategic line to be built to the standard gauge and provide a lateral link to the east-west trajects. As such it never got off the ground, the then main line concern involved humming and hahing until the idea was forgotten. Its successor, the Paris – Orléans company (PO) did, however, accept the concession for a metre gauge version built to standard gauge standards which linked no less than six standard gauge junctions in its 190km course

Location of major surviving minor railways of historical interest in 2000

Calais

2

4

.Reims

• Paris

3

Rennes

1

• Orléans

18

6

Dijon

5

7   9 10

8   9

Lyon

. Bordeaux   12

Grenoble   11

17

13

Toulouse

16

Nice

• Pau

15   Perpignan

14

Commercial Railways	Preservation & Tourist Schemes
1. Réseau Brêton	2. CF de la Baie de Somme
5. CF du Blanc à Argent	3. Musée de Pithiviers
8. Twy de Mont Blanc	4. CF de l'Haute Somme
9. SNCF St. Gervais-Vallorcine	(Froissy-Cappy-Dompierre)
10. CF du Montenvers	6. CF de la Vallée de la Doller
11. CF de la Mure	7. CF de l'Haute Rhône
13. CF de Provence	12. CF du Vivarais
14. CF Corses	17. Twy de Cap Ferret
15. Ligne de Cerdagne	18. CF de la Sarthe
16. CF de la Rhûne	

You can still photograph the lines described in this chapter, so the illustrations are mainly historical. This is the Le Blanc-Argent, conducting its normal business in 1961 with a Verney bogie railcar. (AUTHOR)

from north east to south west: Argent, Salbris, Romorantin where its HQ lay, Gièvres, Buzançais and le Blanc. At one time or another it also linked up with no less than five départemental companies: The SE's Réseau du Centre at Argent, the Tramways du Loiret at Brinon-s-Sauldre, the Tramways de Loir-et-Cher at Romorantin, the CFD's Réseau d'Indre-et-Loire at Ecueillé and the Tramways de l'Indre at Valençay and le Blanc; vestiges of these lines long outlasted their closure and odd buildings can still be seen at junction points. While mentioning odd buildings, the station at Valençay is noteworthy in being in the style of the local château, the Duc de Valençay having funded this whimsical folly, while at Romorantin the line inhabits a full-size standard gauge station which it took over after the standard gauge withdrew. Historically, the original operator, the Cie du CF du Blanc à Argent, was assimilated into the Tartary group who also owned the Tramways de l'Indre and in 1974-5 it merged with the latter to become the Societé des Transports de l'Indre. The system was so complex that it has always been worked as several separate sections: Argent-Salbris; Salbris-Romorantin; Romorantin – Valençay ; Valençay - Buzançais; Buzançais - le Blanc. Originally it had pleasant little 0-6-0Ts and 2-4-0Ts with odd spark arresters but these were retired in the early 1950s and replaced by four 0-6-0D (11-14), two by CFD and two homemade on steam locomotive chassis. For passenger traffic it inherited a variegated set of railcars which it eventually swapped for some standard modern Verneys and ex CFD Billard cars. More recently it acquired, and wore out, some ex-Réseau Breton equipment, and now has four fairly modern CFD/SOCOFER and CFD/Soulé cars with some modernised Verneys in reserve; at the time of writing, new and very modernistic railcar sets are being built to replace these. For many years it ran itself quietly and efficiently while being slowly lopped back at both ends, from Argent to Clémont (1951) and le Blanc to Buzançais (1953). Salbris - Clémont, by then goods-only, followed in 1973 and Buzançais - Lucay-le-Mâle lost its passenger service in 1980 and its goods traffic a few years later. Part of this southern section, from Buzançais, has since been standard-gauged for industrial use and a preservation group has settled on the former route south from Lucay. The remainder has a regular passenger service and is best approached from its remaining main line junction at Salbris.

73

Lines in the south east: the Chamonix group.

This ensemble of three lines – or four if one includes the Swiss Martigny – Chatelard company which interconnects – are all metre gauge, electric and now dependent on passengers, especially tourists. The "ligne de base" (see map opposite) is the former PLM concession from a standard gauge connection at St Gervais-les-Bains – le Fayet up through the mountains via Chamonix (19km, connection with the rack line to the Col du Montenvers) to Vallorcine (34km) and on to the Swiss frontier at km 37. At St Gervais there is a link to the last member of this group, the Tramway du Mont Blanc up to the Glacier de Bionnassay.

Albeit electric and very modern, the **St Gervais – Vallorcine,** as it is commonly known, has much to offer. It runs through spectacular scenery, has plenty of enticing engineering works of which the massive Viaduct de Ste Marie (10.782km) is prominent, has a summit in tunnel at Col des Montets and a fascinating history. It was originally conceded to the PLM and has always been worked by main line companies, first the PLM and now the SNCF. At Vallorcine, about a kilometre before the Swiss frontier, it makes an end-on connection with the Swiss CF de Martigny-Chatelard and for years could only exchange through trailers since the two systems' technical arrangements were incompatible. Opened in 1901, it was unusual in having third rail collection, on 600V DC generated through a specially-built hydroelectric plant at Servoz. The gradients were such that the stock was even more unusual, consisting almost entirely of individual powered vehicles (elements automoteurs) which could be worked singly or in multiple and included both passenger and goods stock; only a few passenger trailers were unpowered. As an additional precaution, a Fell-type centre rail was installed on six of the steeper parts but was used for braking only. Normality started breaking through in 1952 when power supply was transferred to the national grid (EDF), and extended in 1958 with the delivery of eight new bogie power cars (Z 601-08) which had sufficient braking not to use the centre rail; at that time power was increased to 800 volts. The Fell rail was retained for emergency use until the last automoteurs were withdrawn in 1985 but has now been removed and, in 1997, the last links with the old regime were lost when new multi-capable stock was introduced. This, three two car sets owned by

And this is the CFD Réseau du Vivarais doing likewise, albeit at the now closed station of La Voulte-s-Rhone and with a Billard A150D. (AUTHOR)

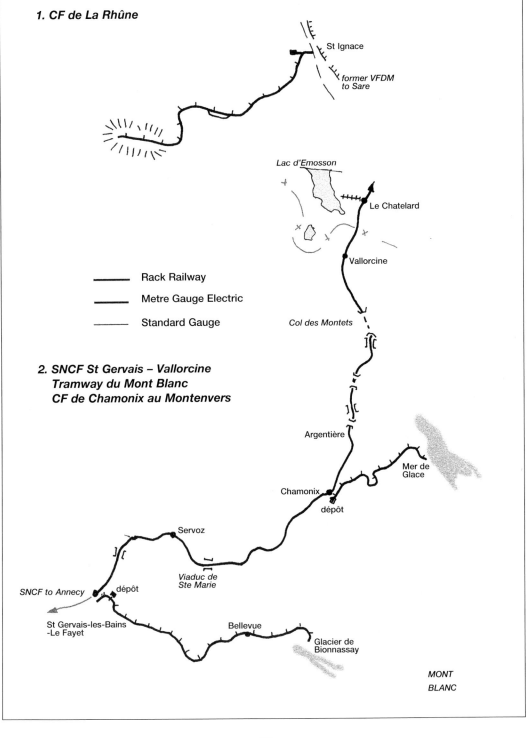

Surviving rack and former Fell-system lines

1. CF de La Rhûne

St Ignace

former VFDM to Sare

Lac d'Emosson

Le Chatelard

Vallorcine

Rack Railway

Metre Gauge Electric

Standard Gauge

Col des Montets

2. SNCF St Gervais – Vallorcine
Tramway du Mont Blanc
CF de Chamonix au Montenvers

Argentière

Mer de Glace

Chamonix

dépôt

Servoz

Viaduc de Ste Marie

SNCF to Annecy   *dépôt*

St Gervais-les-Bains
-Le Fayet

Bellevue

Glacier de Bionnassay

MONT BLANC

SNCF (Z 801/2; 803/4; 805/6) and two by the Martigny – Chatelard, has electrical equipment and current collectors together with rack drive, allowing it to work through over the combined systems.

Both rack lines have been electrically worked for years, although they both started with steam and various locomotives are still "preserved" or "under restoration". The less prosperous of the two is the, until recently rather shabby, **Tramway du Mont Blanc** with its three named two-car sets. Originally intended to reach Mont Blanc itself, the existing line was opened to Col-de-Voza in 1909 and on to the Glacier de Bionnassay (12km) in 1914. The war put paid to extensions and to a proposed electrification which was not carried out until 1957. Initially it ran in summer only but, since electrification, has also run for skiers in the winter although workings may be cut back to Bellevue in case of heavy snow. The line starts from outside the SNCF station, is electrified with overhead collection at 11000v, 50hz from a sub-station at St Gervais and is equipped with single Strub rack on the steeper portions only. One at least of the old steam locomotives is still in existence and, at the time of writing, in process of restoration. One is plinthed in a local park.

The **CF de Chamonix au Montenvers** also starts from near the appropriate SNCF station and is equipped throughout with Strub rack. It was opened in stages as a steam-worked line between 1908-09 and electrified in 1954, also with overhead collection at 11000v, 50hz. It runs, in summer only, for 5km to the Col du Montenvers from which it has a small cable car running down to the Mer de Glace. Normal stock comprises six bogie power cars 41-46 built by SLM and Oerlikon with six matching control trailers, supplemented at peak periods by three 650hp diesel-hydraulic locomotives, Nos. 61-63 delivered between 1967 and 1972 and pushing articulated trailers. Steam locomotive No. 6 is, plinthed at Chamonix.

Lines in the south east: CF de Provence and CF Corses.

Down in the Maritime Alpes, the **CF de Provence** still runs part of the old Sud-France Réseau des Alpes. At its greatest extent this was an extensive Intérêt Général system, consisting of two major routes from Nice, westward to Meyrargues in the Var where it met up not only with the main line but also with the CF

Some continually modernise their existing stock: A CFD railcar just out of shops at the new Nice station of the CF de Provence, with a much rebodied Billard trailer.   (AUTHOR)

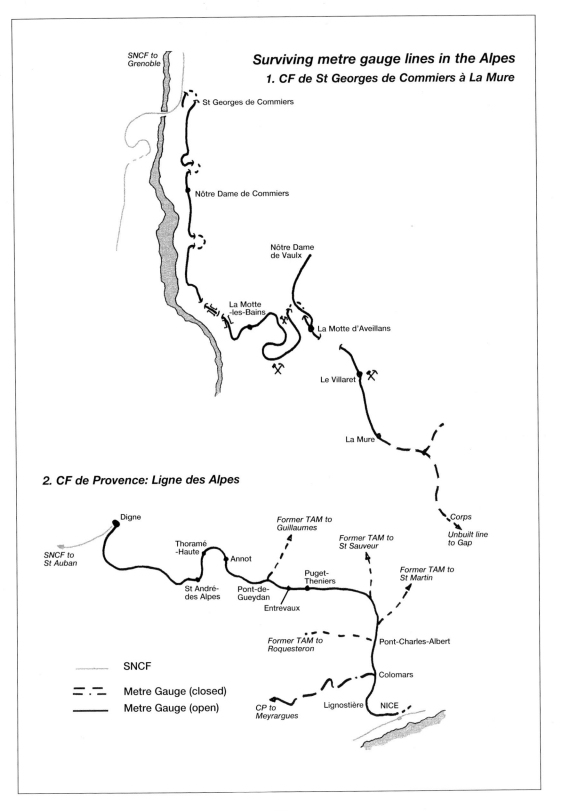

Surviving metre gauge lines in the Alpes

1. CF de St Georges de Commiers à La Mure

SNCF to
Grenoble

St Georges de Commiers

Nôtre Dame de Commiers

Nôtre Dame
de Vaulx

La Motte
-les-Bains

La Motte d'Aveillans

Le Villaret

La Mure

Corps

Unbuilt line
to Gap

2. CF de Provence: Ligne des Alpes

Digne

Former TAM to
Guillaumes

Former TAM to
St Sauveur

SNCF to
St Auban

Thoramé
-Haute

Annot

Former TAM to
St Martin

Puget-
Theniers

St André-
des Alpes

Pont-de-
Gueydan

Entrevaux

Pont-Charles-Albert

Former TAM to
Roquesteron

Colomars

SNCF

Metre Gauge (closed)

Metre Gauge (open)

CP to
Meyrargues

Lignostière

NICE

Some are lucky enough to get new stock. A CFD/Soulé railcar and trailer set at Ajaccio, Corsica. (AUTHOR)

des Bouches du Rhône; and north west along the Var river and through the mountains to Digne where it again met the standard gauge. Initiated under the plan Freyciney of 1879, it opened in stages between 1888 and 1911, originally including stretches of standard and mixed gauge for strategic reasons. At various points, too, it linked with the associated Tramways des Alpes Maritimes. It had a very complex history, being taken over by the CF de Provence in 1925 and modernised in the late 1930s. The Meyrargues line closed after World War 2 and what remains is the metre gauge line from Nice to Digne (Map on p.77) although the SNCF connection at Digne has virtually disappeared; there are on/off plans to regauge the closed SNCF branch to St Auban or to restore the standard gauge service. In recent years, the operator, currently a filiale of the CFTA, has been hampered seriously by lengthy and enervating discussions among the consortium of owning local authorities as to who should have the next concession and by a consequent failure to release funds earmarked for modernisation. As a result, the operator is really having to mark time although, unusually for France, an intense marketing effort is being made to promote the line to tourists and skiers. Having abandoned the former Gare du Sud at Nice, the line now starts several hundred metres along the former roadbed, with a modern station but on a cramped site and in a back-street. Again there are various proposals to move this terminus to one of the SNCF stations. The workshops, originally out at Draguignan on the Meyrargues line, have been resited to an industrial site at Lingostière on the outskirts of Nice and there is a reasonable suburban service past this point and out to Colomars and la Vesubie; the main line has for years seen four trains daily each way. Currently, however, the equipment is insufficient to cope with any increase in traffic although Lingostière is steadily upgrading railcars and trailers to a very high standard of comfort for a metre gauge line. Current stock at 2000 includes six CFD-built bogie cars of varying vintages, a two-car Soulé railcar and trailer set, and several of the old Renault ABH cars which tend to run the suburban service. There are also one Henschel 1200hp DH locomotive bought second-hand from Spain and two Brisonneau et Lotz 600hp diesel electrics, used both for track work and for hauling four refurbished bogie trailers when required. Other equipment is stored derelict at Lingostière. One potentially useful feature is the presence of an amateur steam locomotive preservation group with a depot partway along the line at Puget Theniers; in principle steam trains run over the most scenic part at summer weekends, with rail connections to and from Nice.

Corsica (Map on p.315) is the last of the south eastern systems to survive. Construction was started by the state as long ago as 1878, with two lines, from Bastia to Corte and Ajaccio to Mezzana, which, under the Freyciney plan, were linked by Mezzana – Corte. Branches south along the east coast from Casamozza to Bonifacio and from Ponte Leccia north west to Calvi completed the plan which was achieved by 1894 except for a stretch from Ghisonaccia to Bonifacio. The state not wishing to operate the system directly, the big CFD concern was invited to do so and eventually, in 1933, extended the east coast branch to Porto Vecchio; the last stretch to Bonifacio was never built. Regrettably, the east coast line was badly damaged in World War 2 and the stub of it closed in 1953 (ironically, with EU money available, a project to reopen it was being considered in 1999). Meanwhile the CFD gave up in 1945 and, after a period as a state Régie, the system has been run successively by the Sté Auxiliare pour les Chemins de Fer Secondaires (SACFS); the CFTA and, since 1982, the SNCF on a succession of management contracts – all of which explains the mixed collection of motive power in current use or derelict.

As now constituted, the system is owned by the Region Autonome, the Collectivité Territoriale de la Corse whose title appears on all the modern stock, but is managed for the region by an external contractor. The lines in use are Bastia to Ajaccio via Ponte-Leccia and Corte, and Bastia – Calvi via Ponte Leccia (ie Calvi trains run through to and from Bastia). A modern workshop is installed at Casamozza, some 21km south of Bastia and former junction for the east coast line, while Bastia depot is now basically a running shed. Besides the, fairly sparse, main line services (Calvi has, for years, had only two trains a day) there is a fairly frequent suburban service between Bastia and Casamozza and, in season, a series of short workings between Calvi and the resorts around Ile Rousse (Ligne de la Balagne). These services are not normally advertised outside the island and are usually worked by the oldest vehicles in the fleet. The system currently has a limited goods traffic, mainly parcels and transfer of road vehicles between the three termini – the terrain makes such an operation attractive when needed! For these, three CFD-built BB diesel locomotives are kept, the latest one having come as recently as 1995/6 and being a conversion from standard gauge. The comfortable bogie railcars and trailers are mainly by CFD or CFD/Soule and the newest ones again date from 1995/6; more are planned which may lead to withdrawl of the remaining Renault ABH cars, in 1999 kept to run seasonal services on the Ligne de la Balagne. The line does not appear strongly marketed but does have a useful runabout ticket (Carte Zoom).

The south-west: La Rhûne; Cerdagne

In the southwest, two "commercial" lines survive. One is the ex-VFDM electric rack railway from St Ignace to the summit of la Rhûne (**CF de la Rhûne**) in Pyrénées-Atlantiques, now operated by the CFTA and recently reequipped with modern Swiss-type railcars (Map p.75). This 4.2km-long rack line climbs 718 metres, has gradients of up to 1 in 4, a single Strub rack throughout and has been electrically worked from the start on 3000v at 25hz (now 50hz). It was opened in 1924 by the VFDM using boxy, wood-bodied locomotives and handsome bogie trailers. It performed some exhanges with its, now defunct, Haute-Garonne neighbour, the line from Luchon to Superbagnères as a result of which it now has a total of six machines each capable of pushing two coaches; some are held in reserve for peak periods, the line normally working during summer only but providing service out of season to a television transmitting station near the summit. It is accessible only by road.

The other is the **SNCF Ligne de Cerdagne**, (Map p.77) again recently modernised, although still with what is basically original stock rebodied. This is down in the high Pyrénées (Pyrénées-Orientales to be precise) and runs roughly north-east – south west for some 62km, following the general trend of very mountainous country. Historically it was intended to be standard gauge, carrying on from a CF du Midi branch from Perpignan to Villefranche – Vernet les Bains but the powers that be were eventually persuaded to authorise metre gauge. It was opened over the most difficult section, to Bourg-Madame, in 1911 after a problematic period of eight years which involved many considerable engineering works – the two most famous are the towering and complex Viaduct de Sejourné and a fine example of a Gisclard suspension bridge (there was a similar one on the Tramways de la Corrèze away in the Massif Central). Most works were on the climb to its summit at Bolquere-Eyne (30.2km; 1592m) whence it dropped less sharply to

Bourg-Madame (55.2km). It was not until between 1925 and 1927 that the line was extended to meet the new, electrified Transpyreneen route at the frontier station of La Tour de Carol. Since the Perpignan – Villefranche branch was also electrified in 1911-12 by the Midi as an experiment, it was thus possible to make the complete traverse by electric power; the Perpignan branch, however, wore its equipment out and reverted to steam (or rather diesel) traction in 1971.

The narrow gauge Ligne de Cerdagne was electrified from the start but, rather surprisingly for such a tortuous line, at 850v DC with third rail collection fed by a specially built lake and hydroelectric plant at La Cassagne. Up to the 1950s it had a considerable mineral traffic from mines at the Villefranche end but by 1976 this had dropped off sharply and the remainder was soon transferred to road. Since then the line, which is, alas, deficitary, has been dependent largely on tourists and holidaymakers. It still depends largely on the original bogie power cars and trailers, supplemented by some second-hand coaches and steadily being rebodied or modernised – in which process sadly they have lost their original yellow livery which gave the line its nickname (petit train jaune) in favour of SNCF red/cream. An unusual feature is the use of open (roofless) trailers which are popular with tourists in fine weather. The current operational stock comprises 16 of the original 18 composite power cars (Midi ABDe 1-18) and two of the original ten motor luggage vans, now numbered in an SNCF electric railcar series, plus eight closed and four open trailers; the latter originally had light roofs but are now entirely open above the waist.

Other lines: CF de la Mure; the preservation movement

It is a moot point if one should include the **CF de la Mure (SGLM)** in this category of commercial lines (Map p.77). Once again, administered directly by the State when the standard gauge avoided coal deposits near la Mure in the Savoy Alps, it was actually built by the manufacturing company Fives-Lille, and opened from St Georges de Commiers to La Mure in 1888. Fives-Lille operated it as a steam railway until 1898

Naturally most commercial survivors are electrically powered. This is the CF de la Mure in its original state as a coal haulier.

(AUTHOR)

(with Fives-Lille equipment naturally) when the State took it over directly as the Régie du Chemin de Fer de St Georges de Commiers à la Mure. Increasing traffic led to experiments with electrification in 1903 and conversion of the first stage, from St.Georges to La Motte d'Aveillans in 1907; electrification through to La Mure followed by 1912. Meanwhile, in 1906 it was proposed to extend south-eastward again to Gap in Haute-Alpes – alas it reached no further than the town of Corps, and that not until 1932. Traffic on the extension was so weak that it closed again in 1939. Regular passenger traffic over the stem line ceased in 1950 but a heavy, though declining, coal traffic continued until 1988 when the mines were effectively closed. A private organisation then took over the line for tourist purposes, collecting a certain amount of stock from outside. For the next nine years it was run on an semi-amateur basis but in 1998 the big CFTA thought it worth taking over commercially as a tourist railway on an eight year concession and has great plans for it, so perhaps it can act as a link wth the amateur-run lines. In its present state, the line starts at the old SGLM station opposite the SNCF St Georges de Commiers halt and can be reached quite easily from Grenoble, by train, car or organised excursion. The impressive SGLM station and workshops are intact and in use. The line is still electrified and has most of its former locomotives plus a modicum of original stock which has been supplemented by equipment from Swiss lines including several handsome Noyon - St Cergue motor cars with their trailers. The journey is, to say the least, spectacular including dizzy climbs above sheer drops and views across the several massive lakes and dams of the region. The CFTA has great plans for it and visitors should certainly not be deterred by the lack of steam; this is vintage electric traction at its best with scenery thrown in.

Otherwise, there exist a plethora of enthusiast-run operations which come and go, and which it would not be appropriate to describe here. A few, however, have two qualifications for inclusion: they are based on genuine former minor railway sites and they have stood the test of time. Short commentaries on them inevitably appear in the appropriate regional chapter but for our purposes their history and present condition is noted here.

First, and doyen of the French preservation movement, is the **CF du Vivarais** which has taken over the north-eastern end of the former **CFD Réseau du Vivarais**. This system of Intérêt Général was another outcome of the Plan Freyciney. It was envisaged as a main stem spanning the great watershed, from La Voute-sur-Loire, eastward via Yssingeaux and le Cheylard to La Voulte-sur-Rhône with a branch from le Cheylard north east to Tournon and was conceded from the start to the CFD. Startng as three separated branches at the outer ends, between 1890 and 1891, the bits were joined up in 1902-03 and complemented with a branch off the Yssingeaux line to Dunières, terminus of a PLM standard gauge branch. The CFD always regarded it as one of their star possessions, modernising it from the early 1930s onward and running most of it until 1968 - the western spur from Raucoules-Brossettes to la Voute-sur-Loire being closed in 1952 owing to bus competition.

Fortunately, a group of Lyonnais enthusiasts already running a small 60cm gauge line, decided to "go for the big time", changing their CF Touristique de Meyzieu (CFTM) title to CF Touristiques et de Montagne. After discussions they were granted a lease to operate between Tournon and the intermediate station of Lamastre (one of the original termini and a 'ville gastronomique', which helps to attract the French tourists). Over the next twenty years or so the infrastructure was improved – and finally purchased outright. Original locomotives and stock were revitalised and supplemented by similar equipment from the Réseau Breton and elsewhere and the CF du Vivarais has become a national institution. It is so well established that its veteran promoters are looking for a "commercial" concessionaire to take on operation in conjunction with the Département of Ardéche rather than rely on continuing enthusiast involvement. It operates from its main depot at Tournon, on the Rhône, over a short stretch of mixed gauge and then south west for some 30km to Lamastre in the hills. Long, Mallet-hauled trains run at weekends off-season and daily during high season, normally two going out in the morning and back in the afternoon, allowing a long lazy lunch at Lamastre which suits its French customers perfectly – and is probably the only sensible way to operate a long and steep line. There are supplementary railcar services for the more impatient.

One should mention here that there has, again since 1969, also been a rather more amateur and erratic operation at the western end of the Vivarais between Dunières and the plateau towns. In some years it has

A Z6XX series train of the SNCF St Gervais – Vallorcine line (now in reserve) in days when the Fell centre rail still existed.

Examples of rack lines 1: The Chamonix – Montenvers approaching its top station. (AUTHOR)

not run at all but since about 1996 it appears to have settled down and by the time this is written will either have reached St Agrève or gone under completely. It uses mainly ex-Vivarais/Lozère diesel equipment, with Swiss coaches but has an ex-Corrèze 0-4-4-0T for future use.

Far to the north, on the Channel coast, is the CF de la Baie de Somme. This is the surviving portion of the SE's old "Bains de Mer" system in Region Nord (see Ch 8 for history) running two lines from Noyelles on the Calais – Paris main line, to le Crotoy and via St Valery-s-Somme to the seaside resort of Cayeux. After closure in 1972 it was taken over en bloc by an enthusiast group. It had a somewhat difficult time during the 1970s and early 1980s, mainly due to lack of funding and internal dissensions   but has since become solidly based and is certainly the best surviving example of a metre gauge system of intérêt local. It has a mixed collection of historic – but typical – stock, runs reasonable services in high season and is only just across the channel. What more could one want?

Well, one could ask for a relic of the 60cm gauge. At Pithiviers, on the old 60cm gauge **Tramway de Pithiviers à Toury** southwest of Paris, the Association du Musée de Transports de Pithiviers (AMTP) has taken over the eastern 3km or so of the former line, together with the old terminus and Works at Pithiviers which it has transformed into an excellent museum. A new western terminus has been built at Bellebat, just off the main road, an interesting collection of rolling stock has been assembled from various sugar-beet lines and regular tourist services are run during the summer season. The line itself is very historic, dating from 1892 when it was established as a showcase for Decauville products. Its original main line of 33km was much more than doubled by various goods-only branches over the years and survived for goods, mainly sugar beet, until 1964.

If one wants a standard gauge operation that is still reminiscent of the past, then the (newly constituted) **CF de la Sarthe** (TRANSVAP) is probably the nearest. It is based on the old Mamers – St Calais branch between Connerré-Bielle and Bonnetable, (see ch 7) has a reasonable collection of appropriate locomotives and stock and again runs daily services in summer although mainly with diesel traction. The other lasting

Rack lines 2: The Tramway du Mont Blanc makes its way through the streets to St Gervais SNCF. Note that it is actually adhesion worked on the gentler bits. (AUTHOR)

one is the **CF de la Vallée de la Doller** up near Sentheim in Alsace-Lorraine. If it actually uses a former SNCF branch to Cernay rather than a true light railway, it does have a collection of light railway stock with both steam and diesel traction and regular services in season.

Most of the lines noted above have had detailed individual histories published fairly recently and they are listed for reference in the bibliography. One or two entirely "new" concerns also seem to have a fairly certain future, usually in association with a well-thought out museum and most have a tenuous conection with former railways in that they are laid in whole or part on former trackbeds. The most mentionable are: **Petit Train de l'Haute Somme** (Froissy – Cappy – Dompierre) which uses part of a former World War 1 German military line from a sugar refinery at Dompierre, along a road, down a steep escarpment with a "Z" reversal and tunnel, to finish alongside a canal where the main station and works are located. It is worth visiting particularly because it specialises in WW 1 equipment and has an excellent museum covering that period. In summer it works with mixed steam and diesel traction.

Then there is the Group formerly at Valmondois as the Musee des Transports de la Vallée de Sausseron (MTVS) which, at the time of writing, is moving to the old standard gauge line from Chars to Magny en Vexin and changing its name (but retaining the same intitials). Again, this is a well-established operation which has found and superbly restored a representative selection of intérêt local locomotives and stock on the metre gauge; In fact any operation is subsidiary to this and the main reason for visiting must be the museum exhibits.

Slightly less secure but still worth mentioning are four very narrow gauge lines which appear peculiarly French. Oldest is the 60cm gauge **Tramway de Cap Ferret** mentioned in chapter 5. This was built new in 1952 by a M. Milet who just wanted to run a railway. It runs across a narrow peninsula from town to ocean, has ex-industrial tractors dressed up as steam locomotives and provides a commercial service in summer. Its example was followed in 1963 by the **Tramway de St. Trojan** on the southern end of Ile d'Oleron; this performs a similar role, with similar equipment and neither pretend to be anything but what they are. On the other side of France is the 60cm gauge **CF du Haute-Rhône** which is currently operated by CFTM and has a new line (but partly on old trackbed) between Montalieu and Sault-Brenaz in a country park east of Lyon. This is basically heir to the, now defunct, CF Touristique de Meyzieu, east of Lyon, which was started as long ago as 1963 but was finally put out of action by urban development. It therefore has an interesting selection of steam locomotives on call as well as diesels but, again, does not pretend to be anything other than a tourist operation. Lastly there is the **CF Touristique du Tarn** which occupies part of the trackbed of the former 60cm gauge Tramways a Vapeur du Tarn branch between St.Sulpice and La Ramière, although now using 50cm gauge. It has, over the years, extended both its route and its stock, the latter including Decauville and Couillet steam locomotives as well as a variety of diesels but it does not claim to be a reincarnation of the TVT; again it is a viable tourist operation in its own right. Oh, and perhaps one should not forget the 60cm gauge **CF du Lac d'Artouste** deep in the Pyrenées. Believe it or not, this is an SNCF property and is the relic of a Midi hydro-electrification scheme of the 1930s. Once the dam was built the works railway was turned over to tourist use with diesel locomotives and still runs. You have to take an SNCF train from Pau, then a bus and then a cable car (Artouste – La Sagette) to access it but the resulting trip is spectacular to say the least.

Otherwise one ventures onto dangerous ground – some would claim inclusion on the grounds of preserving bits of a former minor line. Such are the groups on the le Blanc – Argent at Luçay, or the Association hoping to restore at least part of the St Quentin – Guise but their hold on life is somewhat tenuous. One can mention them but only with the old minor railway timetable warning "peut-etre supprimée sans preavis" Fortunately, the Federation des Amis des Chemins de Fer Secondaires (FACS), and the Association Picarde pour la Preservation et l'Entretien des Vehicules Anciens (APPEVA) which runs the Froissy-Cappy line, publish current details of these and others annually in their magazines "Chemins de Fer Regionaux et Urbains" and "Voie Etroite" while from time to time there has appeared an English publication "French Tourist Railways" which is noted in the bibliography. Unfortunately the situation is so volatile that any listing here is likely to be outdated before it is published.

PART 2
Gazetteer by Regions
A historical journey round France

Halte du Tramway.

Notes:

Lines and systems: to accord with Domengie's nomenclature, and the period when most secondary railways were built, the Départements of Seine Maritime; Charente-Maritime and Loire Atlantique are referred to by their original appelations of…Inferieure. Equally, Pyrenées Atlantiques used to be Basses Pyrenées. Note also that, although this causes some complications, the Département of Charente proper is included in the Region Ouest although Domengie puts it in the Region Sud-Ouest because of its main line connections and that Cher is included largely with the Region Sud-Est.

At the end of each chapter are tables of light railways arranged alphabetically by the départements in which they were based and alphabetical lists of urban tramway systems in the appropriate region.

Operators: the first entry is the original concessionaire where this was part of a larger group. Subsequent entries show change(s) of operator and/or points of particular interest (eg. rackline).

CHAPTER 7
Regional Reprises 1: The Region Ouest

Introduction to the region (Map p.295)

The West of France includes a number of largely rural and amorphous Départements and the almost self-contained Bretagne (Brittany) and Cotentin peninsulas. It was also about as typical as one can get from the minor railway angle and therefore a good place to start: Two major state-owned systems of Intérêt Général and several privately conceded ones; no less than eight major – defined as over 250km – départemental systems of Intérêt Local, most with two or even three phases of development; a number of smaller but still substantial systems; and a few isolated lines and systems using between them all the main gauges and forms of motive power. That it also included one of the major railcar makers and one of the more eccentric producers of "homebuilds" was perhaps an accident; after all the Baert and Verney group of concessions which started in le Mans had to get their railcars from somewhere as did the widespread but Colonel Stephens-like empire of M. Tartary and his colleagues. Unfortunately the region is not really a coherent geographical entity and its lines are really only describable in clusters.

The position is complicated by the presence of another "cluster" which is not geographical either, being spread all across the region without rhyme or reason and self-selected by its gauge of 60cm. It included the only really extensive French réseau on the 60cm gauge, the 234km of the **CF du Calvados** on the Normandy coast, with its seven branches, together with no less than five other 60cm gauge public railways, even if four of them were insignificant companies with but a single short line apiece. They will be described in the appropriate places but are highlighted here. The next in significance to the Calvados system was probably the Royan group of lines, way down the west coast just south of la Rochelle in Charente Inférieure. Like the Calvados one, it was an early Decauville Aîné concession which went wrong, and oddly enough, as in Calvados, it was also wartime action in 1944-45, in this case destruction by bombing of the main depot and workshops, which finally sealed its fate.

The other 60cm gauge systems were comparatively insignificant in terms of length though one should certainly mention the Tramway de la Trinité-sur-Mer à Etel in Morbihan which, with only 21km in all, had an eventful, if short life between 1901 and 1914. Perhaps too, for completeness, one should add the curious and very ephemeral Tramway de la Baule, a little sea-front line in south Brittany successively run with steam, forced into liquidation as early as 1903, resuscitated in part in 1905 with early, but unsuccessful petrol cars, followed by equally unsuccessful vertical boilered machines towing the former petrol cars and finally two little DV 0-4-0Ts. Domengie ignores it presumably because of its tramway nature but it is surely worth recording. The other two were miniscule, the very ephemeral Tramway de Rouen-Trianon au Forêt de Rouvray in Seine-Inférieure lasting only two years, and serving only local promenaders before being partly converted into an extension of the metre gauge Rouen tramways, while the Decauville-equipped Tramway de Rotheneuf, linked to a Tramways Bretons branch, had an initial success in the late 1890s but closed in 1914 with a big deficit; the army swooped on its stock with glee and never gave it back.

Brittany: Finistère; Côtes-du-Nord; Morbihan & Ille-et-Vilaine (Map p.296)

The first identifiable geographical cluster is a complete contrast since it was almost entirely metre gauge and completely filled the Brittany peninsuala as far east as the western face of the Cotentin. The core which bound it all together was the five armed star of our first major system of Intérêt Général, the Réseau Breton. The **Réseau Breton** was arguably the French narrow gauge system best known to British enthusiasts since it lasted in its original form and with steam traction for freight right up to 1967 and two lines, standard-gauged and dieselised, still work for passengers and goods at the time of writing. Its importance tended to blind one to the fact that it was once surrounded by, and connected in eight places to, three equally extensive départemental systems, those of Morbihan (414km), Côtes du Nord (334km) and Finistère

In Morlaix the CFD du Finistère (ex CF Armoricains) station was almost beneath the towering main line viaduct.

(FACS)

Un Bonjour de Carhaix

...and over the viaduct ran the mixed gauge track of the mighty Réseau Breton...not quite so mighty in early days as two light trains with 2-4-0Ts await departure from Carhaix.

(FACS)

(427km at its greatest extent), with the equally major system of Ille-et-Vilaine only just off to the east - and tacitly accepted by the state as being within this area since it forms part of the current Region Autonome of Bretagne. The RB was originally conceived in 1879 under the Plan Freyciney and conceded in stages from 1881 to the main line CF de l'Ouest. This, like most main line companies, was not really interested in narrow gauge lines and, having built it, promptly sub-let it, complete with all infrastructure and equipment, to the big Societé Générale des CF Economiques (SE), The first branch, from the central town of Carhaix north west to Morlaix, was opened in 1891 and the sustem was steadily extended, the final extension, from Châtealin to Camaret out in the far west, not being completed until 1925; this latter was interesting in that it was laid from the start in heavy flat-bottomed rail rather than the chaired bullhead track which was then universal on the rest of the system and that the stations were constructed in the traditional west Breton style. As with other parts of the system, the infrastructure was built to standard gauge dimensions and loading gauge to facilitate any future conversion.

At its greatest extent, the Réseau consisted of a "star" of five branches based on Carhaix, three of them having extensions beyond their original termini and spreading across several départements. Anything less like the image of a bumbling light railway would be hard to imagine. Its track was solid and respectable, its stations substantial and its Carhaix Works extensive. As for the rolling stock, at its finest it included two standard classes, twelve elegant 4-6-0Ts by Fives Lille and eight massive 0-6-6-0T Mallets by Piguet of Lyon, together with an impressive set of bogie railcars from various sources. In 1924 a third rail was laid on its Guingamp - Paimpol branch for mixed gauge working, the narrow gauge being kept in for some passenger trains and for transfer workings with the Côtes du Nord system at Paimpol. Since the gangers committed the classic faux pas of starting from each end and laying the third rail on opposite sides, operation involved a rather fearsome adjustment en route (traditionally this is supposed to have involved the narrow gauge but well after that was lifted it was the standard gauge which still jinked sharply at the former crossover point - carefully placarded as saut de mouton). It was the standard gauge which finally won. The SE and its successor the CFTA fought a sturdy rearguard action right up to narrow gauge closure in 1967; after that only the Paimpol branch and a line from the common junction of Guingamp to Carhaix survived

70 BREST-RECOUVRANCE — La Gare des Tramways du Conquet

As a contrast, out in the furthest west, the Tramways Électriques du Finistère at their Brest station.

(Author's Collection)

on the standard gauge as they still do. Goods traffic remained steam-worked on the narrow gauge to the last and, almost up to the end, peak periods were likely to provide the odd steam passenger working as well, with a couple of really handsome if delapidated bogie coaches kept for just such an event. The SE even briefly took over part of the former Finistère system resulting in one of those concessionary complications so dear to the French. Pont l'Abbé – St Guenole was standard gauged for goods only, and in its later days was owned by the département which conceded its operation to the SE which, in turn, as a concessionaire of the SNCF turned operation of this one branch over to SNCF itself.

The RB had a presence in no less than three départements; Côtes du Nord, Finistère and Morbihan but was mainly in Finistère which occupies the whole western end of the peninsula...but then if ever "the leg bone connected to the thigh bone..." in light railway terms, it was in this area which was a total cat's cradle of interlinking lines. From Camaret on the west coast one could reach right to Ploermel in eastern Morbihan and fron there it was only a short branchlne journey to Guer on the Ille-et-Vilaine system; indeed the eastern tip of the RB at la Brohinière was actually in Ille-et-Vilaine although for some reason it never quite connected with the latter's lines.

Ille-et-Vilaine, however, had another of the big départemental systems, a largely connected network of ten branches radiating from the prefecture of Rennes and totalling over 500km. This was the metre gauge **Tramways d'Ille-et-Vilaine,** conceded to the Carel et Fouché groupe in 1896 and built in three stages between 1897 and 1913 – except for the final stretches to Redon which were not completed until 1924 because of the war. It covered the entire département and was almost entirely self contained; only at its northern tip did it connect with a couple of minor lines from St Malo. It was an early user of railcars and, although about half the system closed in 1937, the remainder was further modernised with Billard cars and ran throughout the war. In 1945 the concessionaire even persuaded the département to buy five more railcars but losses still mounted and, soon after the formal concession period expired in 1948, the remaining lines were closed. In general the lines were roadside with curves of down to 50m radius and gradients of up to 30mm/m. Locomotives started with a group of conventional Tubize/Blanc Misseron tramway-type 0-6-0Ts, and then settled on conventional Corpet Louvet light 0-6-0Ts as main motive power.

The CF des Côtes du Nord lasted long enough for even British enthusiasts to photograph it: Corpet Louvet 0-6-0T No. 39 departs St Brieuc (SNCF) in 1956.

(D. TREVOR ROWE)

44 PARAMÉ. — Le Boulevard Rochebonne — LL

Up by St Malo, an early train of the Tramways Bretons noses through Paramé town. (AUTHOR'S COLLECTION)

Interestingly it did have four quite handsome Corpet Mallet 0-4-4-0Ts and two heavier 0-8-0Ts by the same firm for heavy traffic. After experimenting with De Dion and Verney railbuses, the railcar fleet concentrated on the efficient Billard A150D series.

Apart from the TIV, the département had only three minor systems, the short, three branch suburban **Tramways Bretons** at St Malo with a minor branch of a branch from Paramé to Rotheneuf, and the miniscule (9km long) Tramway de **Dinard à St Briac,** up in the north west corner. The Dinard company was a minor oddity, using first two Turgan-Foy steam railcars, together with a most odd six-coupled device (also by Turgan-Foy) which consisted of a very short-boilered 0-6-0T with a luggage compartment built on behind the cab; these were supplemented by a rebuilt Serpollet car wth flash-steam boiler and then by an early petrol-electric bogie car by Westinghouse. Its main motive power, three compound 0-6-0T by Weidknecht, soon proved too light and were replaced by four heavier machines from the same maker. The whole thing was very seasonal and lasted only from 1901 to 1928. The **Tramways Bretons,** a conventional roadside steam tramway with three branches, was actually Ille-et-Vilaine's first secondary line, being opened in part in 1889. It lasted somewhat longer, having a heavy summer traffic pulled by tram locomotives which resisted road competition, and one line was even electrified in 1927. It served throughout the second war and faded away in 1946-47, worn out by its efforts. At Paramé it, in turn, connected to the 60cm gauge **Tramway de Rotheneuf** mentioned above. This, described even by Domengie as "ce curieux tramway", was built but not operated by the Decauville concern and lasted only from 1896 to 1914 when track and stock were commandeered for the war effort and never returned - since it had been in serious deficit since 1912 the concessionaires no doubt heaved a sigh of relief. Its stock was typical Decauville except for a Blanc Misseron 0-6-0T which somehow survives at Pithiviers.

Back on the Brittany peninsula, Finistère itself was home to not one but two fairly extensive systems. First was the **Cie des CF Départementaux du Finistère** (CDF), conceded to Baert & Beldant – predecessors of the Baert & Verney group - in 1891. This started with just three separate branches and between 1893 and 1909 expanded to a total of 214km with systems in both the north and south of the Département. In 1922 it assimilated the **CF Armoricains** (CFA), five lines opened in 1912-13 and including a long north-south traverse from Plouescat to Rosporden, crossing the RB en route at Châteuneuf-du-Faou.

CARNAC. – Arrivée du Tramway

And down in Morbihan, the miniscule 60cm gauge Tramway de la Trinité-s-Mer à Etel pauses en-route. Orenstein & Kopplel 0-6-0WT and Decauville stock.

(AUTHOR'S COLLECTION)

33 LA TURBALLE (Loire-Inf) — Place de la Gare
Arrivée du Train de Piriac

Further south, in neighbouring Loire Inférieure, a train of the CF du Morbihan ambles through the streets of a village. CM 24 is a Pinguely 0-6-0T of 1906.

(FACS)

Other contacts with the RB were at the latter's Morlaix and Rosporden termini. Both systems were true light railways running largely on their own right of way and operated with a collection of Corpet, Louvet 0-6-0Ts; the CDF contributed four-wheeled stock, the CFA some handsome bogie coaches. Their combined railcar stock was, as might be expected, mainly Verney railbuses or the boxy successors of their SCF subsidiary but also included a second-hand Brissoneau et Lotz diesel-electric car. Run as a fermière operation after 1926, the combined systems were gradually replaced by buses and the remnants were only saved by the war. The Département then confided their operation to the SE as the organisation with most experience in the region and the latter ran them until final closure in 1946. The only other light railway was the short, two branch **Tramways Electriques du Finistère** running west from Brest and opened in 1903. It, too, was assimilated into the CFDF in 1922 and was really a rural tramway since it carried only passengers and messageries.

Of the other Brittany départements, Côtes du Nord was entirely colonised by the **CF des Côtes du Nord** which has already been considered in detail in Chapter 2. The southernmost, Morbihan, was in a sense a link with the south since its main concessionaire, the **CF du Morbihan,** also had trackage in Loire Inférieure that was connected with its main system. Its Morbihan system totalled no less than 413km in ten, connected, branches based round the three centres of Ploermel, Lorient and Vannes and built in two stages between 1903 and...1923, the war causing some perturbation to the scheme. Unusually in this region it connected to others at only two points – to its own lines in Loire Inférieure at la Roche Bernard and to the RB's Rosporden branch at Gourin; one of the sadder sights in recent years was its former Gourin station marooned in a carpark. The CM came late to modernisation, serious deficits not appearing until about 1930 when it tried to counter them with first some battery-electric cars and then a small fleet of Brissoneau et Lotz diesel electrics - it was, after all, a Groupe Jeancard concession. The deficit still increased and closure was planned for 1939-40 but again the war intervened and closure was put off until 1947. The CM also took over the former 60cm gauge **Tramway de la Trinité-sur-mer à Etel** in the south of the département which had been built in 1901 and closed in 1914. This had two claims to fame. To start with it was one of the few French companies which dared to patronise foreign makers - three 0-6-0WTs from Orenstein & Koppel supplanted its original Decauville 0-4-2Ts; secondly (and not entirely to the regret of its cash-strapped owners) it was requisitioned lock, stock and barrel on the outbreak of war and its track and material commandeered for the war effort; it all went off to a powder factory at Bergerac and nothing came back except possibly the O&K tank engines and the seven elegant bogie coaches. The infrastructure reverted to the Département which rebuilt it to metre gauge in 1922 and, as noted above, entrusted it to the big CF du Morbihan.

South along the coast: Loire-Inférieure; Vendée (Map p.297)

1947-48 also saw closure of the Morbihan Company's southern empire in Loire Inférieure directly to the south. This département, sitting squarely below Ille-et-Vilaine, was totally different, having no coherent réseaux of its own. Instead it tended to build and equip isolated branches which it then farmed out to various concessionaires. As already noted, the **CF du Morbihan** had no less than six of these in the west, in two groups on both sides of the Loire estuary and totalling some 120km. They were typically Morbihan in structure and equipment and performed adequately until overcome by road competiton in 1948.

The two other main systems in Loire-Inférieure were both two-branch affairs. One was the CF de **Châteaubriant à Erbray,** in the north east corner, which was conceded to M. Lemmonier of Côtes-du-Nord fame and was originally concerned mainly with quarry traffic. It eventually extended to La Chapelle-Glain in the east, and south to Ancenis. It was of the lighter type, mainly roadside and with a narrow loading gauge, had a mixture of tram locomotives and conventional Corpet Louvet 0-6-0Ts together with a De Dion railbus, and should have closed completely in 1938. In practice the la Chapelle branch was reused in the war and survived until 1947. The other two branch system was conceded for operation to the grandly named **Cie Française des Chemins de Fer à Voie Etroite,** a Carel et Fouché subsidiary. It ran south from the prefecture of Nantes to Legé with a branch to Rocheservière, was rather more substantial and on its own right of way, but lasted only to 1935; its single De Dion railbus had only

Again in Loire Inférieure, the Cie Française des CF à Voie Etroite hauled surprisingly heavy traffic over its two brief lines.
(FACS)

two years of use before being sold to the Morbihan. Curiously, this obscure line is known to many British enthusiasts because one of its Corpet, Louvet 0-6-0Ts survived to work at Waltham on an English mineral line. Lastly there was a short standard gauge branch from **Le Pallet to Vallet** which the département conceded to the CF de l'Etat who shuffled off the embarrassment by attaching it to their Tramways de la Vendée (qv) in 1924. Like many of these foundlings it then had a mixed career, losing passenger service in 1933, being taken up by the SNCF in 1938 and then legally passed to the municipality of Vallet; the SNCF ran it as a siding up to 1959.

The big mainline Ouest/Etat company, oddly enough, also promoted a much lowlier, though extensive network of steam tramways as the **Tramways de la Vendée** in the département of Vendée just south of those we have been considering. At a time when mainline companies took some trouble to avoid being lumbered with secondary lines, the Administration des Chemins de Fer de l'Ouest (and then the CF de l'Etat as it became after the CF de l'Ouest collapsed in 1909) accepted the concession from the Vendée Département and kept it right up to incorporation in the SNCF in 1938. True, it made a lot of plaintive noises in later years and SNCF quickly dumped the system back on the Département which enlisted the big CFD concern instead. True, operation by a large national concern did not provide any real benefits in improved stock and services. There it was, however, an eventual 342km of largely roadside steam tramway served by conventional 0-6-0T and 2-6-0T and mostly 4-wheeled stock, its only bogie coaches coming from a taken-over independent line the **CF de Challans à Fromentine** which in spite of its title was not particularly early (1896) but quickly got into debt and had to be bought back by the département in 1914. After experimenting with a truly terrifying machine rebuilt from a coach, together with two imitations on Renault chassis, it also seems to have served almost as a testbed for SCF Verney, whose early railbus-like products were not much appreciated if local comments are any guide; it was left to the CFD to introduce some of their efficient Billard A80D cars and to dabble in diesel locomotives but, alas, that was too late. The last passenger service went over to buses in 1949.

A tangled web: Charente Inférieure, Charente & Deux Sevres (Map p.298)

Going south from Vendée, we meet three départements that are always thought of together in light railway terms, Charente, Charente Inférieure (later Charente Maritime) and Deux Sevres. In truth

Domengie places Charente in the South West Region because of its main line connections but its concessions are so closely entwined with those of the other two that in light railway terms it makes more sense to include it here. We also return to Intérêt Général, for the second IG system in this region was conceded directly to the big Chemins de Fer Départementaux (CFD) company and sprawled over all three départements. As their **CFD Réseau des Charentes et Deux Sevres** it had five main branches, plus an odd line of Intérêt Local in Charente that somehow got attached to the concession and it was very much a mainstream CFD system. Running mainly on its own right of way, it received standard CFD equipment, including bogie coaches and, successively, De Dion Bouton and Billard railcars, it built four locotracteurs out of old steam locomotives at its St-Jean-d'Angely Works and was generally efficient if dull. Like many such systems it was closed in the early 1950s, exporting its more modern stock to other CFD possessions. Even in its own bailiwick it was always heavily outnumbered by the vastly more extensive but much lighter and totally deficitary **CF Economiques des Charentes.** This, (a Jeancard group concession) even caused a conscientious British diplomatic representative to write a long screed to the commissioners drafting our 1896 Light Railway Act to warn them against the dire consequences of intemperate subsidy. (see Consul Warburton's letter: Appendix 2). It had réseaux in both the Charentes, totalling some 397 plus 372km and also boasted two completely isolated offshoots on the neighbouring islands of Il de Ré and Ile d'Oléron. Finally in Charente-Maritime, all on its own at the mouth of the River Seudre, was another of the region's 60cm gauge systems, the **Tramways de Royan.** Always accorded more prominence than its quite restricted size deserved, (it was actually bracketed among the suburban tramways in many official lists) this was basically a network of seaside steam tramways, developed from a Decauville initiative of 1891 and running through the streets, pinewoods and sanddunes, doing much of its business during the summer season and supplementing this with local freight and passenger traffic as occasion offered. It also had the distinction of acquiring and downgauging - if that is the word - a former metre gauge network. This was the so-called **Tramways de la Forêt de la Coubre,** initially started by the Forestry authorities as horse-drawn logging lines as far back as 1865 and then touristified with the French equivalent of Wickham railcars, little boxy

65 — Vendée - CHALLANS-VILLE
Arrivée du train de Fromentine

And further south in Vendée the Tramways de la Vendée runs through a typical village – actually on the once independent CF de Challans à Fromentine.

(FACS)

Just off the coast, there is holiday traffic on the Ile d'Oléron with the CF Economiques des Charentes: stock comprises one of their early Corpet, Louvets and typical sparsely-windowed coaches.   (FACS)

petrol-engined semi-open machines by the firm of Campagne. After WW1, the spidery web of lines was converted to 60cm and joined to the main system as the Tramway de la Grande Côte à Ronce-les-Bains although it still used slightly improved draisines as its motive power. The main system always used steam, first Decauville-supplied 0-4-2Ts by Weidknecht and later some 0-6-2Ts from the same source; as a largely seasonal operation its stock was mainly open-sided baladeuses. Alas, it faded away during the war, its depot and works destroyed in a totally unnecessary air raid in January 1945, together with most of the equipment.

Also among the big spenders was the Département of Charente east of Charente-Inférieure. The CFD had two lines here, an Intérêt Général tongue of its tangled Réseau des Charentes et Deux-Sevres and an Intérêt Local extension of it but the main inhabitant was that Jeancard group so reviled by Consul Warburton, the **CF Economiques des Charentes** which already operated about 400km in the neighbouring Charente Inférieure and Loire Inférieure. In Charente alone it accumulated some 370km of very light, and largely roadside tramway which never really had a chance. Gradients of up to 55mm/m, curves down to 100m radius, a loading gauge of 2.10m and 18kg/m rail were not conducive to long life once road competition grew and even provision of railcars only staved off the inevitable closure. Two lines were briefly saved by the war but closed immediately after. Locomotive stock was entirely conventional Corpet Louvet 0-6-0Ts, rolling stock was four-wheeled. Like other Jeancard group concessions, modern power took the form of a series of battery electric cars from 1927, supplemented by seven Brissonau et Lotz diesel electrics in 1936.

Deux Sevres, the third département in this cluster, also had a roadside metre gauge system of Intérêt Local, the three branch **Tramways des Deux Sevres** (TDS) based on Parthenay. In essence this was a rather drab rural network originally planned to the three-fifteens formula and thus stuck with a lot of deficitary, lightly laid roadside lines. Where it differed was in its eccentric sorties into the early railbus field. It belonged to the Tartary group and M Tartary himself chose it for his first attempts at motor rail transport. In the immediate aftermath of World War 1 there was a lot of military surplus stuff on offer.

In the depths of the Département of Sarthe, a roadside tram of the Tramways de la Sarthe, headed by a Blanc-Misseron bicabine, dozes at a wayside hamlet.

(FACS)

And a rather neater train of the CF de l'Anjou, with its Blanc Misseron 0-6-0T and compartment stock, does the same thing in Maine-et-Loire.

(FACS)

Tartary bought up a job lot of former US Army GMC ambulances and it was these that formed the basis of all his future experiments; indeed the first attempt was simply a standard ambulance with rail wheels and a coat of paint - even down to retaining the canvas tilt... The next batch was a little more sophisticated with an enclosed body resembling a small country bus of the era (and built, it may be said, in the Deux Sevres own Works); a further batch stretched the body and later additions or rebuilds resulted in semi-streamlined (but still four-wheeled and single ended) versions... They were even exported, several Tartary systems including the CF d'Anjou and Tramways de l'Indre being blessed, or cursed, with examples and there was even a single freight pantechnicon version with a massive rear-end overhang. He also seems to have inspired the initial efforts of Baert and Verney who also used surplus GMC chassis at the start. The TDS' other claim to fame was the use of transporter bogies to serve a big customer at Melle which continued to use some track and equipment well after the rest had been declassified.

Rural residue: Sarthe; Maine-et-Loire; Mayenne; Orne; Eure-et-Loir (Map p.299)

The rest of the rural départements inland from the coast are not nearly so easy to group or classify. Sarthe, Orne, Eure-et-Loir, Mayenne, Maine-et-Loire all had their metre gauge systems, often interconnecting into each others' territories but only two had homogeneous ones over 300km in length. The first of these was Sarthe, with its sprawling **Tramways de la Sarthe** spreading from a monumental central station at Le Mans where it had an interesting cruciform crossing with the town tramways...on a pair of intersecting bridges. This extensive system of roadside lines was conceded to what became the Carel et Fouché group and was envisaged in three stages, although the last one was never completed owing to the war. It was originally built to the three fifteens formula and was very poorly placed to fight road competition. It tried, mark you, supplementing its covered and uncovered Blanc Misseron tram locomotives with, first, De Dion railbuses and then some second-hand Verneys but by 1939 only a few lines were left in traffic. These, of course, survived to 1947 and one short section, at Montbizot, lasted longer to serve an industrial customer until 1969; it also helped to keep examples of the locomotives alive until they could be preserved.

On the standard gauge, two railcar trains of the Mamers – St Calais prepare to depart north and south from Conerré-Biellé. Verney railbus in front, CFD 9XX series car behind. (G. J. Hoare's Collection)

Sarthe, in addition, had a standard gauge réseau, the **CF de Mamers à St Calais** with its two branches. Conceived under the 1865 legislation and opened in 1872-73, this even lasted out into the 1970s with a most eclectic collection of railcars – two double-ended Verneys from the Manche département, a CFD designed four-wheeler and a couple of the odd flimsy but genuine buses on rails which Verney was building as late as 1950; sauterelles (jumpers) they were nicknamed by the shaken users. They were designed to work back to back and there is a sneaking suspicion that they might have been intended for easy conversion to road use if required. It also had a curiosity, one of the ex WD 350hp LMS-type diesel shunters which has since been repatriated to England. At one time it even took over a former SNCF branch for freight but closed throughout in 1977. Bits were taken over by a preservation concern which recently lost the original, and historic, workshops by fire but is likely to survive.

The other biggish system in the region was that of Maine-et-Loire, on Sarthe's south western borders. This hid its administrative origins beneath the title of **CFIL de l'Anjou.** The "petit Anjou" was a perfectly normal and quite substantial group of Carel et Fouché lines with neat little 0-6-0Ts and the usual mixture of roadside and private track…but with the distinction of using, almost exclusively, four-wheeled compartment stock which all the neighbours rudely categorised as "type anglais" or, even worse, "cages a poules" (hencoops). Many French main line companies used compartment stock but, by and large, the minor lines fought shy of it and thought it rather down-market (besides being more difficult to heat and monitor!). The Anjou, with 315km, lasted as such until 1928 when it was taken over by the SE who, in turn ran it until 1948, using De Dion railbuses and a few Brissoneau et Lotz cars largely to replace steam working. Maine-et-Loire also had a much smaller concessionaire which linked to the CFA at the old riverside town of Saumur. This was the **Sté des Tramways de Saumur et Extensions** which, under various names – Tramways à Vapeur de l'Ouest; Cie Nouvelle des VFIL de Saumur et des Environs – ran two short steam tramways north and south along the river between 1896 and 1929; it had strong connections with the Tartary companies at the start but ended up in the hands of Verney. Most of its material was normal steam tramway design although it did, for navettes, once have no less than three Purrey steamcars and eventually three Verney railbuses.

If the major systems were fairly bland apart for some oddities, the middling ones (say 100-250km) were pretty average too, and notable in retrospect mainly for their eccentricities rather than their charm. Sarthe was surrounded by lesser – and on the whole blander – systems. There is really not much to say about the three branch **CFD de la Mayenne,** for example, which lay to the west and even linked up at St Jean-sur-Erve just inside the Mayenne border. It was based on the prefecture of Laval, stretched northwestward to meet the CF de la Manche at Landivy, whence it bent back to Mayenne itself with a nice metallic viaduct over the river there; it was a Verney group system with the usual 0-6-0Ts followed by bonneted railbuses. Most of it disappeared in 1938 but the last spur was saved by the war and survived until 1947.

Orne, a long thin département to the north of both these, was served in depth by the main line companies but otherwise had three short roadside lines operated by a Carel et Fouché subsidiary, the **CF des Voies Ferrées Economiques de l'Orne;** these had Piguet 0-6-0Ts for a change and even some centre-entrance coaches but that was about the limit of their individuality. They had a short life, from 1913-1937 and did their job without fanfare. More interesting historically was the short standard gauge branch from **Monsecret via Tinchebray to Les Maures,** just over the border in Manche. This was originally part of a planned east-west link to Cherencé-le-Roussel, the central part of which, between Les Maures and Sourdeval, was snatched by the CF de l'Ouest and incorporated in its system. The western end was later built by the Manche département, but on metre gauge, while the Les Maures - Monsecret line had a very convoluted career. Eventually reduced to Monsecret – Tinchebray it was operated by the CF de l'Etat up to 1930, then by the VFEO to 1935 and then – largely for freight – by two successive Verney Groupe companies to 1951 and finally by a local cooperative which gave up altogether in 1964. Rather more straightforward was Eure-et-Loir to the east whose Tramways de l'Eure-et-Loir managed six steam-worked roadside branches of the lightest kind started in 1889 and not completed until 1931, by which time the first ones were already marked for closure. Originally depending from the Groupe Verney, it was taken over by the SGTD in 1930 and bussified over the next six years.

Up in Manche there was metre gauge: here the CF de la Manche departs from Sourdeval obviously prepared for emergencies if the water tanks run dry. (FACS)

SAINT-JAMES (Manche). — La Gare.

And here the Tramways Normands poses at its St James terminus on the line from Avranches: interestingly the locomotive is actually branded AG (Avranches – Granville) not TN so is pobably from the CF de la Manche. (FACS)

The North coast: Manche; Calvados; Eure; Seine-Inférieure (Map p.300)

All of that leaves just the string of départements along the north coast, from the Cotentin peninsula through Normandy to the mouths of the Seine. The Cotentin itself, effectively defined by the Manche département, provided a rather variegated cluster of its own, and one not easy to sort out. The earliest system of Intérêt Local was the standard gauge line from Barfleur, up in the north east corner, down to Valognes, with a branch to Montebourg. This was originally envisaged under the 1865 act but was eventually conceded to the CFD for its **CFD Réseau de la Manche** in 1883 under the legislation of 1880. It was on its own right of way and had typical branchline stock save for a single St Leonard 0-8-0T (which confused identifiers since it looked very like a contemporary Decauville design). The main "client" of the département was originally the **Cie des Chemins de Fer de la Manche (CFM).** Between 1907 and 1910, this opened five metre gauge branches in three groups, mostly in the south of the département, which eventually totalled some 215km, together with a single standard gauge line from Cherbourg to Barfleur and an urban tramway at Avranches; an extension of the Cherbourg tramways orginally allocated to the CFM was ceded to the Cherbourg company in 1910. The CF de la Manche unfortunately tends to lurk in obscurity but it had its moments. One branch of its metre gauge system, from St Mère-Eglise in the middle of the peninsula was even closed in 1914 and never reopened, its rails and stock being "borrowed" after the war to help lay an extension elsewhere, although it was not declassified for thirty five years. The rest followed in the mid 1930s except for the standard gauge line to Barfleur. Like its neighbours in Calvados, this suffered considerably from the 1944 invasion fighting and, although resuscitated in 1947, closed three years later; at least another western line, the Mamers – St Calais in Sarthe, benefitted from its two modern railcars. Otherwise there were the **Tramways Normands** down in the south west corner which were a Baert & Verney concession and owned two lines – a metre gauge steam tramway from Avranches to St James and a standard gauge line from Pontorson, on the Ouest main line, out across the causeway to the foot of Mont St Michel; they still sell postcards of the latter and there are thoughts of reinstating it in some form to counter motorcar pollution.

The Tramways Normands also ran the standard gauge tourist line up to Mont St Michel. An unusual view looking out along the causeway.

(AUTHOR'S COLLECTION)

101

Collection F. C., Cherbourg

Up in the north the standard gauge held sway: A CF de la Manche train prepares to leave the fort-like station at Cherbourg for Barfleur.
(AUTHOR'S COLLECTION)

The Avranches tramway closed in 1914. All the others bar the stretch from St Hilaire-du-Harcouet to Landivy which was passed to Mayenne, were bought back by the département in the mid 1920s and by 1928 had been handed over to the Cie des Chemins de fer Normands, a specially organised and bus-minded company. This transferred the metre gauge lines to road in 1938, together with the Pontorson line, but partly modernised the others with a fine collection of unusual Verney railcars. These included, among others, a most odd three-section semi-articulated single ender and the two bogie double-end cars which ended up on the Mamers – St Calais. The standard gauge would undoubtedly have closed but for the war but then survived until 1950.

Calvados, to the east, had the biggest 60cm gauge public network in France. Most British enthusiasts probably remember the **CF du Calvados,** if they remember it at all, for one thing only...the fact that its last surviving route perished in the 1944 D-day landings; the pathetic accounts of the morning train abandoned in Luc-s-Mer station and the musings on the origins of that narrow roadside track that appeared in subsequent war documentaries still surface from time to time. Indeed it finished almost where it started in 1890, with a single roadside track from Caen to Dives and, later, Luc-s-Mer intended as a shop window for the products of Decauville Aîné. As such it must have been something of an embarrassment, the concession failing and being transferred to a local company which was stuck with the Département's original choice of gauge. In its heyday, however, it developed into a very complex network based on a central depot at Caen but also having an almost detached group of lines in the west around Bayeux, joined to the originals only by a mixed gauge section along the coast between Courseulles and Luc. It even, for some years, had a considerable mineral traffic from the Saumont plateau down to Caen and its termini are a poignant echo of Allied objectives in the 1944 invasion: Arromanches; Bayeux; Caen; Courseulles; Dives; Falaise; Isigny. The later concessionaire was never very happy - deprived of Decauville's imagination the bureaucrats ordered cutdown copies of light metre gauge designs and the gauge itself proved an insuperable handicap as soon as road competition became serious. Nonetheless its motive power involved not only the original Mallets, but a wide range of both four and six-coupled machines of more conventional type including powerful 4-6-0Ts of both tram and railway pattern. Among its stock were elegant bogie coaches and frivolous seaside trailers; it even had a set of petrol electric railcars for the less lucrative branches.

Otherwise Calvados had three standard gauge lines, of which the first was the early, and always antiquated, **CF de Caen à la Mer** which was promoted under the 1865 act and opened in 1875-76. It ran north from Caen to the coast at Luc-sur-Mer and then west to Courseulles, eventually incorporating the mixed gauge section mentioned above. It had a heavy summer traffic, for which it maintained some double-decker coaches, took through trains off the main line in summer and, following a decision to entrust exploitation to the CF de l'Etat in 1933, had several Micheline rubber-tyred railcars. In 1937 it was entrusted to the bus-minded Sté des Courriers Normands, as was the 60cm gauge, and that should have been the end had not the war intervened and reprieved services. Despite being flattened by the 1944 invasion it was partially resuscitated again in 1945, only to close to passengers in 1951 and completely a year later.

The other two were less sigmificant. The short standard gauge branch from **Moult to Argences** never amounted to much, being opened in 1912 by a local entrepreneur "at his own risks and perils" and transferring its passengers to the road in 1931. It stayed open for goods, mainly for one customer, however, until 1966. During its life it managed to wear out no less than four 0-6-0T - three of them being main-line cast-offs – and end up with an elderly Campagne diesel tractor. The **CF de Caen à Soumont,** opened as late as 1920, was really an industrial railway connecting the Saumont mines of the Sté. Metallurgique de Normandie with their steelworks, and the main line, at Caen but did convey wagonload goods for firms along its route and had an internal passenger service for workers. It lost most of its traffc in 1989 when the mines closed and anything that survived was no more than an industrial siding. In its heyday it was quite heavily trafficked, its locomotive stud including, inter alia, several 2-8-2T and five ex-Reichsbahn 2-10-0s acquired from the SNCF.

All of which leaves us only with the country on both sides of the Seine mouth, comprising Eure and, to the north, Seine-Inférieure (now Seine-Maritime). Eure had only that **CF de Cormeilles à Glos Montfort**

Two birds with one view: A train from the Bayeux lines of the CF du Calvados crosses a CF de Caen à la Mer train at St Aubin on the mixed gauge section betweeen Luc and Courseulles. (AUTHOR'S COLLECTION)

86. - COURSEULLES-sur-MER. - *Place de la Gare*

And a Bayeux-bound train of the CFC erupts from the standard gauge goods yard and across the forecourt of the CF de Caen à la Mer station. An unidentified Tubize/Blanc Misseron tram locomotive heads conventional four-wheeled stock. (C. WALKER'S COLLECTION)

described in chapter 2. Seine-Maritime, like others in this area, was well served by the main line companies and had only minor, scattered branches of its own. For the record, from west to east, these were:

a) the tiny (4km) but metre gauge **Tramway de Etanhuis à St Romain-de-Colbosc.** This was basically a town to station steam tram which, after an unsuccessful flirtation with steam railcars, settled down with three little Corpet, Louvet 0-4-0Ts and a minimum of four-wheeled stock. None the less, it survived from 1897 to 1929 when it was replaced by a bus.

b) the 60cm gauge steam tram from **Rouen-Trianon,** terminus of a town tramway line, **to the Forêt-de-Rouvray.** Being only 2.2km long, and with rail weighing only 7kg/m, it was a catastrophic failure and had only a short life from 1906 to 1908, after which it was partly replaced by a metre gauge extension of the Rouen tramways. It certaily did not help itself by experimenting with two early petrol draisines in an attempt to economise.

c) the two lines of the metre gauge **CF de Normandie,** from Ouville-la-Rivière to Motteville and to Clères. These were a Laborie concession, opened in 1912-13 and were typical rural light railways. They were mainly on their own rght of way but even so had curves of down to 80m radius and gradients of 35mm/m. They did have some handsome Corpet, Louvet 2-6-0Ts, were bought back by the département in 1925 and entrusted to the SE, and survived until 1947, thanks again to wartime needs.

d) The SE's own line, from **Envermeu to Aumale** where it met up with the Somme system of the same company, into which it was effectively integrated. The line was formally run by the SE on behalf of the département and, once again, was saved by the war, closing for passengers in 1947 and completely the following year. Its locomotives, being bought and owned by the département, were similar to those of the CF de Normandie. Together with that line it experimented with a locally built railbus but without success.

Lastly it may be proper to mention two short standard gauge branches that were officially of intérêt local, a freight only line south of Rouen and the CF du Nord-operated line from **Monterolier-Buchy to St Saens.** The Rouen one from **Rive-Gauche to Petit-Quevilly,** was, rather oddly, granted under the 1865 legislation to an industrial concern, the **Societé Bozel-Malera** and opened in 1870. It acquired official status because B-M agreed to carry traffic for other firms and it was basically a long industrial siding; it was closed owing to war damage in 1944. The St Saens line was a straightforward line of Intérêt Local with operation granted to the CF du Nord which worked it with its normal branchline stock. Opened in 1900, it lost its passenger traffic in 1934 and closed, under SNCF auspices, in 1952.

Two escapees from the west coast to finish with

That should finish off the Region Ouest but, both here and in the adjoining Nord region, one has to say that here railways and tramways blur, some lines recognised as railways by enthusiasts being officially classed as "tramways urbains et suburbains" and vice versa. Two little lines especially seem to drop down all the cracks and are therefore mentioned specially here. Both were on the west coast. In Loire Inférieure, west of St Nazaire, was the miniscule **Tramways de la Baule** which for a short 60cm gauge line had a most complex career. It was properly approved from the start, opening an initial line along the seafront in 1887 between the la Pouliguen district and the neighbouring village of Pornichet (achieved by a short extension in 1891). The line appears to have been laid directly on the sand perilously near high water mark and was operated in a rather ramshackle manner with two tiny Decauville 0-4-0Ts pulling "summer" coaches; the operator was, for a reason not clear to the writer, always called "Le Trait d'Union" (the Trade Union Company) its initials giving much mirth to the local press ("Trop Usé" and requires "Transformation Urgente" were two of the politer epithets). It worked fitfully to 1902 and then closed. It was replaced, inadequately, by motor omnibuses and then relaid on a slightly different (and drier) route by a new entrepreneur. For its reopening in 1904 Decauville provided some highly unreliable petrol cars which eventually ended up as trailers for yet more miniscule 0-4-0Ts. "La Navette" (the shuttle) as it termed itself

Representative of the smaller lines in the region: The metre gauge train from Etanhuis poses at its far terminus.

(FACS)

105

Côte d'Amour　　　　　　　　　　;0　LA BAULE (Loire-Inf.) — La " Navette " sur le remblai

And the one that nearly got away: the Tramway de la Baule out on the west coast.　　　　　　(FACS)

had a stormy and, not entirely legal, career up to 1914 and was then summarily closed; postwar efforts to replace it came to nothing.

The quite elegant metre gauge electric line at **Sables d'Olonne** in Vendée even managed its whole career without officially being classified as anything (it ran "by tacit agreement" as one official said) and there is still some mystery about parts of its route – if one wanted to, one could insularly describe it as a sort of French Volks Electric Railway. Basically it ran along the seafront, linking a Casino at the south end of town to one at the north end; just what at that says about the locals' gambling habits is uncertain. It was originally planned to extend to the Etat station (presumably to allow patrons a quick getaway?) but although rails were laid it is dubious if services ever started. It opened in 1901 and when the concessionaire failed after only four years, the town took it over – another parallel with Volks. It was mainly seasonal in operation and closed after the 1925 season when the power plant wore out. The line was laid in the carriageway, with overhead supply at 550v DC and operated by a fleet of seven four-wheelers and two bogie cars with trailers.

Light Railways in Region Ouest

name	ident	gauge	km	lines	dates	cln	operators	
dept: Calvados								
Caen à la Mer, CF de	CM	sg	0028	01	1875-1952*	IL		SCN 1937
Caen à Soumont, CF de	CS	sg	0030	01	1920-1989	-		Ste Metal de Normandie
Calvados, CF du	CFC	60cm	0234	07	1891-1944	IL		Decauville; Empain 1895
Moult – Argences, CF de	MA	sg	0004	01	1912-1966	IL		
dept Charente								
Charentes et Deux Sevres, Réseau des	CFD	metre	0063	01	1889-1950	IL	CFD	
Charentes, CF Economiques des	EC	metre	0370	07	1895-1946	IL	Jeancard	
dept Charente-Inférieure								
Charentes et Deux Sevres, CFD Réseau des	CFD	metre	0242	05	1896-1950	IL	CFD	
Charentes, CF Economiques des	EC	metre	0397	14	1894-1947	Twy	Jeancard	
Forêt de la Coubre, Twy du	TR	metre	0027	01	1863-1913?	Twy		TR 1913.
Royan, Twys de	TR	60cm	0043	04	1890-1945	Twy	Decauville;	CGTR 1895
dept Côtes-du-Nord								
Côtes-du-Nord, CF des	CdN	metre	0334	16	1905-1956	IL	CCFT	
Lannion – Plestin, ligne de	CFA	metre	0021	01	1916-1937	IL		CdN 1921
dept Deux-Sevres								
Deux-Sevres, Twys des	TDS	metre	0154	03	1897-1975*	Twy	Tartary	
dept Eure								
Cormeilles à Glos Montfort et exts CF de	CGM	metre	0075	03	1902-1946*	IL	Laborie	
dept Eure-et-Loir								
Eure-et-Loir, Twys de	EL	metre	0215	06	1899-1936	Twy	Verney;	SGTD 1927
dept Finistère								
Armoricains, CF	CFA	metre	0213	05	1912-1946	IL		CDF 1922
Breton, Réseau	RB	m/sg	0412	07	1891-now	IG	Etat;	SE 1891
Finistère, CFD du	CDF	metre	0214	08	1893-1946	IL	Verney;	SE 1941
Finistère, Twys Électriques du (Brest)	TEF	metre	0024	02	1903-1932	Twy		CDF 1922
Pont l'Abbé-St Guenole, ligne de	CDF	sg	0018	01	1947-1963*	IL	CFDF;	SE 1947
dept Ille-et-Vilaine								
Bretons, Twys	TB	metre	0024	03	1889-1947	Twy		Régie 1923
Dinard à St Briac, Twy de	DSB	metre	0009	01	1901-1929	Twy		
Ille-et-Vilaine, Twys à vapeur d'	TIV	metre	0510	10	1897-1948	IL	Carel et Fouché	
Rotheneuf, Twy de	TR	60cm	0004	01	1896-1914	Twy		
dept Loire-Inférieure								
CF à Voie Etroite, Cie Française des	CFVE	metre	0084	02	1893-1935	IL	Carel et Fouché	
Châteaubriant à Erbray et exts, CF de	TCE	metre	0063	02	1888-1947	IL	Lemonnier	
La Baule, Twy de	TlB	60cm	0002	01	1887-1914	Twy		varied career wth gaps
Le Pallet-Vallet (CF de l'Etat)	PV	sg	0006	01	1912-1959*	IL	Etat;	SNCF 1938
Morbihan, CF du (réseau de Loire-Inf)	CM	metre	0120	06	1906-1948	IL	Jeancard/Verney	
dept Maine-et-Loire								
Anjou, CFIL de l'	ANJ	metre	0315	05	1893-1948*	IL	Carel et Fouché;	SE 1928
Saumur et exts, Twys de	TSE	metre	0020	02	1896-1929	Twy		
dept Manche								
Avranches (Gare-Ville), Twy d'	CFM	metre	0003	01	1907-1914	Twy		Manche CF
Avranches – St James	TN	metre	0017	01	1901-1938	Twy	Twys Normands;	CF Normands 1926
Cherbourg – Barfleur, ligne de	CFM	sg	0033	01	1911-1950	IL		Manche CF
Manche, CF de la	CFM	metre	0215	05	1907-1938	IL		CFN 1926
Manche, CFD Réseau de la	CFD	sg	0044	02	1886-1950	IL	CFD;	CFN 1926
Pontorson – Mont St Michel, ligne de	TN	sg	0010	01	1901-1938	Twy	Twys Normands;	CF Normands 1928
Querqueville – Urville, Twy de	TEC	metre	0004	01	1911-1944	Twy	Manche CF;	TEC 1910

Light Railways in Region Ouest continued...

name	ident	gauge	km	lines	dates	cln	operators	
dept Mayenne								
Mayenne, CFD de la	CDM	metre	0146	03	1900-1947	IL		Verney
dept Morbihan								
la Trinité à Etel, Twy de	TTE	60cm	0021	01	1901-1934	Twy		CM 1934 (to mg 1922)
Morbihan, CF du (Réseau de Morbihan)	CM	m/sg	0414	10	1902-1947*	IL	Jeancard/Verney	
dept Orne								
Montsecret à Cherencé-le-Roussel CF de	CMC	sg	0020	01	1883-1964*	IL	various;	SCF Verney 1935
Orne, Cie des Voies Ferrées Economiques	VFEO	metre	0089	03	1913-1937	IL	Carel et Fouché;	SCF Verney 1935
dept Sarthe								
Mamers-St Calais, CF de	MSC	sg	0077	02	1872-1977	IL		TS 1934; Régie 1947
Sarthe, Twys de la	TS	metre	0440	11	1882-1947*	IL	Carel et Fouché	
Thorigné-Montmirail ligne de	SNCF	sg	0022	01	1955-1977*	IL	Ouest/SNCF;	MStC 1955
dept Seine-Inférieure								
Aumale - Envermeu ligne de (SE)	SE	metre	0051	01	1906-1948	IL		SE
Monterolier-Buchy - St Saens, ligne de	Nord	sg	0010	01	1900-1952*	IL	Nord;	SNCF 1938
Normandie, CF de (Ouville - Motteville)	SE	metre	0066	02	1912-1947*	IL	Laborie;	SE 1925
Rouen à Petit-Quevilly, ligne de	BM	sg	0003	01	1870-1944	IL	Ste Bozel-Maletra	
Rouen-Trianon à La Forêt-de-Rouvray TR	TRL	60cm	0002	01	1906-1908	Twy		
St Romain de Colbosc, Twy de	TRC	metre	0004	01	1896-1929	Twy		
dept Vendée								
Challans à Fromentine, CF sur route de	CF	metre	0024	01	1896-1949	Twy	TV 1914	
Sables d'Olonne, Twys des	SO	metre	0003	01	1898-1925	–		
Vendée, Twys de la	TV	metre	0342	07	1900-1949*	IL	Etat;	CFD 1939

* latterly short portions for freight only

Urban Tramways in Region Ouest

name	power	gauge	km	dates	dept
Angers	e	metre	0025	1896-1949	Maine-et-Loire
Avranches (CF de la Manch)	e	metre	0003	1907-1914	Manche
Brest	e	metre	0018	1898-1945	Finistère
Caen	e	metre	0009	1901-1935v	Calvados
Cherbourg	me	metre	0016	1897-1944	Manche
Elbeuf	e	sg	0009	1898-1926	Seine-Inférieure
Eu-Le Treport	e	metre	0006	1902-1935v	Seine-Inférieure
La Baule	hm	60cm			Loire-Inférieure
La Rochelle	m	metre	0006	1901-1931	Charente-Inférieure
Le Havre	he	sg	0057	1874-1951	Seine-Inférieure
Le Mans	e	metre	0010	1897-1947	Sarthe
Lorient	e	metre	0032	1901-1944	Morbihan
Nantes	me	sg	0042	1879-1958+	Loire-Inférieure
Rennes	e	metre	0018	1897-1952	Ille-et-Vilaine
Rouen	hme	sg	0084	1877-1953	Seine-Inférieure
Sables d'Olonne	e	metre	0003	1898-1925	Vendée
St Malo	m	metre	0010	1889-1927	Ille-et-Vilaine

CHAPTER 8
Regional Reprises 2: The Region Nord

Introduction to the region (Map p.301)

In the 1960s, light railway historians tended to roll the SNCF Regions Nord and Est into one because there was so little left and because they had much in common. Now that history is more important, it seems sensible to split them again and match up with Domengie's boundaries. Briefly, for Region Nord, these comprised the départements of Nord, Pas-de-Calais, Somme, Oise, Aisne and the French "home counties", that sprawling département of Seine-et-Oise which, until recently, virtually surrounded Paris and the heartland of Seine. The latter (saving the tramway enthusiasts' presence) had little of minor railway interest except the inner termini of two standard gauge steam tramways but Seine-et-Oise had some very ramshackle and countrified lines considering its closeness to the capital. Actually the whole Parisian region has now been divided up into a multitude of borough-sized units but since this book is purely historical, we shall ignore the change completely; in any case the Parisian area now includes Seine-et-Marne which, historically belongs to the Region Sud-Est.

The region and its historical complications

Outside the Parisian area, the Region Nord has much of interest from two angles: first it included a considerable part of industrialised France, in particular the extensive coalmining areas of Nord and Pas de Calais; secondly it will be familiar to many British people as having been fought over by British forces in both World Wars: Amiens, Albert, Arras, the Somme basin and Passchendaele...the graveyard plains of Picardy up to and along the Belgian border. In addition to that, many of the most important manufacturers had their headquarters and often their major plants, in the region – Batignolles, Cail, Couillet, Blanc-Misseron and Fives-Lille were names which echoed aross the length and breadth of the land.

From the minor railway historian's point of view this all leads to complications since being fought over, not once but twice, – or three times if you include the Franco-Prussian war, although that was a little early for minor railways – produced all sorts of complications in the concessionary field! Add to this the fact that individual systems sometimes straggled over several départements and the complexity becomes horrendous. Indeed the standard litany of French railway historians is that in the Nord and Est there is no place for describing individual lines, only the results of major groupings...but then the major groupings really only came into prominence after 1918 so how to deal with early history? In this region only, one has to jump around a little between départemental clusters and hope that nothing important drops into the gaps. Even so, it is possible to start with the areas which were least disturbed by the 1914-18 war, and those are the Parisian area and the neighbouring département of Oise.

In and around Paris: Seine; Seine-et-Oise; Oise. (Map p.302)

The most substantial of the local railways around Paris was probably the elaborately named **Cie de Chemin de Fer sur Route de Paris à Arpajon (PA)**. The clumsy title of this standard gauge steam tramway should indicate that it was an early attempt at a minor railway - the "CF sur Route" label was used quite frequently in the mid 19th century, as was the similar "CF Americain", for horse or mechanically worked roadside lines; for some reason, even before the egregious Colonel Train produced his "tramways" label, roadside lines were thought of as typically American. Whether this had any connection with the later French fondness for "trains-tramways" is an interesting subject for speculation... but not here. Anyway, in reality, the PA was not built until the 1890s and in its better moments could look quite impressive with long trains double-headed by massive bicabines and a serious nightly freight traffic into Les Halles, the Paris equivalent of Covent Garden. Partly electrified quite early on, its operation was taken over by a Parisian tramway concern, the STRCP, in 1922 and it was eventually closed down in 1936 when competing forms of transport proved more effective; the electric line was notable for little more than using some demotored double-deck tramcars as trailers. A second batch of two lines to its west was initially operated by a company calling itself, simply, **Cie des Chemins de Fer sur Route.** One, from Epone to Versailles, was never even finished. It got as far as Marel-s-Mauldre (9km) and then closed owing to the failure of its promoters; the second, a tiny line from **Villiers-le-Bel** town to station enjoyed a few years life from 1878 and was then taken over by local interests who made a mess of it, not really helped by some most peculiar locomotives with combined gear and rod drive and an odd gauge of 1,06m (actually 1.10m to rail centres). It closed in 1915, was resuscitated as a metre gauge electric line in 1928 and lasted as such to 1949.

There were several other single branches. One, the standard gauge line from **Magny-en-Vexin to Chars,** was actually very early, being conceded as Intérêt Local in 1868 and opened in 1871. It was bought back by the state in 1900, reclassified as Intérêt Général and passed to the Ouest/Etat which ran it as a standard branch until 1934 and then "affermed" it to the SE which, in turn kept passenger trains going until 1950 and freight until 1952 (under Intérêt Local regulations) after which SNCF operated a section as a siding, once more as Intérêt Général, until 1986. Rather like the Great Western, its operators used mainly equipment from various other light railways they had acquired, including, for the SE, some of the pushmepullyous from their CF de Grande Banlieue (see below). A similar branch from **Chars to Marines** was conceded directly to the CF de l'Ouest and run by them and their successors until 1922 when it passed to the SE. It closed to passengers in 1939 and totally in 1951. At Marines, this line met a metre gauge branch of the SE along the Sausseron valley from **Valmondois to Marines,** opened between 1886 and 1891. The SE graced it with its standard 0-6-2Ts and a fine selection of bogie coaches, followed by three of its later De Dions transferred from the closing Réseau de la Nievre. It lasted until 1949 and more recently its Valmondois depot was taken over by one of the few stable enthusiast-run museums, the Musée des Transports du la Vallee du Sausseron, at the time of writing in process of changing its name and moving to Chars because of a churlish attitude on the part of the local authority. A fourth was the short standard gauge commuter line from **Enghien to Montmorency** which featured in several British railway books because of its elderly double deck coaches and long-funnelled tank locomotives (the funnels had to be long

The Arpájonnais – a typical passenger train of the CF sur Route de Paris à Arpajon on a rare deviation.   (FACS)

3. The CGB as most commonly known, though with a single-cabbed Pinguely in charge. Note the inside cylinders and motion. (AUTHOR'S COLLECTION)

to take the smoke away from the coaches' upper decks). Apart from its habit of propelling its train from the lower station because of the steep grades, this was otherwise a rather boring branch always operated by the CF du Nord and its successors. Lastly, over to the east, was the short, standard gauge line from **Gargan to Livry** which was conceded to the CF de l'Est, run as one of their standard branch lines and lasted only to 1930.

That leaves the standard gauge **Cie des Chemins de Fer de Grande Banlieue (CGB)** which sounds most impressive. In fact it was a highly ramshackle concern, founded in 1911 to build a collection of widely separated branches in the outer purlieus of Seine-et-Oise and to take over sundry existing bits of line, in particular the **Versailles – Meulan** (see below) and the standard gauge branch from **St-Germain-en-Laye to Poissy** which had been built as a suburban tramway in 1896 and bought back in 1911. For a standard gauge system it had the ridiculous loading gauge limitation of 2.10m maximum width (So did the PA but that somehow got away with it). The result was that its trains looked just like metre gauge tramway stock which had been subjected to an overdose of growth hormone – even more so when the locomotives had been stripped of their skirts in later years and exposed their gangly undercarriages, made more obvious because the loading gauge required inside cylinders. Put them on light weedgrown track amid slightly run-down surroundings and the general impression was a bit Colonel Stephensish. True, the CGB was a pioneer in internal-combustion traction, with some Pieper benzo-electric cars as early as 1911. It also had some substantial traffics, including nightly links to Les Halles, but in general it comprised country branches, these actually including one former metre gauge line from **Versailles to Meulan** with a tangled history - it had been built by local effort between 1899 and 1909 as a steam tramway, failed disastrously by 1911 and was then bought back by the Département which handed it over to the CGB instructing the latter to convert it to standard gauge. For the most part the CGB's standard gauge steam stock was quite conventional although there were some odd double-ended locomotives with only the cabs enclosed which irresistably recall Dr Doolitle's Pushmepullyou; one has been preserved for all to see. The SE took the whole network on in 1922 and cautiously introduced a batch of oblong Renault railcars, reducing the old Piepers to trailers. Only a few sections survived the second world war, however, the last closing down in 1949.

MAULE (S.-&-O.) - Halte du Tramway de Maule à Versailles.

Three faces of the CF de Grande Banlieue: 1. the predecessor metre gauge line from Versailles to Maule, with a Pinguely 0-6-0T. (FACS)

POISSY — Sortie de la Forêt.   ND. Phot.

2. an early Pieper bettery electric car on the Poissy – St Germain tramway. (FACS)

Just to the north and north-east of Seine-et-Oise was, quite logically, the Département of Oise which, slightly impolitely, one might class as a rather scruffy agricultural hinterland of the capital - after all, Beauvais right in its heart was formerly classed officially as an alternative airport for Paris and has been used consistently by low-cost flights. As a département, Oise was well served by the main and secondary lines of the big CF du Nord, and was just to the west of the frontlines for most of the 1914-18 war; hence its private secondary railways never amounted to more than five separated metre gauge systems each serving otherwise blank stretches of country and linking at both ends to Nord standard gauge lines. A strong aroma of agriculture and sugar beet hung over them all and kept some of them alive for a surprisingly long time. To take them in some sort of order from south to north they were:

* **CF de Méru à La Bosse.** A largely unremarkable branch conceded to that M.Dequeker who was very active in Nord and Pas-de-Calais, this linked two cross-country routes running south from Beauvais, was opened in 1905, taken over by the VFIL after World War 1 and closed in 1934 without benefit of railcars.

* **CF d'Hermes à Beaumont.** Just east of Méru, this was actually one of the earlier narrow gauge lines in France, conceded under the 1865 laws although not opened until 1879. Once again it escaped serious involvement in the fighting and its concessionaires were even entrusted with other lines in Oise but they ran into financial difficulties and the whole thing was subsumed into the new CGL/VFIL grouping in 1920. It is of some interest in that, while its northern part closed in 1949, the section from Persan-Beaumont north to Ercuis lasted until 1958, helped out by a pair of VFIL-built bogie railcars which went on to the SE's Réseau de la Somme.

* **CF d'Estrées à Froissy et Crèvecœur.** Conceded to Alfred Lambert who was very active in the region, this longish line ran west from Estrées-st-Denis on a four-way junction to the eaqually complex junction of St Just-en-Chaussée where its main depot was and then on to Froissy. Opened in 1891, it extended to Crèvecœur-le-Grand, on another Nord branch, in 1911. It was duly taken over by the CGL in 1920, survived World War 2 but then died a lingering death: Estrées-St Just in 1948, Crèvecœur-Froissy in 1953 and the remainder as late as 1961; the writer kept meaning to visit but put it off too long. It was blessed by Oise with three of the early Billard railbuses (forward control version), two of which were destroyed in the war, and in its final years acquired a motley collection of equipment from other closing CGL lines.

* **CF de Milly à Formerie.** Up in the northwest, this straightforward branch was also conceded to Alfred Lambert and opened in 1894. It gave cross connections to two alternative routes towards Amiens and was initially operated by Corpet 0-6-0Ts and the usual collection of miscellaneous stock. It was financially connected, through Lambert, with:

* **Lignes de Noyon à Guiscard et Lassigny,** up in the north-east corner. Opened in 1895, the two branches were assimilated from the start into the main company, giving it the overly cumbersome, if accurate, title of CF de Milly à Formerie et de Noyon à Guiscard et Lassigny. They were later extended, from Lassigny to Montdidier (1913) and from Noyon to Ham (1912), both involving negotiations with the neighbouring Département of Somme. These were the only départemental lines to suffer seriously from the war, being overrun during the big German offensives of 1918 and having to be subsequently rebuilt before being taken over by the CGL and lasting, except for the western tip, until 1955. They seem to be remembered mainly for the three early Billard railbuses which ran most services in later years. At Bussy, this system also connected with the **CFIL de Bussy à Ercheu,** a nominally independent railway dating from 1897 which was almost entirely in Oise but was actually exploited by the SE and treated as an extension of their Groupe d'Albert; it lasted for passengers until 1954 and for freight to 1955 and was treated as a normal SE branch.

After 1919, all these lines except that to Ercheu were gradually assimilated into the Cie Générale des Voies Ferrées d'Intérêt Local (CGL or VFIL) of which both Lambert and Dequeker were leading lights, and their history is recorded below. Of interest, however, is that the Département tended to purchase and

6943. - *VALMONDOIS (S.-et-O) — Le Passage à niveau. - « Attention au train... »*

A rural moment on the metre-gauge Valmondois – Marines line; to get his human interest the photographer appears to have been short-changed in the railway department but at least the crossing is barriered!　(FACS)

MESNIL-THÉRIBUS (OISE) – La Gare.　　*Pavis-Quillet, nouveau*

While out in Oise, the Méru – Labosse is looking smart enough to be nearly new.　(FACS)

114

retain ownership of equipment while it was also one of the earliest railcar clients of Billard; hence the distinctive snouted and forward control (type longue) railbuses which bore the "Oise No X" blazon on their dark green sides rather than the VFIL logo.

EARLY GROUPINGS: The SE; CEN; The Level, Lambert, Dequecker associations, mainly in Nord; Pas-de-Calais; Somme.

The SE throughout the region (Maps pgs. 302, 303 & 304)

In studying the other départements, perhaps one should start with the Societé Générale des CF Economiques (SE); its rival the CFD had little presence in the north but the SE was there in strength from the beginning. Apart from a number of isolated lines, the SE built up several substantial systems during the late 19th century, mainly in the Nord and Somme départements. The first of these was the sprawling **SE Réseau de la Somme,** conceded in 1882 and begun in 1887 when the company took over a short standard gauge branch of the mainline Nord railway from Noyelles to the little port of St Valéry-sur-Somme. The SE always had excellent relations with the Nord and used these often to negotiate common junction stations and even mixed gauge stretches where needed. The metre gauge Somme network consisted of two major groups of lines and one isolated branch. The latter ran from **Amiens to Aumalle,** on the borders of Seine Inférieure (now Seine Maritime). Opened between 1891 and 1901 it was linked five years later to a line from Aumalle to Envermeu in Seine Maritime and the two were run together. Of the others, the **Groupe de Noyelles** was usually dubbed "réseau des bains de mer" because two of its branches reached the coast at Cayeux and le Crotoy. From Noyelles junction, however, it also ran east to Forest l'Abbaye on a south-north line between Abbeville (junction with the Nord) and Dompierre-s-Authie. The system was actually the last part of the SE's northern fiefdoms to survive, the two seaside lines running partly with steam up to 1959 and with diesel traction up to 1972 while the Forest l'Abbaye spur kept going for freight up to a few years earlier. The system escaped much involvement in the first world war but in the second it was used by the Organisation Todt to carry building materials for the Atlantic Wall. There is evidence of southward extensions from Lanchères and Cayeux and for many years afterward relics remained in the form of a siding full of rusting locomotives near St Valéry. Postwar, as so often in the north, sugar beet was the real saviour, in this case for the Lanchères refinery near Cayeux which retained steam traction to the last and the lines were well known to many British enthusiasts. Happily, all was not lost for enthusiast bodies, now combined as the CF de la Baie de Somme (CFBS), took over and the CFBS now works both the main lines with steam and diesel power in summer. With a collection of locomotives and stock from near and far – as far as Madagascar – the system is still very worth visiting.

The other substantial, and inland, réseau, the **Groupe d'Albert,** came about a decade later and is much less known. Extending to 204km, and coming into contact with various similar lines, mainly in the Oise, it had a comparatively dull career. True, it was fought over and part was closed during the 1914-18 war, including the long line from Albert down to Montdidier, only to be resuscitated afterwards but then so were many others. Otherwise it plodded through the next thirty years or so, with a mixture of steam and diesel traction until being closed throughout in 1949. It should be noted that at Ercheu it linked to the Ercheu – Bussy branch mentioned under Oise.

The other major SE réseau was in the Département du Nord itself and again comprised two separate systems, confusingly designated **SE Réseau du Nord, Groupe Sud et Groupe Nord.** The Groupe Sud, five metre gauge lines in the Cambrai area, was the earlier, being started in 1893 around Solesmes by the CF Economiques du Nord (CEN). The CEN was apparently too preoccupied with other matters to pay much attention to its concession and in 1904 the SE took over. The réseau was largely destroyed during World War 1, reconstructed afterwards but faded away before 1939. The two lines of the Groupe Nord, never completely finished, were opened only just prior to the 1914-18 war. They were conventional metre gauge systems largely running west from the Dunkerque - Hazebrouck standard gauge line although one crossed it to carry on east to Herzeele where it connected with the equally small **CF des Flandres** which ran north from Hazebrouck toward the coast, paralleling the nearby frontier. This latter company was a Lambert concession, opening in 1894 with five light Corpet Louvet 0-6-2Ts and it, in turn, linked at

Hondschoote with an isolated line of the CFIL du Nord de la France to Bray Dunes. The whole tangle gave a rural area connections both to the coastal resorts and toward Pas-de-Calais. During the first war, indeed, military connections were built both to the Pas de Calais lines and eastward to the Belgian SNCV but afterwards the authorities could not agree about them and so a potentially useful opportunity was lost. Thenceforward the systems slowly declined, the last one closing to passengers in 1950 and to goods after the 1951 sugar beet season.

Apart from these "base" systems the SE had a finger in many pies during and after the first war. Firstly, in its own guise, it took over various failing systems or lines - the sprawling CF de Grande Banlieue as already noted, the odd little tramways at Ault, the meandering lines of the CFIL du Nord de la France already mentioned. The NF was a mildly odd arrangement, consisting of three metre gauge lines, one in Aisne, one in Somme and one in Nord; briefly, they were

* **Hondschoote – Bray Dunes** (to SE 1919 and closed to passengers in 1921)
* **Le Catelet – Guise,** in Aisne (to CFS du NE in 1922, after which it lasted until 1951)
* **Roisel – Hargicourt,** in Somme (standard gauged for military use in WW1. Rebuilt as metre gauge and run by SE 1923-27; closed 1932).

The NF also had one proper standard gauge branch, in Nord. This ran from **Don-Sainghin to Fromelles,** was opened in 1906, run by the SE between 1923 and 1927 and then handed to the CF Secondaires company in 1933. The whole thing was slightly confused by the fact that for many years some lines were assigned to the concessionaire M. Michon personally and the final transfer to the NF was not formalised until the late 1920s.

The CF Economiques du Nord

The SE also had an interest in various bits of the national system. It was always a survivor and took over others rather than being assimilated by them. Apart from the SE there were a few other fairly early clusters, however, which stayed outside the later big groupings. One which has, perhaps, received less attention than it deserves was the **Cie des Chemins de Fer Economiques du Nord de la France (CEN)** which had a

Most enthusiasts remember the SE de la Somme in its steam days like this: an SACM 0-6-2T heads a summer holidaymaker's train at Le Crotoy in 1955. (D TREVOR ROWE)

Just as typical was this scene on the Albert system, with an SACM 0-6-2T and train at Mailly-Maillet.
(C WALKER'S COLLECTION)

Along the coast there were other minor lines. A Serpollet steam car of the original standard gauge tramway to Ault pauses at Friaucourt in the snow.
(FACS)

scattered empire in Nord and Pas-de-Calais and even acquired the odd couple of lines outside its home region. The CEN had a slightly odd beginning, being itself a retrospective subsidiary of the great Belgian conglomeration of companies fostered by the Baron Empain. With its SNCV roots, it was probably inevitable that the Groupe Empain would develop urban or interurban steam tramways, in this case around Valenciennes which was not far from the Belgian border. They appear to have been started purely by agreements at local level until in 1885 the French state woke up and insisted on the formation of a French-registered operating company with all the usual legal rigmarole – hence the CEN. Confusingly the CEN legally had two réseaux around Valenciennes, the original one based on that towm under the generic title of **Tramways de Valenciennes à Anzin et extensions** and a later set of more countrified lines **(CEN Réseau du Nord)** granted by the département, most of which were effectively extensions of the former. Once most of the system was electrified, the distinction became blurred and trams ran through to the outer termini, several of the lines crossing into Belgian soil or linking with the Belgian Societé des Chemins de Fer Vicinaux (SNCV). Only the extension from St. Amand to Hellemmes (Lille) and the detached line from Armentières to Halluin remained steam worked and these closed in 1932 and 1935 respectively. The main Valenciennes system lasted in part up to 1966 and, for an electric tram, was quite a jolly affair with cream four-wheelers often towing a gaggle of trailers left over from steam days. The CEN's Pas-de-Calais system , on the other hand, consisted largely of steam tramways. An isolated 53km line from **Lens to Frevent** was very much an product of its urban, industrial neighbourhood, with heavy passenger and goods traffic hauled by Blanc Misseron bicabines; the other two **(Réseau de Boulogne)** comprised an electric tramway from Boulogne to Portel and a metre gauge steam-worked line, partly roadside, from Boulogne down to the Anvin - Calais (see below) at Bonningues.

Other early lines in Nord, Aisne and Somme (Maps pgs. 303 & 304)

Apart from these clusters, most other early metre gauge light railways were either isolated lines belonging to local companies, or smallish clumps of lines conceded by a specific département to a locally based concern; some popped in and out of major groups in the 1920s but became independent again. Of these

Crowds besiege the little 60cm gauge line from Quend on its arrival at Fort Mahon Plage.   (FACS)

Pas-de-Calais — 1 - ETAPLES, Pont sur la Canche

The short electric train of the seaside line from Etaples to Paris-Plage scurries across its bridge over the river Canche. (AUTHOR'S COLLECTION)

perhaps the most substantial were the CF du Cambrésis (CFC) in Nord, the CF Départementaux de l'Aisne (CDA), the CF du Sud de l'Aisne (CSA), which was a Tartary Group possession from the start, and the cluster of loosely associated lines springing from Calais itself (the Anvin – Calais; the Aire – Rimeux – Berck; the Tramway d'Ardres à Pont d'Ardres). The **CF du Cambrésis**, mainly in the Nord Département, eventually ran a straggly cross of four metre gauge lines from Cambrai in the west to Catillon in the east and from St Quentin in the south to the mining town of Denain in the north where it got hopelessly entangled with the standard gauge CF de Somain à la Frontière Belge and with the Valenciennes tram system belonging to the CEN. Its countryside was drab and industrialised, its headquarters at Caudry where the lines crossed was a dismal place of shacks and sheds a good kilometre and a half from the SNCF main line. For British enthusiasts it is probably remembered for three things only: one of its 0-6-0T locomotives (or parts of two, there is some argument) ended up in England as CAMBRAI at Waltham ironstone quarries; it was one of that select band of railways which managed to have a massive boiler explosion (on one of its most modern locomotives, too); it kept the last line, from Denain to Caudry, going with a steam-hauled passenger service right up to 1960 with bright green Piguet 2-6-0Ts ex the CF de la Drôme. So all right, it was simply a convenience for the miners, with a guaranteed captive audience, you were strictly enjoined by enamelled notices not to piss on the coach balconies (on, not off, you note; presumably no one objected to watering the grass), the timetable allowed, whether officially or not, for a lengthy beer stop en route but it was fun and a shame when road transport condemned it to death.

The **Cie des Chemins de Fer Départementaux de l'Aisne**, on the other hand, always had big ideas. It was, in essence, a family affair, founded by the son of that M.Jourdain who was already in charge of a neighbouring standard gauge line from St Quentin to Guise. Its 179km network of lines, all originally metre gauge and of Intérêt Local, were based on the "county town" of Soissons, stretching to north, south and west, with a further one in the north from Romary to Liart. There was nothing particularly special about them, or their working except that during and after the 1914-18 War the networks to the north west of Soissons ran into complications which are described later…

One of the earlier VFIL concoctions, looking very like a cardboard model, awaits its passengers at Calais Ville on the Anvin-Calais (although labelled for the Aire-Rimeux-Berck).

(D. TREVOR ROWE)

The CDA's empire also included one isolated line to the north east of Soissons which had an interesting connection. It started down to the west of the old hill fortress of Laon, in the suburb of Neuville and ran through most of the low-lying parts of that agglomeration before turning southward to its final destination of Nouvion-le-Vineux; indeed its nearest approach to Laon itself was a spur to the Nord station in the valley – hence, no doubt, its flippant local designation of "Laon suburban" (banlieue de Laon). The point was, at the Nord station it did encounter the real **Laon railway** and this, an independent concern, was something rather special - so special in fact that both tramway and railway historians claim it as their own. In the rather flat north there were only two "mountain lines" and this was one of them, the other being at Langres in the Est region. Laon town was 300 metres or so above its station and the answer, after an ephemeral flirtation with Decauville, was.....an electric Abt rack line of metre gauge, served for all its life by similar antique four-wheel cars. It was destroyed in the first world war, resuscitated afterwards with stock reclaimed from Germany and even, so it is said, Poland, and lasted, latterly in municipal control, until 1971 when it was worn out. Then the city fathers decided to become modern and after long arguments replaced the old tramway in 1989 with a featureless people carrier on the "Poma 2000" guided trackway system. It still runs, it does its job but no longer warrants the old Michelin accolade of "worth a detour".

The **CFD du Sud de l'Aisne** was really quite a minor concern but is mentioned here because it was in the Tartary group and because one section hung on into the 1960s and, all right, because the writer was in time to see its last remains and got intrigued by it. Essentially it was a straightforward set of two metre gauge lines from Château Thierry, southeast to Verdelot on a CFD line, and northwest to Mareuil-sur-Ourcq on a Nord branch, with a branch of its own en route, to Neuilly-s-Front. Its own locomotives were numbered in the total Tartary list, it acquired several more from the le Blanc-Argent concern (see ch 6) and was blessed, if that is the word, with some of the earlier railbus conversions from ambulances of the Tramways des Deux Sevres (ch 14). The lines closed down effectively in 1942, only two short sections remaining in place for beet traffic but these were sold to the local refinery four years later and lasted until 1961. The writer was just in time to see the remains and ex BA 22 huddling under an awning at Neuilly.

Pas de Calais and its convolutions (Map p. 303)

The members of the Pas de Calais group, conceded variously to those Messrs Level, Lambert and Dequeker mentioned in chapter 1, who eventually formed a major post-1918 grouping, were originally nominally independent although they had great commanalty of administration and close connections with the big CF du Nord; the latter even provided assistance and a common office at its Paris headquarters according to Domengie. They comprised two major collections, one metre and one standard gauge. The metre gauge one started with the **CF d'Anvin à Calais,** running generally south-east from a bay platform at Calais-Ville station and opened in 1881-82. Conceded to M. Level as early as 1874, it was a conventional metre gauge light railway on its own right of way, with easy gradients (17mm/m maximum) and curvature (100m radius minimum) and powered by staightforward SACM 0-6-2Ts. It was joined in 1893 by M. Lambert's **CF d'Aire à Fruges et de Rimeux-Gournay à Berck** (usually known as the Aire-Rimeux-Berck) which technically had running powers over the AC between the intermediate points named. This was a very similar concern, albeit using mainly Corpet locomotives, as was the third member of the trio, the short **Tramway à vapeur d'Ardres à Pont-d'Ardres** which joined the Anvin - Calais in 1902. Originally the most memorable thing about the AC according to Bryan Morgan was its chocolate brown livery (but then brown, for some reason was almost popular in the north and east; the Ardennes network had it too, though milk chocolate rather than plain). Still even before the Calais lines joined officially they had close links and (if you wanted) you could have had a most tortuous journey which started at Calais-Ville and ended up only a few miles south on the same main line at Etaples. It went like this: Go inland Calais - Bonningues (change for Boulogne over the CEN as an option!) - Fruges by the AC; change to the Aire-Rimeux-Berck and return to the coast via Montreuil, the main line at Rang-du-Fliers and a seaside terminus at Berck Plage. Change again to the almost antique independent metre gauge line north from **Berck to Paris-Plage** (with a side trip over a short 60cm gauge line if you wished); join the electric tramway from Paris-Plage (later le Touquet which sounds more up-market) back east to Etaples. The **Etaples – Paris-Plage** line faded away in 1940 by act of war but thirty years later its offices with their carved legend were

ÉPEHY (Somme) — La Gare ·   Bouchez à Epehy

And the CF de Vélu-Bertincourt-St Quentin connects with the CF du Nord at Epehy – a typical standard gauge light railway train of elderly 0-6-0T and compartment coaches.   (FACS)

still visible from the main line train. Mark you, the link did not last long. Its weakest link was the **CF de Berck-Plage à Paris Plage,** completed in 1912, lifted for military use in 1914, relaid in 1919 and closed in 1927. In making this journey you would also have gone almost right round an odd little 60cm gauge horse tramway from Dannes-Camiers just north of Etaples, to St Cecile Plage but you can't have everything; in any case it ran only from 1898 to 1914 and had parallels with our own Welsh seaside trams - it was built by the **Sté de la Plage de Ste. Cecile** to carry building materials for their resort building operations and thriftily converted for passenger use thereafter.

However, back to Level & co. Their standard gauge collection was also largely in Pas-de-Calais but demonstrates the difficulty of keeping to départemental boundaries in this region. It was down in the south east corner and comprised a veritable cats cradle of short lines which also extended one thread down southeast through a corner of Somme into Aisne, where it connected with another tangle based on St Quentin and conceded to the Jourdain family. It was based originally on three companies. The **CF d'Achiet à Bapaume (AB)** was opened in 1871, extending eastward to Marquoing in the Nord département by 1878. From a point on the latter extension, the **CF de Vélu-Bertincourt à St Quentin (VBSQ)** opened its line south east to St Quentin in Aisne in stages between 1879 and 1880, while, a little to the north, the **CF de Boisleux à Marquion (BM)** had been built between 1874 and 1880; it was effectively extended to Cambrai in 1899 by another nominally independent concern the **CF de Marquion à Cambrai (MC)** which promptly ceded oparation to the BM. All right so far? That, however, was just the beginning. During the 1914-18 war the lines were fought over by both sides, the French building a link between the AB and the BM, from **Quéant to Frémicourt** and the Germans an eastward spur from **Marquion to Aubencheul-au-bac**...oh, and the British double tracked part of both the original lines although this improvement was naturally disposed of after 1918. The military links, however, were retained and in 1927 were officially recognised by the département.

Standard gauge lines

It should be mentioned that there was a considerable presence of standard gauge in the north of the region both because its entrepreneurs were attracted by the original law of 1865 and because of the industrialisation. Various mining branches, départemental short lines and even odd bits of the state system

In more recent years, a typical station of the Achiet – Bapaume drowses in the sun, with a worried looking VFIL railbus in attendance.

(AUTHOR)

At Guise, next door down in Aisne, a more businesslike Renault of the private St. Quentin-Guise prepares to leave.

(G. J. HOARE)

10   LAON. — La Place de l'Hôtel-de-Ville. — The town-hall place.   ND. Phot.

The town square in Laon with two early cars waiting to descend to the main line station.   (FACS)

hired out to private owners, rambled here and there, often connecting in a somewhat random fashion. In this case, for example, the VBSQ connected at St Quentin with quite a substantial part of the Aisne network which was standard gauge from the start. Its stem line was the **CF de St Quentin à Guise** which was actually promoted under the 1865 legislation and conceded to Jourdain (père). Opening was delayed until 1874 by the Franco-Pussian war but it later added a branch from Mézières-s-Oise to la Fère (1898) and assumed operation of the nominally independent **CF de Ribemont à La Ferté Chevresis** on its opening in 1900 – it acquired the full concession when the original concessionaire failed five years later. The group was completed by a further standard gauge line from **St Quentin to Ham** (1910-12) actually run by the CF Départementaux de l'Aisne which was, of course, controlled by Jourdain (fils) – all in the family so to speak.

Other standard gauge lines in Aisne, Nord and Pas-de-Calais (Maps pgs. 303 & 304)

There remains a collection of individual standard gauge branches which have no particular pattern or form and which can easily get overlooked. In no particular order these comprise:

in Aisne:

* The standard gauge **CF de Chauny à St.Gobain** conceded in 1856 and actually opened as early as 1860 as of Intérêt Général and originally operated by the CF du Nord. The St.Gobain glassmaking company took over nine years later and, despite various complications maintained public passenger services until 1950 and freight until 1983 (when the SNCF reclaimed the remains). It was always a nice line with stolid 0-6-0Ts and a couple of handsome Cockerill 2-6-0Ts, used CFD diesels in later years and experimented with piggy-back carriage of road vehicles.

* **CF de Marle – Montcornet:** This, up in the north east corner, was originally an independent company running south east along the Serre Valley to Montcornet where it met the metre gauge lines of the CFD des Ardennes. Opened in 1907 it had links to major sugar refineries at Tavaux and Montcornet – this was always a big sugar-beet area – had some mildly unusual 2-4-0WT locomotives and was subsumed into the CFS du Nord Est after the first war.

in Nord:

a collection – that is probably the word – of scattered lines attributed variously to our old friends Lambert and Dequeker – and hence mysteriously drawn together after the 1914-18 war. They tended to concentrate on industrial goods haulage, passenger traffic being a very secondary consideration and, in one case indeed, being suspended during the war and never restarted. For the record they were:

* **CF de Bettrechies à Hon avec embranchement sur Bavay:** Conceded to M.Lambert and opened in 1895, this was linked to two Nord routes up on the northern side of the département

* **CF de Pont-de-la-Deule à Pont-a-Marcq** (Lambert) was a straightforward line north of Douai opened in 1896. Like the Bettrechies one, the concessionaire cannily arranged with the CF du Nord to provide equipment and personnel although oficially retaining the contract for operation.

* **CF d'Aulnoye à Pont-sur-Sambre** was conceded to Dequeker and opened in 1905; even Domengie can find little to report....

All three of these were heavily damaged by wartime activity and were sumsumed into the Cie Générale des VFIL (CGL) after 1919.

* Last but not least, in this group there were the the 14km of the **CF d'Hazebrouck – Merville,** also conceded to Dequeker, opened in 1906 and stretching south east from Hazebrouck to another junction at Merville. It was more fortunate than the others, continuing to operate until the German offensive of May 1918 overran it and damaged the infrastructure. Like the others it came under control of the CGL after the war.

There was also one further independent line in Pas-de-Calais, the clearly titled **Sté des CF et des Carrières d'Estrée-Blanche.** This was very early, starting as a private mineral railway in 1868 and "going

Up in Nord two different servers to the coal industry.1: A workmen's train of the CF du Cambrésis on arrival at Caudry.
(AUTHOR)

2: A smart passenger train of the HN's heavyweight Somain – Peruwelz line with a modern(ish) 0-8-0T, and bogie coaches from the CF de l'Est.
(AUTHOR)

51. LENS — Boulevard des Écoles

The industrial districts had steam trams too. A typical train of the CEN's Lens-Frevent line makes its slow way through the centre of town.

(FACS)

A train on the detached line of the CEN's Réseau du Nord from Armentieres to Halluin, with a Blanc Misseron bicabine in charge.   (FACS)

public" four years later because of demand from a variety of industrial firms adjacent to the track. It originally started from Berguette, west of Béthune, but, when the CF du Nord built its line in from St Omer, the actual junction was displaced by about 3km to suit. It was always run by the quarry company, acquired most of its locomotives and stock at second-hand and survived for freight until 1950.

There were also various mines railways with public services whch will be discussed later, under the groupings.

A collection of minor oddities

The trouble with concentrating on groupings is that smaller fry tend to slp through the net. Four lines which are in danger of escaping are the region's only genuine 60cm gauge system; that tiny tramway near Ault referred to above, both on the Somme coast; a metre gauge electric line lost amid the tangle of railways in the St.Quentin area in Aisne; and a most peculiar little metre gauge tramway tucked away on the eastern tip of Nord. The 60cm gauge one was the two branched tramway from **Quend to Quend-Plage and Fort Mahon** set up by local promoters to join the Nord main line to the beaches north of the Somme estuary. The stem line to Quend-Plage opened in 1899 with no proper authorisation and was not fully legalised until 1902; the Fort-Mahon branch followed in 1903 – again some two years in advance of official blessing! It was largely a seasonal operation using standard Decauville equipment, was taken over by the Cie des Tramways du Marquenterre (TM) in 1913, spent the war servicing military hospitals in the former hotels and never really recovered although it had an off-season traffic in fish and sugar beet. The **Ault lines** started as a light standard gauge tramway from Feuquières on the Nord to Ault on the coast some miles south west of the Somme estuary. Opened in 1904 for passengers and parcels only, it was badly routed, badly constructed and badly managed – and made matters worse by investing in a Serpollet steam railcar plus some second-hand tank locomotives which included a British 0-4-0ST. It lasted only two years before closing down and although there were attempts to rebuild on a sensible basis they were frustrated by the

VALENCIENNES. - Gare des Tramways

And the original town station of the Valenciennes system in steam days at Marché des Herbes – which seems to be in full swing.

war. It was not reopened, as a proper branch from Woincourt operated by the SE, until 1921 but then lasted until the outbreak of war in 1939; the track was used to bring materials for the German fortifications but the line never reopened to public traffic. The tramway in Aisne was actually two connected lines and can best be describe as a light interurban passenger tram, built to urban norms except that originally it was powered at 5000v 25 cycles – pioneering for 1910 when was opened the first stretch of the **Tramway Electrique de Tergnier à St. Gobain et Anizy-Pinon.** It suffered the usual upset between 1914-18, being partly lifted and only restored, under CFSNE control, between 1931 and 1934. The NE added a branch from Tergnier to Charmes but cautiously converted the power source to the usual 600v DC. It did not last; the St.Gobain – Anizy stretch went in 1938 and the rest got destroyed in the war. The Nord example was the **SA des Tramways de Fourmies à Wignehies,** a short, largely roadside tramway opened in 1884 and serving an industrial district with plenty of private sidings which totalled almost 25% of its overall length. Basically it was too lightly built for what turned out to be a very heavy traffic, used the unsatisfactory Demerbe track system, had problems with troubles in the local textile industry, and was "temporarily" shut down several times - in one case on the excuse that it was to be electrified – before going into receivership in 1904 and failing entirely three years later. In retrospect it might have been better off as a standard gauge line.

Among other minor oddities was a further roadside tram in Pas-de-Calais. Notable because it remained independent, the **Tramways de l'Artois (TA)** had a single route from Béthune to Estaires which led a difficult life between 1899 and 1933. The company had much greater ambitions initially but in practice its only line was virtually destroyed by the war and, although rebuilt afterwards, never really met the increasing road competition. Another oddity only because of our artificial division of France, was the long line in Aisne from Soissons to Rethel which was part of a large metre gauge system based mainly in the département of Marne and operated by another Empain subsidiary, the **Cie des CF de la Banlieue de Reims (CBR)** whose corporate history is covered under Region Est. The Soissons-Rethel line survived partial desrtuction in the first war, was partly reconstructed and regauged to standard and taken over by a large grouping, and, under the Régie des Transports de l'Aisne banner, survived into the 1950s.

The Regional scene post-1918

The war dealt very hardly with most of this region north of the Marne; it was fought over, shattered by artillery, lost and regained. Its railways naturally suffered greatly also and even those that survived were not always what they had been. Metre gauge lines, such as that from Guise to Hirson, conceded faut de mieux to a reluctant CF du Nord and opened only in 1910, had been rebuilt to standard gauge for military convenience; other lines of both gauges, or their remains, had been lifted and replaced either with standard gauge or with parts of elaborate 60cm gauge field railways; stations and structures were unrecognisable in many cases. Equally, many concessionaires had been hard hit financially and were reluctant to struggle with rebuilding their former lines.

So the region Nord arrived at 1918 with not only a devastated landscape but also the GROUPINGS: Perhaps the biggest grouping was an ephemeral one caused entirely by the circumstances of the time. So much was destroyed in this region that the state, in the shape of the **Ministère des Regions Libérées,** (Ministry for the liberated regions)) took a hand in wholesale reconstruction between 1918 and about 1926. In the Region Nord, the MRL immediately took over the former French military 60cm gauge systems in Aisne and Oise and, after suitable negotiations, many of the ex-British lines in the northern départements. At its peak there were over 1000km of 60cm gauge lines in public service; as late as 1964 the Sucrerie de Toury, south of Paris, had a Decauville 0-6-0T still painted in red CFS du Nord Est (NE) livery. As affairs improved, some of the bigger systems were hived off, either to existing operators such as the NE pending regauging or to specially formed companies largely funded and used by the sugar beet industry. The largest of these, the **SA des CF à Voie de 60 du Pas-de-Calais,** acquired a 105km network based on Vis-en-Artois which was a place of pilgrimage for enthusiasts right up to 1957 when it finally closed. Individual sugar refineries also took the chance to acquire ready-made systems, perhaps the best known being that at Froissy in the Somme where the Dompierre refinery's line survived long enough to be taken over by

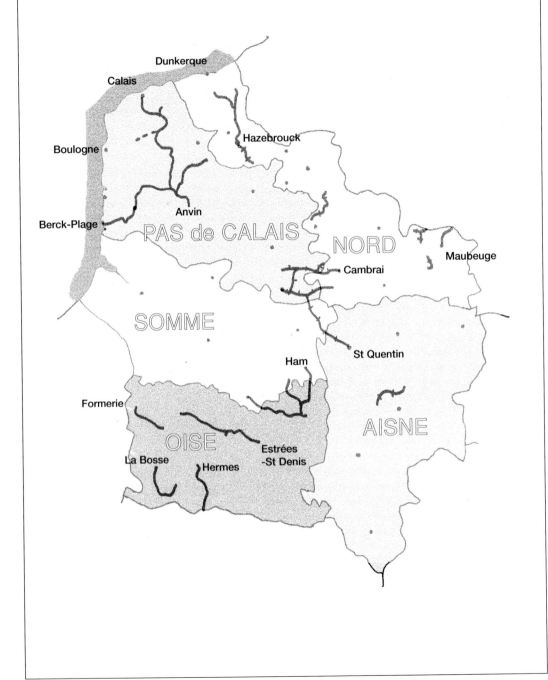

CGL des VFIL. Distribution of lines operated in North France

Dunkerque

Calais

Boulogne

Hazebrouck

Berck-Plage

Anvin

PAS de CALAIS

NORD

Maubeuge

Cambrai

SOMME

Ham

St Quentin

Formerie

OISE

AISNE

La Bosse

Hermes

Estrées
-St Denis

enthusiasts as the, now thriving CF de Froissy – Cappy – Dompierre. Not easily accessible except by car, this unusual line with its reversing "Z" descending from a plateau to the canal bank is worth a visit. Not only does it work with steam – and mainly ex-military steam at that – but it has created an excellent museum of the first world war light railways (see ch 6).

The other groupings were more commercial and longlasting. Most were to some extent geographical in that a Groupe, often an amalgamation of war shattered companies to start with, tended to collect railways in a specific geographical area although it might snap up isolated outliers later on. Probably the two most important ones were effectively formed by a company or association of companies taking over systems whose concessionaires felt unable to rebuild after the war. The biggest was the Cie Générale des Voies Ferrées d'Intérêt Local (VFIL to the British but, more usually, CGL to the French). This was formed by legal amalgamation in 1919 of the three Calais-based metre gauge lines mentioned previously, which was a logical development of their existing status; to this group was added the CF des Flandres in the adjoining Nord département to which physical links had been built for military purposes. The following year it also acquired a whole slew of metre gauge lines in Oise and a collection of isolated branches of both main gauges in Nord. In 1922 it added the standard gauge branch from **Dercy-Mortiers to Versigny** in Aisne and in 1923 the little metre gauge line from **Maubeuge to Villers-Sire-Nicole** in Nord. It finally topped up its empire in 1930 with that group of former standard gauge companies in Pas de Calais which had been particularly hard-hit by the war. These provided a connected network west of Cambrai, with parallel east-west routes through Boisleux and Bapaume and north-south connection down to St Quentin. The total list is given below.

1919	Flandres, CF des	Nord
1919	Anvin à Calais CF d'	Pas-de-Calais
1919	Ardres à Pont-d'Ardres, Twy d'	Pas-de-Calais
1919	Aire à Fruges et Rimeux à Berck CF de	Pas-de-Calais
1920	Estrées a Froissy et Crèvecœur CF d'	Oise
1920	Méru à la Bosse, CF de	Oise
1920	Hermes à Beaumont, CF de	Oise
1920	Noyon à Guiscard et Lassigny, lignes de	Oise
1920	Milly à Formerie CF de	Oise
1920	Hazebrouck à Merville, CF d'	Nord
1920	Aulnoye à Pont-sur-Sambre, CF d'	Nord
1920	Bettrechies à Hon...CF de	Nord
1920	Pont-de-la-Deule à Pont-a-Marcq, CF de	Nord
1922	Dercy-Mortiers - Versigny, ligne de	Aisne
1923	Maubeuge à Villers-Sire-Nicole, CF de	Nord
1930	Boisleux à Marquion, CF de	Pas-de-Calais
1930	Marquion à Cambrai, CF de	Pas-de-Calais/Nord
1930	Vélu-Bertincourt à St Quentin CF de	Somme/Pas-de-Calais
1930	Achiet à Bapaume, CF d'	Pas-de-Calais

The CGL was very forward-looking for its time. As early as 1926, it started building single-ended railcars (ie on railway chassis, not converted buses) in its works at Lumbres, on the basis which the French delightfully call "artisanale" (rather than professional manufacturers one assumes). If that conjours up visions of local jobbing carpenters rushing up the odd vehicle in a backyard shed it is probably unfair. The bigger light railway Works were very well equipped and, if the first CGL efforts did look a bit like rectangular cardboard models, their later ones were very professional indeed - helped, no doubt by the fact that they entrusted the bodywork to firms of professional coachbuilders like Milliom-Guiet. Over a period of thirty years or so, they produced both four-wheeled and bogie cars for metre and standard gauge plus parallel series of six-coupled diesel locomotives; several survive on the Baie de Somme and elsewhere. Certainly they enabled most of the lines to survive into the 1950s and 60s.

REXPOËDE — La Gare

The rural lines are typified by this mixed train of the CF des Flandres with its 2-6-0T at Rexpoede.

(C. WALKER'S COLLECTION)

The other main contender was probably the **CF Secondaires du Nord Est (NE)** which arose from an amalgamation of the CFD de l'Aisne (CDA) and the St Quentin-Guise standard gauge network, both founded by the same family. This effectively took over all the Aisne's remaining départemental lines including the ex Banlieue de Reims one. It was, perhaps, the organisation faced with more copmplications than any other since its railways had been in the very thick of the fighting. Two systems in particular were in need of considerable reconstruction.

First was that ex CBR line east from Soissons already mentioned. This was completely rebuilt to standard gauge on a new alignment between Soissons and Concevreux and then took over the former metre gauge route (with deviations) into Guignicourt. As such it lasted, in part, up to the 1980s, the SNCF eventually taking on various surviving spurs in 1981 as industrial sidings. For much of the time power was provided by a standard series of 0-6-0T by La Meuse, later replaced by CFD and "homebuilt" diesels.

The other system was the old CDA network north and west of Soissons. Here the army had, for its own purposes, in 1917-18 built a new standard gauge link from Appily, south east to the CDA's roadbed at Blérancourt and thence along it to Coucy-le-Château on a north-south main line. After the war, the metre gauge was slowly and painfully restored but the standard gauge was left in, as mixed gauge, between Blérancourt and Coucy for freight. Much of the system lost its passenger traffic again quite quickly, although retained for beet traffic in season. Only Soissons – Coucy and Chauny – Blérancourt – Coucy kept open until about 1942, after which much of the latter had its metre-gauge track lifted by the occupying power; closure of the rest followed in 1948. The standard gauge, however, remained in use until 1963 and the old metre gauge route from Coucy down as far as Montécouvé was relaid to 60cm gauge by the Sucreie Ternynk at Coucy and operated with steam in the beetroot season until the early 1960s; the writer saw the remains in 1962.

As to other groupings, there is some minor confusion in the very similarly named but older **"Cie des Chemins de Fer Secondaires" (CFS)** which ran only a few small rail routes but which later "acquired" some ex-SNCF branches under the system of affermage. Notable among these latter was the long cross country line from Longueville via Provins to Esternay which lasted into the 1960s and whose lower section has now been reassimilated into the SNCF. Apart from these, however, it concentrated mainly on replacement bus services. In any case it had VERY close links with the NE and the two finally merged after World War 2 as the CFSTA (Chemins de Fer Secondaires et de Transports Automobiles).

World War 2 and the consolidation of Groupings

The Second World War, when the whole region was fought over again, twice, caused another round of amalgamations and takeovers. Most prompt of all these was the local region of the newly nationalised coalmining organisation, in this case the **Houillères Nationales du Nord et du Pas de Calais.** Among other things, it inherited five fomer private railways which primarily served coal mines but ran public services on the side. Four were comparatively straightforward affairs of a longish branch from an SNCF line, with outlying spurs, and comprised the **Mines de Marles, Béthune, Lens and Carvin.** Of these only the Mines de Carvin (Libercourt – Carvin) really merits extended mention and that because of its love for large rectangualar railcars. Its first ones were two big Westinghouse petrol-electric vehicles built as early as 1911 and replaced in 1923 by a pair of Renault type KE tricomposites with postal and luggage compartments. The company always seemed very proud of these, emblazoning its name along the sides in large letters, but they clearly did not give entire satisfaction since the Westinghouse cars became trailers and the KEs were soon converted to overhead electrics, surviving as such until 1940.

The fifth line, or rather agglomeration of lines, was different. As the **Cie des Mines d'Anzin,** it actually installed its first railway in 1831, opened the first public sections seven years later, and steadily extended it until by 1874 it ran from Somain in the west through Anzin, Denain, St Waast and Vieux Condé for a total of 38km to Peruwelz just over the Belgian frontier - hence its alternative name of **"Somain à la Frontière Belge".** Even more interesting, its first locomotives were English, two 2-2-2 tender locomotives built by Stephensons in 1836 and some later ones were just as odd, including some big-wheeled 0-4-0Ts with inside valve gear, built by Anzin shops. In its later years the company became quite substantial, largely double tracked on the main line with large imposing stations and a passenger service headed by a class of elegant 2-6-0s with pointed smokebox doors. The long bogie coaches, mainly bought secondhand from mainline concerns, were equally splendid in shining dark green; some of the first class ones still in service at the end even retained the archaic quadrant windows and scarlet leather upholstery of an earlier era. It couldn't last of course. By the late 1950s the chef was getting very impatient with all this passenger nonsense which hampered his coal traffic and it was done away with in 1963 after which matters declined rapidly. Brissoneau et Lotz diesels took over from steam and the line closed down bit by bit as mining declined, the last section going in 1989, three years before the Regional authority itself was dissolved.

In general, the post second world war period was a period of consolidation for the survivors. The CGL turned itself into the Cie Générale des Enterprises Ferroviaires et Routières (CGEFR) in 1956 to concentrate on road transport, at the same time losing most of its remaining concessions in Aisne to direct control by a newly constituted Départemental transport authority the Régie des Transports de l'Aisne (RTA) which carried on, mostly for goods, into the 1970s. The Calais group and the Oise lines faded out by the mid 1950s. Most of the rest of its empire, in particular the standard gauge complex round Cambrai (Boisleux-Marquion-Cambrai; Achiet-Bapaume; Velu-Bertincourt-St Quentin) was taken on in 1961 by an association of former employees calling itself the Régie Départementale du Pas de Calais. All are now closed save the stretch from Achiet to Bapaume which has been taken over by a local cooperative as virtually an industrial siding. Of the other major players, the NE and the CFS, as noted above, did the logical thing in 1960, amalgamating as the Cie des Chemins de Fer Secondaires et de Transports Automobiles (CFSTA) and in 1966 that in turn merged with the SE to become the Cie de Chemins de Fer et Transports Automobiles (CFTA) which is still very much in existence (although taken over by the big conglomerate Cie des Eaux which in turn has been recreated as Vivendi). Its rail operations have more recently been largely confined to running some ex-SNCF branches, mainly in the Est region, but it also makes bids from time to time to run other systems - it has in recent years had periods of operation on the CF de Provence and Corsica, and is currently (2000) running the Réseau Breton, the Provence, the CF de la Mure in Savoie and the rack line from St Ignace to la Rhûne in the Pyrenées.

Light Railways in Region Nord

name	ident	gauge	km	lines	dates	cln	operators	
dept: Aisne								
Aisne, CF Départementaux de l'	CDA	m/sg	0179	07	1907-1963*	IL	Jourdain (fils);	NE 1922
Banlieue de Reims, CF de la (in Aisne)	CBR	m/sg	0168	04	1903-1981x	IL		NE1922/RTA1952
Chauny - St Gobain, CF de	CSG	sg	0015	01	1860-1993*	IG		SNCF 1983
Dercy-Mortiers - Versigny, ligne de	DMV	sg	0022	01	1878-1959	IL		CGL 1922
Guise - le Catelet	NF	metre	0040	01	1900-1951	IL	NF;	NE 1922
Guise-Hirson, ligne de	Nord	m/sg	0039	01	1910-1969x	IG	Nord CF du;	NE 1938
Laon, CF de	CFL	metre	0002	01	1899-1971y	Twy		rack
Marle à Montcornet, CF de (CDA)	MM	sg	0020	01	1907-1959*	IL	Jourdain (f) CDA;	NE 1922/RTA1952
Mezieres à Tergnier CF de (StQG)	MT	sg	0017	01	1898-1963	IL	Jourdain (p);	NE 1922/RTA1952
Ribemont à la Ferté-Chevresis, CF de	SQG	sg	0018	01	1900-1958*	IL	Jourdain (p);	NE 1922/RTA1952
Soissons - Guignicourt, ligne de	NE	sg	0060	02	1919-1990	IL	new line;	NE 1922/RTA1952
St Quentin - Ham, ligne de	CDA	sg	0021	01	1910-1981*	IL	Jourdain (f) CDA;	NE 1922
St Quentin à Guise, CF de	SQG	sg	0040	01	1874-1968z	IL	Jourdain (pere);	NE 1922/RTA1952
Sud de l'Aisne, CF du	CSA	metre	0083	03	1910-1961*	IL	Tartary;	NE 1934
Tergnier-St Gobain et à Anizy-Pinon Twy de	TTA	metre	0038	02	1910-1940	Twy		CDA 1913; NE 1927
dept: Nord								
Anzin, Mines d' (Somain à Peruwelz)	SFB	sg	0040	01	1838-1989*	IL		HBNPC 1946
Armentières - Halluin, ligne de (CEN)	CEN	metre	0026	01	1895-1935	Twy	Empain; CEN	
Aulnoye à Pont-sur-Sambre, CF d'	APS	sg	0006	01	1905-1948*	IL	Dequeker;	CGL 1920
Bettrechies à Hon...CF de	BH	sg	0009	02	1895-1967*	IL	Lambert	CGL1920/UUCF1956
Cassel, Twy de	TC	metre	0004	01	1900-1934	Twy		
Don Sainghin - Fromelles, ligne de (NF)	NF	metre	0018	01	1906-1951	IL	NF;	CFS 1933
Flandres, CF des (lignes d'Hazebrouck)	CF	metre	0043	02	1894-1954	IL		CGL 1919
Fourmies à Wignehies, Twy de	TFW	metre	0006	01	1884-1903	Twy		
Hazebrouck à Merville, CF d'	HM	sg	0014	01	1906-1962*	IL	Dequeker;	CGL 1920
Hondschoote - Bray Dunes, ligne de (NF)	NF	m/sg	0015	02	1903-1951*	IL	NF;	SE 1919
Maubeuge à Villers-Sire-Nicole, CF de	MV	metre	0013	01	1896-1951	IL	Lambert;	CGL 1923
Nord, CF Economiques du (réseau du Nord)	CEN	metre	0074	05	1892-1966g	IL	Empain;	CEN from new
Pont-de-la-Deule à Pont-a-Marcq, CF de	PDPM	sg	0029	01	1896-1955z	IL	Lambert;	CGL 1920
SE Nord (gpe Nord) Herzeele gpe	SE	metre	0050	02	1910-1951*	IL	SE	
SE Nord (gpe Sud) Solesmes gpe	SE	metre	0100	04	1907-1944	IL	SE	
Valenciennes à Anzin et exts, Twys de	CEN	metre	0052	04	1881-1966	Twy	Empain;	CEN 1885
Cambrésis, CF du	CFC	metre	0120	04	1881-1960	IL		SE 1921-24
dept: Oise								
Bussy à Ercheu, CFIL de (SE)	SE	metre	0013	01	1897-1955*	IL	Lambert (explSE);	SE 1913
Estrées à Froissy et Crèvecœur CF d'	EFC	metre	0054	02	1891-1961	IL	Lambert;	CGL 1920
Hermes à Beaumont, CF de	HB	metre	0031	01	1879-1958	IL		CGL 1920
Méru à la Bosse, CF de	ML	metre	0032	01	1905-1934	IL	Dequeker;	CGL 1920
Milly à Formerie (lignes de) CF de	MF	metre	0032	01	1894-1935	IL	Lambert;	CGL 1922
Noyon à Guiscard et Lassigny, lignes de	NGL	metre	0058	02	1895-1955	IL	Lambert;	CGL 1922
dept: Pas-de-Calais								
Achiet à Bapaume, CF de	AB	sg	0033	01	1871-1969z	IL	Level;	CGL 1930; RPdC 1961
Aire à Fruges et Rimeux à Berck CF de	ARB	metre	0088	01	1893-1955	IL	Lambert;	CGL 1919
Anvin à Calais CF d'	AC	metre	0095	02	1881-1955	IL	Level;	CGL 1919
Ardres à Pont-d'Ardres, Twy d'	TAP	metre	0006	01	1902-1955	Twy		CGL 1919
Artois, Twys de l' (Béthune-Estaires)	TA	metre	0018	01	1899-1933	Twy		
Berck-Plage à Paris-Plage CF de	BP	metre	0017	01	1909-1927	IL		
Béthune, Mines de (Bullay-Grenay)	BG	sg	0010	01	1862-1970*	IL		HBNPC 1946
Boisleux à Marquion, CF de	BM	sg	0026	02	1878-1969	IL	Lambert;	CGL 1930; RPdC 1961
Carvin, Mines de (Libercourt - Carvin)	LC	sg	0005	01	1865-1970*	IL		HBNPC 1946
Estrée-Blanche, CF et Carriéres d'	EB	sg	0014	01	1872-1950*	IL		EB 1880

name	ident	gauge	km	lines	dates	cln		operators
dept: Pas-de-Calais								
Etaples à Paris-Plage, Twy d'	TEP	metre	0006	01	1900-1940	Twy		
Frémont - Quéant/Marquion - Aubencheul	CGL	sg		02	1918-1964*	IL	ex military;	CGL 1930; RPdC 1961
Lens - Frévent, ligne de (CEN)	CEN	metre	0054	01	1895-1948	Twy	Empain;	CGL 1935
Lens, Mines de (Lens - la Bassée)	LlB	sg	0017	01	1868-1986*	IL		HBNPC 1946; SNCF
Marles, Mines de (Lapugnoy-Rimbert)	LR	sg	0007	01	1862-1980	IL		HBNPC 1946
Marquion à Cambrai, CF de (expl BM)	MC	sg	0020	01	1899-1964	IL	Lambert;	CGL 1930; RPdC 1961
Paris-Plage - Casino Golf, Twy de	TPC	60cm	0004	01	1910-1925v	Twy		
Plage de Ste Cecile, Sté de la	TsC	60cm	0003	01	1898-1914h	Twy		
Réseau de Boulogne (CEN)	CEN	metre	0048	02	1895-1948	IL	Empain;	CGL 1935
dept: Pas-de-Calais/Aisne/Somme								
Vélu-Bertincourt à St Quentin CF de	VBsQ	sg	0040	01	1879-1969*	IL	Level?;	CGL 1930; RTA 1956
dept: Region nord								
Ministére des Regions Libérées	MRL	60cm	1007	06	1919-1927	IL	Régie;	ste de 60 1926
Voie de 60, CF de la (Vis-en-Artois)	VA	60cm	0105	05	1926-1957	–		Sugar refinery lines
dept: Seine-et-Oise								
Chars – Marines, ligne de (SE)	SE	sg	0006	01	1911-1951	IL	Ouest/Etat;	SE 1922
Enghien à Montmorency, CF d'	EM	sg	0003	01	1886-1954	IG	Nord;	Nord/SNCF
Epone – Marel-s-Mauldre	EM	metre	0009	01	1883-1884	Twy	CF sur Route	
Gargan-Livry, ligne de (EST)	Est	sg	0003	01	1890-1930	Twy	Est	
Grande Banlieue, CF de	CGB	sg	0174	09	1911-1953s	IL		SE 1933
Magny à Chars, CF de (ETAT)	SE	sg	0011	01	1871-1986*	IG	Ouest/Etat/SNCF;	SE 1934-52
Paris à Arpajon, CF sur Route de	PA	sg	0035	02	1893-1936	Twy		STRCP 1922
St-Germain-en-Laye – Poissy, ligne de	CGB	sg	0005	01	1896-1933	Twy		CGB 1911
Valmondois à Marines, ligne de (SE)	SE	metre	0022	01	1886-1949	IL	SE	
Versailles-Maule-Meulan, Twy de	TVM	metre	0042	11	1899-1913+	Twy		CGB 1911;sg 1913
Villers-le-Bel et Exts, CF de	TV	1.06m	0003	01	1878-1915	Twy	CF sur Route; see next record	
Villers-le-Bel, Sté des Twys de	TVB	metre	0003	01	1928-1949	Twy		rebuild.
dept: Somme								
Feuquières-Fressenville-Ault CF de	FA	sg	0012	01	1904-1906	Twy		
Quend et Fort Mahon Twy de	TM	60cm	0013	02	1899-1931	Twy		TM 1913
Roisel-Hargicourt, ligne de (NF)	NF	m/sg	0007	01	1894-1931	IL	Lambert;	SE 1921-27
SE Somme – Groupe d'Albert	SE	metre	0067	04	1888-1949*	IL		SE
SE Somme – Groupe d'Amiens (to Aumale)	SE	metre	0058	01	1891-1948*	IL		SE
SE Somme – Groupe des Bains de Mer	SE	metre	0204	04	1887-1970*	IL	SE;	CFBS 1970
Somme, Réseau de la (SE)	SE	m/sg	0329	10	1858-1989*	IL	Nord to 87;	SE 1887
Woincourt-Ault	SE	sg	0013	01	1921-1946	IL	SE; SE exp	

Urban Tramways systems in Region Nord

name	power	gauge	km	dates	dept
Amiens	h/e	metre	0019	1891-1940	Somme
Armentiéres	e	metre		1901-1914	Nord
Boulogne-sur-Mer, Twys electriques	he	metre	0020	1881-1951	Pas-de-Calais
Calais et extensions, Twys de	he	metre	0020	1879-1940	Pas-de-Calais
Cambrai	e	metre		1903-1914	Nord
Cassel	e	metre	0004	1900-1938	Nord
Douai, Twys electriques de	e	sg	0021	1898-1950	Nord
Dunkerque, Twys electriques de	HBE	sg	0016	1880-1952	Nord
Lille	HVE	sg	0133	1874-1966	Nord
Lille-Roubaix-Tourquoing, Twy elect	HE	metre	0106	1877-date	Nord
Maubeuge	e	metre	0010	1903-1951	Nord
Paris (all)	HSE	sg	0612	1855-1938	Seine-et-Oise/S
St Quentin, Twys de	ae	sg	0008	1899-1956	Aisne
Valenciennes	me	metre	0064	1881-1966	Nord
Versailles	hme	sg	0015	1876-1957	Seine-et-Oise

CHAPTER 9
Regional Reprises 3: Region Est

Introduction to the region (Maps p.305)

The area designated by Domegie and Banaudo as their Region Est de la France, was certainly one of the more intriguing areas for minor railways even if not the most prolific one. All along its eastern border it was inextricably entangled with its neighbouring countries - with Belgium and its Societé Nationalé des CF Vicinaux (SNCV) in the north, briefly with Luxembourg, with Germany all up the Rhine and even, in a couple of places, with Switzerland at the southern tip. As an additional complication, parts of several départements in the old geographical provinces of Alsace and Lorraine were sequestrated by the Germans following the Franco-Prussian war of 1870-71 when they, quite naturally, became Elsass-Löthringen and had their formative years, for minor railway development, very much under German influence. The result in practical terms included a considerable batch of station-to-town lines which got classified as minor railways because they could take goods but which are also claimed by the urban tramway historians. Between 1914 and 1918, the whole area was part of the battle zone and its light railways were often alternately commandeered for military use or destroyed in the fighting. After the war, when the lost territories returned to France, there was muddle and confusion which was not helped by Germany again claiming much of the disputed area from 1940 to 1944.

The northern départements: Marne; Ardennes; Aube; Haute-Marne; Meuse (Maps p.306)

So what does one have? In the north are the very French départements of Marne, Ardennes, Aube and Haute-Marne, slap in the path of any invader from the east or north and thus fought over three times – in 1870-71; 1914-18; 1939-45. Their comunications systems can only be described as shell-shocked and it is

20cm makes a difference – but not much so far as the stock is concerned. A typical train of the CFD des Ardennes on an 80cm gauge line, with an even more standard Corpet, Louvet 0-6-0T. (AUTHOR'S COLLECTION)

Connections along the frontier. A CDA train, with one of their handsome Corpet Louvet 2-6-0Ts at the exchange station of Corbion; SNCV stock on the nearer track.   (AUTHOR'S COLLECTION)

surprising that so many of them lasted as long as they did. The lines of Marne were a typical example. They were entirely conceded to one company, the **CF de la Banlieue de Reims (CBR)** which we have already met running Soissons – Rethel on the Marne – Aisne borders, and opened from 1896-on. The company had, by 1913, as Banaudo says, built up a "standardised and rationally worked" system of roadside lines radiating from Reims toward places such as Chalons, Fismes, Asfeld, Rethel and Montmirail, where it linked to the CFD's Seine-et-Marne line to la Ferté-sous-Jouarre. It was operated by tramway-type 0-6-0Ts and a collection of four-wheeled stock and the company was just considering a complementary set of extensions when war came, the invading Germans arrived and the front stabilised more or less in the middle of the system. Not a good time to be a horse tramway either, that at Epernay immediately losing its horses and stock to the military. Reims itself was under seige and, consequently, much knocked about, although the surviving lines, largely taken over by military engineers, made considerable contributions to forward supply. The end of the war saw the concessionaire in a parlous state, operating what remained on behalf of a départemental régie while the rest was painfully rebuilt. Even so, it soon gave up, operation being handed in 1927 to the Sté Général des Transports Départementaux (SGTD) a notoriously bus-minded body which managed to close most of the lines by 1939. The remainder, as always, had a brief renaissance during the second war but the last passenger services over CBR lines in Marne finally disappeared in 1947. Only the Rethel - Asfeld stretch, transferred to CFD des Ardennes control, lingered on until 1949 and then until the early 1960s for freight and that had very little traffic outside the sugar-beet season, though it did keep some Corpet, Louvet 2-6-0Ts in operation until the end.

At Asfeld, just over the départemental border, the CBR made contact with the **CFD des Ardennes, (CA),** a link which proved useful when the army needed hurriedly to evacuate the latter's stock in the face of a German advance. Mark you, if the army had had its way that evacuation would not have been possible because originally the Ardennes system was to be...800mm gauge; as related in chapter 3, someone had had the bright idea that if the gauge was different from all others, then an invader would not be able to make much use of any lines he captured. Fortunately, after only a few branches had been built, this plan proved so inconvenient that future schemes were hastily converted to metre gauge.

Apart from three short standard gauge branches conceded under the formula of Intérêt Local to the big **CF de l'Est,** the whole of the Ardennes system was the fiefdom of the locally organised **CF Départementaux des Ardennes;** here was the genesis of the Baert & Verney group which, in this case, after World War I, founded the Sté Centrale de Chemins de Fer et d'Entreprise which also built SCF Verney railcars – many of which were tried out on the Ardennes system. The département built up a system of some 342km in three stages; the second and third were effectively metre gauge from the start, the army authorities having perceived the error of their ways, and the first was slowly converted from 1903-on as occasion offered. They formed two major networks serving the heart of the département and a series of separated branches reaching out to, and across, the Belgian frontier where they made contact with outliers of that country's SNCV at Petite-Chapelle, Sorendal, Corbion and Pussemange. They were, basically, typical roadside tramways with nice little Corpet, Louvet 0-6-0Ts and 2-6-0Ts and a selection of both four-wheeled and bogie stock. From 1914 to 1918 the Germans used the existing lines for their own purposes, employing Belgian and other equipment to make up for the evacuated stuff, simply turning any surviving 800mm gauge track into 600mm – so much for military theory! After the war, the département laboriously rebuilt the whole thing, generating new links into Belgium and acquiring smallish railcars including several Verneys (SCF Verney being just up the road at Prix-les-Mezières) and, for some odd reason, seven peculiar little German four-wheeled cars which could be semi-permanently attached via corridor connections to miniscule two-wheeled trailers – a sort of railway bendy bus cut off short. The 1939-45 war brought further problems and, in 1947, the surviving lines were taken over en Régie, by the Régie Départementale des Transports des Ardennes (RDTA). This proceeded to close all but three lines by 1950 but kept the remainder in use for sugar beet traffic until 1957-61.

Aube, alas, hardly got off the ground, mainly because of indecision and arguments among the départemental authorities. The départemental opened the **Tramways de l'Aube,** two short metre gauge

Connections further south. The ill-fated CF de la Banlieue de Reims shunting; note the overhead gantry for goods transfer.

(FACS)

lines in the south from Polisot to Les Riceys and Cunfins, in 1901-02 and entrusted them to the Tartary group but an attempt to build an electrified network centered on Troyes, the **CF Électriques de Champagne,** was frustrated by a whole collection of problems. First, the actual decision on what to build lasted for years, being finalised only in 1912 with concession to the Groupe Giros & Loucheur who had similar interests in Haute Vienne and the south west. Then there were arguments and changes of plan regarding the type of power car required and some difficulties in acquiring land. Some earthworks had been built and most of the trailer stock acquired by the outbreak of the 1914-18 war when all work stopped. What had been built was commandeered for use elsewhere; the power cars "in preparation" disappeared when their builders works were overrun. Only the electric power station was brought into use and, as in other such ventures, this was theoretically a separate company. After 1918 some attempts were made to restart the venture, the scattered stock being reclaimed, refurbished, stored on the existing CDA and then hired out here, there and everywhere on short period contracts – a sort of rural metre gauge ROSCO by the sound of it! Eventually the bits of infrastructure that had been constructed decayed and the remaining stock was sold off, the project being wound up in 1930-31. The two existing lines at Polisot lasted until 1947 for passengers and 1949 for goods; their equipment was largely conventional Pinguely 0-6-0Ts and four-wheeled stock, latterly supplemented first by a couple of Tartary's home-build railbuses and then by De Dions.

To the east of Ardennes and Aube was basically a frontier region where France juts out to the Rhine and was, between 1871 and 1918, very much a disputed area. Haute Marne and Meuse were still French but now "in the front line." The former départements of Meurthe and Moselle, plus a part of Vosges, were all arbitrarily split between German and French administrations; Haut-Rhin and Bas-Rhin were assimilated almost entirely by the German occupation, only a small section of Haut-Rhin remaining French. The result was twofold: those areas under German control saw their secondary communications developed in German style; the remaining French sections, which became Meurthe-et-Moselle and Territoire-de-Belfort had to adapt themselves to coping with long, thin tracts of country that were not necessarily geographically coherent. Hence the remaining railways of the region are not rationally coherent either. Indeed Haute Marne never really had a départemental network, just a couple of standard gauge branches, a distinctly pottering and antiquated metre gauge line, and its one plum, the metre gauge Riggenbach rack railway which joined Langres station, down on the plain, to the préfecture of Langres itself some 100m above. Started in 1887, and always operated by the **Régie Municipale du CF de Langres,** it was steam worked until 1935 when the equipment wore out and then electrified with single-unit cars. It climbed straight up the hill, its most enjoyable feature being the graceful viaduct by which it jumped the former moat before plunging through the old fortifications to its single track station. When the infrastucture also showed signs of wearing out, in 1971, the town council closed it without further ado. The two standard gauge lines, for the record, were the **CF de St. Dizier à Wassy et Doulevant** (le Château) up in the northern apex and the SE's ligne de **Gudmont – Rimaucourt.** The Wassy line was actually operated by the CF de l'Est until 1933 when the CFS took it on as an "affermage"; passenger traffic ceased in 1952, the freight traffic duly passed to the CFTA in 1966 and the SNCF called time in 1991. The Gudmont branch, opened in 1887 and always worked by the SE, linked a string of industrial villages to two CF de l'Est lines. It closed in 1950, but has left a nice memorial in the shape of restored 0-6-0T RIMAUCOURT. The metre gauge line was the independent CF de Foulain à Nogent-en-Bassigny, a rural branch opened in 1904 which appears to have worked uneventfully all its life with the same Corpet Louvet 0-6-0Ts and classic 4-wheeled stock until they just wore out in 1947; a nice quiet line to model!

More coherent were those secondary lines in the département of Meuse but only because they were grouped around the great frontier fortress of Verdun, latterly developed as a sort of galvanic reaction to the German conquests of 1870-71. Most well-known of the départemental system were the lines of the **Compagnie Meusienne de Chemins de Fer,** itself, in 1891, an inheritor of various metre gauge branches built earlier whose concessionaire, the **CFIL de la Meuse** had failed. Grouped largely to the south west of Verdun, and based firmly on the main line junctions of Revigny and Bar le Duc, these rather antiquated steam tramways gained considerable fame during 1914-16 as part of the military supply system that helped

LANGRES — La Crémaillère reliant la Gare à la Ville, située 140 m. plus haut.

A. Veyssière, phot.-édit.

Early years in Haute-Marne. The CF de Langres in its steam-worked days.   (AUTHOR'S COLLECTION)

The Langres rack line in later days; an electric car preparing to cross the city ramparts.   (AUTHOR)

to sustain the fortress complex of Verdun during its interminable siege. Operated by the famous 10th Section of the military engineers, they were much developed and stock was commandeered from all over France to meet their needs. Almost needless to say, by 1918 the whole system was in a terrible state and the concessionaire, quite reasonably, gave up. The département bought its lines back in 1922 and entrusted them to the SE who already had a two-branch system in operation. By 1936, the whole Meusienne system had closed, save for part of a branch south from Revigny, which had been standard-gauged from **Robert-Espagne (junction) to Haironville.** This survived, at least for freight, until 1971.

The **SE's** possession was its **Réseau de la Woevre,** from Verdun north to Montmédy and south to Commercy, with a common stretch out to Vaux-devant-Lamloup. It came late, being opened just in time to have to evacuate all its stock onto the Meusienne as the Germans advanced. They, in turm, worked the northern line mercilessly, commandeering stock from all over the place, while the French military did what they could with bits of the rest. The SE painfully rebuilt it after the war and ran it until the late 1930s; even then the military had plans to use the formation for 60cm gauge lines but these were cut short by the next wave of German invasion.

Like Haute-Marne, Meuse also had two detached standard gauge lines. Down in the south-west corner was the **CF de Guë à Menaucourt,** built largely for mineral traffic and actually comprising a main line plus two short branches. Independent in the beginning, it was taken over by the CFS in the 1920s; passenger traffic stopped in 1932 but the quarry traffic survived to be assimilated into the CFTA and lasted until 1969. The **Aubréville – Apremont-sur-Aire** line in the north was basically a military branch built in 1918 and handed over to the SE in 1922. Apart from a very brief fling with mixed trains it never carried passengers and was closed to all traffic in 1937.

The French side of the frontier: Meurthe-et-Moselle; Vosges; Territoire de Belfort; Haute-Saône (Map p.307)

East of Meuse and Haute-Marne we come to the true frontier area, where Alsace-Lorraine had been divided in 1871. Immediately east of Meuse was the long thin remnant Meurthe-et-Moselle. Only in the south of this was there really any room for minor lines and these were confined to a single SE possession,

867-1. CUNFIN — La Gare (Point terminus)

A typical scene on the little Tramways de l'Aube with a short passenger train at Cunfin terminus. (FACS)

142

Over in Meuse, an antiquated train of the Cie Meusienne trundles along a village street between Haironville and Revigny; the double buffers are prominent. (AUTHOR'S COLLECTION)

from **Toul to Thiaucourt;** a gaggle of suburban tramways round Nancy; a couple of brief steam tramways around Lunéville **(Lunéville – Einville and Lunéville – Blamont – Badonviller)** and the standard gauge **CF d'Avricourt-Blamont-Cirey,** whose name must have been deliberately contrived! Avricourt-Cirey would have done just as well. Still not many private standard gauge lines could boast of being a frontier marker, which part of the ABC was until 1918, and not many had Mallet locomotives (two 0-4-4-0T by Henschel). Of the others, the line from **Toul to Thiaucourt** always seems underservedly in obscurity. It was essentially an SE venture of the more substantial sort, with nice heavy (24.5 tonnes tare) Corpet, Louvet 2-6-0Ts and handsome bogie coaches. Its development was long delayed owing to military worries and when it opened in 1910 it was on the understanding that all viaducts would be mined in advance and that certain sectors were covered by fire from neighbouring forts! One has to say that the concerns were justified in that it found itself squarely in the front line during the 1914-18 war and was virtually destroyed. It was rebuilt but never really recovered. Passenger traffic finished in 1932 and the line was closed in stages up to 1940; blown bridges spelled the end.

The two Lunéville lines differed in several ways. **The Lunéville – Einville** with its short spur to Jolivet was almost an urban tramway with little 0-4-0Ts – indeed one was an early SLM tramway locomotive. The **Lunéville – Blamont – Badonviller,** actually two branches, had rural reaches and 0-6-0Ts plus, later, a few De Dion railcars. Both suffered in the first war and were reconceded to the Tramways de l'Aube thereafter. The Lunéville end closed in 1937, the rest was closed by force majeure in 1940 except for a brief renaissance in 1942.

The **Nancy suburban lines** were really extensions of the urban system and the first one, out to Pompey, was run by the big CFGT from the start. The other two, from 1910-on, were the responsibility of a separate concessionaire, the **Cie des Tramways Suburbains** which, alas, went belly-up during the difficulties of wartime when it ran out of money. The municipality took both systems on en Régie and then confided them to the CFGT who kept the whole thing going until after the war; the suburban lines closed in 1952.

COUSANCES aux FORGES (Meuse). - La Gare

Suite G. Vernet - Cliché A. Humbert, photo, St-Dizier

Standard gauge was not ignored. The Gúe-Menaucourt pauses to shunt en-route   (FACS)

And the Avricourt-Blamont-Cirey flaunts its 0-4-4-0 Mallet in its last years of operation.   (FACS/M. GEIGER)

So that was Meurthe-et-Moselle. Also still to the west of the new frontier in 1871, were most of the Vosges département and that chunk of Haut-Rhin which, since it surrounded Belfort, logically became the Territoire de Belfort. The Vosges never had a unified system, just three detached standard gauge branches and three similar metre gauge lines.

The standard gauge ones were the **Etival – Senones**, the **Senones – Moussey** and **Charmes – Rambervillers.** The latter was initially operated by the CF de l'Est until 1934 when the CFS took it over as part of an agreement for affermage of Est lines in the area, notably the line from Mont-sur-Meurthe (in Meurthe-et-Moselle) down through Rambervillers to Bruyères. Except for a siding at the Charmes end, the Rambervillers line closed in 1939 though the affermage survived to come under CFTA control. It closed in turn to passengers in 1980 and to all traffic in 1988. **Etival – Senones,** opened in 1885, was always run by the company of that name and was a dead-end branch up in the northeast corner of Vosges. Like other Vosges lines it was closed by fighting in 1914 and only revived in 1919. It survived into the 1940s, even acquiring a Billard railcar but was summarily closed during the German advance when Senones depot was destroyed and most of the staff deported. It was briefly revived in 1945 but passnger traffic ceased three years later. The rest remained open for goods traffic until 1975 and then saw a short flowering as the touristic CF à vapeur de la Valleé du Rabodeau until 1989. The derelict track was lifted in 1993-94.

While the Etival – Senones achieved some fame in its later years, the same cannot be said for the **CF de Senones – Moussey** which was virtually an extension of it and exchanged traffic – though the Etival company refused the concession which was taken up by local interests and opened in July 1914...to close shortly after as the area was overrun. It was reconstructed and reopened in 1928 and, apart from the usual hiccup in 1944, actually outlived the Etival line for passengers, lasting until 1951. As a line it was a sort of French roadside Easingwold, with minimal locomotives and stock and serving entirely local needs.

Not far away was that metre gauge **Tramway de la Valleé de Celles,** from Raon l'Etape to Raon -sur-Plaine which got itself into the history books by having to borrow coal off the main line (or as one source has it, a local factory) when it had cash-flow problems. That image is a little unfair. It was opened in 1907 as a perfectly reasonable means of local transport for a valley up in the northeast corner of the département and apart from an unfortunate experiment with second-hand Purrey steam railcars, it was a normal metre gauge steam worked tramway which just had the misfortune of being chopped in half by the Front from 1914-18. After the war it was resuscitated but went steadily downhill (metaphorically speaking; most of its trouble lay in the high cost of coal for going uphill). In 1935 it was reconceded to the big Cie des Chemins de Fer Secondaires (CFS) who brought in railcars and tried to make a go of it; they even provided a new Brissoneau-et-Lotz petrol-electric car in 1937. Regrettably a vital bridge near the SNCF station was destroyed in 1944 and not rebuilt; the detached line lasted only six years more, closing in 1950 except for a short standard gauge stretch which remained as an industrial siding.

Otherwise there were two other metre gauge lines from Gerardmer in the south east. One, the steam-worked **Tramways des Vosges,** joined Gerardmer, terminus of one Est branch line, westward to the middle of another at Remiremont. Bult in 1890, it actually stayed intact during the first war, being used as a line of supply by the French army. Afterwards, following the usual financial embarrassments, it was entrusted to the SE in 1926 and they ran it up to closure in 1935, using the original equipment which comprised four Batignolles 0-6-0T and four-wheeled stock. The other line, the **Tramways de Gerardmer à Retournemer, la Schlucht and Hoheneck** was rather more complex, starting in the 1890s as a steam tramway eastward to Retournemer. This was apparently so successful that a steeply graded electric continuation was built up to the saddle of la Schlucht and the French/German frontier (where it met the Munster - la Schlucht: see p.153) and thence back up again to Hoheneck summit. The war actually saw expansion, with links to the Remiremont and Munster lines. After financial difficulties and a fatal accident, the SE took over in 1925, extending electrification to Gerardmer but giving up in 1935 in favour of a local bus company; the Gerardmer - la Schlucht line closed in 1939, never to reopen...all of which leaves one unresolved mystery; there exists a photograph, but no details, of a pre-1914 "road train" connection consisting of a splendid open-cab prime mover with a six-wheeled trailer of very railway-like appearance which is said to have connected at Remiremont...

Two faces of Lunéville: The Lunéville – Einville in an urban moment.   (FACS)

The Lunéville – Blamont with a children's special in 1913.   (FACS)

The Vallée de Celles line not only experimented with a Purrey railcar but got it photographed in service. (FACS)

Around Gerardmer: the Gerardmer – Remiremont steam tram in an idyllic moment. (FACS)

Tramways de Gérardmer. - Entre Retournemer et la Schlucht
Cliché Marchal, Granges (Vosges

and the Gerardmer – La Schlucht with its elegant electric car in typical scenery   (FACS)

South of Vosges was that odd bit of land, the Territoire de Belfort which for once did have a rational system radiating from Belfort town, although thoroughly mixed up with the local trams and a military 60cm gauge network. Conceded to (what else!) the **CFIL du Territoire de Belfort,** a Verney connection, this came late on the scene and was electrified from the start. It had three main branches, to Sochaux over in Doubs, to Réchésy and to Etueffont-Haut, from which latter sprang a further two short spurs to the Rougemonts (Rougemont le Château and la Chapelle-sous-Rougemont). Opened in 1913, it was effectively taken over by the army after French advances in 1915 and used intensively as a line of supply; it was even temporarily extended, both by a steam worked branch at the western end and by a steam, later electric, link from la Chapelle over the border to Sentheim. A massive influx of steam locomotives and stock came to reinforce the indigenous equipment but electric services appear to have continued. After the war, however, electricity prices rose so high that for a time the concessionaire used steam, mainly in the form of ex-Army Baldwin 0-6-2Ts. Post-war operation, however, was increasingly deficitary and the Réchésy line plus outlying branches to the Rougemonts were closed between 1932 and 1936. Electricity was largely replaced by steam power and Verney railcars on the other lines but these slowly dwindled away as well, the final services to Etueffont going in 1948. There remains only to mention a funny little metre gauge electric tram at Beaucourt, south west of Belfort, which carried both goods and passengers and operated from 1904 to 1940 when it was destroyed by the fighting.

The final part of the "French side", to the west of Belfort, demonstrates the historical problem that occurs if one takes any arbitrary boundary - in this case that between the old CF de l'Est and the PLM. In many ways the sprawling area of Haute-Saône, bracketed as it was by Doubs, Jura and Côte d'Or, belonged geographically in the Sud Est. Certainly its extensive départemental system was operated entirely by one concessionaire, the **Cie Générale des CF Vicinaux (CFV),** which, as one might expect from its name, was largely controlled by the Groupe Empain. The CFV is much better known for its linked system in Jura. Haute-Saône, however, was the CFV's main base, with a connected metre gauge, steam worked system of some twelve lines totalling almost 500km. It started very early, an independent operator opening a stretch from **Gray to Gy** officially in 1878 but being subsumed in the CFV only nine years later. Between then and 1912, the remainder was opened in three stages, and there would have been a fourth but for the war; this may have been a blessing in disguise since the region was very sparsely populated and traffic was low. The system was behind French lines during the war but was quite important as part of the forward lines of communication. After the war, it suffered early from road competition and was closed between 1937 and 1939. As a system it was largely roadside, operated by conventional Pinguely and Corpet, Louvet 0-6-0Ts, towing both four-wheeled and bogie stock.

Although not directly connected with the CFV, it should be mentioned here that, partly to relieve unemployment following its closure, the SE was granted affermage of a considerable kilometrage of SNCF lines in the area, basing its **"Réseau de Franche Comté"** on Gray and setting up major workshops there; they still operate, overhauling equipment for both CFTA and other railways. As conceded, they formed a star, from Gray to Is-sur-Tille, to Culmont-Chalindray and to Troyes totalling some 185km and covering parts of four départements, Aube, Cote d'Or, Haute-Marne and Haute-Saône. They are discussed in chapter 5.

The German side of Alsace-Lorraine: Moselle; Haut & Bas Rhin (Map p.308)

The three areas of Alsace-Lorraine taken over by Germany in 1871 were different from almost anywhere else in France. They had been among the earliest to explore the idea of secondary railways, the CF de l'Est taking advantage of the 1865 legislation to build light branch lines on the standard gauge. While several private attempts were also made to construct lines under the 1865 Law, their subsequent development was almost entirely in typically German style and does not have any real départemental affiliations – the "new" départements post 1918 just absorbed what was already there. It is probably easier to categorise them by type rather than location.

Basically there were

* **Two small metre gauge systems controlled by the State Railway Authority** – in this case the Kaiserliche Généraldirektion der Eisenbahnen in Elsass-Lothringen (EL). The first, largely in

Moselle, from **Lutzelbourg to Drulingen** in Bas-Rhin with a short branch to Phalsbourg, actually started as an industrial line to Vilsberg and Phalsbourg, and had a few short years under the control of the Societé Suisse locomotive firm (alias SLM) before, effectively, being nationalised in 1891 and extended to Drulingen in 1903 under the guidance of the EL. The other, in Haut-Rhin, eventually comprised four lines radiating from Colmar **(lignes de Colmar)** and, again, was initially privately worked by locomotive builders Krauss who, naturally, provided the first locomotives. This lasted only until 1890 when the EL took it over. Both had to make do with a miscellaneous collection of tram and conventional locomotives until the EL acquired a series of thirteen standard 0-8-0Ts by Hagans, with articulation to the rear axle only; this was basically a Klien-Lindner device but modified by Hagans who claimed a patent. Subsequently both passed under control of the SNCF, then the Deutsches Reichsbahn during the second war, and finally the SNCF again. The Drulingen line lost its passenger services in 1949 and closed for goods in stages, in 1951 and 1953. The Colmar group had a more complex career, the Bollwiller branch being converted to standard gauge during the 1914-18 war and then assimilated into the AL while the Wintzenheim line was transferred to the municipal tramways and electrified in 1934. The two surviving metre gauge steam lines were passed to the AL in 1931 but apparently did not survive World War 2 although there are references to occasional goods traffic for a few years thereafter.

* A few typically German kleinbahnen: Thus Thionville, up near the Luxembourg border, had town trams but also a typical German steam operated metre gauge kleinbahn, the **Thionville – Mondorf.** This ran north and connected wth the metre gauge CF Luxembourgois at Mondorf. It was originally run by the Vering & Waechter group who also controlled the two short lines of the urban system in Thionville which started with steam traction and were electrified in 1912 and, prior to 1914, it used their tracks to reach the main line station; after 1918 it connected for passengers to the St.Francois tram terminus instead. There was also a gaggle of suburban electric trams to the west of Thionville town, under the generic title of **Tramways de la Valleé de la Fentsch.** These opened around

Another electric réseau; the CFIL de Belfort at its town station in Belfort.   (FACS)

In a more rural moment, the CF Vicinaux in Haute Saône with a mixed steam train. (FACS)

CFV with a typical train of its Haute-Saône network. (FACS)

1911-12 and were taken over in 1922 by the Societé d'Electricite ét de Gaz de la Basse Moselle (SBTM) who opened a final branch, to Neufchef, as late as 1932. The Mondorf line closed in 1934, the urban routes in 1944 by act of war, but the remainder lasted until 1950-51, latterly in control of the nationalised Electricity Authority.

A standard gauge line somewhat similar to the Thionville – Mondorf operated between **Farschviller and Puttelange** from 1912 to 1936 while Bas Rhin had the standard gauge **Rosheim-Ottrot-Nabor.** Both were typical German bummelbahnen with small well-tank locomotives and four-wheeled stock and the latter connected at Ottrot with a short-lived metre gauge branch eastward to Erstein; this latter died in World War 1 but was later partially resuscitated as a Strasbourg Tramways branch. The Rosheim – Nabor line is still with us for mineral traffic but probably not for long; the quarries are scheduled to close in 2002. There was also the **Strasbourg – Schiltigheim,** a largely industrial line.

* a number of short passenger carrying lines – often station-to-town – usually operated either by a municipal authority or by a local company: **Novéant-Gorze; St Avold; Hagondage,** in Moselle, were all standard gauge electric and **Ribeauvillé** (Rappoltsweiler) in Haut-Rhin was always steam worked. Morhange was steam but did not survive the 1914-18 war. **Dornach – Morschwiller,** also in Haut-Rhin, was standard gauge electric but considered itself a proper railway despite using massive four-wheeled power cars rather than locomotives. Like Morhange, it did not survive the 1914-18 war.

Of these, perhaps the most interesting was the **Ribeauvillé** line. It started as metre gauge, conceded to the SLM locomotive building company and was of note in being probably the first line to use transporter wagons (as opposed to bogies). Several of these Alsacienne lines used daft patent methods of permanent way, including the Hartwich system where bullhead rail was fastened directly to moulded sleepers without chairs intervening, or, as here, the Demerbe system. This used comparatively heavy bridge rail ("U renverse") laid directly in the street without sleepers and was not successful. In any case, although the concessionnaire failed, traffic was heavy enough for the line to be relaid to standard gauge; since it was only just over two miles long, it should, with hindsight, have been that from the start. After the war it was run first by a local company and then en Régie until its closure in 1938.

Over on the German side, the Munster – La Schlucht is decorated for its opening. (FACS)

The Tramway de Ribeauvillé in holiday mood must represent all the miscellaneous Kleinbahnen. (FACS)

And the Colmar – Wintzenheim represents the suburban lines. (AUTHOR'S COLLECTION)

* Some quite substantial **urban and suburban tramways round Mulhouse, Colmar and Strasbourg.** The Strasbourg one in particular had quite an intensive network, used both steam and electricity and was linked to a doppelganger in Baden across the Rhine.

* Some miscellaneous lines which are not so easy to categorise. There was for instance an electric rack railway from **Munster to la Schlucht** at the top of a mountain where it met, but did not connect with, the Tramways de Gerardmer à Retournemer, la Schlucht and Hoheneck ....but then la Schlucht was actually on the border so until 1918 the lines just stared at each other. The German one was opened in 1907, using elegant bogie power cars; it stopped all services on the outbreak of war, was linked to the Gerardmer group in 1915 when French troops overran the region and was finally destroyed in the fighting. Postwar attempts to rebuild came to nothing. Another railway of possible interest not far away was the short electric line from **Turckheim to Trois-Epis** which offered seasonal transport to Colmar folk seeking the cool hills in summer. It was very much a tourist operation, with short, balconied motor-cars capable of working in multiple, and some airy baladeuse trailers. It did not reopen for the 1934 season... Lastly the Swiss **Birgstalbahn** stuck a cheeky tongue into France between Flüh and Rodersdorf but that is hardly a French minor railway!

After the 1914-18 war, of course everything changed. The lost départements were restored to France, most German-owned transport was sequestrated or put under administration, and retrospective legislation made everything respectable. Those private systems and lines which survived were either operated as local Régies or conceded to the larger French groupings – the SE was prominent. The state-owned narrow gauge systems were taken on by the Alsace-Lorraine main line company and, in due course, passed to the SNCF except for the suburban Colmar-Wintzenheim stretch which was electrified in 1935, linked to the town centre and ceded to the municipal tramways. As noted above, since the Colmar - Bolwiller branch had been standard-gauged during the war, this left only two steam-worked lines in Colmar. They indeed, had a final fling under Reichsbahn control during the 1940-44 period but did not survive the war; too many bridges were destroyed. Elsewhere, most of the town trams were municipalised, the only really unfortunate one being Strasbourg which saw its whole system east of the Rhine severed for good and reincarnated as the Mittelbadische Eisenbahn Gesellschaft.

Postwar and the Regions Libérées

Lastly, as in the north, the end of the 1914-18 war found a huge kilometrage of 60cm gauge field railways in existence and often usurping the trackbeds of former standard and metre gauge lines. Again as in the north, these were in general released to the **Ministère des Regions Libérées** and played a large part in the restoration programme. There is, so far, not a great deal of information about this disputed area. The French are, in any case, somewhat naturally sensitive about the whole matter and the bitter fighting in two world wars has led to many local records being destroyed. Nonetheless it is clear that in Ardennes, Haute Marne, Meuse and the Alsace-Lorraine area, the systems of both sides (and all combatants, for British, American, French and German troops fought here) were widely used with a most comprehensive collection of locomotives and stock of virtually every military type. Their life was briefer than those in the north, most having been removed or superseded by 1924; fewer provided passenger services of any note, the only one worth remembering being a French-built line between Bussang and Amarin, down on the Vosges - Haut-Rhin frontier. This cunningly used an existing road tunnel to get over the Bussang saddle and its western end was used by Vosges, being formally conceded to the operator of the Tramways de Gerardmer. Even then passenger traffic lasted only to 1922 and it was closed throughout two years later. Indeed, few lasted very long thereafter, even as private industrial lines. On the other hand even prior to the war the great French fortresses around major centres such as Verdun, Toul and Belfort had had extensive, permanent 60cm gauge military systems and these continued; some, with the development of the Maginot line, were even expanded but that is another story.

Light Railways in Region Est

name	ident	gauge	km	lines	dates	cln	operators	
dept Ardennes								
Ardennes, CFD à VE des	CA	metre	0342	13	1895-1961*	IL	Verney;	RDTA 1947
Est, CF de l' (IL concessions)	Est	m/sg	0017	03	1871-now	IL		SNCF 1938
dept Aube								
Aube, CDF de l'	CDA	metre	0035	02	1901-1949	IL	Tartary	
Champagne, CF Électriques de	CEC	metre	0152	03	not opened	Twy	Giros & Loucheur; never completed	
dept Bas-Rhin								
Erstein - Ottrot ligne de	EO	metre	0019	01	1907-1918x	Twy	DEBG	
Rosheim - Ottrot - Nabor	RN	sg	0012	01	1902-now	IL	DEBG;	CTS 1924
Strasbourg - Ottrot, ligne de	SO	metre	0035	01	1930-1955	Twy	CTS from new	
Strasbourg - Schiltigheim, ligne de	SS	sg	0002	01	1860-1967	IL	Sch.Ebn;	EL 1885/AL/SNCF
Strasbourg Tramways (suburban lines)	CTS	metre	0109	06	1886-1957	Twy	SSB;	CTS 1919
dept Haut-Rhin								
Colmar, lignes de	LC	m/sg	0066	04	1885-1992*	IL	Krauss;	EL 1890/AL/SNCF
Dornbach - Morschwiller-le-Bas, Twy de	TDM	sg	0004	01	1910-1917	IL	DNE	
Flüh - Rodersdorf (Birsigtalbahn)	BB	metre	0004	01	1910-now	Twy	Swiss coy	
Mulhouse, Twys de (suburban lines)	TM	metre	0036	04	1883-1957	Twy	SLM;	TM 1922
Munster - la Schlucht (rack rly)	MLS	metre	0010	01	1907-1914	Twy		rack
Ribeauvillé (Gare-Ville), Twy de	TR	m/sg	0004	01	1879-1938	Twy	SLM;	TR 1923
Turckheim - Trois-Epis, Twy de	TTT	metre	0009	01	1899-1933	Twy		SET 1923
dept Haute-Marne								
Foulain à Nogent-en-Bassigny CF de	CFN	metre	0012	01	1904-1947	IL		
Gudmont-Rimaucourt ligne de (SE)	SE	sg	0021	01	1887-1950*	IL	SE	
Langres, Régie municipale du CF de	CL	metre	0001	01	1887-1971	IL		rack
St Dizier à Wassy et Doulevant, ligne de	Est	m/sg	0040	02	1868-1991*	IL	Est CF de l';	CFS 1933;CFTA 1966
dept Haute-Saône								
Gray-Ville - Bucy-les-Gy, ligne de	CFV	metre	0022	01	1878-1938	Twy	Empain; CFV 1988	
Haute-Saône, CFV Réseau de la	CFV	metre	0499	11	1894-1938	IL	Empain	
dept Marne								
Banlieue de Reims et exts, CF de la	CBR	metre	0278	08	1896-1947*	IL	Empain;	SGTD 1927;
								régie 1937 see also Aisne
dept Meurthe-et-Moselle								
Aubréville-Apremont S.Aire, ligne de	SE	sg	0012	01	1918-1937	IL	military;	SE 1922
Avricourt-Blamont-Cirey CF d'	ABC	sg	0018	01	1870-1969*	IL	Est (expl);	ABC 1937
Lunéville-Blamont-Badonviller	LBB	metre	0046	03	1911-1942	IL	Tartary;	CDAube 1921
Lunéville-Einville	LE	metre	0011	02	1902-1942*	Twy	CDA;	LB.B 1921921; CDAube 1921
Nancy tramways (suburban line)	CGFT	sg	0010	01	1908-1948	Twy	CFGT	
Toul-Thiaucourt, ligne de	SE	metre	0047	01	1910-1940*	IL	SE	
Tramways Suburbains, cie des (Nancy)	TS	sg	0029	02	1910-1952	Twy		CFGT 1921
dept Meuse								
Cie Meusienne des CF	CM	metre	0107	04	1891-1936	IL		SE 1922
Guë à Menaucourt, CF de	GM	sg	0045	03	1882-1969*	IL	CM (1891); CFS 1932;CFTA 1966	
Meuse, CFIL de la (lignes de Révigny)	CM	metre	0062	02	1878-1936x	IL	CM 1888; SE 1922	
Robert Espagne – Haironville (SE)	SE	sg	0022	01	1933-1971x	IL	SE;	CFTA 1966
Woevre, Réseau de la (SE)	SE	metre	0123	02	1914-1938	IL	SE	
dept Moselle								
Farschviller – Puttelange, Twy de	PF	sg	0005	01	1911-1937	Twy	Régie municipal;	1923 Régie m. 1923
Hagondange – Mezières-les-Metz, Twy d'	THM	sg	0006	01	1912-1964	Twy	Thyssen;	UCPMI 1920
Lutzelbourg – Phalsburg - Drulingen	LD	metre	0022	02	1883-1953*	Twy	EL;	AL 1919;SNCF 1938
Morhange (Gare-Ville) Twy de	TMO	metre	0003	01	1911-1914	Twy	Strbn Morchingen	

Light Railways in Region Est continued...

name	ident	gauge	km	lines	dates	cln	operators
Novéant – Gorze, Twy de	SE	sg	0006	01	1912-1933	Twy	LEAG; · SE 1925
St-Avold (Gare-Ville)	TSA	metre	0003	01	1910-1944	Twy	Régie municip 1925
Thionville, réseau de (SE)	VWEB	metre	0030	02	1903-1935+	Twy	DEBG; SE 1924
Valleé de la Fentsch Twys de la	STBM	metre	0029	04	1912-1951	Twy	Vering & Waechter; see Thionville
dept Territoire de Belfort							
Beaucourt (Gare-Ville) Twy de	TB	metre	0004	01	1904-1940*	Twy	
Territoire de Belfort, CFIL du	CFB	metre	0085	07	1913-1948*	IL	Verney
dept Vosges							
Celles, CF de la Valleé de	CVC	metre	0024	01	1907-1950	IL	CFS 1935
Charmes – Rambervillers, CF de	CR	sg	0028	01	1871-1939	IL	CFS 1934
Etival – Senones, CF d'	ES	sg	0009	01	1885-1975*	IL	tourist 1975-89
Gerardmer, Twys de	TG	metre	0020	01	1897-1939	Twy	SE 1925; SATE 1935
Remiremont – Gerardmer, (Twy des Vosges)	TV	metre	0026	01	1900-1935	Twy	SE 1935
Senones – Moussey, Twy de	TSM	sg	0006	01	1914-1951	Twy	destr 1914-19; reopened 1928

* latterly short links for freight only
x part of some system

Urban tram systems in Region Est

name	power	gauge	km	dates	dept
Beaucourt	e	metre	0004	1904-1935v	Territoire de Belfort
Belfort	e	metre	0004	1898-1952	Territoire de Belfort
Chalons-sur-Marne	e	metre	0004	1897-1938	Marne
Charleville-Mezières	e	metre		1900-1914	Ardennes
Colmar	e	metre	0005	1902-1960	Haut-Rhin
Epinal	e	metre		1906-1914	Vosges
Forbach	e	metre	0009	1912-1950	Moselle
Longwy	e	metre	0006	1902-1935	Vosges
Metz	he	sg	0031	1880-1948	Moselle
Mulhouse	hme	metre	0010	1880?-1956	Haut-Rhin
Nancy	he	sg	0043	1874-1958	Meurthe-et-Moselle
Reims, Twys electriques de	he	m/sg	0020	1882-1939	Marne
Sedan	e	metre		1899-1914	Ardennes
Strasbourg	hme	metre	0155	1878-1960	Bas-Rhin
Thionville	e	metre	0028	1911-1953	Moselle
Troyes	e	metre	0012	1899-1950	Aube

CHAPTER 10
Regional Reprises 4: Region Sud-Est

Introduction to the region (Map p.309)

The Region Sud-Est – basically the area covered by the old Paris-Lyon-Mediterranée (PLM) main line company – is different again from all the others and in many ways more substantial. Certainly it had the usual admixture of small, penurious concerns and single départemental systems but it was, first and foremost, the stamping ground of the big groups, in particular our old friends the SE/CFTA and the CFD. Added to that, there was a strong tendency before and after the first war for larger départements to take over or amalgamate diverse lines into Régies Départementales rather earlier than elsewhere – and these régies tended to be progressive instead of defeatist.

All this was aided by the "shape" of the region; in the comparatively easy country east and south of Paris the lines of Intérêt Local were thick on the ground, often nominally interconnecting for considerable distances. Further south, in the rugged uplands, they grew much sparser, with widely separated systems creeping up into the hills either side of the Rhône valley and threading the mountainous terrain near the Swiss border. Lastly, as the Alpes descended to the coastal plain, there was another concentration, including most of the serious standard gauge concerns. Mainly because of the terrain, some are, just, still with us (see chapter 6). The region, therefore, lends itself to a geographical treatment and the logical place to start is directly east of Paris where the départements of Seine-et-Marne and Yonne abut on both the Regions Nord and Est.

Parisian hinterland: Seine-et-Marne; Yonne (Map p.310)

Seine-et-Marne was almost equally divided between the CFD and the SE with only one minor independent, the **Tramways du Sud de Seine-et-Marne.** This latter, which always had close connections with the Verney Group and was assimilated by it in 1925, ran two brief lines south from the prefecture of Melun (where it kept carefully away from the neighbouring SE line); the earliest, to Barbizon was opened in 1899, the long branch from Chailly, where the workshops were, to Milly-la-Forêt (where it did NOT connect with the CF de Grande Banlieue) followed only in 1910. In essence it was a simple roadside tramway with Corpet Louvet 0-6-0Ts and four-wheeled stock and which never modernised beyond two of the earliest Verney railbuses; it died, exhausted and bankrupt, in 1938.

The CFD and SE, on the other hand, both started early but differently. The CFD tended to run isolated lines which it either started from new – such as that straightforward branch from la Ferté-s-Jouarre to Montmirail on the borders with Marne which later became famous simply because the CFD continued to use Montmirail as its main Works even after the line died – or took over as concessions came due. Most of these lines were quite substantial, running on their own rights of way, with reasonable traffic. They comprised:

* **Lagny – Mortcerf,** taken over in 1896 but originally one of the first true metre gauge lines of Intérêt Local, dating from 1865 as a horse-drawn mineral line to quarries near Neufmoutiers and from 1872 as a steam-operated public railway between Lagny and Villeneuve-le-Comte, where the quarry branch turned south. Its early history is somewhat complex but, briefly, the original concessionaires went bankrupt and the line was run in administration until 1896 when the CFD agreed to take over. They did so in 1900, extending to Mortcerf two years later and running it with a mixed bag of steam locomotives until the end of 1933.

* **La Ferté-s-Jouarre – Montmirail,** conceded directly to the CFD and a straightforward unprofitable line which struggled on from 1889 until 1947. It started on an Est branch, linked up with the SE's Seine-et-Marne system at Sablonnières, the CF du Sud de l'Aisne at Verdelot and the CF de la Banlieue de Reims at Montmirail itself where the depot and works were situated and there was another

284. MELUN — La Station du Tramway de Verneuil   E. L.

The SE's Seine-et-Marne detached line at its southern terminus: a typical scene where a substantial light railway connected with both road and main line.   (FACS)

link to the CF de l'Est. Its locomotives were four little 0-6-0T by Couillet, its stock comprised classic CFD four-wheelers and its fame, as noted above, resides in the fact that, after closure, the CFD retained Montmirail Works as its main construction base.

* **Meaux – Dammartin,** originally conceded to the CF de l'Yonne but "acquired" by the CFD in 1931 following ten years in the wilderness after the Yonne gave it up as too deficitary; the CFD agreed and closed it in 1936 though a short stretch was used for another twenty years by the Meaux sugar refinery to shift sugar beet. It was a light roadside line with few distinguishing features, had four Corpet Louvet 0-6-2Ts designed to run cab-first, acquired two Verney railbuses and later a single Renault-Scemia bought by the département. There were vague thoughts of linking it to the Lagny line at Villeneuve-le-comte via Crecy but they never came to anything.

* **Montereau – Egreville – Château Landon.** This last was a true light railway, on its own right of way, and opened in 1888-89. It is best known to enthusiasts since, alone of these lines, it was modernised after World War II with Billard railcars and 0-6-0D tractors rebuilt from steam locomotives. Its proprietors even took over part of a former line of the Yonne département, between Cheroy and Egreville in 1948-9 and experimented with mixed gauge sections at Montereau and Souppes for freight. The main line between Montereau and Egreville lasted until 1959 although in its final years it was notorious for its delapidated condition.

The SE, on the other hand, stuck to roadside tramways and a single cluster of connected lnes for its **SE Réseau de Seine-et-Marne** based on the windswept village of Jouy-le-Châtel (notable for its massive cast-iron pissoir on the station platform), with only one isolated branch from Melun to Verneuil-l'Etang. It was a generally standardised system, substantially equipped with bogie coaches and a class of 0-6-2T not enclosed but designed as tram locomotives to work cab-forward; the cab shelters were constructed appropriately which gave them a rather odd appearance to many eyes and one has been preserved on the tourist CF de la Baie de Somme. The system was generally prosperous as these things go, in a largely agricultural and rural area with considerable goods traffic, in particular sugar beet, and a string of private sidings and branches. This even ensured the continuance of the last sections, from Jouy to Nangis and Rogenvillers, right up to 1965 although, as might be expected, passenger traffic had ceased in 1934 as road competition in such easy country won the day. With such an early cessation there was no use of railcars but two 0-6-2Ts were converted to diesel power in later years for use on the goods trains.

It must be said that Seine-et-Marne seems never to have got its act together completely. Although the SE's réseau had some coherence, the remainder were built more or less haphazardly and fell into the hands of the CFD more by accident than design.

In Yonne the pattern was somewhat different. The CFD had its own fiefdom, a 75km-long line between **Laroche-Migennes and L'Isle-Angély** which seems to have escaped most of the histories. It opened in 1887 and was due to close in 1939 but was saved by the war...and is memorable to the writer mainly because of the curious roof-radiators wth which it adorned its (borrowed) Billard railcars in the post-war years; built-in headwinds comes to mind as a description. The CFD also briefly ran two lines running east from **Sens,** conceived prior to the 1914-18 war and conceded to the **CFIL de l'Yonne** but opened only in 1925-26 (they were doomed by road competion even before they started) and eventually took over the Yonne's other lines which formed a straggly "A" south from an apex at Joigny, together with a single line from Sens to Egreville. These had a long gestation between 1901 and 1914 and their life was not without complications. Slated for closure in the 1938 coordination plan, three stretches were acquired by local cooperatives under the names of CF du Gâtinais (Sens – Egreville) and CF Auxerre – Joigny – Toucy (for lines from Toucy). The latter, set up as a result of wartime pressures, operated only from 1943-47 but the Gatinais ran for all traffic from 1938-1949 after which the Cheroy-Egreville portion was assimilated into the neighboring CFD line for beetroot traffic only; it lasted as such until 1956.

The central area: Nièvre; Allier; (Cher); Loire and a digression to Puy-de-Dôme (Map p.311)

Immediately south of the Paris region, the **SE** held sway, with its **Réseau du Centre,** a huge, rambling affair which most inconveniently for historians, spanned both the Sud-Ouest and Sud-Est regions. This was intended to be based firmly on three départements, Allier, Cher and Nièvre and included systems of

And a rural moment on the CFD's equally busy line from Montereau to Château Landon   (AUTHOR'S COLLECTION)

57. - SEMUR. - Le Viaduc

Even rural networks had their moments; a train of the CFDCO crosses an ordinary river valley at Semur.

The CFDCO was quite rural even in its electric guise – a summer train on the Dijon – Gevrey Chambertin line. Now why did they call the trailers buffaloes?

both Intérêt Général and Local. In reality, the **SE Nièvre** system never got properly assimilated and there was always a physical gap between it and the nearest Allier railhead at Moulins although a connnection between Moulins and St Saulge was planned. Anyway, it was quite substantial enough in itself, comprising as it did a connected set of lines stretching from Nevers itself in the west to Saulieu right over the eastern border in Côte-d'Or and, with its branches, extending over 212km. Together with a short isolated line from Cosne-sur-Loire to St Amand-en-Puisnaye right up in the département's north west corner, it comprised the whole départemental system save for a tongue from neighbouring Saône-et-Loire which reached Château-Chinon. For the record, the first line of all, from Saulieu to Corbigny, was actually conceded to the **CF de la Nièvre** who opened it in 1901 but squabbled with the département and so handed it over to the SE. The eventual system was a fairly typical SE concern with its neat 2-6-0Ts, handsome wooden-bodied bogie coaches and, later on, De Dion railbuses of the later marks. Between 1903 and 1939 it gave good service but, as so often happened, the deficit grew so great that a road minded council then closed the whole thing down. Exit the SE Réseau de la Nièvre.

West and south of the Nièvre, however, the SE was even more ambitious. The parts of its Réseau du Centre sprawling through Cher and Allier totalled no less than 679km, of which some 284km comprised the **SE Réseau de l'Allier Intérêt Local** system and 220km the very similar **Intérêt Local network** in neighbouring **Cher** to the west. The remainder comprised **175km of Intérêt General** about half of which was the Cher-Allier link line from Lapeyrouse north through Cosne sur-Oeil to Sancoins. Cher, technically, is in Domegie's Region Sud-Ouest but its light railway history has to be taken here to make much sense; the equipment of both systems was similar and used in common, they were run from a common headquarters at Moulins, with a central Works at Cosne d'Allier, while the combined PW department was based at Bourges in Cher. The first portion to be completed, after several unsuccessful offers, was two linked lines of Intérêt Général, from La Guerche, in the south east corner of Cher, south west to Châteaumeillant, with a north-south offshoot from Saïncoins down into Allier at Lapeyrouse. This was a conscious effort to link the two départemental systems and the metre gauge was deliberately chosen for the Cher Intérêt Local lines to foster this ambition. The **SE's Cher Intérêt Local** system itself opened its first

LE PERRÉON (Rhône) — Gare du Chemin de fer du Beaujolais

CHAMBION, ÉDIT., VILLEFRANCHE-SUR-SAONE

Representative of the many smaller systems; a typical train of the CF du Beaujolais in its habitat. (FACS)

section in 1888 and comprised four separate branches connecting with the Intérêt Général lines and serving the prefecture at Bourges, and the south-west and northern parts of the département; the latter line, on from La Guerche, actually linked up with the well-known CF du Blanc à Argent at its Argent terminus. The **Allier Intérêt Local** system, depending from this link, resembled nothing so much as a ball of string after a kitten has been at it, sorting out eventually as six straggling lines, one of which, from Lapalisse to Le Mayet, connected slightly confusingly with a concern calling itself the Chemins de Fer du Centre, opened in 1908-09, which had a 38km link from Vichy through Cusset and Le Mayet into the neighbouring département of Loire where the bulk of its lines were situated. Its final section, from Cusset to Vichy, was actually added as mixed gauge in 1912 over an existing PLM branch and also served a large stone quarry at Les Malavaux some kilmetres east of Cusset. Suffice here to say that its Allier stretch was ceded to the SE after the Loire lines became a Régie in 1928 and, after closure in 1949, the section from Cusset to Les Malavaux was taken over by the quarries, transhipment being made at Cusset where the crushing plant was located. In 1963 the quarry extension was standard gauged, allowing through working via the SNCF and crushing was then done at the quarry. Most of the Allier system proper was closed in 1939, except for the Cosne – Moulins branch but the Cher system and the Intérêt Général section worked throughout the war – the latter line under some difficulties since it was partitioned between the occupied and the unoccupied zone. It all closed at much the same time in 1950-51. The combined fleet of locomotives, unusually, comprised a mixture of SACM, Battignoles, Buffaud et Robatel, Schneider and Weidnecht - not a Corpet in sight and the only Pinguelys were four taken over from a private company. Their wheel arrangements ranged from 2-4-0T through 0-6-0T, 2-6-0T and 0-6-2T and even a couple of 0-4-4-0T Mallets. Its quite substantial total fleet of railbuses were all late-model De Dion single enders of the MH and NJ series while the typically SE bogie coaches ran the gamut of layouts comprising 1/luggage; 1/2 composite; 1/2/luggage; 2; 2/luggage. At least they did not, like the Frenchified Portuguese Vale do Vouga, have third class as well to worry about. There was nothing particularly exciting about the SE in Nièvre, Cher and Allier; it just did its job solidly until coordinated out of existence – or nearly so, since the local agence got a few SNCF standard gauge lines to occupy the staff instead under the "affermage" principle.

There were curiosities in Rhone and in Loire. The quaint line from Feurs to Panissières, alas, never opened although it got photographed. (AUTHOR'S COLLECTION)

SAINT-GALMIER (Loire) — Le Tramway - Place de l'Hôtel de Ville

Borel, éditeur

And the little metre gauge line at St Galmier was really just a shuttle, though it had the cheek to use German locomotives for a time

(FACS)

And that confusing **Cie des CF du Centre,** down in Loire to the south east? It started life as the **CF Départementaux de la Loire** (CFDL) in 1901 with three metre gauge lines from Roanne and St.Etienne and had a slightly vague existence until the CF du Centre (CFC) was formed in 1908 specifically to take it over – which, after several démarchés, it did in 1911. The CFC's own réseau came on stream between 1910 and 1912, the CFDL being assimiliated into this. There was nothing particularly special about the CFC except that it initially ordered a class of Decauville 2-6-0T which it was persuaded, for use in Allier, to change for some Cail 4-6-0T which were looking for a home. Four of the five Decauvilles wandered off, via a contractor, to end up in North Africa and Portugal and cause widespread historical confusions in the process; the fifth actually got delivered and the CFC became so enamoured of it that they put in a repeat order for another four (class was CFC 50-54). Most of the system was closed during the 1930s but the Allier bit survived until 1949.

Loire was something of an oddity in several ways. A long, thin département, it ranged from the rural north where the CFC held undisputed sway with a tangle of lines around Roanne to the long-industrialised area round smoky St Etienne where, naturally, the CFC, in the shape of former CFDL lines, also had a presence. Here it actualy tangled with the interurban lines of the **CFVE de St Etienne à Firminy, Rive de Gier et extensions** which was one of three tramway operators in the St Etienne area. The CFVE started as interurban steam tramways, later electrified itself and assimilated the town trams, and still runs one long interurban route, so rates a mention. En route to St.Etienne, there were several mildly peculiar short lines, the oddest, the **CF de Feurs à Panissières,** never actually entering service although it was built and trials were run over several years. This was the only real example of the Lartigue monorail system to be publicly funded in France – a sort of French Listowel and Ballybunion that never came to fruition. The département had long wanted to connect Feurs, on a PLM main line, with the neighbouring administrative centre of Panissières but the difficult terrain and the subsequent cost inhibited them. M.Lartigue sold them the monorail idea on the grounds that it was an economical way of solving the problem. Construction started in 1895 and from then until about 1902 various, but largely unsuccessful, trials were held – not helped by the train derailing when carrying a party of local notables come to view progress. The concessionaire gave up, noone else wanted to take it on and the whole thing was summarily scrapped. Later attempts to replace and extend it on the metre gauge came to nothing.

Some way south on the same PLM line was the town of **St Galmier,** notable to us for its short, station to town, metre gauge steam tramway whose major goods traffic was bottled mineral water...passenger working ceased in 1930 but the water kept the line afloat until 1954, aided, unusually for France, by a gaggle of second-hand industrial diesels replacing the original Orenstein & Koppel 0-6-0Ts. And to the east, and actually belonging to the neighbouring Rhône département, was the quaint, electrified tramway from **Viricelles-Chazelles to St Symphorien-sur-Coise** which ran from 1899 to 1933 and was sustained mainly by the goods traffic from its many private sidings.

A short digression into the odd: Puy de Dôme (Map p.311)

So much for Loire but, while we are on the subject of oddities, we might as well digress briefly westward to Clermont Ferrand where the otherwise blank département of Puy-de-Dôme was stuffed with them (well, all right, four short lines then but if that's all you've got you have to flaunt it). The more conventional of these were a metre gauge line from **Riom to Volvic** which used bullhead rail, almost unheard of for Intérêt Local metre gauge in France, and ended in a steep climb past the Volvic mineral springs (another source of water traffic)... and two short standard gauge spurs, from **Gerzat to Maringues** and from **Billom to Vertaizon.** They were all eventually run by the grandly named CF de la Limagne, which was set up to take over the first two in 1903, were all quite early (the Billom one as early as 1873) and kept their increasingly antiquated stock up to the end. In its last days, up to 1964, the Vertaizon line was quite famous for its elderly four-wheeled compartment coaches and archaic 0-6-0Ts, some of which were inherited from the Gerzat company. In 1965 the SNCF took over and has subsequently worked it as an ordinary industrial siding for freight.

The real oddity, however, started in Clermont Ferrand itself. Imagine the Isle of Man Snaefell lime operated by steam and you have that curiosity of curiosities the **CF du Puy-de-Dôme.** Built and operated by the town tramways company, this purely tourist line climbed 1000m in 15km to spiral up round the, equally peculiar Puy de Dôme itself, which is essentially the remaining core of an old volcano. To cope with the gradients it used not a rack as might have been expected but the "Systeme Hanscotte", which was effectively a derivative of the Fell centre rail system. It did not have a very happy life. Opened only in 1907, it was closed and partly dismantled in 1917 so the army could use track and locomotives to haul heavy artillery in the Vosges. Rebuilt in 1923 it lasted only for three more years before a toll road to the summit took most of its traffic. While it lasted, however, it was quite impressive with big, chunky 0-6-0Ts and both open and closed coaches.

East of centre: Côte d'Or, Doubs, Jura, Saône-et-Loire (Map p.312)

So, returning to where we started from, what of the country to the east of Nievre and Yonne? This was that splendidly vinous Côte d'Or of which Bryan Morgan once remarked that the station names alone were worth a bottle a mile ....Since they included such as Beaune and Nuits-St-Georges that seems a fair comment. Its départemental system, all of a piece except for an electrified stretch from its prefecture, **Dijon, to Gevrey-Chambertin** (now there's a name) was originally conceded not to the SE or CFD but to something unexpected.... the big CF du Sud de la France whose ostensible purpose was to operate lines down near the Mediterranean coast. As a set of, largely roadside, steam tramways the first Côte d'Or lines were operating as early as 1891 and were repossessed by the Département in 1910 to form the **Régie des Tramways Départementaux de la Côte-d'Or (TDCO)** which, in turn bcame the **Régie des CF Départementaux de la Côte d'Or in 1921-22.** Presumably someone in office thought that tramways didn't sound quite the thing, although that is what they were. At the same period the Régie took over operation of the Gevrey-Chambertin line which was the last portion to survive - to 1953 when it closed because the stock, some of it very second-hand, was literally falling apart. The main system was slightly out of the ordinary in its locomotive stock. Its basic machines were quite distinctive, skirted, Piguet-designed

Electric lines were common around Lyon but they were not all trams: A Vaugneray-bound train of the Fourvière Ouest Lyonnais. (FACS)

The standard gauge Est de Lyon in its earlier years. (FACS)

2-6-0Ts, three of which were eventually sold to the CF du Cambrésis and survived there up to 1959. It also had two massive Orenstein & Koppel 0-10-0Ts for goods work which were eventually transferred to Algiers and are said to have ended up in Corsica and, at the other extreme, a peculiar steam railcar on the Scotte system built by the local firm of Petolat which fortunately did not stay long. The system's own ventures into railcars were confined to a couple of, equally short-lived, Purrey steam cars prior to World War I and some oddities in the 1930s – plus, of course, the electric motor cars of the Gevrey-Chambertin line.

So where does one go from Côte d'Or? East then south seems best, for a quick look at the Swiss frontier and then back to a system which nearly, but not quite, connected with the Allier/Loire group. There really wasn't very much at all east of Dijon (at least not in Region Sud-Est) until one reached Besançon and the département of Doubs up against the Swiss frontier. Doubs was either a mess or a fascinating historical tangle depending on your point of view. It started life with a whole collection of independent metre gauge lines, such as the **Tramway de Pontarlier – Mouthe (1900); CFIL d'Andelot à Levier (1901); CF Regionaux de Franche-Comté (1908); CF du Doubs (1910)** most of which were physically linked in some way, all but the Franche-Comté being assimilated at various times into the CF du Doubs. After 1945, all were taken over by the Régie des CF Départementaux du Doubs which really tried to make them pay. Only the short, three-branch **Tramway de la Valleé d'Herimoncourt,** up in the north, held out but then, once road traffic in its built-up area became intense, an elderly steam tramway was just a nuisance and it closed in 1932. Shades of the Glyn Valley; it also had a war-surplus (metre gauge) Baldwin which caused more trouble than it was worth.

The new proprietors embraced the railcar era enthusiastically, first with conventional De Dion railbuses and then with successive experiments on semi-streamlined vehicles produced by Jean Laborie and using rubber "tyres" interposed between hub and rim. They had a reputation for comfort and speed, were apparently liked by travellers and rejoiced in the nickname of blue arrows (or blue birds if you prefer an alternative source!) from the colour of their two-tone paintwork. The Doubs was also the victim of the old canard that because everyone knew the destination but not what the vehicle was, all cars bore "autorail" on their blinds. So they did and, since there was road competition and the lines ran along roads it was a very

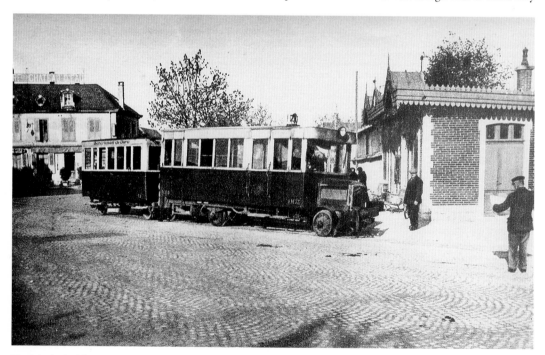

Most typical of the eastern départements was the railcar train – in this case a De Dion JM and matching trailer of the Pontarlier – Mouthe.

(FACS)

In the foothills of the Alpes one had a choice – traditional tortillards, as here on the Voiron – St Béron.

(AUTHOR'S COLLECTION)

sensible idea..."wait for the autorail" has a catchy marketing tang about it even now. After the war the Régie did its best, acquirng modern petrol-electric cars from Anjou and partly replacing steam with diesel tractors but the road still beat it; the lines closed progressively between 1950 and 1953.

Just south and west of the Doubs, that system connected at Lons-le-Saulnier with.... the **CF Vicinaux, Réseau du Jura.** One automatically thinks of the Jura as Swiss but here, where Switzerland pokes a western tongue into France, is the French département of Jura with its formr extensive systems of steam and electric tramways. Apart from the odd fleeting reference in Bryan Morgan's "The End of the Line", these appear to have been little chronicled until recently. They actually comprised two related réseaux, with an isolated line from Dôle in the north of the département which is usually classed with those of Haute-Saône. The earlier of the two main systems was steam and largely roadside, being built between 1898 and 1907. It started from Lons-le-Saulnier and ran south and east to St Claude, with branches from Clairvaux to Foncine-le Haut and from the imaginatively named Bifurcation (junction) to Arinthod; presumably there was no distinguishing settlement within kilometres! Foncine was also a junction (le-Haut to le-Bas) with the second system of two short lines northward to Champagnole and Boujailles with a common stretch to Sirod. These, conceived in 1914, were not built until after the war and not electrified until 1928 even though that was in the original plan. A third réseau, to extend the Lons one, was started but never completed although substantial earthworks were built. The steam lines used proper tramway-type locomotives, both enclosed and bicabine, originally had a heavy goods taffic, particularly in timber, and most survived until the late 1940s; the last electric line closed in 1950.

There remains to mention the French part of a well-known international electric railway the **Nyon – St Cergue – Morez.** The French part, from Morez to la Cure, was opened only in 1921, administered first by a private company and then by a régie and appears to have caused constant pain and grief to the Swiss operating company. Somehow it survived currency fluctuations, the war and even motor competition until 1958 when the French gave up and closed their section. Fortunately some of the old power cars and trailers were sold back to France when the Swiss company modernised and can still be seen at St Georges de Commiers on the CF de la Mure (qv).

Or modern electrics, as shown by the Tramways de l'Ain, here at La Cluse.   (FACS/CHAPUIS COLLECTION)

Thence we turn west to complete the circle. Lying along the eastern edge of Nièvre and Allier is a rural département, Saône-et-Loire. North from the prefecture of Mâcon ran just one of the five widely scattered branches that made up the empire of the metre gauge **CFIL de Saône et Loire,** dating from 1901. What with the need to maintain five separate depots and some disastrous roadside locations, this was a rather unhappy company which ran so deeply into debt by 1924 (the PLM was even supplying coal on credit) that it was taken over en Régie. The département settled its debts but closed it in stages during the 1930s in favour of road transport, save for the Chalon – Mervans branch which struggled on for goods until 1945; in any case, there was little unusual about it, with its standard 17-tonne Corpet Louvet 0-6-0Ts and its four-wheeled stock. On the west of the département, however, was another pair of metre gauge lines which seen unfairly neglected by historians. These comprised the **CFD's Réseau de Saône-et-Loire,** created mainly to service the Forges de Guegnon in the Arroux valley - the Forges ended up by owning a useful collection of metre gauge preservables, hence their mention here!. One route, from Toulon-sur-Arroux to Bourbon Lancy, failed early, with mixed road and rail services from 1932 and final closure in 1939 except for a mixed gauge section at Bourbon Lancy which was, rather hurtfully, conceded to the CFD's great rival the SE. There was a reason, the SE just having rceived also the affermage of the SNCF branches from Cercy la Tour to Bourbon Lancy and on to Gilly-sur-Loire; it retained these for goods trafic well into the 1980s. The CFD main line, from Digoin to Etang, however, was profitable, mainly because of the Forges traffic, and was modernised by the CFD with its usual Billard cars and 0-6-0Ds rebuilt from steam, lasting until 1953.

The Lyonnais, east & west: Rhône; Ain; Savoie & Haute Savoie; Hautes Alpes (Map p.313)

South and east from Saône-et-Loire is an east-west collection of Départements which need to be taken together, grouped as they were around and between France's second city of Lyon and the equally important (in its own esteem at least) city of Grenoble over by the Swiss border. The link perhaps comes with the aptly named **CF de Rhône-Saône-et-Loire.** Its two metre gauge lines linked La Clayette and Cluny in Saône-et-Loire with Monsols in Rhône immediately to the south. A collaborative venture between the two départements, this metre gauge system was conceived at the beginning of the century but opened only in 1911. It got into a horrible financial mess during the war and went into receivership, ending its life as a Régie Interdépartementale in 1934. Its equipment comprised a series of Piguet 2-6-0Ts unusually painted brown and pulling long-wheelbase four-wheelers with De Rechter radial axles; it had one railcar which Berliet knocked up out of a coach body and that is all there was to the RSL.

At Monsols, however, the RSL met up with the **CF du Beaujolais** which carried on southward to Villefranche with a winding line west from Villefranche to Tarare and another probing east across the PLM to Port-de-Frans where it met the Ain system. Conceded to the Cie Central des Chemins de Fer et des Tramways (CCFT) it opened between 1901 and 1903, used neat little Pinguely 0-6-0Ts and a very crude Saurer railbus, was much put out by the war and bought back by the Département as a Régie Départementale. Like the RSL it was summarily closed in 1934.

Not content with almost ruining itself over the RSL and CFB, the département had a number of other railways. Just north west of Tarare, there was an odd cluster of three independent branches, one metre gauge **(St Victor – Thizy)** and two standard gauge **(St Victor – Cours; Amplepuis – St Vincent de Reins).** St Victor-s-Rhins was actually just in Loire and both its lines wandered about the Trambouze valley, crossing each other at intervals. The metre gauge came first, in 1882, and went first, in 1932 for passengers and two years later for goods. It was just a small local railway with nothing more unusual about it than using twin, close-set, buffers instead of the more normal centre ones. The St.Victor – Cours, however, had a thriving goods traffic exchanged with the main line, actually used the PLM station and lasted to 1960 for passengers and 1969 for goods – although latterly worked by SNCF as a siding. It was served throughout its independent life by a quartet of solid little Schneider 0-6-0Ts and had a penchant for mixed trains. The last of the trio, the Amplepuis – St Vincent-de-Reins, was a nondescript affair pottering up the valley of the Reins which, (just in case you thought we got the spelling confused) sometimes got called the Rhins in the neighbouring département of Loire). It bought its locomotives second-hand from the big CF du Nord (but named them), never had railcars and came to an abrupt end in 1935 following a derailment - presumably, like the American Wiscasset line, the proprietors, by then the Département, didn't think it worth repairing. Lastly, south of Tarare the **CF de Rhône-et-Loire (CRL)** were granted but never completed a four-branched system, achieving only a single line from St Symphorien in the west to Messimy where it met an outlier of the western Lyons group of lines. To be fair, its owners probably regretted even this one line, which was deficitary from its opening in 1914 to its sequestration by the Département in 1926 and its closure in 1933; even a most odd little producer-gas powered railbus knocked up by the workshops from an unwanted brakevan didn't help.

Lyon itself was in Rhône but just on the northwest borders of Isère and most of its associated lines were in that Département. Around and about the city the municipal tramways company, the **Omnibus et Tramways de Lyon, (OTL)** had an extensive urban system of tramways, trolleybus, buses and funiculaires, now complemented and partly replaced by the inevitable light metro. It also operated several associated suburban départemental electric lines, the metre gauge **Fourvière et de l'Ouest Lyonnais** in Rhône being the most extensive. This was originally a steam tramway, starting at the top of a most peculiar electric rack railway from St Just and running south west to Ecully, to Vaugneray, to Messimy and on to Mornant (where it would have met another unbuilt Rhône-et-Loire line if all had gone well). In OTL control it was electrified with handsome vestibuled bogie cars and, until 1935, had a healthy goods taffic. The last line closed in 1954.

There really is not space to deal in depth with the OTL whivh has been thoroughly chronicled elesewhere. Suffice to mention here the metre gauge electric, almost imterurban **Lyon - Neuville** "le Tram bleu"; and the long standard gauge line east through Isère to **la Balme** and Sault-Brenez which survived until 1957 and 1951 respectively. The last part of the la Balme line was never electrified and was actually worked by a very rural outlier of the **CF de l'Haut-Rhône** which paralleled the départemental boundary south-east to Bregnier-Cordon.

From Lyon one has a choice of routes eastward: Ain, trapped between Isère and the Jura, or Isère itself which tends to take one off course to the south...Ain it is, then with a quick circle through the Savoies before returning to Isère and the Lyonnais. The hilly and complex département of Ain started with no fewer than seven independent concessionaires and had to rationalise after the first war by joining them all in a Régie Départementale and building various connecting links to make some sense of the whole. They started with a Jeancard group concession of seven metre gauge branches, the **CF Economiques du Sud-Est** in the easier and more lucrative western regon around the prefecture of Bourg. The lines were conventional steam-operated roadside tramways, opened from 1897-on, and appear to have operated without much incident until after the first war. Once established, the département started a second réseau, of five branches, conceded to a new venture the **Cie des Tramways de l'Ain** but also partly linking separated parts of the original system. From 1918 on, the département gradually took over all these lines into a Régie and set out to unify and modernise them. An efficient central workshops was built at Bourg, experiments were made with petrol and diesel traction and, more importantly, the mountain lines from Nantua to Amberieu and to Hauteville were electrified at 10,000V 25 cycles with modern bogie power cars and tractors; most of the infrastructure for a further link between Hauteville and Tenay was also completed, but the final bridge was not built and rails were never laid. The last lines survived until 1954.

Even all this still left the occasional oddity: the early **Marlieux – Chatillon** steam tram (1879-1934) which predated the 1880 legislation and never even tried to modernise; Its tiny Schneider 0-4-0Ts and clerestoried cars (a novelty for France) served it to the end, supplemented only by a single Corpet, Louvet and an odd double-deck steam railcar which – rather like our own Wantage tram – was quickly converted to a high-capacity trailer for fair days. Then there was the equally pottering **Tramway de Pont-de Vaux – Fleurville,** five metre gauge kilometres which carried passengers only (at least, en principe), had to be taken over by Fleurville municipality and then passed en-régie. It supplanted its original (de-frocked) tram locomotives by De Dions in 1932 but closed only four years later beaten by the bus. Not that far away was the standard gauge steam operated **CF du Haut-Rhône** which extended a tramway of the Lyon municipal company. It was a straightforward line with four solid, 0-6-0Ts by Buffaud-et-Robatel and was never, alas, profitable. Like the PVF it got taken over by the RDTA in 1920 but was never assimilated into the main

Or a mixture. At Vizille Terrasse, the VFD's electric trains (left) mingled with newfangled Crochat railcars (right)

(FACS)

170

1700 — Clairvaux-du-Jura - La Gare - Les deux Lacs

In Jura you could use various means: here a pushmepullyou Pinguely of the CF Vicinaux shunts languidly at the little station of Clairvaux. (FACS)

system. The metre gauge **Gex – Ferney Voltaire** steam tram up in a salient to the north east was mostly a passenger carrier, effectively an unelectrified link to the Geneva tramways, and always had close links with them. Its main problem was the hassle involved in crossing the frontier and, despite thoughts of electrification, it gave up in 1932. Lastly, in the same salient, there was the **Bellegarde – Chézery** metre gauge electric line up by the Swiss frontier. Again largely a people-carrier it did have a short stretch of mixed gauge to a factory, was self-contained in that it made its own power, and lasted until 1937; its pride and joy was a single Jeumont-built bogie car bought as late as 1932, which was then sold to the tramway de Valence à St.Peray in Drôme. Since it touched the border at Bellegarde, it actually had customs facilities.

From that border it is but a short step south to the Département of Haute Savoie, also with lines connecting into Switzerland and individualised by the mountain terrain through which they ran. They included one of the three former Fell lines in France, the PLM's metre gauge electric railway from **St Gervais to Vallorcine.** This, though now conventional, is fortunately still with us and described in chapter 6, as are its two associated rack railways the **CF de Chamonix au Montenvers** and the Tramway du Mont Blanc at St Gervais. Otherwise there was a complex of lines grouped round the international city of Geneva with its spreading system of urban and suburban tramways. Firstly, there was a further rack line. The **CF du Salève** was electrified with a third rail and, like the Revard line in nearby Savoie, was built in 1892; it connected at Veyrier and Etrembières with the CGTE's Geneva tramways. Unusually for such lines, its stock consisted of a dozen six-wheeled single-unit cars with end balconies but side doors to the two-class saloons and they always ran singly. The final one of its two branches to the Salève summit closed in 1937 beaten by road transport and a competing cable car. Then there was the local réseau of none other than the **CF Economiques du Nord (Annemasse -Sixt).** Opened as a steam tramway in 1892 from a CGTE connection at Annemasse to Samoens with two branches, it was due to be greatly extended but was frustrated by the 1914-18 war, only a short extension, from Samoens to Sixt, being completed in 1926. The following year it closed throughout to passengers .....to allow of electrification of the main line which reopened in 1932 with modern bogie stock. It lasted until 1959, being finally closed by the road lobby despite a very intensive local campaign. Lastly there was a metre gauge steam tramway, from **Annecy to Thones,** out to the south west which should have been part of a bigger system cut short by the war. It was a conventional roadside line with enclosed locomotives, and with little to note apart from the spectacular scenery along part of its route. Sadly it did not pay and faded away in 1930.

Rationally enough Savoie is directly south again from Haute Savoie and with its prefecture at Chambéry. What one would have found there was another of the curiosities of French minor lines, the **Tramways de Savoie, later the CFDIL de Savoie.** Their founder was greatly impressed by the Decauville exhibit at the 1889 Paris exhibition and, from 1892, there grew up a network of four roadside lines around Chambéry on the 60cm gauge. They were frankly not a financial success, making a loss from 1907-on, and, despite an attempt at modernisation involving petrol electric railcars, vanished in 1932; they were replaced by trolleybuses. Otherwise, the département had a only a scattered collection of very minor lines – the terrain was not helpful to light railways unless rack-assisted and the French never tried to emulate the Swiss in that fashion. On the western borders were the **Pontcharra – la Rochette – Allevard,** two metre gauge and mildly industrial branches opened in 1895 and later standard-gauged; and the little metre gauge **Tramway du Pont de Beauvoisin** notable for its four very neat Pinguely 0-6-0Ts and its two, very crude, Saurer buses on rails – and even more, perhaps, for daring to try out a Mekarski compressed air car (from Aix-les-Bains, so it is said). Since the records are very quiet about this presumably it was not successful. Again it ran along the western border and, eventually, connected with the **Est de Lyon** at St.Genix d'Aoste. Further east was an odd little electric tramway from **Moutiers to Brides les Bains;** always geared to the seasonal needs of its little mountain resort it was replaced in 1930 by a trolleybus with the splendid name of "Electrobus de Savoie" which also replaced the Chambéry lines. There was one more, isolated, rack railway, a conventional Abt line established as a private company and running from **Aix les Bains up Mont Revard** . It ran with little trouble from 1892 to the early 1920s but then there was some financial jiggery-pokery and it ended up by being taken over by a filiale of the PLM. It closed in 1936 after a competing funicular was built. Oh, and the département did host most of the short lived **Fell** railway over the **Mont Cenis** pass to Italy whose history has recently been comprehensively chronicled in English but it is dubious if that would have considered itself a minor railway.

Isère: Split between two geographical regions; the east Lyonnais and the mountains round Grenoble (Map p.314)

West from Savoie brings us back to Isère and the biggest concentration of minor railways in the Lyonnais – the département is complex enough to warrant a section of its own although one might have included Hautes-Alpes if that remote place had ever had any light railways. Two of the three substantial systems in Isère had a Lyon terminus and, together with a Sud-France concession, filled the space between Lyon and Grenoble. One of them, the standard gauge **CF de l'Est de Lyon** will also divert us briefly eastward again toward Savoie, the Swiss border and the international city of Geneva. The Est de Lyon was a fairly solid concern, founded with Belgian capital in 1878 and tapping a rich traffic throughout the east lyonnais. But for the 1914-18 war it might even have got right through to Chambéry in Savoie. As it was its eastern termini were at Montalieu and at St Genix-d'Aoste up against Isère's eastern borders and it contented itself with a lucrative stone and industrial traffic into Lyon-Est. It did great service for the region up to and during the 1939-45 war but in 1947 passenger traffic was withdrawn and the system cut back to Bouvesse. The remainder, however, was thoroughly modernised with diesel locomotives and centralised control via radio, surviving up to the mid-1990s when the last stub was taken over by the SNCF and its buildings at Lyon-Part-Dieu, occupied since 1983, destroyed.

From Lyon, south, the minor lines otherwise thin out drastically as the central massif, to the west, and the Savoie Alpes to the east create their own barriers to easy communication. Those companies which did manage to get started divide fairly neatly into two groups – those which had their origins in the Rhône valley and those which radiated (more or less) from Grenoble. In the middle, between Lyon and Grenoble were two rambling metre gauge systems, one of which was the "other" line to have a Lyon terminus. This was the so-called **Tramways de l'Ouest du Dauphiné, (TOD)** originally two lines conceded to the

Tramways de l'Isère and opened in 1899 but but quickly taken over by the Sud-France in 1903 when the TI became insolvent. The Sud France, initially under the title **Tramways Départementaux de l'Isère,** added a further line, completing one of the originals as well, and then ran the combined system under, eventually, the banner of **Sud-France - Réseau de l'Isère. (SF-I).** Basically one long straggling line with branches, and two short outliers connected via other réseaux, it was quickly deficitary, in administration by 1914 and taken over "en-Régie" by the Régie des Voies Ferrées du Dauphiné (whom we shall meet soon) by 1922; The VFD it was who ran it under the "Tramways de l'Ouest Dauphine" label though that was never a separate company.. The last line closed in 1939. It was notable mainly for its widespread use of, non-skirted, bicabine locomotives – a sort of rural relative of the CGB pushmepullyous – one of which is preserved on the CF du Vivarais and for an eccentric collection of railmotors.

At various points in its system, the SF/TOD interacted with an earlier Isère départemental réseau operated by our old friends from the north, the CEN. Just why organisations specifically formed to run regional réseaux elsewhere concentrated around here is not clear but they obviously did. The **CEN's Réseau de l'Isère** opened its first line, from Grenoble to Veurey, in 1895 and eventually had three other branches in central Isère forming a connecting line from Vienne in the west across to Voiron in the east where it met the independent **Voiron - St Béron.** This made a huge loop (with one short branch) round the eastern tip of Isère and tangling with the CEN at one end and both the Pont de Beauvoisin company and the Sud-France at the other. It was a typical roadside tramway with conventional 0-6-0Ts and was eventually assimilated into the VFD in 1932 but by then was very much on the decline, its last trains running only four years later. For the writer it is memorable chiefly for the odd way in which it actally cut through a shop building in St Laurent du Pont to get round a sharp corner. The CEN lines were also roadside tramways in an area suited to road competition and were turned over to buses in the early 1930s.

This really leaves us with the various lines around Grenoble and another slight confusion. That city had, and now has again, an extensive urban tramway system and also had two suburban metre gauge electric lines owned by independent companies, the **Tramway de Grenoble à Chapareillan** opened in 1895 amid severe squabbling with local tramway operator, the SGTE, and the **Tramway de Grenoble à Villard-les-**

While at Sirod junction, on the same company's Champagnole system, electric trains prepare to depart.

(FACS/CHAPUIS COLLECTION)

Lans which was equipped and operated by the CGTE from the start and which also handled goods in its outer reaches with some quite respectable electric locomotves. More importantly, it was also home to the **Sté des Voies Ferrées du Dauphiné** which ran heavily trafficked lines out to Froges and, via Vizille, up the Romanche valley to Bourg d'Oisans. There was always tension between the SGTE with its electrified passenger lines, and the steam-powered VFD which eventually electrified the Froges and Vizille lines on its own account. Freight traffic on the Romanche line in particular was very heavy, most exiting via a mixed gauge link from Vizille town to Jarie-Vizille station on the PLM. The confusion arises because, in the difficult times after World War 1, the département bought this system back, setting up a Régie which not only steadily acquired other Isère systems but continued to use the VFD name. Post 1920, therefore, it should really be referred to as the Régie Départementale des Voies Ferrées du Dauphiné. In general, passenger services on the "old" VFD faded away during the 1930s, only being saved for a period by the 1939-45 war which saw a massive traffic into and out of Grenoble. After the war, the remaining line, up the Romanche as far as Livet, concentrated on freight. As a short term measure to overcome wartime depresations, it acquired several heavy tank locomotives from Swiss sources but, from 1951, replaced them with home-built diesels on ex-steam chassis and four Brissoneau et Lotz diesel electrics. Vizille-Livet was abandoned as late as 1964 and the standard gauge between Vizille and Jarrie was still in occasional use in 2000 when it was being refurbished.

The only other significant line in these eastern Alps was, and is, the metre gauge **CF de St Georges de Commiers à la Mure.** Opened in 1888 by the Fives-Lille company, this scenic line of Intérêt Général was intended to open up coal deposits in the hills and passenger traffic was always secondary. It was originally steam-worked by cab-first Fives Lille 0-6-2Ts (what else) but was not profitable and only ten years after opening, it was taken under state control as a national Régie. Its history and current state are described in chapter 6 but it needs to be mentioned here because it was originally intended to carry on up the Route Napoleon to Gap in Hautes-Alpes and that would have been Hautes-Alpes sole claim to light railway fame; shame about that.

The Rhône corridor: Drôme; Ardèche; Haute-Loire; Lozère (Map p.314)

Down the Rhône, the secondary routes were much more strung out and rarely connected but did appear at intervals all the way down to the Mediterranean coast. Working down the river, on the east bank there was first the spread-out system of the metre gauge **CF de la Drôme,** the first line of which was opened in 1893 with a connected réseau based on Tain l'Hermitage and Valence and with various isolated branches linking administrative centres to the nearest PLM artery. A standard départemental concern run with light, six-coupled locomotives, it had a reasonable traffic but fell into difficulties during the first world war. It was taken over, en bloc, by a Régie Départementale which still operates replacement road transport. The Régie also took over the tiny **Chamaret-Taulignan** line in 1928 but that was so deficitary that it was closed the following year. It also agreed to run a new electric interdépartemental tramway from **Valence to St-Peray** , across the river in Ardèche, opened in 1927. This, indeed, survived the general closure in 1933 but was sharply truncated in 1940 by destruction of the river bridge. Cut off from its workshops, the line staggered on until 1950, then being replaced by a bus.

On the left or west bank there was virtually nothing south of Lyon until one came to the sleepy town of Tournon but then, in compensation, one met one of the greatest of the French secondaires, the **CFD's Réseau du Vivarais.** This was of Intérêt Général, being conceived as a strategic route spanning the high watershed between Rhône and Loire and was always the pride of the CFD's narrow gauge empire. Its history has been faithfully chronicled in both French and English, and portions of it still remain as tourist lines so it is described in chapter 6.

Associated with this system, under the generic title of **"Réseau du Vivarais-Lozère"** was an isolated line not of the Rhône but which will get missed out if not mentioned here. That was the sole secondary railway of the Lozère département over to the west from Ardèche. It was promoted in 1904 as a line of Intérêt Général to join the PLM ligne du Bourbonnais to Florac, sous-prefecture of the département and isolated among the crazy crags of its Causses de Mejean. The PLM flatly refused to get involved at all and it was

LE COLLET-de-DEZE — La Gare

The CFD's Vivarais system has been often illustrated. Its Lozère line, here at a typical station, has been much more shy. (AUTHOR'S COLLECTION)

left to the CFD to build and operate it, as an adjunct to the Vivarais system. It was certainly a line with its own rugged charm and benefitted by constant exchanges of equipment with its larger neighbour, although its own Mallets were the unusual 2-4-4-0T variety. Like the Vivarais, deficits started mounting in the 1950s and, again like the Vivarais, it closed in 1968; its two final diesel locomotives survive on the western end of the former, a local attempt to run the Lozère line as a tourist route having come to nothing.

Back on the Rhône, just south of the Vivarais' southern terminus at La Voulte-s-Rhône, there was a complete contrast, the river terminus of the purely départemental **Tramways de l'Ardèche.** In an ideal world this should not have been built at all since the countryside was almost unpopulated and the terrain would have tested even the powerful machines of the CFD. Still, the département wanted to connect its major (sic) administrative centres and in 1910 opened a 104km long main line, struggling up from the Rhône southwest to St Paul-le-Jeune and throwing off a branch to Largentière en route; the system was completed by two isolated lnes, from Ruoms to Vallom in the south east and from St Peray to Vernoux. Its history is catalogued in chapter 2 as a typical example of how (or perhaps why) not to run a minor railway! The only other narrow gauge effort was a funny little metre gauge electric tramway from Aubenas to Vals les Bains surviving from 1898 to 1932 mainly on seasonal traffic to Vals (which originally had to reach the line via the Tramways de l'Ardèche – not a promising source one would assume!).

The Rhône delta: Vaucluse; Bouches-du-Rhône; Gard: an offshore excursion to Corsica (Map p.315)

Carrying on south, on the right bank the département of Vaucluse had no railways of its own, just a single line of Intérêt Général which ran east from **Orange to Buis-les-Baronnies.** As usual this was originally projected as standard gauge but the PLM muttered and prevaricated so much that it was eventually built to metre gauge; hence the operation was quickly dumped on the SE who opened it throughout in 1907. Unusually it had a fairly uneventful life, lost its passenger services to the coordination policy in 1938 and was closed altogether in 1952.

Again typical, in this case of the ambling standard gauge lines in Bouches du Rhône. St Rémy-en-Provence station in steam days.

(FACS)

Then there was a long gap until one reached the easier country round the widespead Rhône delta with the historic towns of Tarasçon, Arles, Nîmes and Marseilles. Arles itself had no less than three stations of which the western one (Trinquetaille) was home to the metre gauge **CF de la Camargue** whose three major routes radiated south and west to Salin-de-Giraud, Stes-Maries-de-la-Mer and Nîmes. The first two lines, opened in 1892, were actually promoted by a company working salt deposits along the coast and that was always a staple traffic; the Nîmes line, with its branch to St Gilles, was an afterthought agreed amicably by Bouches du Rhône and Gard. Gard, whose sole line it was, went all progressive in 1920 and electrified its bit, Bouches du Rhône following somewhat tardily in 1930. Alas the saltworks proved fickle when a direct SNCF link from Trinquetaille was destroyed in 1944 and eventually substituted water transport for rail. With passenger traffic declining and deprived of its lifeblood, the system wilted and died, closing progressively between 1949 and 1958.

Arles was also the western terminus for part of the Bouche du Rhône's major concessionaire. Starting as the **CF des Bouches du Rhône** this and its sister concern the **CF Regionaux des Bouches du Rhône** were repossessed very early, becoming a Régie in 1913 and are still in existence as such. The Régie Départementale des Bouches du Rhône had a number of quite widely separated standard gauge branches including a very industrialised one east of Marseilles (Pas-des Lanciers – Martigues) which is still in partial use and a town to station tramway at le Ciotat which was electrified for part of its life and used ironclad cars appropriate to its shipyards destination. While we are on the subject of tramways the BdR also took over in 1920 an interurban electric tramway from Aix to Marseilles which lasted as such until 1948 when it was replaced by....a trolleybus line which in turn survived up to 1964. Marseilles itself had an extensive system of town trams, of which one line still runs to complement its metro and out to the west was a short-lived standard gauge line, from Miramas to Port-de-Bouc which was eventually supplanted by a PLM branch.

However, back to the **Régie Départementale des Chemins de Fer et Tramways Électriques des Bouches-du-Rhône,** as it became. It also had a vaguely interesting property depending, as they say, from the east bank of the Rhône a little to the north of Arles. Tarascon, which hosted one end of this, is an odd place with a station so horribly complicated that even the French made jokes about it. Not the least of the complications was that down in the middle of all the embankments lurked the insignificant terminus of a standard gauge light railway belonging to the resident départemental company. This was part of a two-branch setup (from Barbentane and Tarascon) which joined up way out east at Plan d'Orgon and went on to Orgon itself. Latterly, however, it ran only to St Rémy-en-Provence, a sleepy town dominated by its Roman remains (the Romans were prolific builders around here) which at least gave one something to look at between coming out on the daily goods and returning in the evening. Its only memorable feature in later years was the reserve motive power, a box-like Berliet railcar painted a garish yellow with a red stripe. It has been preserved. The line is one of the last remnants since after 1945 the Régie's services were steadily cut back, recognising an altered status by becoming the Régie Départementale des Transports des Bouches du Rhône in 1965. Parts of several lines nominally survived in 1999 but are really long industrial sidings with none of their former character.

Marseille is also a convenient place to leave the mainland for a short while since it is the main exit port for ferries to the island of **Corsica.** The island of Corsica is, indeed, technically mainland territory, with two départements now united under a région autonome but for all practical purposes it is self contained. Its extensive metre gauge system, eventually comprising three long lines and never quite completed, was of Intérêt général and built by the state. Operation was given to the CFD who regarded it as on a par with their Vivarais network and equipped it accordingly. The Mallets were four-coupled but otherwise the equipment was very similar and was modernised in the same way. The longest route was down the east coast to Porto-Vecchio with an unbuilt extension to Bonifacio in the far south, but this suffered geatly during the 1939-45 war and was never fully reopened; it closed completely in 1951. The other two, from Bastia to Ajaccio down on the west coast, and a branch off that line to Calvi are most fortunately still with us and are described in chapter 6.

Trams in the hills: A train of the Tramways des Alpes Maritimes on one of its scattered lines.   (FACS)

Eastward to the Italian frontier:
Var; Alpes-Maritimes; Alpes-de-Haute-Provence (Map p.316)

And so back to Arles and the last long line of the BdR which once set off east from here. If you then had time you could have travelled by non-PLM metals from here all the way to Nice with only a single change at Meyrargues where the BdR and our old friends the Sud-France faced each other across the main line station forecourt, at least until 1936 when the BdR closed down its passenger service.

On to Meyrargues, then. This was the westernmost outlier of the huge **CF du Sud de la France** which once owned three completely separate réseaux east of Toulon in the départements of Var and Alpes Maritimes and which, apart from various electric tramways, had a virtual monopoly in the area. Its main system, the line from Meyrargues via Draguignan to Nice **("Central Var" 211km)** and a subsequent line from Nice to Digne **("des Alpes" 151km)** in common with the former as far as Colomars, was conceived as a strategic system of Intérêt Général under the Plan Freyciney and, for some years, parts of the Central Var line were mixed standard and metre gauge. Reason prevailed, however, and the metre gauge soon reigned alone; for the same reasons, a projected strategic cross link between Draguignan and St Andre des Alpes on the Digne line was never built. The Sud-France, incidentally, had a passion for substantial stations and its termini at Nice and at Toulon were positively monumental, quite out of keeping with the status of a secondary railway. The history of the CF de Provence, as it became in 1925, is outlined in chapter 6.

From this double system, there briefly sprang a series of dead-end electrified metre gauge départemental lines of intérêt local, conceded from 1906 under the title of **Tramways des Alpes Maritimes (TAM)** and opened from 1909-on. One connected group linked Grasse and Veynes, on the Central Var line, with the coast at Cagnes; four others struggled west, east and north from the ligne des Alpes, some wth a common link over it between Pont-Charles-Albert and la Tinée; a seventh should have gone into the hills from the Central Var but was never completed. They were true mountain goats with curves down to 25m radius and gradients of up to 80mm/m; hence the use of electric power since steam would have got nowhere. Unfortunately the traffic, though originally quite substantial on the earlier lines, in no way justified the

As a complete contrast, the busy scene on the coal-hauling La Mure railway at its St. Georges de Commiers transhipment point.   (AUTHOR)

massive investment in earthworks, tunnels and viaducts required to traverse a very rugged country and was minimal on the final stretches opened as late as 1923-24. Power was provided at 6600V, 25cycles and equipment included some very neat four-wheeled power cars with matchng trailer stock. The lines closed successively between 1929 and 1932 as road competition increased.

So far as the Sud-France is concerned, that leaves its third major possession, the départemental **Réseau du Var** running east along the coast from Toulon towards Fréjus and St Tropez. It was the foundation line of the Sud-France, dating from 1889 and a mix of Intérêt Local railways and tramways so far as regulations were concerned. Up to the first war the réseau, a conventional steam tramway, appears to heve been reasonably profitable but afterwards, as road competition in the easy, well-populated region increased rapidly, it soon became deficitary. By 1925, when the Sud-France was replaced throughout its possessions by the Sté des CF de Provence, it was in trouble. The CF de Provence (CP) certainly did its best, providing an excellent series of Brissoneau et Lotz articulated railcars between 1934 and 1938 which substantially improved usage and reduced the loss. Regrettably the second war, especially events connected with the allied invasion of southern France in 1944, caused considerable damage and afterwards the département lost little time in changing over to road services. The lines closed in 1948, the modern stock being quickly snapped up by Spanish metre gauge lines where they worked well into the 1970s; one example is being preserved on the Vivarais.

The CP also modernised the Intérêt Général lines, first with some powerful bogie railcars of Renault's ABH series both before and after World War II, and in 1951 with four Brissoneau et Lotz diesel electric locomotives to replace its ageing 4-6-0Ts. Both lines would probably have continued indefinitely but many engineering works on the Meryrargues route were destroyed in 1944 and were never rebuilt; disconnected bits continued for a few years and then were abandoned. In contrast the Nice - Digne line was steadily developed as part of a major transport link from the Grenoble area, SNCF trains connecting with a special express serice, the "Alpes-Azur", at Digne. Eventually taken over by the CFTA in 1974, the line has survived despite all that political machinations and disastrous floods could throw at it; its present position is discussed in chapter 6.

The CP almost, but not quite, closes the chapter since there were two rural tramway systems which just about qualify for inclusion. To the west of Toulon, in Var, and closely connected to the city tramways, was the two-branched standard gauge réseau of the **Tramways Ouest-Varois.** It was built in 1914 but opened only in 1917, its Belgian-built cars having been diverted by the war so that it had to scrounge second-hand material from Lyon and Paris; quaintly this included a double-deck car which is said to have lost its top deck in a minor avalanche in the Ollioules gorge. After the war it struggled on for a time but was never profitable since it served a largely country area with feeble traffic. It succumbed finally about 1936.

Further east, based on Nice itself and extending both along the coast to Garavan near the Italian frontier, and inland over increasingly difficult country, to Grave-de-Peille, Levens, Bendejun and Sospel, was the départemental, or country, réseau of the metre gauge electric **Tramways de Nice et du Littoral (TNL).** Domengie virtually ignores this extensive system which in many ways paralleled that of the TAM; this is presumably because it was basically a passenger carrier and thus, technically, a suburban tramway. In practice it was analagous to the TAM and conceded under the same plan - seven lines to the TAM, seven to the TNL. As with the former, the routes were spectacular and heavily engineered, the traffic was, alas, minimal and the deficit was large. Some of them certainly conveyed wagonload goods behind special tractors and the Sospel line, for example was as spectacular and heavily engineered as any mountain railway....if only, from the tourist point of view, it still existed! Like the others, however, it died in the 1930s.

On the mainland there then remains but one minor line to chronicle but that had, for the writer at least, a peculiar distinction. Long before he knew much of France there was a mention in a boy's book (was it one of the Biggles series?) where our hero, fleeing from something, stood in a derelict station and observed "the rails of the old mountain railway to Monte Carlo dropping sharply between his feet" (Or similar words; the exact quotation has long gone, though the vivid impression remains). It was some years before it became clear that this had been one of France's few steam-operated rack railways, the **Monte Carlo - la Turbie**

And a relic of former glory among the big contenders: the old Gare du Sud at Nice on the CF de Provence.

(AUTHOR)

metre gauge Riggenbach line established in 1894. It was basically a straightforward climb from town to plateau but for some years it was complicated by a stretch in common with a short electric rack line from Place St Michel to the Riviera Palace hotel. Since this was on the Strub principle the complications must have been horrendous and the hotel line duly had a serious accident soon after opening; it survived only to the First World War. The main company did rather better and was under consideration for electrification in 1932 when the drive mechanism on one of its four-wheeled locomotives broke and it, too, had a horrible accident; the train descended out of control, smashimg through the lower station and resulting in two deaths. Services were terminated and, despite various negotiations lasting into the 1950s, were never restarted.

A gesture more

That should close the chapter but perhaps one should mention France's overseas possessions, several of which were considered integral départements of metropolitan France. Most had sugar-cane lines, Mauritius is thinking of reviving one with an old Corpet Louvet and La Réunion did so for a while so it can serve as an example. Although separated from the mainland by several thousand miles, this Indian Ocean island is still technically a French Département and had, for many years, a metre gauge secondaire running round much of its coastline (as indeed did other French possessions). The two lines of the Chemin de Fer et du Port de la Réunion from St Denis were opened by a private company as early as 1882; it promptly went bankrupt and was taken over by the state which ran it henceforth en régie. 1963 saw total closure . It has to be mentioned, since the last section from St Denis along the coast to la Possession was retained for emergencies until 1976 since it ran mainly in tunnel while the old coast road was susceptible to storm damage. In recent years a local group was been set up to conserve what remains - the track, one, formerly plinthed, 0-6-0T, and the surviving railcars with their trailers. It is not entirely in accord with the authorities at the time of writing but has hopes for the future.

Light Railways in Region Sud-Est

name	ident	gauge	km	lines	dates	cln		operators
dept Ain								
Ain, Régie Départementale des Twys de l' (new lines)	RTA	m/sg	0039	03	1920-1938	IL		RDT Ain new; new lines of RDTA
Ain, Twys de l'	TA	metre	0174	05	1911-1954	IL		Régie 1919
Bellegarde à Chézery, CFIL de	BC	metre	0020	01	1912-1937	IL		?
Gex à Ferney-Voltaire, Twy de	GF	metre	0010	01	1900-1932	Twy		Régie 1920
Haut-Rhône, CF du (Begnier - la Balme)	HR	sg	0035	01	1911-1939	IL		Régie 1920
Marlieux à Chatillon, CF de	MC	metre	0011	01	1879-1934	Twy		Régie 1919
Pont-de-Vaux à Fleurville, Twy de	PVF	metre	0005	01	1900-1936	Twy		Régie 1920
Sud-Est, CF Economiques du	ESE	metre	0183	07	1897-1933	IL	Jeancard	Régie 1920
dept Allier								
Allier, SE Réseau de l' (IG)	SE	metre	0088	01	1890-1950	IG	SE; (see Allier, SE (IL)	
Allier, SE Réseau de l' (IL)	SE	metre	0241	07	1887-1950	IL	SE; also Allier SE (IG) qv.	
Centre CF du (in Allier)	CFC	m/sg	0038	03	1910-1949	IL		SE 1928
Dompierre-s-Besbre a Lapalisse, CFIL de	CDL	metre	0043	01	1893-1939	IL		SE 1900
dept Alpes-Maritimes								
Alpes, Sud-France Réseau des	SF	metre	0350	02	1889-now	IG	Sud France;	CP 1925
Alpes-Maritimes, Twys des	TAM	metre	0146	06	1911-1931	Twy		CP 1925
Monte-Carlo à la Turbie, CF de	MCT	metre	0003	01	1894-1932	IL		rack line
dept Ardèche								
Ardèche, Twys de l'	TA	metre	0138	04	1910-1930	Twy ?		CFD 1922
Aubenas - Vals-les-Bains, Twy de	TAV	metre	0006	01	1898-1932	Twy		electric
dept Ardèche; Haute-Loire								
Vivarais, CFD Réseau du	CFD	metre	0203	04	1890-1968	IG	CFD;	CFV 1968
dept Bouches-du-Rhône								
Aix-en-Provence - Marseille, Twy de	AM	sg	0021	01	1903-1948	Twy		Régie 1921
Bouches du Rhône, CF des	BDR	sg	0177	06	1874-now	IL		Régie 1913
Camargue, CF de la	CFC	metre	0123	04	1892-1958	IL		Régie 1913
dept Corse								
Corse, CF de la	CC	metre	0363	03	1888-now	IG	CFD;	complex.
dept Côte-d'Or								
Dijon - Gevrey-Chambertin, ligne de	TED	metre	0010	01	1909-1953	Twy	TE Dijon;	Régie 1921
Côte d'Or, Sud-France Réseau de la	SFCO	metre	0342	06	1891-1948	Twy	Sud France;	Régie 1910
dept Doubs								
Andelot à Levier, CFIL d'	AL	metre	0033	01	1901-1953	IL	Laborie;	CFDoubs 1935; Régie 1945
Doubs, CF du	CD	metre	0101	03	1910-1953	IL	Laborie;	Régie 1947
Franche-Comté, CF Regionaux de	RFC	metre	0045	01	1905-1952	IL	Schlumberger;	Régie 1947
Herimoncourt, Twy de la vallée d'	TVH	metre	0020	03	1887-1932	Twy		
Pontarlier à Mouthe, Twy de	PM	metre	0030	01	1900-1950	Twy	Schlumberger;	CF Doubs 1927
dept Drôme								
Drôme, CF de la	CD	metre	0195	08	1893-1936*	IL		?; Régie 1922
Taulignan - Grignan - Chamaret, CF de	TGC	metre	0011	01	1907-1928	IL		Régie 1922
Valence-St Peray, Twy de	VSP	metre	0006	01	1927-1950	Twy		Régie 1927
dept Gard								
Aigue-Vives, (station - ville) Twy d'	TAI	60cm	0002	01	1892-1901	Twy		
dept Haute-Savoie								
Annecy – Thones, Twy d'	TAT	metre	0022	01	1898-1930	Twy		

Light Railways in Region Sud-Est continued...

name	ident	gauge	km	lines	dates	cln		operators
dept Haute-Savoie continued...								
Chamonix au Montenvers, CFIL de	CM	metre	0005	01	1906-now	Twy		rack line, now electrified
Mont-Blanc, Twy du	TMB	metre	0012	01	1909-now	Twy		rack line, now electrified
Salève, CF du	CFS	metre	0009	02	1892-1937	Twy		rack 3rd rail electric rack line
Savoie, CEN Réseau de la (Annemasse)	CEN	metre	0070	03	1892-1959	Twy		Empain
St Gervais - Vallorcine, ligne de	PLM	metre	0034	01	1901-now	Twy	PLM	Fell rail SNCF 1938
dept Isère								
Dauphiné, Voies Ferrées du	VFD	m/sg	0074	03	1894-now*	IL		VFDRégie 1920
Grenoble à Chapareillan, Twy de	TGC	metre	0043	01	1899-1947	Twy		VFDRégie 1930
Grenoble à Villard-de-Lans, Twy de	GVL	metre	0037	01	1911-1951	Twy	SGTE	
Isère, CEN Réseau de la	CEN	metre	0100	04	1891-1954*	IL	Empain;	SGTE 1902
Isère, Sud France Réseau de l'	TDI	metre	0119	04	1909-1937	IG	SF;	VFDRégie 1922 (TOD)
Isère, Twys de l' (then TOD)	TI	metre	0058	02	1899-1937*	Twy		SF 1902; régie 1922
Lyon, Cf de l'Est de	EL	sg	0105	03	1881-1998	IL		to SNCF
Lyon, Omnibus et Twys de (la Balme)	OTL	sg	0067	01	1907-1951*	Twy	OTL;	suburban line of Twys co.
St George de Commiers à la Mure...CF de	SGLM	metre	0069	03	1888-now	IG	Fives Lille;	state 1898;CFTA 1998
Voiron à St Béron, CF de	VSB	metre	0036	02	1894-1936	Twy		VFD Régie 1933; VFDRégie 1932
dept Jura								
Jura, CF Électriques du (Morez-la-Cure)	CFV	metre	0012	01	1921-1958	IL		Noyon-StCergue-Morez international line
Vicinaux, CF des, Réseau du Jura	CFV	metre	0193	05	1898-1950	IL	Empain;	see also Haute-Saône
dept Loire								
Centre CF du (in Loire)	CFC	metre	0116	04	1912-1939	IL		Régie 1928
Feurs - Panissières, Monorail de	MFP		0017	01 1895-1899	IL not opened			
Loire, CFD de la	CDL	metre	0120	07	1901-1938	IL		CFC 1911; Régie 1928
St Etienne, Firminy, Rive-de-Gier cfve	CFVE	metre	0046	03	1881-	Twy		interurban Twy.
St Gaulmier, CF de	CSG	metre	0003	01	1913-1954*	Twy		
dept Lozère								
Lozère, ligne de la	CFD	metre	0049	01	1909-1968	IG	CFD	
dept Nièvre								
Nièvre, CF de la	CFN	metre	0062	01	1901-1939	IL		SE 1902
Nièvre, SE Réseau de la	SE	metre	0150	04	1902-1939	IL	SE; plus CF de la Nievre (qv) 62km	
dept Puy-de-Dôme								
Gerzat - Maringues (Sté Batignolles)	GM	sg	0020	01	1889-1950	IL		Limagne 1903
Puy-de-Dôme, CF du	CPD	metre	0015	01	1907-1926	Twy		TCF; - centre rail systeme Hanscotte
Riom-Volvic (Sté Batignolles)	RV	metre	0018	01	1890-1936	IL		Limagne 1903
Vertaizon à Billom CF de	VB	sg	0009	01	1875-1964+	IL		Limagne1939; SNCF1965
dept Rhône								
Ampelpuis - St Vincent de Reins, CFIL d'	ASV	metre	0016	01	1907-1935	IL		Régie 1927
Beaujolais, CF du	CFB	metre	0094	03	1901-1938	IL	CCFT?;	Régie 1924
Fourvière et de l'Ouest Lyonnais, CF de	FOL	metre	0034	03	1886-1954	Twy		OTL 1911
Lyon à Neuville, Twy de	TLN	m/sg	0016	01	1890-1957	Twy		OTL 1922.to mg 1932
Rhône-et-Loire CF du (Messimy-St Symphorien-s-Coise)	CRL	metre	0031	01	1914-1935	IL		Régie 1926
Rhône, Saône-et-Loire CFD de	RSL	metre	0063	02	1911-1934	IL		Régie 1924
St Victor à Cours, CF de	SVC	sg	0013	01	1882-1969*	IL		
St Victor à Thizy CF Routier de	SVT	metre	0007	01	1882-1934*	IL		
Viricelles à St Symphorien et exts, Twy	VCS	metre	0010	01	1899-1933	Twy		

Light Railways in Region Sud-Est continued...

name	ident	gauge	km	lines	dates	cln		operators
dept Saône-et-Loire								
Saône-et-Loire CFIL de	SL	metre	0192	05	1901-1945*	IL		Régie 1924
Saône-et-Loire, CFD Réseau de	CFD	metre	0098	02	1893-1953*	IL	CFD;	3km to SE 1939
dept Savoie								
Aix-les-Bains - Mont-Revard, ligne de	AMR	metre	0009	01	1892-1936	Twy		rack PLM 1924
Mont Cenis Rly Co	MC	1067mm	0078	01	1868-1871	IL	ephemeral Fell line	
Moutiers - Brides-les-Bains, ligne de	MBB	metre	0006	01	1899-1930	Twy	VF des Alpes Fr.;	Régie 1911; electrobus 1930
Pont-de-Beauvoisin, Twy de	TPB	metre	0017	01	1897-1933	Twy	EL	
Pontcharra-La Rochette-Allevard, Twys de	PLA	m/sg	0017	02	1895-19??	Twy		
Savoie, Twys de	TS	60cm	0031	04	1892-1932	Twy		Régie 1914
dept Seine-et-Marne								
La Ferté-s-Jouarre - Montmirail, ligne	CFD	metre	0045	01	1889-1947	IL	CFD	
Lagny - Mortcerf, ligne de	CFD	metre	0017	01	1872-1933	IL		CFD 1896
Meaux-Dammartin, ligne de (CFY)	CFY	metre	0029	01	1910-1936	IL	Yonne CF;	CFD 1931
Montereau-Egreville-Château Landon	CFD	metre	0051	01	1888-1959	IL	CFD	
Seine-et-Marne, CFD Réseau de	CFD	metre	0116	03	1872-1959	IL		CFD from 1900; (all lines)
Seine-et-Marne, SE Réseau de	SE	metre	0131	04	1901-1965*	IL	SE	
Seine-et-Marne, Twys du Sud de	TSM	metre	0034	02	1899-1938	Twy		Verney 1925
dept Var								
Var, Sud-France Réseau du	SF	metre	0116	02	1889-1948	IL	Sud-France;	CF de Provence 1925
dept Vaucluse								
Orange - Buis-les-Baronnies, ligne d'	SE	metre	0041	01	1907-1952	IG	SE for PLM;	SE/SNCF 1938
dept Yonne								
Laroche-Migennes - L'Isle-Angély CFD	CFD	metre	0075	01	1887-1951	IL	CFD	
Yonne, CFD Réseau de l' ???	CFD	metre	0071	03	1925-1938	IL		CFD 1923
Yonne, CFIL de l'	CFY	metre	0180	06	1901-1956*	IL	CFY;	CFD 1923; CFG 1939

* latterly sections for freight only

Urban tram systems in Region Sud-Est

name	power	gauge	km	dates	dept
Aix-les-Bains	m	sg	0021	1896-1911	Savoie
Aubenas – Vals-les-Bains	e	metre	0006	1898-1932	Ardèche
Avignon	e	metre	0017	1901-1932	Vaucluse
Besançon	e	metre	0009	1897-1952	Doubs
Cannes	e	metre	0025	1899-1933	Var
Cannes-Grasse	e	metre		1915-1926	Var
Clermont-Ferrand	e	metre	0018	1890-1956	Puy-de-Dôme
Dijon	e	metre	0013	1895-1961	Côte-d'Or
Fontainbleau	e	metre	0012	1896-1953	Seine-et-Marne
Grenoble	e	m/sg	0101	1897-1952	Haute-Savoie
Grenoble TGC	e	metre	0043	1899-1947	Haute-Savoie
Le Puy	e	metre		1896-1914	Haute-Loire
Lyon	hme	m/sg	0347	1880-1957	Isère
Marseille	hme	metre	0177	1876-now	Bouches-du-Rhône
Melun	e	metre		1901-1914	Seine-et-Marne
Nice et du Littoral	he	metre	0144	1878-1953	Alpes-Maritimes
Nimes	he	sg	0014	1880-1950	Gard
Roanne	e	metre	0012	1901-1935v	Loire
Saint-Chamond	e	metre	0002	1906-1931	Loire
St Etienne	me	metre	0084	1881-1949	Loire
Toulon OV	e	sg	0023	1917-1936v	Var
Toulon STVG	he	sg	0067	1886-1955	Var
Toulouse	he	sg	0089	1905-1957	Haute Garonne
Vichy	m	metre		1895-1925	Loire

CHAPTER 11
Regional Reprises 5: Région Sud-Ouest

Introduction to the region (Map p.317)

The Region Sud-Ouest, at least as delineated by Domengie's boundaries, did not really form a geographical whole, being bounded rather by the territories of the old Paris-Orléans and Midi railway companies. Its topography was very varied, its light railways and their operators often spread over more than one département while two of its départements, Cher and Charente, sit more comfortably with other regions. South and south west of Paris in topographical terms were first the rolling, fertile plains of the Beauce – often called France's grain basket, although sugar beet was equally important both for the economy and for railways. Stretching thence down the eastern flank was the western side of the central massif, rugged upland country terminating at its southern end in the Carcassonne Gap between Mediterranean and Atlantic coasts. Down the western coast and along the Mediterranean were easy, vine-growing regions quickly colonised by both standard and metre gauge and along the bottom were the high Pyrenées, again a difficult region for minor railways, although they certainly tried...while down the centre was a collection of rural départements, lush rolling country very lightly populated in the 19th century and hence not a very good place to run light railways – it is a characteristic of the region that many départemental systems came late, were never finished and closed early; the 1930s were a graveyard of hopes.

Within the geographical frame, there was another, operational, one. The region had a surprising number of electrified lines and systems largely, though not entirely, inspired by a single financial grouping, that of Messrs Giros and Loucheur who left their own "stamp" on widely separated lines. Other indigenous groupings, if they may be so called, were confined mainly to the Verney, Tartary and Jeancard groups, all of whom we have already met in the neighbouring Région Ouest; the Groupe Ortal, a family business which had a finger in various pies at different times but came down latterly to running one isolated standard gauge branch; the big manufacturing concern, the Societé des Constructions de Battignoles which eventually gave way to the Societé pour Construction et Exploitation des Transports Auxiliares (SCETA), virtually a subsidiary of SNCF and its predecessors; and the Cie des Voies Ferrées Départementales du Midi (VFDM) depending from the Giros et Loucheur group. The VFDM was, for no fault of its own, an unfortunate concern in spite of being sponsored and supported by the main line CF du Midi. It acquired, or was conceded, a variety of projects in no less than four départements; in addition, it took over and ran several existing systems but they all went sour and virtually nothing survived the second world war. Otherwise, there were both the SE and the CFD, both of whom had considerable interests in the region; indeed the CFD actually took up its first serious concession here, in the département of Indre-et-Loire. The main line companies as usual were also active almost despite themselves, occasionally getting their arms twisted by the state to promote lines seen as of strategic value although they usually passed their concessions on to smaller operators on a fermière basis or subsidised what effectively became subsidiary companies.

The northern cluster: Loiret, Loir-et-Cher, Indre, Indre-et-Loire, Vienne and Cher (Map p.318)

So how to start? Logically one starts wth the central cluster of rural départements and their equally rural – and very typical – systems. At the northern tip of the region, based largely around the old city of Orléans, was the Département of Loiret. It had one unusual isolated outlier to the north in the well-known **Tramway de Pithiviers à Toury** which survived long enough to become cherished by British enthusiasts. In itself this was an oddity. Dating from 1892 and actually built by the département, it was one of three lines which the Decauville company promoted as a showcase for its 60cm gauge products. As usual, alas, Decauville failed to make a go of it and it quite quickly became a régie départementale which it remained for the rest of its surprisingly long life; indeed its direct operation by the départemental Highways Department actually preceded the official concept of Régies and so may be considered a pioneer in that field. It had an

OUTARVILLE — La Gare

The most famous 60cm gauge line of all was the Tramway de Pithiviers à Toury in Loiret. Here a typical early Decauville Mallet poses at an equally typical wayside station.

(FACS)

505. Chambon (L.-et-C.) — La Gare du Tramway

More typical of the northern rural départements, however, were the bucolic Tramways de Loir-et-Cher with their narrow bicabines and shacklike stations.

(FACS)

assured traffic in agricultural products, especially sugar beet to the refineries at either end. As a result of the first world war it was able to reequip itself cheaply in the 1920s and when the Calvados system failed it acquired a couple of quite reasonable petrol electric bogie railcars. Passenger traffic even survived into the early 1950s and seasonal freight kept it going for another ten years...In the last resort, however, it was small (33km main line), isolated and non-standard so when its neighbouring sugar refineries went over to road transport in 1964 it died immediately - though it bequeathed much of its usable stock to tourist railways or private collectors and a short portion became base for one of the longer-lasting preservation operations described in chapter 6.

The main pride of the département, however, was its metre gauge **Tramways du Loiret,** four roadside lines radiating from Orleans city and at times wandering into the neighbouring départements of Cher and Loir-et-Cher. Built to the "three 15s" formula, this was a tramway of the lightest type and its short career, from 1905 to 1934, was typical of many such systems: its tortuous roadside locations, its restricted loading gauge of only 2 metres and its miniscule Corpet Louvet 0-6-0Ts made it incapable of meeting road competition despite a half-hearteed foray into railbuses in the 1920s. Its only notable feature was its use of de Rechter radial axles rather than bogies on some of its coaching stock.

The same story can be repeated with variations all down the central corridor. Immediately south west of Loiret was Loir-et-Cher, an even more rural area which embraced light railways over-enthusiastically. The Département eventually had no less than 438km of metre gauge track straggling through the countryside around its centre of Blois, comprising two largely independent systems let to different operators. The nine branch **Tramways de Loir-et-Cher (TLC)** had some excuse, being started as early as 1888 under the Carel et Fouché group. Again, apart from a line from Blois to St Aignan actually granted to the Paris-Orléans comany and technically of Intérêt Général, but hurriedly dumped on the TLC, it was largely roadside, mostly to the three 15s formula and wildly uneconomic from the start. Stock was typical tramway, even though its Tubize-built tram-type locomotives had only one driving position (not uncommon on rural lines) and its only railcars were unusual – six boxy but double-ended machines by Campagne who are usually thought of as draisine manufacturers. Like the Loiret concern it died quickly in 1934 despite investing in two diesel locomotives, but even then it outlived the second group of lines. These, the **Tramways**

98. - VOUVRAY (I.-et-L.). - La Gare des Tramways

Other départements were not much more imposing: the Twys d'Indre-et-Loire at its Vouvray depot.   (FACS)

Électriques de Loir et Cher, lasted only from 1913 to 1933 and there is a case for saying they should never have been built in the first place. Just why did the département, suddenly, in 1910, approve construction of a separate group of electrified rural lines which could never pay their capital cost - bucolic rambling routes with an average of only three or four trains daily but all the expense and complication of overhead wiring, a massive generating plant and sub-stations to provide the line voltage of 6000 AC at 25 cycles ...the answer appears to be that they were seduced by the concessionaire's offer to provide electric power to villages en route as a by-product (it didn't work of course. Having got the double concession he then proceeded to charge almost extortionate fees for supplying the tramways with power). Even experiments with a lightweight, single-ended car in the 1920s could not save the Tramways Électriques de Loir-et-Cher and, after repurchase by the département in 1933, they were summarily closed and their routes turned over to buses.

South and east from Loir-et-Cher is a cluster of three départements which might well be taken together – from west to east they are Indre-et-Loire; Indre; and Cher to the east of that. All had substantial systems and their operators included not only the Verney and Tartary groups as might be expected around here but also the CFD and the SE. They were all knit together by the continuous 190 kilometres of the metre gauge Intérêt Général **CF du Blanc à Argent** which is fully described in chapter 6. Suffice to say here that it started over in the north of Cher, curved southwestward to its headquarters at Romorantin in Loir-et-Cher and then curved back into Indre for the rest of its route to le Blanc near the Vienne border and is a line of such importance and complexity that it is still, in part, with us though now reduced to a shadow of its former self. It linked no less than six standard gauge junctions in its course from north east to south west: Argent, Salbris, Romorantin, Gièvres, Buzançais and le Blanc. There or en route it also linked up with no less than five départemental companies in the areas we are considering. It met the SE's Cher system at Argent itself; the Tramways du Loiret at Brinon-s-Sauldre between Argent and Salbris; the Tramways de Loir-et-Cher at Romorantin; the CFD's Indre-et-Loire system at Ecueillé; the Tramways de l'Indre at Valençay and again at le Blanc itself.

GRAÇAY (Cher) — La Gare

And the Tramways de l'Indre at Graçay, wih a conventional Pinguely 0-6-0T. (FACS)

In its younger days even the CF du Blanc à Argent could look quite casual, with its little 0-6-0Ts – though the track was noticeably better! (FACS/Chapuis Collection)

Also largely in Indre were, quite naturally, the **Tramways de l'Indre,** a fiefdom of the Tartary group. They had three detached lines, with a short branch off one, were conceived in the early 1900s and might have had extensions if the war had not intervened. Their roadside lines were not particularly memorable, unless it was that they used Pinguelys rather than Corpets and were later blessed, or cursed, with some of M.Tartary's home made railbuses - which they quickly swapped for De Dions. The last line closed just before the second world war. This one actually ended at Vierzon in the neighbouring Cher département where it met an outlier of that département's system, a west-east line actually run by the Jeancard group under their **CF Economiques des Charentes** banner. This isolated possession, from Vierzon to the resoundingly named Neuilly-Moulin-Jamet, was only opened in 1914 but was surprisingly little disturbed by the war. Afterward it suffered rather more and had to be bought back by the département in 1929 and allocated to the TI as an extension of their line to Vierzon. It closed in 1938-39 and the track was lifted for use elsewhere. Most of Cher, however, was occupied by the big SE which had both Intérêt Local and Intérêt Général concessions there. Its réseaux formed part of the SE's massive "SE Réseau du Centre" which covered both Cher and the neighbouring département of Allier (which is in Domengie's South East region) and their history is best related there.

Indre-et-Loire, on the opposite side of Indre, was also largely in the hands of a big concern, in this case the two-cluster **CFD Réseau d'Indre-et-Loire.** Indeed it was the CFD's first real concession. Its four lines, of Intérêt Local, surrounded the prefecture of Tours but never actually reached it, although one did get access from Fondettes via the town tramways. This was a complex arrangement, the CFD being physically linked to one of three long suburban lines of Tours Tramways and freight was hauled over the latter to the PO interchange in Tours; passengers either changed to an electric tram or on occasion stayed put, coaches apparently being hauled into town. Certainly in World War 2. CFD railcars penetrated into the centre. The CFD lines were formally divided into the Réseau Nord and the Réseau Sud, the north one being conceded in 1882, only a year after the CFD was formed, and opened in 1885; the southern system followed in 1889. They were always favoured by their parent, receiving the first of the really effective Billard railcars (501-03) generally known as "Porcinets" owing to their very pig-like snouts, and later supplemented with some more streamlined cars from the same firm. The Neuillé-Pont Pierre workshops were even chosen to build the first series of diesel locomotives although, alas, the lines were closed in 1949 before

Regional oddities included two close together: The 60cm gauge Tramways de Royan train pauses on its journey through town to the seaside.   (AUTHOR'S COLLECTION)

the last one was finished. The département also had two isolated standard gauge lines originally run for it by main line companies – **St Maure (station to town)** which was operated by the PO from its inception in 1913 to its closure in 1945 and a branch of a branch from **Ligre-Rivière to the old walled town of Richelieu** which is now a tourist operation after a spell under CFD auspices. Slightly confusingly, it was PO and then SNCF right up to 1950 when the CFD took it over as some compensation for losing its metre gauge network. CFD promptly introduced diesel traction but, even so, had to discontinue passenger services in 1960 and gave up altogether in 1972. A local "régie municipale" then took over for goods under the name Régie Ferroviaire Richelaise and more recently the tourist operation "Trains à Vapeur de Touraine" has operated steam passenger trains in season.

That leaves us with Vienne, to the south of Indre-et-Loire and abutting on Indre. Vienne, again, had one of those "typical" rural systems. After more or less succeeding with a shortish steam-worked line near Poitiers in the 1890s, the **Tramways de la Vienne** conceded to the predecessors of the Groupe Verney, it plunged heavily and disastrously with the three branched CF Economiques du Poitou (a Groupe Verney concession) as late as 1914. With minimal traffic, a network not completed until after the war and roadside track served by light Corpet, Louvet 0-6-0Ts it never had a chance and closed in 1934.

The last of the big metre gauge systems: Haute-Vienne, Corrèze, Dordogne and ...a couple of empty départements, Creuse and Cantal (Map p.319)

Vienne's next door neighbour to the east, Haute-Vienne, was different...Haute Vienne thought it through properly and decided on a substantial system of electrified lines radiating from the préfecture of Limoges. The **CFD de Haute-Vienne (CFDHV)** opened from 1911-on. With difficult country to cover and availability of hydro electric power for its two generating stations this could be seen as a sensible decision, as was the choice of high tension current - 10,000V at 25hz/s. With over 340km and eight branches, the réseau was substantial by any standards. The equipment, comprising excellent 4-wheeled and bogie power cars with matching trailers and goods stock, running on rail of between 20 and 35kg/m was also substantial and the system survived two wars only to be closed in 1949 because the equipment was worn out and the highways department wanted to widen the roads. It is a pity, although natural, that it is remembered not for its benefits but for a poignant relic; in 1944 the SS panzer division "Das Reich", struggling toward the Normandy front, was held up by maquis action. In revenge, a unit surrounded the little village of Oradour-sur-Glane and massacred all its inhabitants; a CDHV tram was actually turned back only minutes before and escaped. After the war the deserted village was preserved as a memorial and, among its contents, were the rails and overhead wires of the former tramway.

Immediately south of Haute-Vienne was Corrèze which contained both the other major system of Intérêt Général and a widely dispersed but completely hopeless set of rural steam tramways. The **PO Lignes de Corrèze (POC)** have been fully described in Chapter 2; the **Tramways de la Corrèze (TC)** were intended to fill in the gaps. The TC was sad. The first concessionaires gave up before they started and the four separated lines with a single short branch off one were not complete until 1913. War broke out, a projected second réseau was hastily dropped (traffic on the first was minimal) and all but part of one line were closed in 1932. The survivor, from Neuvic d'Ussel to St Bonnet-Avalouze, kept going partly because it traversed very difficult country, partly because it was run by the concessionaire of the PO Corrèze, partly because, thanks to the latter, its trains could run through to Tulle. By dint of inheriting railbuses from the POC and concentrating its surviving Piguet 0-6-0Ts it lasted right up to 1959; the département even bought two narrow-bodied Billards at third hand from Pas de Calais but the track by then was almost worn out. Its great glory was a fine example of the Gisclard suspension bridge at La Roche-Taillade which still exists.

Now those Billards were narrow bodied because they came originally from the Dordogne, which is west of Corrèze and south of Vienne. It started off in 1886 with granting the Groupe Empain the three-branched **CF du Perigord (CFP)** radiating from its major town of Perigueux and supplemented this with four more scattered lines, leased to the **Tramways de la Dordogne** in 1911; three of them started from outer termini of the CFP. The first group had tramway-type locomotives, the second had conventional Pinguely 0-6-0Ts but both were largely roadside and neither prospered. As early as 1921, the Département took back control and amalgamated them into a **Régie des CF Départementaux de la Dordogne.** They might well have

...where it connected with the 60cm gauge (née metre) lines through the Fôret de la Coubre with their boxy draisines.
(FACS)

191

Over in the centre were lines substantial…such as the PO Lignes de Corrèze, here fulfilling its function by steam as late as 1960. (AUTHOR)

…and insubstantial: The Tramways de la Corrèze, rather uncomfortably gracing Platform 1 at Tulle SNCF station.

(D. TREVOR ROWE)

closed in the 1930s but in 1925-26 the big CFD concern took over and, while closing down some portions, modernised the rest with no less than twelve identical Billard A80D railcars; it was the original loading gauge which dictated their narrow width of 2.20m. With their help the remainder survived until 1949 when road competition forced final closure. Most of the modern railcars went to the PO Corrèze, the rest to the CGL in Pas-de-Calais.

Finally among the big spenders there was the Département of Charente, to the west of Dordogne, but it was so inextricably mingled with its neighbours of Charente-Inférieure and Deux Sevres that it is better dealt with in the Region Ouest. The other two départements which fall naturally into this cluster were Creuse and Cantal but they were barren. Creuse, it is true, thought vaguely about a départemental system in 1907 and got as far as having two longish routes declared as Intérêt Général and conceded to that reluctant suitor the CF de Paris – Orléans (PO) but this was in 1912 and they somehow never got built. Cantal never got even that far, just a half-promise of a POC extension east from Argentat to Drugeac-Salers.

Smaller systems and nil returns: Lot-et-Garonne; Lot; Tarn-et-Garonne... plus Gers and Aveyron for luck. (Map p.320)

Besides the prolific départements already mentioned, the region had a plethora of smaller systems, and the further south you got the smaller and more isolated they tended to become. Smallish départements such as Gers and Aveyron even had no serious minor lines of their own, relying on the main line companies and on occasional tongues of other peoples' systems poking into their area – although Aveyron did have an urban tramway, at Rodez, with elegant bogie cars. Others had fair-sized systems but not particularly memorable ones: **Tramways de Tarn-et-Garonne and de Lot-et-Garonne, Tramways de l'Aude** and others trundled their standard 0-6-0Ts and four-wheeled stock along the roadside until the deficit got too great (often three or four times the receipts) or road competition got too fierce; a few diversified into road transport. In this little group, Tarn-et-Garonne and Lot-et-Garonne each had their sleepy roadside metre gauge systems, both very similar. **The Tramways de Tarn-et-Garonne** were conceded to those MM Fougerolle who had fingers in several light railway pies and had a central star of three lines based on Montauban with three other isolated branches, totalling some 182km. Opened in stages from 1913 to 1927 (the war intervened, of course, and most of the stock was requisitioned), they were always deficitary and lasted only to 1933. The **Tramways de Lot-et-Garonne,** originally granted to a local who failed to make a go of them and then passed to the Groupe Ortal, eventually came under the latter's VFDM banner in 1923. They dreamt of a Réseau of some 325km but eventually managed just 130 and lasted only from 1911 to 1933 with interruptions (and their last years, ironically, were devoted to carrying roadstone). Both were mainly roadside, had a mixed bag of light 0-6-0T locomotives and four-wheeled stock and each had a single Horme-et-Buire railcar which caused them pain and grief.

Lot had only the tiny metre gauge steam tramway on its northern border from **Bretonoux-Biars to St Céré,** otherwise known as the **Tramways de Quercy.** Opened in 1907 it was, oddly for such a short line, greatly affected by the war and was turned into a "Régie Départementale" in 1924 - surely the shortest on record. Originally steam-worked, it was always in motive power trouble and finally closed in 1934 because both its railcars had broken down... Aveyron never had a real light railway; it is mentioned only because it was home to that early industrial line, from Salles-la-Source to Mondalazac, which sparked off all the gauge controversy and because it did have that small urban tramway, at the hill town of Rodez...and Gers? Gers, alas had nothing at all in the way of light railways of its own, just playing partial host to a couple of branches from other départements. Even the main line Midi company found it too difficult to conquer and left various projects umcompleted.

The west coast and other digressions: Gironde and Landes; Basses and Hautes Pyrenées.
Standard gauge in the south-west: Gironde and Landes (Map p.321)

To the west of the lost départements, however, lay two of the three major standard gauge systems in the region, sprawling directly inland from the Atlantic coast, generally southwards from Bordeaux with one outlier. These were the **SE's Réseau de la Gironde** and the complex of companies which fused in 1916 to become the **Cie des Voies Ferrées des Landes (VFL):** both have had excellent individual histories written about them for those who are seriously interested.

Even in outline, the history of these lines is complex. Although the Gironde ones appear physically connected on the map, in truth a number of companies was involved and the first route was actually constructed under the 1865 act, so was a pioneer. This was the **Cie du CF de Nizan à St Symphorien,** which, from 1873, ran west from Nizan on the Midi main line and later extended itself southward to Sore and, under the 1880 act, on to Luxey in the Landes département in 1886. To complete this story, although out of sequence, another standard gauge line, promoted by the Ortal group, was opened in 1906 south from **Luxey to Mont de Marsan.** It became a régie départementale in 1951 and lasted until 1964. Meanwhile a long semi-circular route from St Symphorien west and north to Lesparre, above Bordeaux, plus a couple of branches, had been authorised in 1877, followed shortly by a detached, but still standard gauge line on the north bank of the river Gironde (the "ligne du Blayais"). Alas neither concessionaire was able to proceed and in 1881 the département, in desperation, asked the SE to take on the whole thing. It duly did so, assimilating the Nizan - Sore company in 1888 and adding a short branch at Lacanau. The final standard gauge route, a spur off the **CF du Medoc (CM)** from Margaux to the SE's Bordeaux branch remained in other hands and in any case closed in 1933. (The Medoc, bought out by the Midi in 1912, was largely of Intérêt Général but had several Intérêt Local branches conceded by the département).

Back at the ranch (or rather the main line of the CF du Midi south to Hendaye) several small companies in the Landes had developed standard gauge branches off that main line. Based around the former **Cie du CF du Born et du Marensin** (1909) which changed its name to suit, they included also the **CFIL du Département des Landes** (1888) and the **CF de Soustons à Leon** (1904); in 1916, they effectively fused to become the Voies Ferrées des Landes. Unlike the Gironde system they were largely separated branches off the Midi route to Hendaye frontier although run from a common HQ at Dax.

All the standard gauge systems bar the **Margaux-Castelnau** (itself taken over by the CF du Born et du Marensin from the CF du Medoc) modernised themselves from the 1930s-on and survived World War 2. Although passenger services for the most part disappeared in the 1950s and 60s, both main systems survived in part for goods traffic up to recent years and one branch of the Landes hosted a tourist operation. All had various oddities - the Gironde kept in reserve up to the 1970s a rake of eight wheel parallel axle (ie: not bogie) coaches from the English Metropolitan Railway and in 1946 acquired a set of ten ex-US Army General Electric bogie diesel electric locomotives – several of which survive. Otherwise they were just reasonably trafficked secondary lines serving their communities and hauling the timber provided by the pinewoods through which they ran. Yet there was one independent standard gauge oddity in the Gironde that deserves mention. This was the short **CF de la Teste à Cazaux Lac** down near the terminus of a Midi branch from Bordeaux to the coast at Arcachon. This, originating in 1874 under the 1865 rules, was the first, and eventually the last concession operated by the Ortal group which took it over from its bankrupt concessionaire in 1886. Ortal made it pay up to about 1930, largely because it served a military base....and when he started getting back into deficit the département promptly ceded the whole thing to the army who still, effectively, run most of it for their own purposes. It was always mildly intriguing partly because of the security aspect and partly because of its two antiquated Corpet 0-4-0Ts with their huge spark arresters which featured in photos and lasted until 1955.

Other digressions on the way south

While we are in this area perhaps one should mention four other oddities:
* The **Tramway de Bordeaux à Cadillac** a 32km-long metre gauge steam line running south from that city which somehow evaded the attentions of the Bordeaux electric tramways (TEOC). It was conceded to M.Fougère, opened in 1897 and had a good suburban passenger traffic well into the 1930s, when road competition caused a sudden catastrophic decline so that it closed in 1935. It was run throughout its life mainly by a set of conventional Tubize/Blanc Misseron 0-6-0Ts, prided itself on having vestibuled coaches (although they were otherwise primitive four-wheelers) and never invested in railcars.

In the forgotten Rural depths there were forgotten rural tramways – The Tramways de Tarn-et-Garonne were typical.

(FACS)

* **The Tramways à Vapeur de la Chalosse et du Bearn.** This was basically a perfectly normal metre gauge affair on the borders with Basses Pyrenées with three branches; two, (to Peyrehorade and to Orthez via Amou) were centred on Dax the third, longer one joined Amou to Aire-s-l'Adour where it linked with a line of the Pau-Oloron-Mauleon. It had Corpet Louvet 0-6-0Ts and some quite elegant bogie coaches. It came late, in 1909, had ideas of expansion but ran into financial difficulties and, after a disastrous war, declined rapidly during the 1920s and early 1930s; its last freight service ran in 1937 and that was the end.

* France's only public railway built to the 75cm gauge – which was one of those theoretically allowed by the 1880 rules. Only 12km long, the **Cie des CF Economiques Forestiers des Landes** ran between Roquefort and Lencouaq-Jourets and dated only from 1907. Its gauge, so it is said, was determined by the two light 0-4-0Ts picked up second-hand; its traffic was always feeble and after 1918 it slowly dwindled away, closing finally in 1934.

* The various seaside tramways around the Arcachon peninsula, mainly grouped around its southern tip at **Cap Ferret.** These seem originally to have been purely local enterprises which slipped through the regulatory net and (apart from a forestry line to the north) were based around the up-and-coming holiday resort of Belisaire on the sheltered eastrn side. The peninsula, in the 1920s, appears to have been somewhat similar to our own Dungeness spit apart from being sand rather than shingle, with a lengthy scatter of holiday cottages and fishermen's huts, but all these habitations were in the sheltered Bassin d'Arcachon while the dunes and beaches were out to the west where the Atlantic breakers rolled in. The first tentative horsedrawn lines appeared before 1914 and the SE thought the area promising enough to propose a standard gauge branch down from its Réseau de la Gironde although it never came to anything. The 1920s saw an explosion of holiday developments and two mechanically powered lines of 800mm gauge, from Belisaire to the Pointe – the peninsula tip – and from Belisaire across to the Atlantic. They were powered by a delightful collection of home-made machines including some

Fordson tractor conversions and used mainly baladeuses as might be expected. Continuing delevopment and road demands closed them in 1936 and that seemed to be the end.

Not so. In 1952 the Belisaire-Ocean line was virtually reborn as the **Tramway de Cap Ferret** which was never a historic line but a 60cm gauge tourist ralway built by a man called Milet who felt there was a need and it might be fun... It ran, and still runs in summer, down on the Arcachon peninsula joining town to sea; it has quaint industrial diesels lightly disguised as steam locomotives; it inherits its history from the network of previous similar lines in the area. It is thus the grandparent of French tourist railways and so worth remembering.

So what else is worth considering in any detail along the western seaboard? : certainly the electric lines. The Region was particularly rich – if that is the word – in electric light railways, most of which were wildly deficitary from the start and lasted for comparatively short periods. We have already encountered two major players, in Loir-et-Cher and Haute Vienne. Most of the remainder were short isolated lines or unfinished systems which still present plenty of historical loose ends. The Gironde had two – the two-route tramway from **Bordeaux to Camarsac and to Beychac,** and the **Tramways Électriques du Libournais.** The choice of electric traction for the former was natural since it was operated by the Tramways Électriques et Omnibus de Bordeaux (TEOB); just why the latter, two rambling lines out in the hinterland, settled on overhead wire collection at 6,600V, 16 2/3hz, is not quite so clear...perhaps the fact that Ortal had a finger in both pies had something to do with it. In any case, both systems appear to have served their areas satisfactorily until the stock and equipment wore out, when they were turned over to road transport.

The western Pyrenées and their light railways: Basses Pyrenées; Hautes Pyrenées (Map p.321)

Down the coast, in Basses Pyrenées (now Pyrenées Atlantiques), however, the twin resorts of Bayonne and Biarritz had since the late 19th century been joined by two alternative secondary routes. These were the metre gauge **Bayonne-Lycée-Biarritz (BLB)** opened in 1888 and the standard gauge **Bayonne-**

105. - SAINT-CÉRÉ. - Départ de l'Autobus pour Figeac

While the tiny train from Bretonaux-Biars to St Ceré in Lot was clearly so insignificant that the photographer didn't even wait for it to couple up as he concentrated on the new roadbus. (AUTHOR'S COLLECTION)

Nearer the coast there were minor electric lines...here a motor fourgon of the Tramways du Libournais shows the relative importance of passengers and parcels! (FACS)

Anglet-Biarritz (BAB), opened in 1877, the BAB having the distinction of using double-deck coaches with locomotives which sported improbably long chimneys to carry their smoke away. The BLB, essentially a suburban passenger line, electrified itself in 1912 and in 1922 the BAB followed suit, converting to metre gauge for easier interworking with both the BLB and the VFDM's Réseau Basque (see below). In 1944 both were bought in by the Département and operated as a régie départementale until their closures in 1952 and 1948 respectively.

At both Bayonne and Biarritz, both lines connected from 1922 with another electric metre gauge system, the **VFDM Réseau Basque.** The VFDM, coming comparatively late into the field, was much enamoured of electric lines for which the Pyrenéen rivers were expected to provide a convenient source of electric power. This system, originally conceded to a Belgian syndicate in 1910, became the predecessor of the VFDM, reorganising itself under that name in 1913-14. How many enthusiasts now realise that the Spanish "El Topo" from Hendaye south to St Sebastien had its origins in this (unsuccessful) Belgian effort which was soon replaced by a French group, and how many realise that, from 1924 to 1939, Hendaye Gare was also served by a VFDM line down the coast from Bayonne - which in itself stemmed from a 60cm gauge horse tramway linking Hendaye Gare and Casino? Alas the system was typical of the unfortunate VFDM. No sooner had it planned a grand design than the first war broke out. Its Hendaye line, and a branch inland from St Jean de Luz to Ascain and Sare, with a rack line to la Rhûne, were not finally achieved until 1924 and a projected line from Ascain north east to Peyrehorade on the Landes border was never finished. Inland a projected inland system based on St Jean Pied du Port (no relation to St Jean de Luz) never got beyond incomplete earthworks save for a short stretch down to Mendive which was used as an industrial siding.

A short digression while we are in the Basses-Pyrénées (or Pyrenées-Atlantiques as they are latterly known): although not electric, the département also had two other secondary metre gauge groupings which remained independent and which tangled with the electric lines at various points. First was that conventional, steam-worked **Tramways de la Chalosse et du Béarn** already mentioned, which was really based in the Landes but which was conceded a Pyrenéean réseau that was never fully completed..... For

105 ARCACHON- Côte d'Argent - Le Tram conduisant de Bélisaire à l'Océan   *Edit. N. G.*

Even more minor was the 80cm gauge Tramway de Belisaire à l'Ocean, precursor of the present Tramway de Cap Ferret.

completeness it is mentioned again here since its three lines, based on Dax and Orthez, would have met the VFDM and the POM (see below) at several points.

The other was the accurately named **CF de Pau-Oloron-Mauleon (POM)** which flowered briefly around the inland town of Pau between 1901 and 1931. Classed officially as a tramway under the 1880 act, it had two separated groups of lines. One, based on Oloron, ran to Mauleon and to Sauveterre-de-Bearn where it should have connected to an unbuilt line of the Chalosse et du Bearn company. The other ran four branches centred on Pau and later took over the only completed part of another CduB line. The whole system fell into the hands of the big Societé Générale des Transports départementaux (SGTD) in 1929 and, since the latter was primarily a bus operator, had been summarily closed by 1931.

However, back to the electrics. South of the Landes, the ground started rising towards the high Pyrénées and these, although generally inimical to railways of any description, did appear to favour the use of electric power if railways of any sort there were to be; hydro electric power was available and electric cars could surmount the formidable grades easier than asthmatic steam locomotives. Hence, all across the French side of the Pyreneen range, tentative attempts were made to comquer the terrain and the VFDM was, naturally, involved as were two of France's comparatively few rack lines. These were that VFDM construction from **St Ignace to the summit of la Rhûne,** already mentioned, and a similar line further east from **Luchon to Superbagnères** which was actually in a dangling bit of Haute-Garonne and, for most of its life, was run by the Département. Both were electric, used 4-wheeled locomotives pushing bogie coaches, were purely touristic and have been linked by a very detailed history ("Les Cremaillères Jumelées des Pyrenées"). The Luchon line foundered in 1966 when the equipment was very run down and the département decided not to spend money on renewals. The line to la Rhûne, however, is still very much with us, now energetically administered by our old friends the CFTA and sporting new, Swiss style, rack railcars.

Hautes Pyrenées, because of the terrain, never had much light railway trackage but, east and south of the famous spa town of Lourdes, there were two minor systems. Most northerly and little known were the two lines of the **Tramways Électriques de la Bigorre** from Lourdes to Bigorre and on, via Gripp, to the seasonal resort of Artigues. Again they came late, the first section not opening until 1914 and the remainder a year later. It was an unfortunate set-up, the company having to give way to a Midi filiale, the **Sté des Voies Ferrées d'Intérêt Local des Pyrenées (VFP)** in 1918, having its depot, with most of the stock, burnt down in 1921 and sustaining a succession of fatal accidents owing to the terrain and, one suspects, quality of the infrastructure. The Artigues extension was closed in 1924, the remainder, despite considerable realignments, following in 1932-34.

To the south of Lourdes, at the end of a Midi branch to Pierrefittes, was another two-line group which the writer would dearly have liked to have seen in its prime. This was the **CF de Pierrefitte à Cauterets et à Luz (PCL)** whose title showed where it ran but made no mention of its most intriguing section, the steeply graded, double-track extension tramway between Cauterets and the spa of la Raillère. Because of differences in level this was not actually connected to the rest but ran happily right up to 1970 with three elegant bogie cars with end balconies for the crew but side-door compartments for the clients. (all three were eventually preserved). It is a pity it did not last even five years longer since it would now be a curiosity at least as great as any rack line. The remainder was still quainter, even after it got rid of an inconvenient double reversal. Its stock, both goods and passenger, consisted almost entirely of motored cars (elements automoteurs) and in its later years, hardly any two were alike. The Luz line closed in the 1930s and the Cauterets one would have done so in 1939 if it had not been for the war. Instead, it struggled on to 1949 although latterly presumably illegally since it was actually declassified in 1944.

Between the western Pyrenées and the Massif: Ariège, Haute Garonne, Tarn (Map p.322)

These three départements are taken together because they more or less fill the space between the west coast ones and the Carcassonne gap. Ariège was a rather cut-off département hard up against the Spanish border and was not well endowed with light railways. The least unimportant was another of those isolated tramways, in this case the metre gauge **Tramways de l'Ariège** which ran two brief, separated, lines and appears to have been electric because it was originally promoted by the local power generation company.

There were also substantial standard gauge networks. This is the SE's Réseau de la Gironde at Cabanac in the golden years with a passenger train.

(FACS)

One branch, between Oust and Aulus, closed in 1933; the other, from St Girons to Sentein, followed four years later. One must confess it was marginally less ephemeral than the département's only other line, a roadside steam tramway from **Tarascon-s-Ariège to Auzat,** which ran between 1911 and 1932, only lasting till then because the local industries were slow to go over to road transport.

Haute Garonne, however, had the only really substantial electric line of intérêt local; alas, it came far too late, and had only a brief life cut short by politics. This was the final flowering of the VFDM, a modern, well-equipped interdépartemental route from Toulouse in Haute-Garonne east to Castres in the Tarn, with a branch en route to Revel. This **VFDM Réseau de la Haute Garonne** was in some ways a bit of a puzzle. It actually spanned two départements, Haute-Garonne and Tarn, with a substantial depot at Castres which it shared with the , then VFDM operated, CFD du Tarn. It was built as late as 1930 with the most modern bogie equipment and using industrial frequency alternating current.. and it never really got anywhere; it was probably too late to snatch traffic back off the roads and so was a prime candidate for "co-ordination" in 1938-39. One might say it was born of politics and died from them.....but its power cars were really splendid affairs and one feels that it deserved better than the fate it received.

Yet even if one forgets the Toulouse – Castres electric line, there was still quite a lot to see in Haut-Garonne in the olden days. Toulouse itself, capital of the south west, had an extensive urban tramway system and was home to a spreading départemental network. The **CF du Sud Ouest,** incorporating also the **CFIL de Toulouse à Boulogne-s-Gesse,** and with eight lines and over 300km, was quite conventional but it did use some very neat little MT series de De Dion railbuses and it did have the "train blanc", composed of heavyweight battery electric cars towing bogie coaches specially painted white; indeed it served as the proving ground for the battery-electric concept and, effectively, ran competitive trials of different makers' offerings. As with other systems, alas, it came late, suffered from road competition as soon as that arose, and was well on the way to closure in 1939. The surviving branches lasted out the war but but went in 1947 and 1949. In contrast, Haute Garonne also had the little metre gauge electric **Tramway de Marignac au Val d'Aran,** a 15km long line opened in 1914 and only just escaping the status of an international railway – a projected extension across the Spanish frontier never happened.

And east of Toulouse, briefly linked to it by that ill-fated electric line of the VFDM already described, was Castres and the Département du Tarn. For the most part, the modest four-branch system of the **CFD du Tarn,** split between the Groupe d'Albi and the Groupe de Castres was conventional too. Its early railcars were Verneys rather than De Dions, the Groupe d'Albi, in fairly easy country, expired before 1939 and the Castres system was only saved by the war and its diffcult terrain. It was then being run by the VFDM who hung onto it until 1953 when it should have closed. Instead a concern calling itself the Societé Auxiliaire pour les Chemins de Fer Secondaires (SACFS) took over and tried to revive it by thorough modernisation – single manning, reduction of stations to unstaffed halts, dieselisation with modern equipment from all over the place. Sadly the deficit was only slowed and in 1962 the road lobby won. All of those facts are true but ignore that, in its final years at least, the Castres system had a great deal of charm and a journey by it into the green heart of the Agout valley was almost an adventure - in fact if you didn't read the highly complicated timetable correctly (or confused Thursday with Tuesday) it might have become a challenge as to how to return...

What was really unusual, however, was that ihe Tarn département also created not one but two 60cm gauge lines. One, the miniscule branch from **Réalmont to Laboutarié,** was a horse tramway for much of its life, only aspiring to a rather unsuccessful Berliet tractor a few years before it died in 1933; unkind souls said it was only built because the folk of Réalmont, to the east of Laboutarié, didn't see why Lavaur should have a tramway and not them. Lavaur, out to the west, was on a proper system, the **Tramways à Vapeur du Tarn (TVT).** This met the horse tram at Laboutarié but eventually stretched west and south for some 46km with three branches centred on Graulhet and might have gone further. Its final stretch from La Ramière to St. Sulpice was intended to turn north to Salvagnac but was never completed. The TVT was, as one might suppose, inspired by the 1889 Paris exhibition, had standard Decauville stock hauled by Weidkecht 0-6-2Ts and 4-6-0Ts just like those of the Calvados, and, not to be left out, had a boxy bogie railcar by Berliet. More to the point, one can still get a feel for it since part of the trackbed including a

Eventually all the major border players converted to electricity. Here a typical train of the Bayonne – Anglet – Biarritz shows its self off.

26 – Route de PIERREFITTE à LUZ-St-SAUVEUR
Le Pont de Pescadère

The Pyrenéen lines are represented by the two-branched system from Pierrefitte to Luz and St. Sauveur, here seen in typical scenery.

Down on the Spanish boarder there were further electric lines; in this case the Tramways de l'Ariege.　　(FACS)

A typical scene on the CFD du Tarn in the 1950s with a Verney railcar.　　(AUTHOR'S COLLECTION)

splendid viaduct has been reused by a tourist railway the CF Touristique du Tarn (CFTT), although on the 50cm gauge. It definitely meets the Michelin standards for "worth a detour".

The Mediterranean: Pyrenées Orientales, Aude and Hérault. (Map p.323)

Way over in the east between France and Spain, there was a further cluster of lines that tend to get forgotten. These were the two possessions of the **CF des Pyrenées Orientales (CPO),** started intriguingly by that M.Level who had extensive interests in the north but for most of its life a subsidiary of the CF du Midi company and with a group of three standard gauge steam lines radiating from Perpignan. Most had gone by 1950 but the Thuir branch survived for passengers to 1952 and was still operated for freight for many years more. Indeed the remnants of this were active well into the 1980s and the last stub, worked by the SNCF, only closed in 1994.

The CPO's second possession, to revisit our electric theme, was its electric, metre gauge "Réseau de Montagne", or "du Haut Vallespir", with two tramway-type routes starting at the end of a PO branch and running from Arles sur Tech to Prats de Mollo and to St Laurent de Cerdans, right up on the Spanish frontier. Built late, in 1913, it lasted only to 1937 but looks fascinating in photographs.

And, right in the Pyrenées – indeed abutting on the neighbouring republic of Andorra at one point - was one last electric line which, astoundingly, is still with us. Domengie considered it so much "of the main lines" that he deliberately omitted it but it is a secondary railway for all that, although of Intérêt Général. From Perpignan an isolated standard gauge electrified branch of the Midi ran upward and westward to Villefranche – Vernet les Bains and from there a metre gauge electric line cut dizzily across the upper slopes to another standard gauge junction over on the Toulouse-Barcelona transpyrenéen line at la Tour de Carol. This **Ligne de Cerdagne** has always been operated by the main line companies and their successor the SNCF; it has its eccentricities – the power arrangements are nearer those of the Paris metro than anything else, using third rail collection, it has several of the more imposing viaducts of France, including a Gisclard suspension bridge; it has traditionally included completely open coaches in its rakes and its tourist potential is thought sufficient to have warranted wholesale modernisation of the elderly stock in recent years. It has a detailed history written about it and it can still be visited; it is noted in chapter 6

Finally, or almost so, debouching onto the Mediterranean coast north of Pyrenées Orientales, were two further substantial départemental systems, one metre and one standard gauge. The metre gauge **Tramways à Vapeur de l'Aude** were specifically intended to link its countryside with the single Midi line from Toulouse to Narbonne through the Carcassonne Gap and comprised a dozen shortish lines totalling no less than 336km and opened between 1901 and 1910. All except one were roadside tramways, deficitary and over difficult country and, after the concession passed to the bus-minded Societé Générale des Transports Départementaux (SGTD) in 1932, closure was swift. Stock was always conventional, comprising mainly 17-tonne Corpet Louvet 0-6-0Ts towing four wheeled vehicles plus a few De Dion KG series railbuses.

At one point the TA stuck a quick loop into the neighboring département of Hérault, which completes our tour of the southwest. Hérault was different, the home of the third big standard gauge system, the **CFIL de l'Hérault** which covered the southern part of the département with a connected network of lines. Its first line, from Montpellier to Palavas, opened as early as 1872, its last in 1913. It had two main bases, working from Montpellier and Béziers, a more interesting than usual collection of motive power including some spindly Mallets, and was taken over by the SE in 1929. The system was largely intact until after World War 2 but then degenerated into two remnants based on Béziers (for the wine traffic) and Montpellier - Palavas (for the seaside trippers). Its final motive power included a series of handsome 0-8-0Ts by Schneider which were active into the 1960s; six hideous BB diesel elctrics based on war-surplus components; a fascinating collection of railcars including conventional De Dions, single-ended Verneys which ran back to back, and a genuine De Dion push-pull set of motor and control trailer. The latter were needed because Montpellier Esplanade terminus, reached over a long viaduct, had only a single dead-end running line. Coaches, unusually for a standard gauge line, were latterly all four-wheeled, balcony ended saloons. The Palavas line lasted with diesel traction until 1968 although those in the Béziers group lost their passenger services in 1954 and became little more than industrial sidings.

CARCASSONNE. - Tramways de l'Aude

A train of the metre gauge Tramways de l'Aude in Carcassonne town, with admirers. (FACS)

The final standard gauge system as most remember it: A packed holiday train of the CFE de l'Hérault as it runs along the Etang side to Palavas.

(D. TREVOR ROWE)

Light Railways in Region Sud-Ouest

name	ident	gauge	km	lines	dates	cln	operators
dept Ariège							
Ariège, Twys electriques de l'	TEA	metre	0039	02	1911-1937	Twy	
Tarasçon-s-Ariege à Auzat, Twy de	TTA	metre	0016	01	1911-1932	Twy	
dept Aude							
Aude, Tramways à vapeur de l'	TA	metre	0336	12	1901-1932	IL	SGTD 1930
dept Aveyron							
Salles-la-Source – Mondalazac, ligne de	PO	1.10m	0007	01	1861-1882	Twy	PO; mineral rly
dept Basses-Pyrénées							
Chalosse et du Bearn, Twys de	CB	metre	0067	02	not opened	IL	
VFDM Réseau Basque (Bayonne - Hendaye)	VFDM	metre	0066	04	1916-1948	IL	Giros & Loucheur; complex: see also Tarn; Lot-et-Garonne
Artouste, ligne de	SNCF	50cm	0010	01	1924-now	Twy	CF du Midi/SNCF
Bayonne-Anglet-Biarritz, CF	BAB	m/sg	0008	01	1877-1952	IL	Régie 1944
Bayonne-Lycée-Biarritz, Twys de	BLB	metre	0011	01	1888-1948	Twy	Empain; Régie 1944
Pau – Oloron – Mauleon CF de	POM	metre	0216	05	1901-1931	IL	Empain
St Ignace – la Rhûne, ligne de (VFDM)	VFDM	metre	0004	01	1924-now	Twy	VFDM; rack
dept Charente							
Charentes et Deux Sevres, Réseau (CFD)	CFD	metre	0063	01	1889-1950	IL	CFD; see ouest also
Charentes, CFE des (Réseau de Charente)	EC	metre	0370	07	1895-1946	IL	Jeancard
dept Cher							
Charentes, CFE (Réseau du Cher)	EC	metre	0068	01	1914-1939	IL	Jeancard; TI 1930
Cher, IL réseau du (SE)	SE	metre	0220	04	1888-1951	IL	SE; SNCF 1956
Cher, réseau d'Intérêt Général (SE)	SE	metre	0091	01	1890-1951	IG	SE; see also Allier
dept Corrèze							
Corrèze, lignes de (PO)	POC	metre	0095	03	1904-1970	IG	PO/SNCF; SE 1962
Corrèze, Twys de la	TC	metre	0181	05	1912-1959	Twy	Laurent; SCETA 1944
dept Dordogne							
Dordogne, Twys de la	TD	metre	0159	04	1911-1949	IL	RD 1921;CFD 1926
Perigord, CF du	CFP	metre	0128	03	1890-1949	IL	Empain; RD 1921;CFD 1926
dept Gers							
GERS - no lines of its own							
dept Gironde							
Bordeaux à Beychac et Cailleau Twys de	BBC	sg	0016	01	1908-1949	Twy	TEOB 1913
Bordeaux à Cadillac, Twy de	BC	metre	0032	01	1897-1935	Twy	Faugère et Bernard
Bordeaux à Camarsac, Twy de	TEOB	sg	0016	01	1908-1949	Twy	SE; TEOB 1913
Born et du Marensin, CF du	BM	sg	0011	01	1912-1933	IL	became VFL 1916 see Landes
Gironde, Réseau de la (SE)	SE	sg	0313	06	1884-1978*	IL	SE; complex origins
La Teste - Cazaux, CF de	LTC	sg	0013	01	1876-now*	IL	Ortal; military
Libournais, Twys electriques du	TL	metre	0038	02	1913-1949	Twy	Ortal
Margaux - Castelnau (Medoc)	MED	sg	0011	02	1884-1933	IL	Medoc CF; BM 1912; VFL 1916
Nizan à St Symphorien et à Sore, CFIL de	NS	sg	0039	01	1873-1978*	IL	Faugère et Bernard?; SE 1888 part of SE Gironde system
dept Haute-Garonne							
Luchon – Superbagnères, ligne de	LS	metre	0005	01	1912-1966	IL	rack
Marignac au Val-d'Aran, Twy de	MVA	metre	0015	01	1914-1954*	Twy	
Sud-Ouest, CFIL du	SO	metre	0305	08	1903-1947	IL	Régie 1942
Toulouse à Boulogne-s-Gesse CFIL de	TB	metre	0105	02	1900-1949	IL	SO 1903
dept Haute-Garonne; Tarn							
Toulouse – Castres et Revel (VFDM)	VFDM	metre	0103	02	1930-1939	IG	VFDM

Light Railways in Region Sud-Ouest continued...

name	ident	gauge	km	lines	dates	cln	operators	
dept Haute-Vienne								
Haute-Vienne, CFD de la	CDHV	metre	0330	07	1912-1949	Twy	Giros et Loucheur	
Limoges – Aix-en-Vienne, ligne de	CTL	metre	0015	01	1908-1949	Twy	Twys de Limoges;	CHDV 1912
dept Hautes-Pyrenées								
Bigorre, Twys electriques de la	TEB	metre	0041	02	1914-1934	Twy		VFP 1918
Pierrefitte, Cauterets, Luz, CF de	PCL	metre	0025	03	1897-1970	Twy		
dept Hérault								
Hérault, CFIL de l'	SE	sg	0202	07	1872-1968	IL		SE 1929
dept Indre								
Indre Twys de l'	TI	metre	0182	04	1902-1939	IL	Tartary	
dept Indre-et-Loire								
Indre-et-Loire, Réseau d' (CFD)	CFD	metre	0242	04	1885-1949	IL	CFD	
Ligre-Rivière - Richelieu, ligne de	Etat	sg	0016	01	1884-now*	IL	Etat/SNCF;	CFD 1950;RFR 1972. now a tourist line
Ste Maure (stn-ville) (PO)	PO	sg	0003	01	1913-1945*	IL	PO for dept.	
Tours-Fondettes (Twys de Tours)	TT	metre	0011	01	1899-1949	IL	expl CFD	
dept Indre/Cher/Loire-et-Cher								
Blanc à Argent, CF du	BA	metre	0190	01	1901-now	IG	PO;	TI 1975
dept Landes								
Born et du Marensin CF du (Landes)	BM	sg	0135	09	1909-now**	IL	Ortal;	to VF des Landes 1916(qv)
Chalosse et du Bearn, Twys à vapeur de la	CB	metre	0143	03	1909-1937*	Twy		
Landes, CF Economiques Forestiers des	EFL		0012	01	1907-1934	Twy		only 75cm gauge line
Landes, CFIL du Département des	CFL	sg	0188	10	1888-now**	IL		VFL 1916
Landes, Voies Ferrées des	VFL	sg	see individual components			IL		VFL by amalg 1916
Luxey à Mont-de-Marsan CF de	LM	sg	0045	01	1906-1964*	IL	Ortal;	Régie 1951
Soustons à Leon, CF de	SL	sg	0022	01	1904-1969*	IL		VFL 1916
dept Loir-et-Cher								
Blois-Vienne - St Aignan, ligne de(PO)	PO	metre	0038	01	1899-1934	IG	TLC;	conceded to PO but sub-let
Loir-et-Cher, Twys de	TLC	metre	0247	09	1888-1934	Twy	Carel et Fouché;	Régie 1927
Loir-et-Cher, Twys electriques de	ELC	metre	0153	04	1913-1933	Twy		
dept Loiret								
Loiret, tramways du	TL	metre	0135	04	1905-1934	Twy	Fougerolle	
Pithiviers à Toury, Twy de	TPT	60cm	0033	01	1892-1965*	Twy	Decauville;	Régie d. 1901
dept Lot								
Bretonoux-Biars – St Céré (Quercy)	TQ	metre	0010	01	1907-1934*	Twy		Régie 1922
dept Lot-et-Garonne								
Lot-et-Garonne, Twys du	TLG	metre	0130	03	1911-1933*	IL	Ortal;	VFDM 1923
dept Pt Pyrenées-Orientales								
Cerdagne, ligne de (Midi)	Midi	metre	0062	01	1910-now	IG	Midi;	SNCF 1938
Pyrenées Orientales, CF (Haut Vallespir)	CPO	metre	0029	02	1913-1937	IL		
Pyrenées-Orientales, CF des	CPO	sg	0046	05	1910-1998	IL		SNCF 1953
dept Tarn								
Laboutarié a Réalmont, Twy de	LR	60cm	0005	01	1905-1933	Twy		
Tarn, CF Départementaux du	CDT	metre	0149	04	1905-1962	IL		VFDM 1933;SAFCS 1953
Tarn, CFVE et Twys à Vapeur du	STT	60cm	0046	02	1895-1937	Twy		part to 50cm gauge tourist line.
dept Tarn-et-Garonne								
Tarn-et-Garonne, Twys de	TTG	metre	0182	06	1913-1933	Twy	Fougerolle;	STAMidi 1932
dept Vienne								
Poitou, VF Economiques du	VFEP	metre	0164	03	1914-1934	IL	Verney	
Vienne, Twys de la	TV	metre	0052	01	1895-1934	Twy	Verney	

Urban tram systems in Region Sud-Ouest

name	power	gauge	km	dates	dept
Angoulême	e	metre	0017	1900-1935v	Charente
Arcachon	e	metre	0007	1911-1930v	Gironde
Béziers	he	metre	0020	1879-1948	Herault
Biarritz	me	metre	0006	1888-1948	Landes
Blois	e	metre	0007	1910-1934	Loir-et-Cher
Bordeaux	he	sg	0168	1880-1958	Gironde
Bourges	e	metre	0006	1898-1949	Cher
Hendaye	me	metre	0003	1906-1935	Pyrenées Atlantiques
Limoges	e	metre	0020	1897-1951	Haute-Vienne
Lourdes	e	metre	0003	1899-1930v	Hautes-Pyrenées
Montargis	m	metre	0002	1912-1914	Loiret
Montpellier	e	metre	0017	1897-1949	Herault
Orléans	he	sg	0021	1877-1938	Loiret
Pau	e	metre	0007	1900-1929	Basses-Pyrenées
Perpignan	e	metre	0027	1900-1955	Pyrenées-Orientales
Poitiers	he	metre	0006	1895-1947	Vienne
Rodez	e	metre	0002	1902-1920	Aveyron
Sète	e	metre	0009	1901-1935v	Herault
Tours	hme	metre	0049	1887-1949	Indre-et-Loire

PART 3

Technical History

Equipment and infrastructures; a general survey

CHAPTER 12
Technical development – a general survey

Parts 1 and 2 of this volume have dealt with the political and social history of minor railways in France. What of the equipment and fittings? With such a large potential market, did they develop during the formative years?

The crude answer is Yes, but really only on the metre gauge. On the other gauges, things were rather different. In most cases the standard gauge lines were prepared to buy locomotives and stock very similar to those already in production for the big companies' branch lines since these were cheaper and readily available. Only a few, such as the SE de l'Hérault, went in for Mallets or similar exotic machines, and then only in small numbers. Standard gauge coaching stock was also similar to normal branchline vehicles although it tended always to be obsolescent by main line standards and, for freight, most preferred to use main line vehicles which could (axleloads permitting) be easily interworked, thus removing the need for transhipment.

That being acknowledged, it must be said that in the very early days – the 1850s and 1860s – everything had to be developed "from new", so to speak. Hence the first narrow gauge railways were, effectively, industrial and their initial locomotives were simple 0-4-0 side-tank machines with uncomplicated valvegear and little or no crew protection. For the light standard gauge branches of the CF de l'Est an equally simple design of light 0-6-0T was developed from the start, to accord with the need for an axleload not exceeding 10 or 11 tonnes, and this was taken up by the early "private" lines such as the CF de Caen à la Mer. Its advantages were, in due course, noted on the narrow gauge also, both by industrial concerns such as the Greek CF d'Ergasteria (much cited by French exponents) and by early French public railways; for some years Gouin, Koechlin and Schneider in particular waxed rich (or at least solvent) on supplying such lines with motive power of a very similar pattern, whoever built it. Others soon got into the act, however, and then the standard gauge just took what was available. Branch line coaches had always been either light by design or hand-me-downs from earlier main line stock which was, perforce, light and simple because of contemporary motive power limitations. So much for the standard gauge.

The 60cm gauge, when its turn came, was almost entirely dominated by the firm of Decauville Aîné, who produced standard ranges of four and six-coupled locomotives, and by such firms as Weidknecht or SA les Ateliers Metallurgiques at Tubize/Blanc Misseron, both of whom were often subcontracted by Decauville. Probably because of the Decauville influence, more use was made of bogie passenger and goods stock but there was not really sufficient market to attract any of the big firms and, after about 1890, the general trend was one of improving existing designs rather than new development. Any chance of development was not helped by the 1914-18 war, whose aftermath provided large quantities of ex-military stock to fulfil most future needs - at heavily discounted prices.

The metre gauge, however, provided a large home and export market. For most people interested in railways, motive power usually comes first and the common enthusiast vision of French metre gauge railways at least is of a conventional 0-6-0 side tank by the firm of Corpet, Louvet or a Blanc Misseron tramway-type bicabine trundling 4-wheeled, end-balcony coaches. That is not really a true picture. Certainly Corpet, Louvet in their different incarnations provided, perhaps, almost half of the motive power for the intérêt local lines but that included 2-6-0s, 0-6-2s, 0-8-0s, Mallet articulateds and sundry other wheel arrangements as well as the "standard" 0-6-0T design that was built in varying weights to order. The other half, however, was supplied by a variety of specialist makers: Decauville, Pinguely, Buffaud et Robatel, SACM (Sté Alsacienne), Ateliers de Tubize, Piguet of Lyon - Piguet products, with their curved cab roofs, were oftem mistaken for Corpets but, to the writer's eye, were generally better proportioned and more handsome. The big companies such as the CFD, and the Intérêt General concessionaires, often bought from others - usually those supplying power for the appropriate main line companies. Thus SACM; SLM of Switzerland; Cail; Battignoles; Franco-Belge; St Léonard... all featured prominently although, for an unexplained reason Piguet also got into the act once with a series of very handsome Mallets for the CF de l'Etat's Réseau Breton.

Development was in any case limited to some extent by the dead hands of the "cahiers des charges" which were designed not only for standardisation but to minimise the cost to public funds - or at least to keep it within reasonable limits. Nonetheless, on the larger lines especially, there were some very fine locomotives. The Sud-France had a series of excellent 4-6-0Ts as did the Réseau Breton; some very handsome large 0-6-6-0T Mallets were produced for the CFD by the Societé Suisse/SLM and there were plenty of their just-as-efficient four coupled relatives. A long distance secondaire with its Mallet tank and its quite luxurious bogie vestibuled coaches could hold its own with any similar European line.

Nor was rolling stock nearly as stereotyped as is sometimes suggested. It may not be entirely appropriate to talk about development in this aspect. Certainly there was development in the early days from the primitive designs of the 1870s but, once a standard pattern was established, it was largely adhered to for both passenger and freight stock; innovation was, again, largely stultified by the, almost standard, cahiers des charges that were imposed on the different categories of secondary railway and this was especially true of the metre gauge. Therefore the stock tended to be similar right up to the autorail era. This applied to the goods vehicles in particular; unless the company asked for bogie vehicles (they almost never did) the standard patterns of 10-tonne capacity four-wheeler were almost bound to be similar. The standard continental fashion was for the very sensible multi-purpose van with sliding ventilation flaps and open wagons usually had hinged, rather than sliding, doors while it was only common sense to make lowsides convertible to bolster wagons. Many, too, had the distinctive feature of brakesman's huts or chairs since continuous brakes were comparatively late in arriving and were often fitted mainly to passenger stock.

Passenger stock, however, had wide variety. The bigger lines were quite happy to go in for bogie coaches – more often than not elegant affairs with smart wooden bodies and fancy ironwork – and some groupings used them even for more humble lines; the SE was a great believer in them. The advantages were that you could have two or three classes in one vehicle and they rode much better. The converse was that a heavily loaded train could not alter its composition so easily whereas with four-wheelers you just dropped one off when traffic was light and picked it up again on the way back. The end-balcony saloon was certainly very popular but compartment coaches were by no means uncommon up to the early 1900s although they were usually rudely categorised as English type or hen coops, while vestibuled vehicles often with side corridors and proper sanitary facilities were not unknown in later years especially among the lines of Intérêt Général.

In general, it was the metre gauge, too, which saw most of the interesting experiments with self-propelled vehicles in an effort to reduce working costs. Initially these were largely attempts at steam-propelled railcars for both standard and metre gauge, although compressed air was also tried – but mainly on urban lines. Scotte, Purrey, Rowan and Serpollet four wheeled, vertical-boilered cars saw a brief flowering especially on "navettes" where a system had routes running from a main line station through the neighbouring town but their inherent disadvantages, lack of power and capacity, need for frequent refuelling, the delicacy of their internal workings, discouraged their users. From about 1910-on, however, serious trials were started with internal combustion engines, in particular with petrol electric drives, and with battery electrics. In retrospect these were a little premature, their success having to wait until the war produced massive development in the design and production of petrol engines in particular. Afterward the French makers were certainly in the forefront of railcar development as will be described in chapter 14.

As to electric lines, as can be seen from chapter 4, after the early, and impressive, experiments with high tension AC current,there was very little real development in electric traction in the way that the Belgian SNCV, for instance, developed. Many of the smaller lines were essentially electric tramways carrying only passengers and small goods (messageries). The smallest, often station to town lines, simply used the contemporary patterns of urban trancar which, since they rarely reequipped, became more and more antiquated and delapidated as the years went by. Those slightly larger were mainly in the nature of suburban trams and, again, tended to use appropriate stock - four-wheeled or bogie passenger trams capable of pulling one or more trailers; the main difference from urban lines was that they often had two or more classes of accommodation. The rural systems of some départements, in turn, acquired a fairly boxy patterm of 4-wheeled or bogie power car based on such heavy trams but, again, developed surprisingly little when compared to the equivalent makers in, say, Belgium or Switzerland where the use of electricity made a real impact.

The main trends of development and design of motive power and stock will be illustrated in the following chapters. To avoid constant repetition, short forms of the main makers' names have been used and the full names will be found in appendix 5. Chapter 16 discusses the main features of light railway infrastructure which remained surprisingly constant throughout the period.

CHAPTER 13

Steam, internal combustion and electric locomotives and tractors

1. Steam locomotives

This chapter really needs to start with a health warning: The number and variety of French secondary railways was so great that for any general statement there are bound to be numerous exceptions and general statements are all one can really make in the space available. As a general statement, therefore, standard gauge minor railways produced very little that was not mirrored elsewhere by industrial users or by the main line companies. In many cases (cf Caen à la Mer; VF des Landes) the locomotive stock was almost identical to contemporary machines produced for branch line work by main line companies; indeed the locomotives for the CF de l'Est branches in Bas-Rhin (1864-65) can be said to have set the pattern for much that followed. Six-coupled machines by firms such as Koechlin, Schneider, Cail, Fives Lille and Battignoles predominated and the variations were mainly in such eccentricities as hugely tall funnels to take smoke and steam above the upper decks of double-deck coaches. A few standard gauge lines had distinctive light railway designs - the CF de Chauny à St Gobain had a couple of handsome 2-6-0T by Cockerill for example to complement their archaic Koechlin 0-6-0Ts and the SE de l'Hérault a series of equally handsome 0-8-0Ts. Other railways with heavy traffic, mostly in the north east, followed suit – the CFS had some heavy 0-8-0Ts and Mines branches, plus the Somain – Peruwelz, also favoured them for coal hauling and heavy shunting work. A very few lines experimented with articulateds as described below but they were definitely exceptions to the rule. Most of the detailed comments in this chapter, therefore, refer to metre gauge or, where appropriate, to the 60cm gauge, and consider locomotives in increasing order of size and complexity.

As to general typology, on all gauges, the tender locomotive was very uncommon; the Somain – Peruwelz standard gauge line had a class of quite elegant 2-6-0s, the Sud-France had some 0-6-0s in its earlier, strategically minded days, the French military had some splendid 0-6-6-0 Mallets for their North African

The quintessential early standard gauge 0-6-0T, RIMAUCOURT, of the SE's Gudmont-Rimaucourt branch, here seen in industrial service but hardly altered apart from the cab. (AUTHOR)

NG 4-coupled 1: The standard Decauville/Weidknecht 60cm gauge 0-4-2T as supplied to the Tramway de Pithiviers à Toury.   (AMTP/FACS)

NG 4-coupled 2: Gouin light 2-4-0T as retained for shunting on the PO Corrèze in 1960.   (AUTHOR)

lines, but in general tank locomotives were preferred even though they were religiously turned to face chimney first where turntables were available. The side-tank design was paramount with only a few well-tanks (though these included some rather British-looking Cockerill 2-4-0WTs on the Aisne lines associated with the St.Quentin - Guise (Nos 32-43) which vaguely recalled Adams practice) and hardly any saddle-tank machines save for a few British imports.

Four-coupled locomotives

After the early years, where it was common on industrial railways, such as those at Modalazac and Trebiau, the four coupled locomotive was not common on French light railways except for three specialised purposes – as shunters for those with industrial sidings, as motive power for short lines with very sharp curvature and, on a very few systems, as motive power for light, fast passenger workings. The shunters and short line machines, on both standard and metre gauge, were mainly standard or lightly modified industrial 0-4-0 tank engines and those are much the same anywhere; an unusual standard gauge variant was provided by the early Mines d'Anzin which homebuilt a small series of oddities with truly enormous wheels. One survives in preservation which is why they are mentioned here.

The light fast 2-4-0T as used by the SE on its own account, and by a few metre gauge lines of Intérêt Général – the Réseau Breton and PO Corrèze among them – was of rather more interest. It was always a side tank locomotive, usually with large coupled wheels, and was really of use only where dedicated passenger trains were required; hence it fell rapidly from use as soon as railcars appeared, although two examples remained in use at Tulle (Corrèze) for works shunting up to the 1960s. The only common example of this type was on the 60cm gauge where Decauville, often sub-contracting to Weidknecht, designed a neat 0-4-2T which was a standard product of the company for many years and used on several of the lines they equipped. Calvados, Pithiviers and Royan all had examples.

Six-coupled locomotives

Basic motive power for the average light railway of Intérêt Local or Tramway category was undoubtedly the light, six-coupled side tank 0-6-0T locomotive and once the general pattern was established, whether

The bog-standard Corpet, Louvet 0-6-0T, in this case No. 55 of the CFE des Charentes.   (FACS)

213

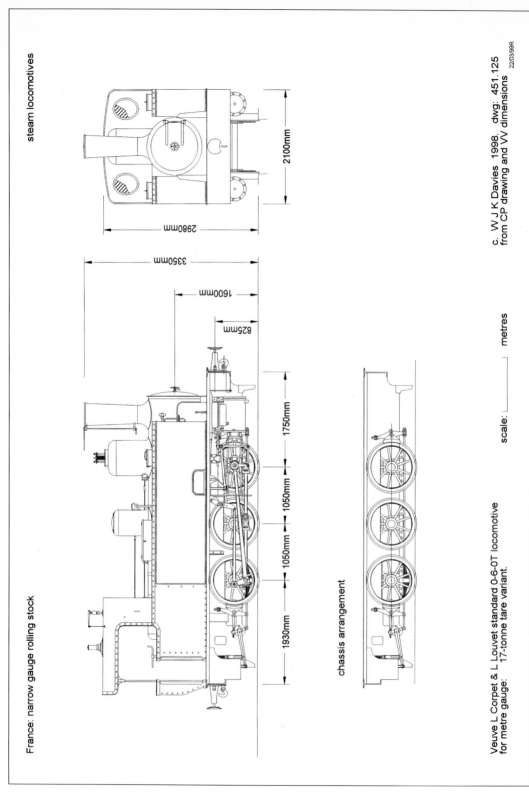

steam locomotives

France: narrow gauge rolling stock

2980mm

2100mm

3350mm

1600mm

825mm

1750mm

1050mm

1050mm

1930mm

chassis arrangement

Veuve L Corpet & L Louvet standard 0-6-0T locomotive
for metre gauge: 17-tonne tare variant.

scale: |_____| metres

c. W J K Davies 1998.   dwg: 451.125
from CP drawing and VV dimensions

22/03/99R

214

A herd of pushmepullyous: Pinguely bicabines on the Tramways de l'Ouest du Dauphiné   (FACS)

imposed by the manufacturers or the cahiers des charges, or both, there was very little development; a Corpet, Louvet 0-6-0T of the 1920s was instantly comparable with a similar machine of the 1880s except for the (marginally) improved cab and different valve gear. A tramway-type locomotive (bicabine) was....a bicabine whoever built it; Tubize and other makers had standardised that design way back although Pinguely added a little variation by uncovering the boiler portion and installing a separate cab at each end. In most cases the tramway-type was the classic "Vicinal" design with a full-length superstructure, canopied roof, and with working platforms fore and aft of the boiler assembly. The wheels and motion were, in theory, covered by hinged side skirting although many lines in practice either left this hooked up or dismantled the hinged covers. A variant, for example on the Tramways de la Sarthe and the Côtes du Nord, was a conventional single-cab locomotive with motion covers. A slight cause of confusion is that many apparent bicabines for rural lines had only one driving position, normally, though not always, in front of the smokebox; they presumably had overall covering "to avoid frightening the horses". In any case, the basis of all was a simple, six-coupled, plate frame chassis with smallish wheels, an unsuperheated boiler designed for minimum maintenance, two outside cylinders with Allan, Stephenson or, later, Walschaerts valve gear driving slide valves. 11-18 tonnes was a realistic range of tare weights. Most makers had standardised outlines and so far as conventional locomotives are concerned, you tended to recognise a Pinguely, a Corpet or a Tubize/Blanc Misseron by whether it had a square or rounded cab, or whether the side tanks were full length or stopped at the smokebox rear; Piguets were a trap for the unwary since they looked somewhat like a Corpet. As to dimensions, the makers were so blasé about scaling up or down to meet demand that their publicity shots usually did for the whole range - just fill in the right weight on the caption and there you were. The 60cm gauge had only a few 0-6-0T although Decauville designed a standard range from 8-tonnes upward which was extensively used by both the military and industrial concerns.

The next "step" up for the more ambitious metre gauge lines was to add a leading or trailing axle, usually in some form of Bissel truck. Given a slightly higher axleload, this allowed for more weight and power and was an effective means of guiding locomotives round the inevitable sharp curves at somewhat higher speeds than before. Tare weights of between 18 and 25 tonnes were common and both 2-6-0T and 0-6-2T found

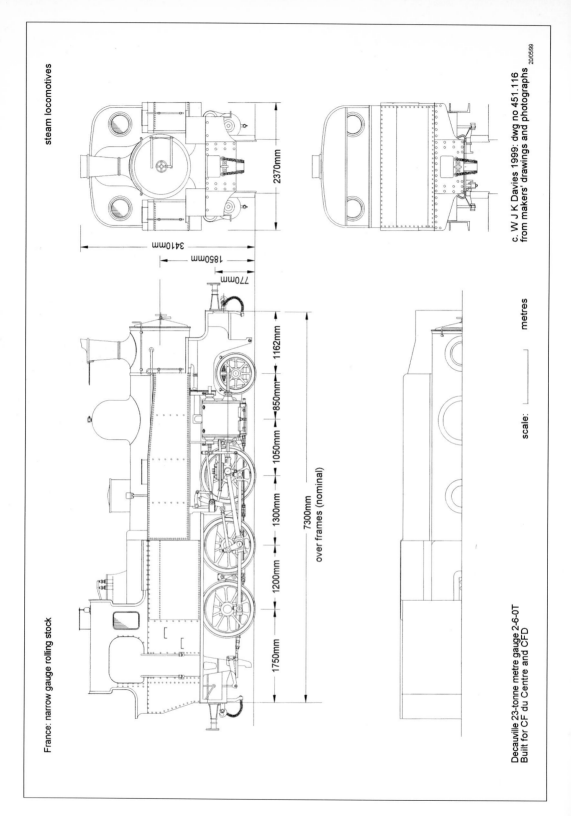

steam locomotives

France: narrow gauge rolling stock

2370mm

3410mm

1850mm

770mm

1162mm

850mm

1050mm

1300mm

7300mm
over frames (nominal)

1200mm

1750mm

Decauville 23-tonne metre gauge 2-6-0T
Built for CF du Centre and CFD

c. W J K Davies 1999: dwg no 451.116
from makers' drawings and photographs

20/05/99

scale: |_____| metres

216

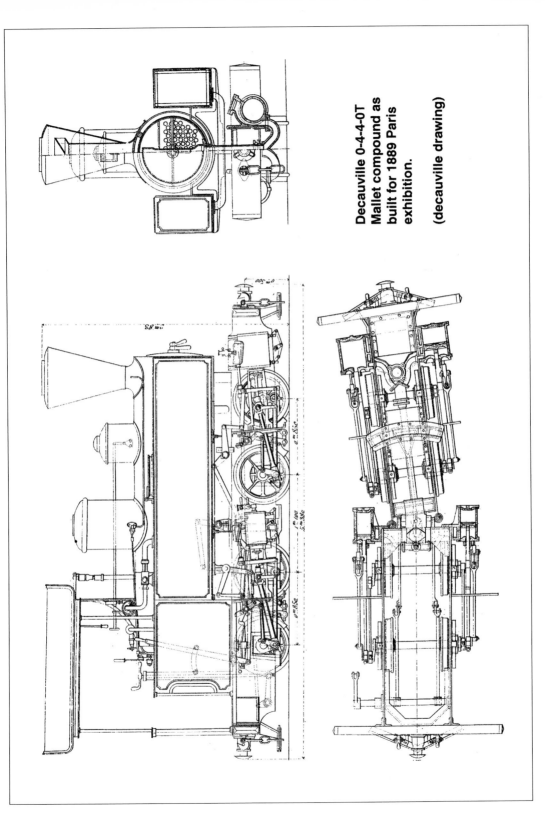

Decauville 0-4-4-0T Mallet compound as built for 1889 Paris exhibition.

(decauville drawing)

217

A typical metre gauge 2-6-0T, in this case a Schneider product for the SE's Réseau de Centre   (MAKER/FACS)

favour with different companies. Some very handsome locomotives resulted, the Corpet and Piguet examples in particular appearing nicely proportioned while the neat 23-tonne Decauville design had a rather Germanic look. The big CFD tended to go for a rather chunky and squared off appearance with series from main line makers SACM, St Léonard of Liége, Sté Franco-Belge and Cail, while the SE added its own particular flavour with a standard 0-6-2T actually designed – and some built – by the main line CF du Nord, plus a series of 0-6-2Ts from Cail and from Buffaud et Robatel which were intended to work bunker first so had their cab shelters back to front. Decauville produced a lengthened version of its 0-4-2T which found some favour on the 60cm gauge. An interesting feature was that a few designs were actually two-cylinder compounds.

What one might call the intermediate types - 4-6-0; 2-6-2 - were not very common at all. The writer can think of only four purpose-built light railway 2-6-2T, No 251 of the CFD on the metre gauge and a class of three on the standard gauge Pas de Calais system. This may have been because turntables were common and French lines always preferred to run their locomotives chimney first where possible – it is rare to see a photo of a metre gauge light railway with the locomotive running bunker first unless it was designed to do so and the SE de Seine-et-Marne used to refer to their cab-first 0-6-2Ts as 2-6-0s which shows their perceptions. The 4-6-0 was used a little more widely but the major series even of that reached the CF de Provence and the CF du Centre by accident – traded against other potential stock when the Portuguese Vale do Vouga concern decided it could not afford them after all. The Réseau Breton also had an excellent class, two of which still survive in preservation. On the 60cm gauge, Weidkecht produced for Decauville a series of 4-6-0T which was used by the Calvados and the Tramways à Vapeur du Tarn, while Tubize (via Blanc Misseron) built a few 4-6-0 tram locomotives for the Calvados too.

Heavy locomotives: 8 & 10 coupled, articulated

Then one comes to the heavy brigade, intended for goods work or for long distance haulage on the bigger lines. On the standard gauge, railways tended to take what was available second-hand. Thus the heavy coal-

French curiosity: the cab-first 0-6-2T, represented here by Buffaud et Robatel 3714 on the SE's Seine-et-Marne system.

(AUTHOR)

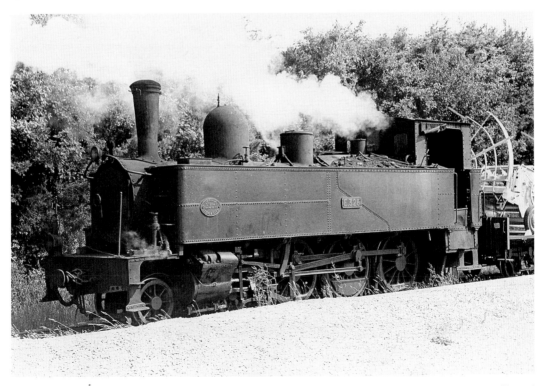

The next step: a 4-6-0T of the Réseau Breton's 32X series.

(AUTHOR)

Heavy power: standard gauge Schneider 0-8-0T of the CFE de l'Hérault.

(MAKER'S PHOTO)

A lighter Mallet: 0-4-4-0T 404 of the Réseau Breton.

(G. MESGOUEZ/CFTA)

Piguet 0-6-6-0T Mallet E 415, also on the Réseau Breton.

(AUTHOR)

hauliers of the north east used industrial type eight or ten coupled machines, or bought similar designs superannuated by main line companies; on the "lignes affermées" such as the étoile d'Autun, or the system based on Gray, they even leased current machines and held on to them after they disappeared from main line use – hence the 130B 2-6-0s and the 140C class 2-8-0s so beloved of enthusiasts in the early 1970s, although heavy tank locomotives were also popular.

On the metre gauge, a very few concerns, for differing reasons, settled for 0-8-0T or even 0-10-0T, usually where there was heavy mineral traffic: the Tramways d'Ille-et-Vilaine; CF du Côte d'Or; the CF de la Drôme; CF de Cormeilles à Glos Montfort and the CF du Cambrésis found them useful. Even here there was no unanimity: the le Blanc – Argent, 190km long and with heavy traffic, stuck faithfully to a series of lightish 0-6-0Ts and spurned the offer of an 0-6-6-0T Mallet from the Tramways de l'Ain. On the whole, however, most of the bigger systems, given their curvature and gradients, opted for articulation and, in France, this was almost exclusively to M. Mallet's compound design which came in various wheel arrangements and sizes. The essence of the Mallet design was a fixed rear frame carrying the cab, boiler and high pressure "engine," with an articulated sub-frame and the low pressure "engine" in front and pivoted on the boiler assembly; that minimised the problem of flexible connections for high pressure steam. The simplest and most widely used, largely for lines of Intérêt Local, was the 0-4-4-0T but the CFD especially had a number of 2-4-4-0Ts in the Lozère and Corsica, while 0-6-6-0Ts were certainly not uncommon. Again the CFD had a very handsome series (401-08) on its Vivarais system, together with six modernised examples and the Réseau Breton acquired eight heavy Piguets which served it well until the end. The standard gauge rarely needed the complexity and only the CFIL de l'Hérault and the CF d'Avricourt-Blamont-Cirey deliberately experimented with small numbers; the experience was not repeated.

The 60cm gauge actually started with Mallets, miniscule 0-4-4-0Ts built for the Paris exhibition, and the military even had a series of quite powerful 0-6-6-0 tender locomotives for export to Tunisia of which one,

A typical CFD-built diesel 0-6-0D converted from a steam locomotive. No. 12 (CFD Neuillé) on the le Blanc – Argent.

(AUTHOR)

converted to a tank locomotive, ended up on the Pithiviers - Toury. Most 60cm gauge eight or ten coupled machines, however, were ex military equipment of WW1 or WW2 and cannot really be counted as French designs!

2. Internal-combustion-engined locomotives

Up to the mid 1930s, i/c engined locomotives were very rare but the savings generated by railcars made some concerns think again. Cost of developing such things new and the depressed condition of many minor lines did not encourage the big manufacturers but some of the larger railway groupings decided to act on their own account; a useful byproduct of the comparatively late start was that reliable diesel engines were available from the beginning.

Most inventive was the big CFD company, many of whose systems had very well equipped workshops and – because it was a railcar pioneer - surplus steam locomotives which belonged to the company not the département or could be purchased cheaply. The first attempt, by the Charentes works at St Jean d'Angély, was something of a blind alley consisting as it did of the motor/generator set from Crochat petrol electric railcar Ae 51 mounted directly on its power bogie and matched to a new 75hp CLM diesel engine. It worked but was not really powerful enough and, anyway, surplus Crochat cars were few and far between. It did set the style of a bonnet at one end, an off-centre, full width cab and a rear "boot" containing the fuel tank and other useful items. It also inspired the Toulon-s-Arroux depot on CFD's Saône-et-Loire system to convert the chassis of 0-6-2T 204 into a machine capable of replacing it on line work. The result was a single-ended 0-6-0 with mechanical drive from a 150hp CLM engine to the centre axle, the coupling rods being retained. So satisfied was the CFD that it decided to equip its Neuillé-Pont Pierre shops on the Indre-et-Loire system to start series production. A group of six (to be 11-16) was envisaged but production was disrupted by the war and only five were completed, the last one in 1948 soon before the system closed....meanwhile, back in Charente another four were produced for the owning bodies (State and Département), in Dordogne three lighter 180hp versions were produced for the Département (650-52) and the Central Works at Montmirail eventually built another four. Since they travelled widely and several still exist the listing is given below:

No.	source	date	hp	first user	notes
11	A51	1935	75	Charentes	Scr 1944
204	204	1936	150	Saône-et-Loire	to Tunisia 1954
4	4	1940	75	Indre-et-Loire	to Mines de Carmaux (8)
11	8	1941	130	Yonne	to le Blanc-Argent
12	2	1942	135	Yonne	to le Blanc-Argent (9)
13	6	1948	150	Indre-et-Loire	scr 1968 (1)
14	7	1948	150	Indre-et-Loire	to SILEC, Montèreau (sg)(2)
15	1	1951	150	Saône-et-Loire	to Senegal
16	3	not built; components used as spares			
50	50	1944	150	CFD Charentes	St Béron steel via B-A
62	62	1946	150	CFD Charentes	to CFD Lozère (3)
70	70	1948	150	CFD Charentes	to CFD Lozère (3)
650	11	1946	180	CFD Dordogne	to Haubourdin cement
651	17	1947	180	CFD Dordogne	to Haubourdin cement (4)
652	26	1947	180	CFD Dordogne	to Haubourdin cement (4)
201	201	1949	180	CFD Vendée	to Haubourdin cement (5)
851	17	1948	150?	CFD Seine-et-Marne	scr 1955
852	18	1948	150?	CFD Seine-et-Marne	Ouvre sugar, Souppes
X	23	1949	150?	CFD Vivarais	CF du Vivarais
Y		1949	150?	CFD Vivarais	CF du Vivarais

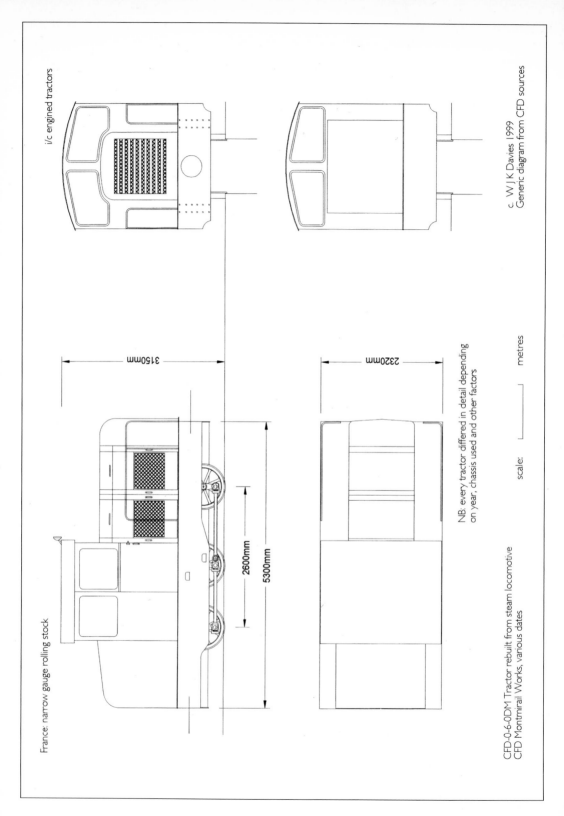

i/c engined tractors

France: narrow gauge rolling stock

3150mm

2600mm

5300mm

2320mm

NB: every tractor differed in detail depending on year, chassis used and other factors

scale: |_____| metres

CFD-0-6-0DM Tractor rebuilt from steam locomotive
CFD Montmirail Works, various dates

c. W J K Davies 1999
Generic diagram from CFD sources

diesel locomotives

France: narrow gauge rolling stock

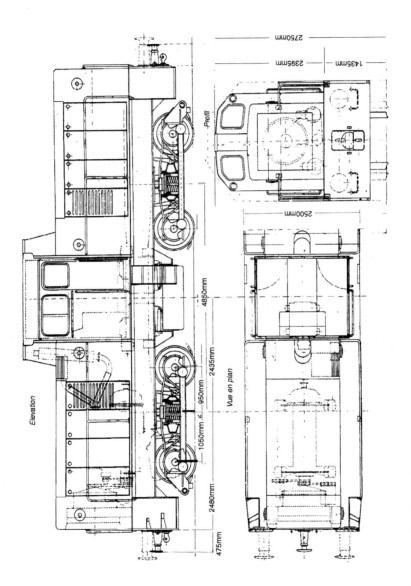

Elevation

Profil

Vue en plan

4850mm

2435mm

950mm

1050mm

2480mm

475mm

2750mm

2395mm

1435mm

2500mm

400hp BB locomotive for metre gauge
Cie des Chemins de Fer Departementaux 1962

source: Maker's photo, redimensioned

225

No.	source	date	hp	first user	notes
built for other companies (not using CFD chassis)					
101	12	1948	150	CF du Doubs	to CFD du Tarn LT1 (6)
102	14	1948	150	CF du Doubs	to Guadeloupe
103	13	1948	150	CF du Doubs	to VFD 1954
51	-	1949	180	CF de Provence	derelict 1999
82	82	1950	159	Colvay & Dombasle	to CFD du Tarn LT2 (7)

(1)   via work at Toulon-s-Arroux; Egreville; Vivarais
(2)   via Toulon-s-Arroux & Egreville
(3)   in tourist use on west end of Vivarais 1999
(4)   via CGL Pas de Calais & the Ardennes network
(5)   via Blanc-Argent and St Beron
(6)   thence to Corsica. Scr.
(7)   thence to CF de Provence as 52. scr.
(8)   to Luçay-le-Mâle for preservation, 2000
(9)   to Baie de Somme, 1989

Possibly inspired by the CFD, several other concerns converted stean locomotives to tractors in small numbers. The CGL fabricated two quite handsome machines (351-52) which still exist on the Baie de Somme; the le Blanc-Argent, after finally settling on a couple of machines from the CFD's Indre-et-Loire batch, had two of its own design built at Perigueux Works; the Voies Ferrées du Dauphine built two narrow and two standard gauge machines – though the latter were rather in the nature of a Johnson rebuild with only the wheel centres and some frame parts being reused. Even the SE converted two of its 0-6-2Ts into 0-6-2Ds. By the time all this was happening, however, it was really too late; the small concerns which might have benefitted were closng or had already gone and there remained only the big systems of Intérêt Général as a market for future narrow gauge machines. The CFD partially met this need with a series of 400hp bogie 0-4-4-0 tractors with their patented Asynchro hydraulic/mechanical transmission, one for the Vivarais, two for the Corrèze and one for Corsica; all survived in 2000, two derelict at Nice and two in use at Bastia, together wth a similar, but non-coupled machine which is actually a standard gauge version rebuilt for Corsica as late as 1995.

The only other major developers of diesel locomotives for the French metre gauge railways were Brissoneau et Lotz, as a spin-off from their successful petrol electric railcars. Their first effort was a simple, boxy 0-6-0D tractor for the Tramways des Deux Sevres which was successful enough to be sold on to an industrial company and has since been preserved. Their main contribution was a series of ten BB 600hp double-cab DEs built after the war for the Union des Vois Ferrées, for Corsica, Provence and the Voies Ferrées du Dauphiné plus two tractors for the CF de Provence's Var system but they also produced some standard gauge machines - for example for the Régie des Bouches-du-Rhône and for the Anzin lines.

The CFD was also a major provider of diesel power for the standard gauge, developing first some four-wheeled examples and then a range of double-bogie, double-ended machines which found several buyers. Otherwise standard gauge diesel tractors were largely standard or lightly modified industrial probucts from firms such as Moyse, Valermi and Battignoles. Battignoles produced an interesting set of 0-6-0Ds for the Est de Lyon designed to work in multiple when required; the SE bought ten ex-US Army General Electric BB tractors for their Gironde system and commissioned six new BBs from COFERNA (Ste des Constructions Ferroviares et Navales), using similar parts, which must have been the ugliest diesels ever produced; they even looked as though laid down in a shipbuilding yard! In more modern times the few remaining lines have used SNCF-type locotracteurs and even lease SNCF BBs at times.

3. Electric locomotives

As for electric traction, electric locomotives and tractors were not common since they were really required only where the system had either heavy mineral traffic or dfficult gradients (Tramways de l'Ain)

CFD-built 4-wheeled and bogie standard gauge diesel locomotives at Autun, on the afformed Morvan lines.

Big, ugly but practical: One of the SE's DE1-6 series of diesel electric machines built mainly from General Electric parts. (AUTHOR)

or both (SGLM) or there were special reasons (CF de la Rhûne rack railway). Most lines preferred to use heavy power cars which could carry passengers or freight besides hauling extra coaches and/or wagons. Fairly common as a compromise, however, were the motor baggage cars (fourgons automoteurs). Those lines which did use tractors – such as CF de la Camargue and Tramways de l'Ain – tended to include a luggage compartment somewhere; only the CF de la Mure made a point of heavy bogie locomotives by Sécheron and that was because it was essentially a coal-hauler. The second generation of these still exist and now haul tourist trains on the line.

1 LE MONT SAINT-MICHEL. — Le Côté Sud et la Digue. — LL.

Seaside lines tended to go in for tinted cards: This is Mont St. Michel on the standard gauge line from Pontorson, in Manche.

SAINT-MALO. — Le Casino. -

And this is the St Malo station of the metre gauge Tramways Bretons, in Ille-et-Vilaine.

516. Cherbourg – La Divette et ligne Cherbourg Barfleur

Just inland, the standard gauge CF de la Manche line from Cherbourg to Barfleur with a Weidknecht 0-6-0T.

(C. WALKER'S COLLECTION)

GRANVILLE. — Le Chemin de fer de la Manche. — ND Phot.

And the same company's metre gauge line from Granville, again with a Weidknecht 0-6-0T. (C. WALKER'S COLLECTION)

A tram-train of the Cherbourg – Urville line, originally conceded to CF de la Manche as a railway, then taken over by Cherbourg tramways.

A train of the Tours tramways line out to Luynes and Fondettes – officially a railway of Intérêt Local and used by both tramways and the CFD. This is a St Leonard 0-4-0T of the tramways company.

Old and modern views of another semi-urban system, the CEN's Valenciennes network – here with a steam train at its Bonsecours terminus

(AUTHOR'S COLLECTION)

...and here at Lourches with an electric tram-train on the long interurban line from Valenciennes.

(AUTHOR)

13. LA TURBIE. — Chemin de fer à Crémaillère de Monte-Carlo. — Le Grand Cintre — LL.

Two historic rack lines: A steam train of the ill-fated Monte-Carlo – la Turbie Riggenbach line.

J.J. 5685 Chemin de fer du Salève. Château de Monnetier

The electric CF du Salève, near Geneva

Two ways of climbing hills: 1. The cremaillère from Langres station to town, in Haute Marne ended up right on the battlements. (AUTHOR)

2. The funicular de St Hilaire du Touvet, down in the Alpes east of Lyon. (AUTHOR)

Links from past to present: The CF de Chamonix au Montenvers in steam days.　　(K. TAYLORSON'S COLLECTION)

The CF de Chamonix au Montenvers in modern times with a two-car electric set.　　(AUTHOR)

A goods train of the 60cm gauge Tramway de Pithiviers à Toury headed by an ex-War Department ALCO 2-6-2T.

(AMTP/GEIGER)

A regular passenger train on the CF du Cambrésis pauses at a wayside station as late as 1959.

(AUTHOR)

Steam mixed train of the PO Lignes de Corrèze in SNCF days, awaiting departure at Tulle SNCF. Mallet 101 in charge.
(AUTHOR)

The CFD Réseau du Vivarais was using steam traction on goods work well into the 1960s. Here SLM Mallet 403 leaves St jean de Muzols on the regular Tuesday morning goods to Tournon.
(AUTHOR)

On the ligne affermées, a Billard car of the CFSTA waits at Provins station on the Provins – Longueville branch in 1967.

And a hired SNCF 130B leaves a station near Gray, on the CFTA's Franche Comté network, with a special working.

The 60cm gauge Crochat petrol electric railcar now restored to former glory by the AMTP. (AMTP/GEIGER)

The boxy standard gauge Berliet in reserve at St Rémy-en-Provence, on the Régie des Bouches du Rhône.

(AUTHOR)

A Billard A50D2 articulated car at Le Cheylard, on the CFD du Vivarais. (AUTHOR)

Two types of De Dion bogie cars at Carhaix on the Reseau Breton: OC1 in the shed and OC2 on the right.

(AUTHOR)

The countryside of the CFD du Tarn, with Billard A80D car crossing Le Boiussas viaduct. (AUTHOR)

A De Dion railbus pauses at St. Privat de Vallongue on the CFD's Ligne de la Lozère; a two-wheeled trailer is being unloaded. (D. TREVOR ROWE)

Traditional liveries on the CF de Provence; Brissoneau et Lotz diesel electric locomotive and Renault ABH railcar.

(AUTHOR)

And the standard gauge steam train to Palavas, on the SE's Hérault system.

(AUTHOR'S COLLECTION)

242

A packed train on the CF de la Mure, with Secheron T7 in charge, pauses at a photographic stop en route.

(AUTHOR)

A colourful train of the CF du Vivarais, with SLM Mallet 403.

(CFTM)

The Soule motor and trailer set of the CF de Provence, in new livery, enters the new station at Nice. (AUTHOR)

A Calvi – Bastia working on the CF Corses entangled with the seafront at Ile Rousse on the Ligne de Balagne; CFD 2XXX series cars. (AUTHOR)

CHAPTER 14
Railmotors and Tramcars

Early attempts: steam; battery and i/c electric

Railmotors, as such, first appeared on French secondary railways in the first decade of the 20th century when several designers - but mainly Purrey, Rowan, Scotte and Serpollet – produced self-propelled four-wheeled or bogie tramcars powered by a vertical boiler at one end. Several systems experimented wth one or the other – CFD de la Côte d'Or; Tramways de l'Ardèche; Twy de la Vallée de Celles; Tramways de Saumur et Extensions all had multiple examples and the Lyon tramways had some Rowan bogie cars. All found that the "delicate" nature of their mechanism, and the very limited passenger capacity, restricted their use to short urban navettes or shuttles; the same applied to attempts to utilise the Mekarski compressed air system which had been tried out on the urban tramways at, for example, Nantes, La Rochelle, Aix-les-Bains and in Paris. For rural work, which was what most lines wanted, the idea was a non-starter.

Steam and compressed air having proved largely unacceptable, there remained electricity which was a special case and will be discussed later, and the up-and-coming internal combustion engine with its problems of unreliability and power transmission. Two systems were then paramount. First was mechanical transmission via a gearbox and some form of final drive – chain or shaft and gearing – which reacted badly to inexperienced drivers or poor track; the other, building on tramway practice, was i/c electric using a petrol, diesel or gas engine to drive a generator which provided power to electric motors mounted either on the underframe or an axle; interestingly, the tramway design of maximum traction drive was not commonly used. A variant of this method was to use a bank of accumulators to replace, or supplement the petrol engine. Since this was, in essence, a dead end we may as well dispose of it first.

i/c-electrics: The battery-electric railmotors of French light railways form a very specific but interesting case. Given the very crude nature of early mechanical transmissions it was always to be expected that experiments with other types would be made. Petrol or benzol-electric drive was being tried as early as 1911, the design with most potential probably being the Pieper system which combined some battery power with a petrol engine. A series of Pieper cars was used by the Belgian Vicinal and a French company – the Cie des CF de Grande Banlieue – was briefly seduced but the whole thing was subject to many breakdowns and was, as its users said "delicate" – a favourite euphemism of the period; demotorised, however, they made quite good trailers. Westinghouse also tried their hand early on with the Tramway de Dinard à St Briac but their cars were not developed. The only serious attempts that lasted were pure-battery cars developed by consortia led by De Dion, Satramo and SACM – who later joined with Thomson to form Alsthom - which had a vogue during the 1920s and early 1930s on a few systems – CF Economiques des Charentes, CF du Morbihan, CF du Sud-Ouest near Toulouse had smallish fleets, the Sud-Ouest machines in particular arousing some interest because of their ability to pull three or even four bogie trailers. Unfortunately, the weight of batteries required to provide any reasonable radius of action was considerable. If there was also a requirement to haul one or more trailers, which there often was, then the result was invariably a massive bogie machine of "ironclad" appearance, an axleload perilously near the permitted maximum and a restricted range. In addition, running costs were not entirely favourable and the charging requirements made them inflexible in operation. The electric drive, therfore, did not become generally interesting until reliable petrol-driven generators became available. Then two firms took it up and developed it in different ways; they were Henri Crochat, in association with Decauville, and Brissoneau et Lotz.

Crochat built petrol-electric devices for all gauges, wth examples of 60cm, metre and standard gauge being produced in small numbers, although his railcars were confined to the narrow gauge. His design stemmed from a series of centre-cab locomotives produced for the military during the first war and comprised a motor-generator set of from 16 to 40hp driving one or more axlehung motors, all set in a very boxy body on a conventional channel frame. All the narrow gauge cars had limited accommodation because of the room taken up by the power unit and were not greatly liked because of the additional complication of the drive. However a variety of railways bought them as evidenced below although Crochat himself retired from the fray in 1924; Decauville took over his patents and customers:

Crochat Petrol-electric railcars

Year	Customer	Type	No	Notes
60cm gauge				
1922	TPT		1	single-end, 4w
1923	Twys de Savoie		1	type TPT
1923-24	CF du Calvados	CL	3	double-end, 4w
1923-24	Twys de Savoie	CL	1	type CL
1926	Twys de Savoie	SV	2	single-end, bogie
metre gauge				
1923	Twys de Loir-et-Cher	LC	1	single-end, 4w
1925	Twys d'Eure-et-Loir	LC	1	type LC
1925	CFD Indre-et-Loire	IL	1	double-end 4w
1924	CF de la Drôme	DR	1	single-end 4w
1927	Dept de la Meuse	DR	2	single-end 4w
1923	Dept de la Dordogne	DD	2	double-end, bogie
1925	CFD	VV	3	double-end, bogie (1)
1926-27	Saône-et-Loire	SL	4	double-end, bogie
1927	VFD (Réseau TOD)	SL	1	double-end, bogie

(1) one to Vivarais, then Charentes; two to Corsica

The light that failed: A typical Purrey steamcar, of the Tramways de l'Ardèche.   (FACS)

Early cars had to pull ordinary coaches: The railway-type Renault-Scemia RS series could do so reasonably well: This is a standard gauge RS4 of the CF de Grande Banlieue. (RENAULT/FACS)

Others, such as this gas-powered Campagne device of the Tramways de Loir-et-Cher had to have special light trailers provided. The odd cylinder is the gazogene apparatus. (FACS)

All these, however, were really variations on a theme, the main development consisting in use of bogies rather than four-wheels and in provision of two driving positions; technically they remained faithful to Crochat's original concept.

The main development of i/c electric drive for secondary railways was taken up by the firm of Brissoneau et Lotz who had produced much of the electrical equipment for Crochat's experiments. During the early 1930s they developed what was, for the period, a sophisticated power unit based on either a Berliet or Saurer diesel engine of 125-150hp coupled to electrical equipment of their own design; in some of the more powerful cars the sets were duplicated and arranged side-by-side in a special compartment. This equipment was installed in an excellent chassis, with compensated springing to the bogies, axlehung motors and a high standard of coachwork and passenger comfort. The standard car for French lines, derived from a series built for the CF de l'Anjou in 1934-35, was modern in appearance with metal clad bodywork and roof radiator; a development was an articulated motor-trailer set built in 16 examples for the Sud-France's Var system. Customers included:

CF de l'Anjou	5	1934-35	later to CF du Doubs
CF du Morbihan	7	1934-37	to CdN/Germany
CFE des Charentes	7	1936	scr/Germany
CF de la Vallée de Celles	1	1937	scr
CF de Provence (Var)	16	1935-38	to Cantabrica, Spain

Two of those were Jeancard Group lines with experience of battery-electric traction. Despite some problems with the electrical systems owing to overloading, the cars generally served well and found a good second-hand market when their original owners closed - to Doubs and Côtes du Nord in France for the standard cars, and to the northern coast lines in Spain for the articulateds. Three were even sold to Germany during the war and ended up as DR class VT 137.562-564 on the Franzburger Kreisbahnen. Further developments were sold to French Africa but they are outside the scope of this work.

i/c engined railbuses and railcars

Railbuses: Almost contemporaneous with Crochat's early work was the development of the single ended, mechanical-transmission bus-on-rails which was taken up by a plethora of lines and systems. As related elsewhere it all started with M.Tartary whose group were concessionaires for a number of dubiously viable steam tramways. The end of WW1 released cheaply onto the market a great many road motor vehicles, among them a set of ex US Army GMC ambulances on offer at a disposals site near Romorantin. M Tartary recognised that these with their, for the period, reasonable suspension might form the basis for an economical rail vehicle, bought a job-lot and took them to the workshops of his Tramways des Deux-Sevres at Parthenay. Here, over a period, he developed his ideas, first with a simple conversion of a complete ambulance and then with successively more sophisitcated bodies on the basic chassis. His patents essentially consisted of mounting the chassis on specially designed rail wheels in such a way that the front axle had some longitudinal play through the former steering mechanism and in providing a crude built-in turning plate so that the single-ended vehicle could be turned anywhere on the line. This initially involved a separate circular "track" that could be laid down but was later completely integral and actuated by means of a jack.

All Tartary's bus bodies were slightly idyosyncratic and had a home-made look. At the same period, however, the firm of Baert & Verney, which ran several concessions nearby, also bought a job-lot of 50 ambulances, designed or adapted a proper road bus body to suit them and started series production; they were probably the first proper railbuses and served on a variety of lines. They were followed by a few very crude conversions from Saurer and a much larger number of purpose-built vehicles from the car firm of De Dion Bouton which bought up Tartary's patents and produced over 100 during the next ten years (in all De Dion built 195 cars for secondary lines, of which 89 - nearly half - were J series railbuses and many of the rest were the closely related K, M and N series cars). The main lines of development were two-fold; replacement of the bus-type front axle by a four-wheeled bogie to improve riding and ease the battering given

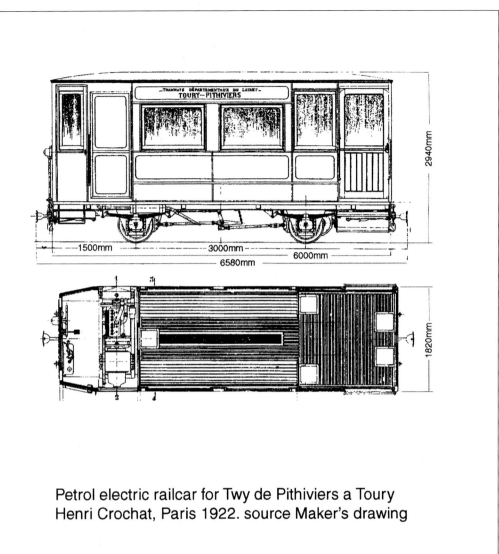

Petrol electric railcar for Twy de Pithiviers a Toury
Henri Crochat, Paris 1922. source Maker's drawing

to already fading track; and movement of the driver's seat to the forward control position, thus releasing space within the body and giving a more modern full-fronted appearance. The De Dions in themselves show the linear development of the concept. First were the J series (JA & JM) which were basically a De Dion bus chassis suitably strengthened and equipped, and then fitted with a squareish bus body often built by outside contractors - Carel et Fouché were a favourite. The first JM series (JM2-4) which were most common were four-wheeled but then came the K series with a front bogie and full-fronted cab grafted on, followed by the more rounded M series and finally the quite impressive NC and ND for the CFD in 1934 and their standard gauge analogues for the SE and the CF de l'Est. These were effectively the final railbuses, De Dion moving on to bogie double-enders of proper railway construction. It should be said here that railbuses have, perhaps, had an undeservedly bad press. Certainly their ride was less than perfect but then the alternative - the same bus jolting alonmg the unmade roads or pavé of the period - was even more bone-shaking. When compared to conventional railway coaches, at least railbus passengers tended to have upholstered seats and reliable heating (off the exhaust) rather than footwarmers or a fumy coke stove.

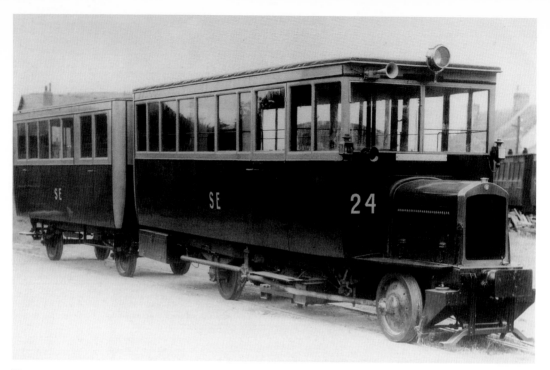

The most common early vehicle was the genuine railbus. This is a typical De Dion JM series car of the CF de l'Anjou with its matching trailer.

(FACS)

Biggest competitor to the De Dion was probably the equivalent Verney design, here represented by car No. 5 of the CFD du Finistère with its odd (but by no means uncommon) single axle trailer.

(FACS)

Certainly even the JM series had long and useful lives so they clearly served their purpose. Even a partial list of initial customers is a rollcall of the French secondaires:

Twy de Châteaubriant à Erbray	1
CF des Côtes du Nord:	11
VFE de l'Orne	4
Tramways de Loir-et-Cher	1
Tramways d'Ille et Vilaine	5
CF du Doubs	7
CF Vicinaux	7
SE (various systems)	35 mainly M/N types
CFD (various systems)	15 mainly N types
Tramways du Loiret	3
Tramways de l'Indre	3
Tramways de la Sarthe	2
CFD de l'Aube	2
CF de Cormeilles à Glos Montfort	1
CFS du Sud-Ouest	11 all type MT
CF de l'Anjou	8

and many among this illustrative list had repeat orders

De Dion were by no means the only maker to enter this particular field. Billard of Tours started their railmotor career with some very bus-like vehicles for Oise – but on proper railway chassis; Renault had an initial period of developing rather crude bus-type single enders, and pioneered the replacement of front wheels by a bogie before producing the railway-type Renault-Scemia RS series; Verney developed the concept into some quite modern looking vehicles which included semi-articulated designs. M Laborie, another innovator/entrepreneur, after playing with souped-up draisines, experimented with rubber-tyred wheels and produced a series of fast, semi-streamlined versions for his Doubs system; a spin-off which only affected one or two standard gauge lines in France was the Micheline, effectively a luxury road coach on six or eight wheels, with drive to a rear bogie and rubber-tyred wheels to improve suspension. Most went abroad or to the main lines but the standard gauge Caen à la Mer had two and some main line companies bought them for secondary routes.

As regards railbuses in general, a few were even produced for standard gauge lines – not many because the single-ended format was unwieldy with heavy vehicles. All however, were essentially similar under the skin. Their common characteristic was that they were single-ended, with only a low reverse gear, and that, in the final analysis, the chassis of most of them was designed for road work – it was comparatively flimsy and the suspension was somewhat bone-shaking...In the end it was these features which terminated development in favour of purpose-built, double ended designs which we will consider in a moment.

First, however, there was an odd hybrid which seems to have been almost unique to France – the Belgian SNCV is the only other serious contender known to the writer and their effort was a bit of a cheat. This was the conversion, by several lines, of ordinary four-wheeled passenger coaches into self-propelled vehicles. There was, supposedly, something of a precedent in the old steamcars which were often basically powered coaches but the i/c engined conversions had only cheapness to commend them. They retained all the discomfort and spartan nature of their origin with noise, vibration and jerkiness added, so the idea was a dead end. The Lyon firm of Berliet started in this way and their fairly small production all had boxy echoes of that origin.

The main line of development, however, from the mid-1930s was in purpose-built motor railcars and in these French manufacturers excelled. Leaving aside Brissoneau et Lotz already mentioned, two makers dominated the scene in the 1930s and 1940s – Renault and Billard, both of whom also had considerable overseas markets to aid their development – the demands of the longer French colonial lines in Africa and Indo China led to provision of more powerful engines, rugged drive trains and comfortable interiors. In France, development took two different paths.

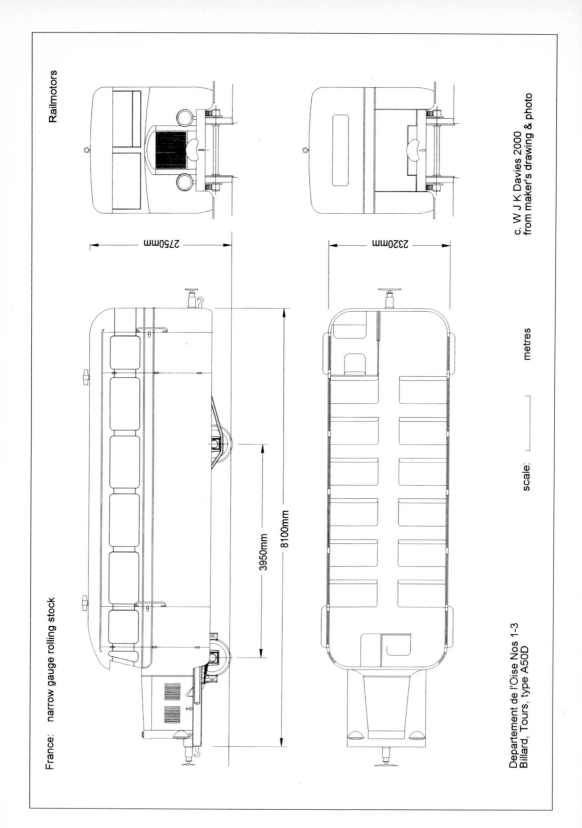

Railmotors

France: narrow gauge rolling stock

2750mm

2320mm

8100mm

3950mm

c. W J K Davies 2000
from maker's drawing & photo

scale: _____ metres

Departement de l'Oise Nos 1-3
Billard, Tours, type A50D

Logical conclusion of the railbus was the full-fronted De Dion N series produced for the CFD in particular. This is CFD 201 still operating on the Lozère in the 1960s. (AUTHOR)

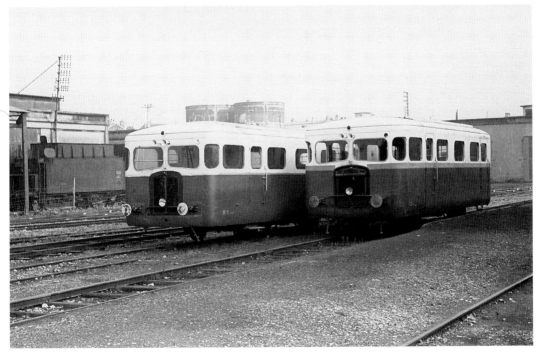

The standard gauge equivalents were probably the VFIL-built single-ended cars: These two are on the Achiet – Bapaume in Pas-de-Calais. (AUTHOR)

Renault were very much involved in building for the main line companies and their products showed it. Following the successful four-wheeled RS series, built for both standard and metre gauges, they steadily developed large double-ended bogie cars, normally using Renault engines and capable of pulling a reasonable trailing load. The final result, so far as secondary railways were concerned were the VH and ABH series used by main line companies and some substantial secondary companies such as the St Quentin-Guise, and their metre gauge analogues the ABH and ABJ cars. Between 1935 and 1950 these were purchased in some quantity by the CFD (for Corsica), the CF de Provence and, in three examples, by the CF des Côtes du Nord. They were intended for long distance work and their quality was such that examples were still in use in 1999 on relief duties in both Corsica and Provence.

After experimenting with a few single-ended railbuses (A50D and DL; A75D) Billard (more precisely the Sté des Anciens Etablissements Billard) of Tours took a completely different approach. Largely at the instigation of the big CFD concern, they developed a low-slung, lightweight diesel-powered bogie vehicle capable of running fast over light secondary trackwork and of hauling a matching trailer. These little cars, ranging from 80hp to 210hp, were double-ended with a low centre of gravity, had provision for luggage and small goods, and revolutionised timetables on many secondary systems. The CFD took the lion's share of production but the Tramways d'Ille-et-Vilaine and the CFS du Nord Est (on the standard gauge) bought some and came back for more and they were always in demand second-hand when their original systems closed; some went through half a dozen owners. The final logical development came too late for the French market but was built in some quantity - and also under licence - for Spain. Billard also produced scaled up versions for the standard gauge and designed a lightweight standard gauge four-wheeler (9XX series) which was later built also by the CFD for their Morvan lines. The metre gauge programme showed a steady development, successive series being (by nominal horsepower):

The larger standard gauge cars were often single-ended too. Here one of the slightly odd Verney semi articulated, three-section cars dozes on the CFE de l'Hérault.
(AUTHOR)

A80D	1937-38	12	CFD Charentes	31-33; 311-15
			CFD Indre-et-Loire	511-13
			CFD de l'Yonne	801
A80D1	1938	12	CFD Dordogne	601-12
A80D2	1938-38	5	CFD Vendée	701-04
			CFD Seine-et-Marne	705
A80D3		1	CFD Charentes	316
A80D4		2	CFD Indre-et-Loire	514-15
A135D	1935	3	CFD Indre-et-Loire	501-03
A150D	1936-37	9	CFD Corsica	111-16
			CFD Vivarais	211-213
A150D1	1937	5	Twys d'Ille-et-Vilaine	AM20-25*
A150D2	1939	4	CFD Vivarais	221-24**
A150D4	1939	1	CFD Vivarais	214
A150D6	1946-47	4	Twys d'Ille-et-Vilaine	AM21/26-28
A210D	1935	6	CFD Corsica	101-06

*   essentially an uprated A135D
**   articulated cars, essentially two A80D combined

Of these the A80D series (sub-series 1-4) was the most well-known, variants being produced in two widths (2.200 and 2.400m) to suit existing loading gauges and with engines of from 80hp to 100hp. Most were eventually fitted retrospectively with the latter. The numbering was not quite as simple as it seems since vehicles were sometimes diverted between systems before delivery and others ordered in replacement. The gaps in type designation for the A150D series are accounted for by three standard gauge cars (A150D3/5) for the CFS du Nord Est; the postwar ones for Spain (A150D7) and three for la Reunion (A150D8). The success of all these cars was such that they lasted long and had a succession of owners; even in 1999 preservation groups were still using them in normal traffic.

Perhaps one should not neglect the firm of SCF Verney altogether. During the 1930s they concentrated on exploring the single-ended design which they brought to a high pitch of development. Their market was always smaller than the others but the Tramways de la Vendée, CFD du Tarn, and some others had several each and put in repeat orders. The position is somewhat confused since their distinctive bodywork was very similar to that of a railway company which built its own cars during the same period. That was the Compagnie Générale des Voies Ferrées d'Intérêt Local, whose Lumbres Works busily rebodied various railbuses and built new a number of four-wheeled and bogie cars, both metre and standard gauge. They used the professional coachworks of Milliom-Guiet extensively and it may be that SCF Verney, when they were based in the Ardennes, used the same firm. The CGL, however, extemporised rather than developing; Verney did make a final contribution with eight large bogie double-ended cars for the SNCF after World War 2. They were split between the PO Corrèze and le Blanc-Argent and several, rebodied, were still in reserve on the latter in 1999.

In a way, one should stop there since the market faded away. Several lines of Intérêt Général, however, refused to die - Provence; Corsica; le Blanc-Argent – and, in the 1970s these needed replacement railcars. There has, therefore, been a final flowering, mainly through the big CFD who now specialise in building equipment rather than running railways. They have produced successive improvements of a standard bogie railcar, normally with CFD Asynchro transmission; successively there are the X1200; X2000; X5000 series and, in recent years a very efficient motor-trailer set in collaboration with Soulé of Bordeaux who have now been taken over. Provence, the le Blanc – Argent and Corsica have all benefitted; the latest cars were delivered as recently as 1998 to Corsica and even more modernistic ones are currently in production for the Le Blanc – Argent. On the standard gauge, the main experiment was a series of three lightweight, four-wheeled railbuses built by Soulé at Bagneres de Bigorre in 1990 for secondary lines in Brittany. Designed to work in multiple if required and incorporating as many standard fitments as possible, these were, in

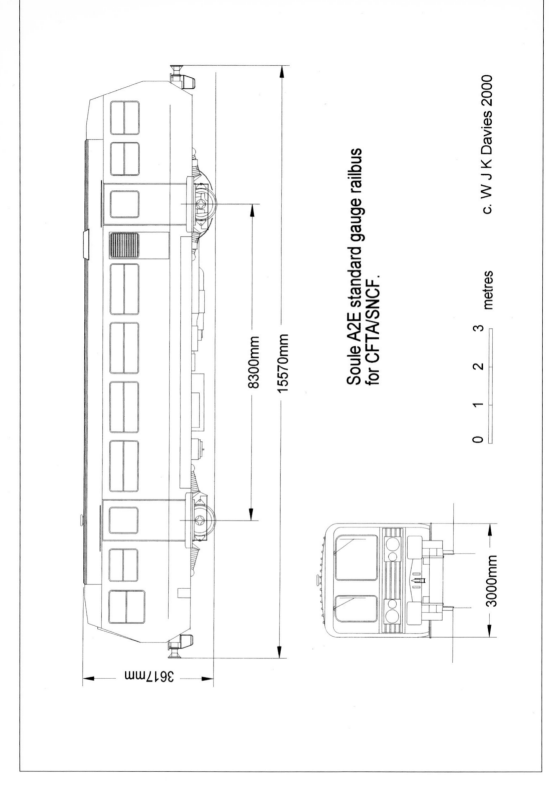

Soule A2E standard gauge railbus
for CFTA/SNCF.

c. W J K Davies 2000

0   1   2   3   metres

15570mm

8300mm

3617mm

3000mm

256

The later successful double-ended metre gauge design must here be represented by the one that lasted best: A Billard A150D of 1937. (AUTHOR)

More "artisanale", perhaps, were the VFIL Lumbres-built bogie cars bodied by Milliom-Guiet and looking very like Verneys. This is M41 in its later days at Noyelles on the Somme. (AUTHOR)

France: narrow gauge rolling stock

diesel railcars

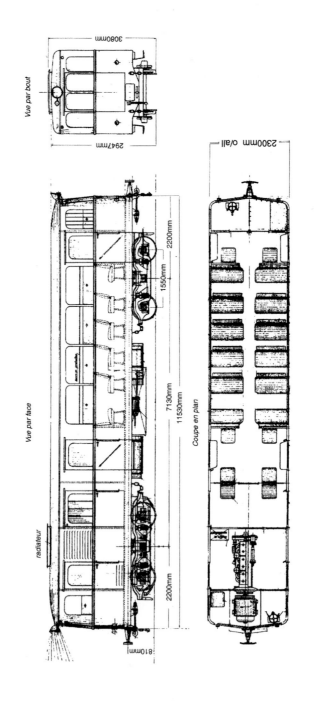

Diesel-electric railcar for CFIL de l'Anjou
Ets. Brissoneau et Lotz, 1937

source: maker's drawing simplified

258

effect, modern equivalents of the CFD's 9XX series. They appear to have suffered from the same problems as light railbuses elsewhere and have not been perpetuated.

Motor luggage vans

An interesting variation not common outside France was the motor luggage van or fourgon automoteur. This was in essence, an offshoot of the type quite popular on electric lines (qv) where it was effectively a heavy power car with space for goods instead of passengers and capable of towing either coaches or goods vehicles. On non electrified lines, however, it was usually a self-contained vehicle intended to provide a more regular and faster service for small goods than could be given through the periodic mixed train especially once railcars took over passenger workings. The first one recorded was actually a Turgan-Foy steam car on the Dinard – St Briac line but the real ancestor was probably the rather odd device dreamed up by M. Tartary on one of his lengthened ambulance chassis.This was, visually, a large furniture pantechnicon on wheels and the massive rear overhang must have led to some very judicious loading at times. It was not repeated but, as steam services declined, several systems converted surplus railcars to run messageries services. A typical single-ended one was Verney railcar A3, on the CFD du Tarn, and the CFD converted several double-ended Billard cars in much the same way.

Electric railmotors – tramcar and railway patterns

Many of the smaller electric lines were essentially electric tramways carrying only passengers and small goods (messageries). The smallest, often station to town lines, simply used the contemporary patterns of urban trancar. Those slightly larger were mainly in the nature of suburban trams and, again, tended to use appropriate stock – four-wheeled or bogie passenger trams capable of pulling one or more trailers; the main difference from urban lines, as already noted, was that they often had two or more classes of accommodation.

The main railway development was in power cars for large départemental systems: The serious lines and systems were really of two main types – the conventional départemental light railway radiating from a centre or with a group of disconnected rural lines; and the very few true interurban (or at least inter-ville) systems. The latter tended to come late and, as would be expected, run between two agglomerations or a city and its suburbs: Lyon – Neuville; Annemasse – Sixt; Toulouse – Castres and Revel were of this type. Classic examples of the former were: Tramways Électriques de Loir-et-Cher; CFD de la Haute Vienne; CF

Electric cars 1: a "train" of elements automoteurs at Chamonix, on the SNCF St Gervais – Vallorcine line.

(AUTHOR)

France: narrow gauge rolling stock

electric power cars

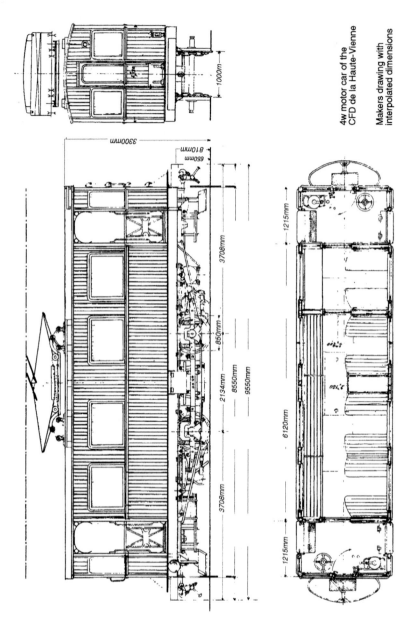

4w motor car of the
CFD de la Haute-Vienne

Makers drawing with
interpolated dimensions

Source: maker's drawing

Power car for CFD de la Haute-Vienne
Ste. Franco Belge, Raismes 1909

Electric power cars

France: Narrow gauge rolling stock

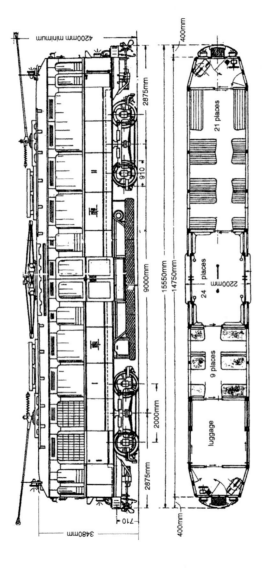

Power car for metre gauge Tramway de Lyon a Neuville
Les Constructions Electriques de la France, Venissieux 1932

source: TCL diagram redimensioned

261

Electrics 2: Modern power car of the Tramways de l'Ain.   (FACS)

de la Camargue; CFIL du Territoire de Belfort; or (among the smaller operators) Tramways du Libournais.

The "rural" départemental systems divided again between those which favoured four-wheeled designs and the bogie advocates. The four-wheelers were used particularly by lines in mountainous country such as the Tramways des Alpes Maritimes. These could be built by well-known makers such as Decauville but tended to be equipped electrically by others such as SACM or Thomson. They were oftem mounted on tramway-type trucks and accommodation varied; the TAM, for example had 1st/luggage cars (which then towed 2nd class trailers) and all-2nd class ones (which towed composites). The systems in flatter country (eg: Haute-Vienne; Loir-et-Cher) tended to favour bogie vehicles with multi-class accommodation and specifically designed to tow goods wagons as well as passenger trailers.

In the middle was that small group which had equipment characteristics of both – Fourvière Ouest Lyonnais with its Vaugneray-type motor cars; Tramways de l'Ain which superimposed modern electric railcars on a typical rural system; the Voies Ferrées des Pyrenées Orientales in the Haut-Vallespir; the main-line-owned Cerdagne and Chamonix systems; even, perhaps, the odd branches to Cauterets and Luz in the central Pyrenées. Their equipment was individual and, indeed, sometimes idiosyncratic in character. The FOL, for example, had large, elegant bogie vehicles with end vestibuled entrances and a clerestory; the Tramways de l'Ain examples were definitely specially built railcars and motor luggage vans with neat, round-cornered steel bodywork, full pantographs and modern control equipment and had very little of the tram in their ancestry; the St Gervais-Vallorcine originally had boxy, balconied four-wheeled stock, almost every item of which was motored, with its own controls and could be used independently or in multiple; the Cerdagne had large oblong bogie motor cars very clearly designed by a main-line railway company; the VFPO had narrow bogie steel-clad railcars and the Cauterets lines had a strange combination of open control platforms (later enclosed!) and side door compartments in their bogie cars. In most cases these soldiered on either until closure or, in the Cerdagne's case, to the present day with a modicum of rebuilding. Only the St Gervais – Vallorcine saw first a series of railway-type bogie cars and trailers and, more recently, some very modern multi-capable stock for interworking with the neighbouring Martigny – Le Chatelard company.

262

CHAPTER 15

Rolling Stock

1. Passenger rolling stock

Passenger stock of French light railways tended to be determined by three factors: the gauge; whether the railways were roadside or on their own right of way; what the major manufacturers were ready to offer. The main manufacturers were either French or Belgian and, in both cases, had a flourishing market not only at home but in the colonies and in other European countries – for example Spain and Portugal. Like the locomotive makers, they, therefore, tended to settle on fairly standard designs which fitted common specifications and could be offered more economicially than bespoke models.

Locomotive hauled enclosed coaches

These are probably best discussed by gauge, since the three main gauges developed very differently:

Standard gauge: it may be unkind to say that there was no real development on the standard gauge but it is true. Just as in Britain, minor standard gauge railways tended to buy obsolete or obsolescent vehicles from main line companies and run them into the ground – as late as the 1950s coaches could still be seen running around in the north east with the quadrant windows characteristic of the very early days of railways and, at places as far apart as Mamers, Bayonne, Caen and Paris, double-deckers ("à l'Imperiale") were by no means unknown well into the twentieth century. A few lines, such as the CFE de l'Hérault, bought end-balcony four-wheelers but the typical standard gauge minor railways coach was a shabby compartment vehicle, often with windows in the doors only and with hard wooden seating in the third class. After each

Both 4-wheeled and bogie coaches with the antique quadrant windows were still around in the early 1960s. This is an example in workmen's service in the HN Valenciennes group. (AUTHOR)

Nombre de places assises : 1ʳᵉ Classe, **6** ; 2ᵐᵉ Classe, **14**. Au total, **20**.

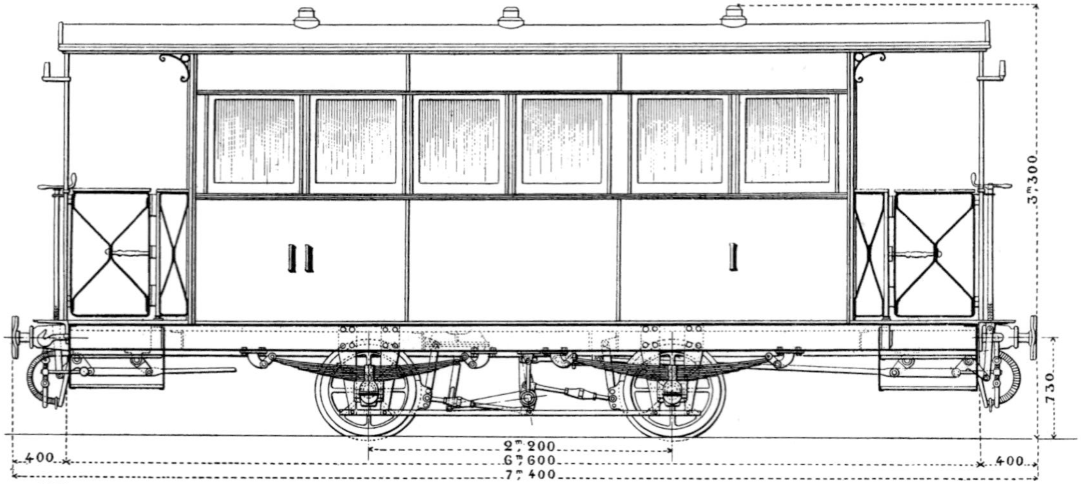

Ce type de voiture a été construit pour la **Cⁱᵉ des Chemins de Fer du Tarn-et-Garonne.**

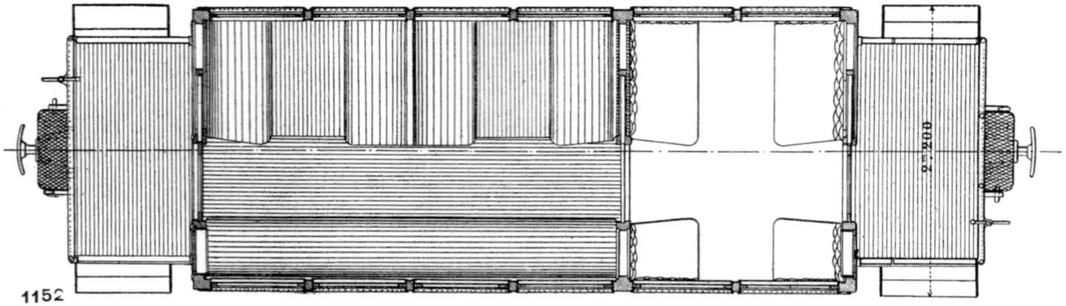

1151
1152

4w balcony-end metre gauge coach for Twys de Tarn-et-Garonne – Decauville.

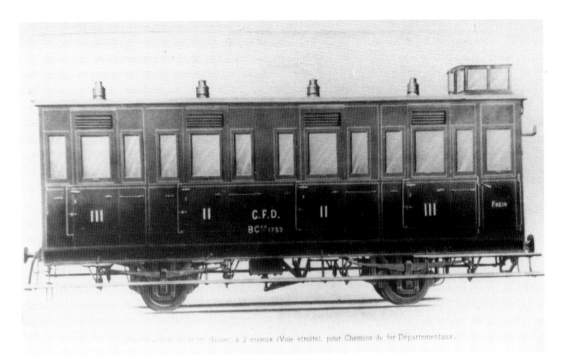

Its narrow gauge equivalent, the "cage aux poules" as used by the big CFD company. (AUTHOR'S COLLECTION)

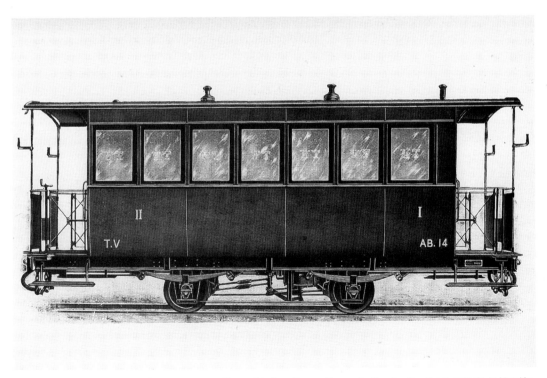

The most common 4-wheeler for metre gauge lines: this is a Decauville production for the Tramways de la Vendée.

(AUTHOR'S COLLECTION/DECAUVILLE)

of the two wars, German branch line coaches were frequently used, having been acquired as war reparations and for some unfathomable reason the SE's Gironde system ended up with some ex-Metropolitan Railway eight-wheeled parallel-axle coaches. As to bogie coaches, frequently they were second-hand cast-offs of a main line company although it must be said that just occasionally this resulted in something rather special; the Houillères line from Somain to Peruwelz for instance, as late as the 1960s, had immaculately maintained compartment bogie coaches from the CF de l'Est which put their main line cousins to shame – even if they did, quaintly, have quadrant windows (and red leather buttoned upholstery) in the first class only.

Metre gauge: Early passenger vehicles for the metre gauge (for example on the Lagny – Mortcerf line or the early CFD concessions like Indre-et-Loire) were invariably crude compartment stock originating in contemporary road vehicle design, with small, infrequent windows and, often, with external wood framing to the body. As lines developed, however, they too developed in two different ways – four-wheeled or bogie (six-wheeled was never popular although a few lines used long-wheelbase four-wheelers with De Rechter radial axles); compartment or end-balconied saloon. In some ways there was considerably more progression than on the standard gauge; at its best the later bogie coach for the bigger Intérêt Général systems was as well built and comfortable as any of its European contemporaries.

A number of lines settled on compartment vehicles for various reasons, mainly in imitation of main line companies. Typical examples were the CF de l'Anjou, which used them almost exclusively and the CFD which used them even on its Intérêt Général systems as initial equipment. Typical examples of both composite and third class four-wheeled stock survive in preservation on the CF du Vivarais and show the standard features of side-door compartments with small windows each side of the door and droplights in the doors themselves; partitions might be full-height or, in lower classes especially, where shared lamps were common, three-quarter-height only. They had the advantages of body rigidity and privacy, particularly for superior class passengers but the triple disadvantages of being difficult to heat; considerably impeding the chef-de-train in his passages through the train (or along the footboards in this case); having

Intermediate type: a 4-wheeler with extended wheelbase and radial axles on the CFD du Tarn.

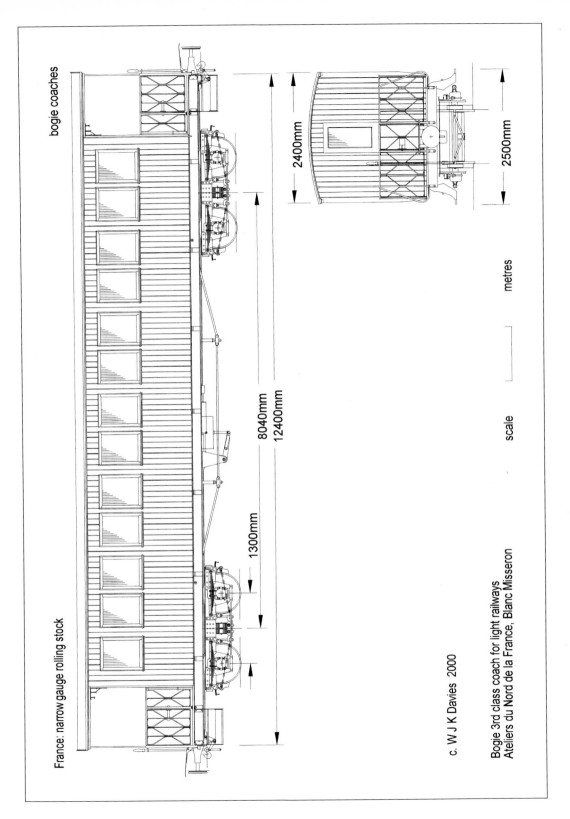

France: narrow gauge rolling stock

bogie coaches

2400mm

2500mm

8040mm
12400mm

1300mm

scale

metres

c. W J K Davies 2000

Bogie 3rd class coach for light railways
Ateliers du Nord de la France, Blanc Misseron

France: narrow gauge rolling stock

coaches

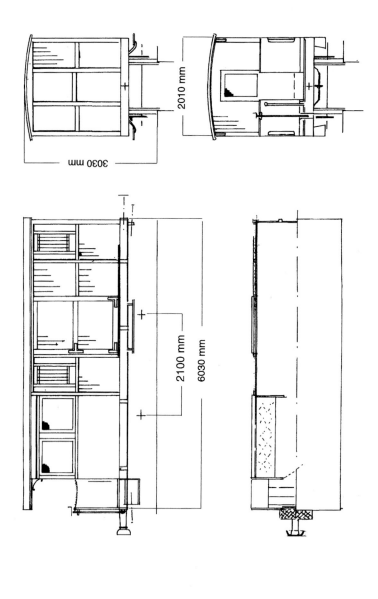

3030 mm

2010 mm

6030 mm

2100 mm

W J K Davies 1995

scale |_____| metres

Typical metre gauge 4w luggage/coach
Tramways de la Correze

Decauville bogie coach for Twy de la Trinite-s-Mer à Etel (60cm gauge)

swing-doors which could be inconvenient at roadside halts. Nonetheless both four-wheeled and bogie versions were used by companies with their own right of way and unencumbered stations.

Tramways, and other lines with a proportion of roadside running, soon settled on the end-balcony saloon coach as meeting their requirements more fully. It was much easier to board from roadside locations since steps could be recessed into the balcony structure; it could be heated more or less adequately from a solid fuel stove sited within the saloon; the chef de train could move easily through the train via its end doors and fallplates between vehicles. In addition, on lines with restricted loading gauge, the seating could be arranged either longitudinally or along one side with transverse seating opposite, allowing a narrower body. Differing classes were catered for by transverse bulkheads with internal doors. There were plenty of spartan third class examples with only a few, widely spaced droplights each side, including some bogie vehicles – for example on the CF du Cambrésis which catered extensively for industrial workers. It is noteworthy, however, that even early examples more commonly had contiguous windows along each side, often with droplights for ventilation.

There were variations on the theme – the CF de la Drôme, for example used centre-entrance four-wheelers, and bogie composites sometimes had one or more entrance platforms between classes, often in conjunction with end balconies – but once the "rules" were established by standard cahiers there was little real development. The big manufacturers such as Carel et Fouché, Dyle et Bacalan, Desouches et David, SA la Metallurgique (later SA les Ateliers Metallurgiques) and other French/Belgian concerns were quite happy to build essentially similar vehicles well into the 1920s when increasing use of railcars effectively stopped further purchases. Ironically Decauville, who were so advanced on the 60cm gauge, tended to concentrate for metre gauge lines on very traditional four-wheeled or bogie tramway-type cars, often with reversed semi-elliptic (ie "upside down") springing on the bogies. Only a few big companies, such as the CFD for its Vivarais, Lozère and Corsican systems, took the logical step of ordering vestibuled, steam-heated saloons or mixed compartment/saloon corridor coaches fitted with toilet facilities for their long distance workings but several concerns took advantage of the bogie coach to have a train in one vehicle – 1st, 2nd, 3rd class plus luggage was certainly not unknown.

Charge : 5 tonnes.

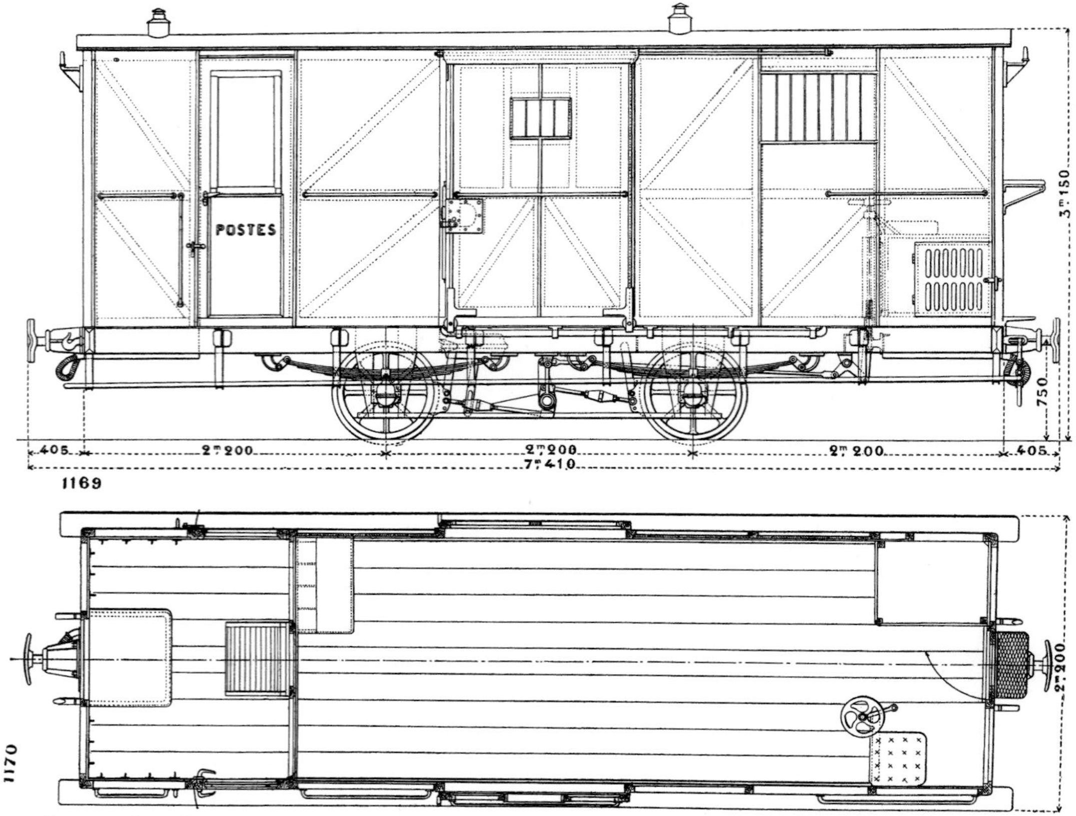

3ᵐ150

750

405.

2ᵐ200.

2ᵐ200

7ᵐ410.

POSTES

2ᵐ200

405.

1169

2ᵐ900

1170

Ce type de voiture a été construit pour la **Compagnie des Tramways du Tarn-et-Garonne.**

4w luggage van, metre gauge, for Tramways de Tarn-et-Garonne – Decauville.

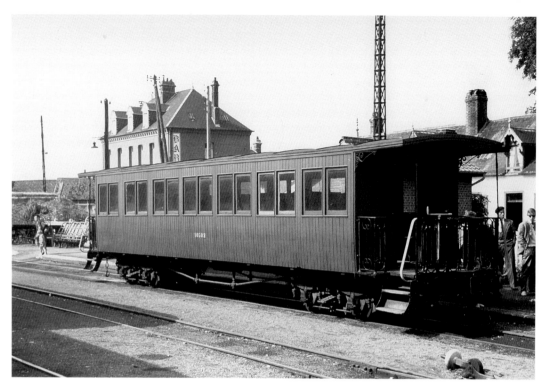

And a metre gauge bogie coach of SE pattern, by Ateliers de Manage.

(AUTHOR)

Elegance on the metre gauge; a 1st/2nd lavatory composite of the Réseau Breton, for the up-market holiday traffic.

(AUTHOR)

60cm gauge: In some ways this stock was developed further and earlier than on other gauges. This was almost entirely due to the energy and imagination of the Decauville company which, from the start tried to combine low tare weight with the maximum capacity allowed by the prevailing axleload. Hence Decauville lines, even in the early 1890s, had long, elegant bogie coaches, sometimes with secondary suspension. The one oversight was in luggage van design, this being restricted mainly to rather crude adaptations of a standard four-wheeled van. Most 60cm gauge lines retained this stock to the end, only the Tramway de Pithiviers à Toury building some quite modern-looking centre entrance vehicles on old chassis in the 1920s and 1930s. It is also notable that, when other makers entered the 60cm gauge market, stock regressed rather than developing; Blanc Misseron designs for the later Calvados lines were simply scaled down versions of metre gauge four-wheeled stock.

Open and semi-open coaches

The one aspect in which the narrower gauges excelled was in the provision of "baladeuses", open-sided vehicles with transverse seating of "toastrack" pattern and much in vogue among the coastal or spa-resort lines. Most common on the 60cm gauge, although some metre gauge "tourist" lines had them, these could be either four-wheeled or bogie and might be fitted either with back-to-back seating or with tramway-type swing-over seat backs. Many also had vestigial end balconies to accommodate handbrakes (and a few standing passengers) while some side protection was provided by either drop-down blinds or, more commonly, curtains. Only one line, so far as is known, officially had completely roofless trailers, this being the metre gauge Ligne de Cerdagne in the Pyrenées but there are photographs from various sources showing open wagons in use as improvised passenger accommodation in times of stress. Most baladeuses were third class but the CF du Calvados had a number of 1st class vehicles with half-doors, some screening between compartments and upholstered seats.

Typical metre gauge goods stock 1: a ventilated van with brakesman's hut. (AUTHOR)

Voiture de 1ʳᵉ Classe
à bogies
Type KG

Voie de 600 ᵐ/ₘ

Nombre de places assises **30**

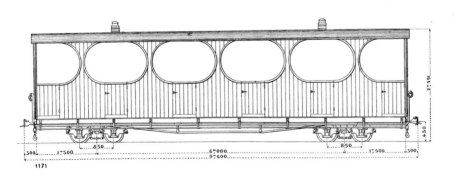

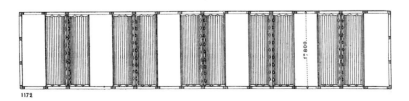

Ce type de voiture a été adopté par de nombreuses compagnies de **Chemins de Fer d'Intérêt local.**

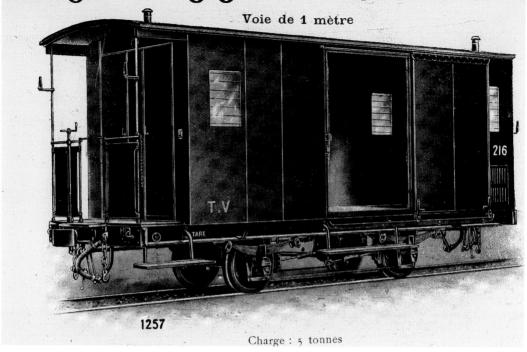

Fourgon à bagages avec compartiment pour la

Voie de 1 mètre

1257

Charge : 5 tonnes

4w luggage van for Twys de Tarn-et-Garonne.

Less usual were single-axle railcar trailers. Here are three differing examples, one insulated, on the CFD's Ligne de la Lozère.

Luggage, brake and postal vehicles

Here, irrespective of gauge, there was a clear difference of opinion between operators. Some wanted composite passenger/luggage vehicles, others preferred separate luggage/brake vans; in either case it was normal to insert a postal compartment for carriage - rather than sorting - of mail instead of having dedicated postal vehicles. There was no "typical" design of luggage van, as can be seen from the accompanying illustrations. Four-wheelers were most common, and could have end-balconies or simply blank ends, but often with a narrow personnel door allowing access to other vehicles by fallplates. In general the interior was one large space which the chef de train had to share with the luggage and any livestock - although a common feature for dogs especially was an integral ventilated box, usually with external access via a small, mesh or ventilated-panel, door.

Because it never expanded very much, the 60cm gauge market tended to parallel the metre gauge one. Thus the Calvados system had both four-wheeled and bogie passenger/luggage vehicles in the same bodyshells as full coaches, but also converted some bogie chassis to full-luggage vans for the summer traffic. Full luggage vehicles were mostly four-wheeled, however, and these were rarely more than ordinary goods vans crudely converted for their new role by inclusion of a brake valve and a stove.

2. Trailer stock for railcar haulage

When railbuses and railcars became common, one of their main deficiencies was lack of accommodation, particularly on market or fair days; lines therefore had to build or improvise some form of trailer to augment this. The first attempts were, naturally, converted or lightly modified coaches now surplus to requirements (one of the main specification requirements for many railcars was that they should be able to pull an ordinary coach). Sometimes these were unaltered except possibly for being painted in a matching livery, sometimes they were modified, particularly to suit railcar braking or heating systems. Despite specifications, however, railbuses and the lighter tramcars were often not capable of taking much of a trailing load. For them it was necessary to provide matching lightweight trailers and these took a number of forms. Passenger trailers were usually purpose-designed lightweight shells matching the railbus and sometimes including a luggage compartment. In later years there was a certain amount of cannibalism, demotorised railcars of both Brissoneau and Billard design being used as trailers (and sometimes reconverted if need arose). In 1999 two of these conversions could still be seen acting as control trailers for "rames reversibles", or push-pull rakes, at Calvi in Corsica. Baggage/parcels trailers might be simply passenger ones with some windows deleted and a sliding door in each side or they might be purpose-designed. Of the latter, perhaps the oddest were the not uncommon single-axle variety rather like an ordinary road motor-car trailer. Otherwise a light four-wheeled van or even an open wagon might be adapted for trailer use and repainted.

3. Freight and Service Rolling Stock

As with other categories of rolling stock, standard gauge lines either used main line vehicles without transfer or/and had a few rather archaic examples for internal use, so there is little to report.

On the metre gauge, standard patterns were quickly established. As a general rule, all major varieties of goods stock had the following characteristics:

* They were 4-wheeled with laminated springing, oil or grease axleboxes and some form, at least, of parking brake usually via a lever acting on the wheels of one side only.

* The payload varied from about 7 tonnes (light tramways) to a fairly standard 10 tonnes on the more substantial lines

* a proportion either had pillar handbakes acting on all four wheels, operated from a raised seat or hut at one end, or were fitted with continuous brakes (air or vacuum), or had both hand and continuous brakes. In the latter case, non-braked vehicles were normally piped.

* Frequently a standard underframe was used for all goods stock, easing the spares position and making conversion from one type to another practicable if traffic conditions changed.

France: narrow gauge rolling stock

four-wheeled goods vans

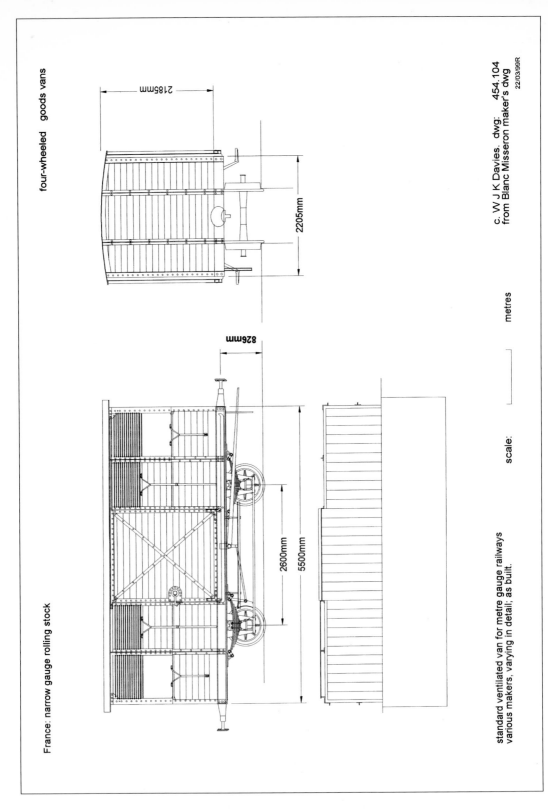

2185mm

2205mm

826mm

2600mm

5500mm

standard ventilated van for metre gauge railways
various makers, varying in detail; as built.

scale:

metres

c. W J K Davies. dwg: 454.104
from Blanc Misseron maker's dwg
22/03/99R

276

France: narrow gauge rolling stock

four-wheeled open wagons

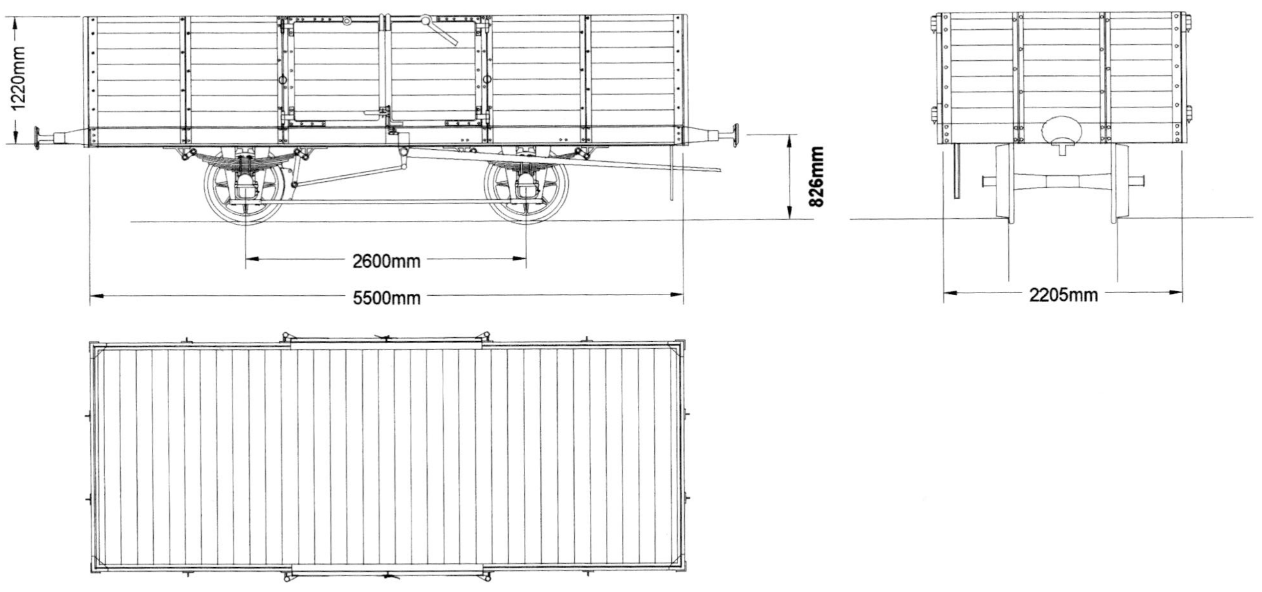

2205mm

826mm

2600mm

5500mm

1220mm

standard open wagon for metre gauge railways
various makers, varying in detail; as built.

scale:

metres

c. W J K Davies. dwg: 454.103
from Blanc Misseron maker's dwg
22/03/99R

277

four-wheeled lowsides

France: narrow gauge rolling stock

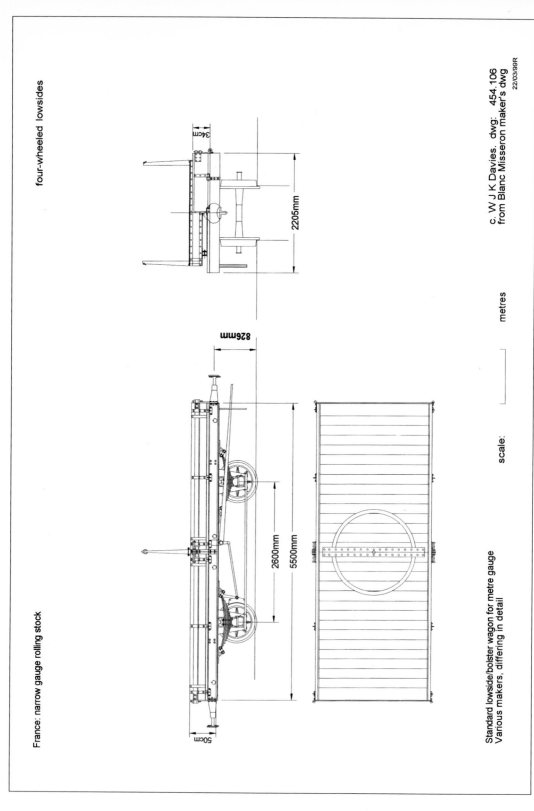

34cm

2205mm

826mm

2600mm

5500mm

50cm

Standard lowside/bolster wagon for metre gauge
Various makers, differing in detail

scale:

metres

c. W J K Davies. dwg: 454.106
from Blanc Misseron maker's dwg

22/03/99R

A fairly common fate: a Campagne railcar converted to a service draisine on the CF du Cambrésis. (AUTHOR)

As to special features, the French lines early on adopted the very sensible continental pattern of multi-use van, with one or two ventilation apertures each side of a central sliding door and covered by adjustable metal flaps over a fixed grille. Given the rural and agricultural nature of most of their traffic, this provided a considerable saving in vehicles and much needed flexibility in scheduling. Most high-sided wagons had twin hinged, rather than sliding, doors each side but this was probably dictated by the makers rather than operational reasons. Operational needs certainly did dictate the very common curved or triangular tops to each end of a high-sided wagon, and the hinged metal bar running along many such wagons which allowed loading to above side-height and easy covering with a tarpaulin, for which ring bolts were normally provided. Lowside wagons usually had split dropsides and many could be fitted with removable bolsters.

On the 60cm gauge, miniature versions of the above were quite common but Decauville also pioneered the use of bogie wagons and vans which could carry the standard 10-tonne load within normal axleloadings. The most common bogie wagon in early years was lowsided with split dropsides but the Pithiviers line later developed a high-sided version in steel plate or mesh for its specialist beet traffic. Livestock carriage was perceived to be a problem and Decauville developed a special bogie van on a well-frame, examples of which worked at both Pithiviers and on the Calvados. In practice, however, it was found that livestock could be safely transported in normal goods vehicles so the idea was not pursued.

In later years it is noticeable that there was a demand for higher capacity vehicles, especially on metre gauge lines. By the time this arose, it was not economic to buy new equipment but, on the other hand, passenger traffic was declining. Consequently many lines converted the chassis of former bogie coaches to flat wagons which were used particularly for timber traffic and for maintenance purposes. A few were also used in attempts to develop container traffic but this never really caught on.

A final type which must be mentioned was the transporter bogie or transporter wagon for carrying standard gauge vehicles on the metre gauge. Both types were used on a small scale, mainly but not entirely by railways in the former German sphere of influence. They were normally used only for short workings

A typical hand-worked rail crane, in this case of the CFD.

(AUTHOR)

where an important industrial customer was just out of reach of any standard gauge siding and did not form the staple stock of any significant railway. A number of railways also had mixed gauge sections where adapted four-wheeled vans or wagons were used as connectors between a metre gauge locomotive and standard gauge stock.

A note on service vehicles

Unlike British lines, almost every French system of substance had a purpose-built, hand-operated breakdown crane and some form of breakdown tool van. For permanent way work, hand-operated and, later, motor trollies (draisines) were normal. One or two firms, in particular Billard and Campagne, specialised in building these which were normally four-wheeled and fitted with boxy, utiltarian bodies; the body might be fully enclosed or open-sided. In later years powered service vehicles were sometimes supplemented with obsolete railcars, but otherwise tended to tow small-wheeled "lorries" or trollies. For general service purposes, ordinary goods stock, sometimes crudely modified, was usually used.

CHAPTER 16
Infrastructure, layouts and buildings; a brief note on operation

Track and fittings

Secondary railway infrastructure was, by and large, similar in principle throughout France but differed in detail according to the whims of architects and regional styles. Although a few lines (for example the Réseau Breton) went in for bullhead chaired rail, track was normally Vignoles-pattern flat-bottomed rail on wooden sleepers with a variety of ballast depending on what was available locally. Rail weights were fairly well standardised. 60cm gauge could, in extremis, use 7.5kg/m semi-portable track but more commonly used 12.5kg/m (either prefabricated or conventionally laid), 15kg/m or even heavier rail. The lightest metre gauge lines used 15kg/m rail; better metre gauge, and even some standard gauge, might use 18kg/m (very common), 20kg/m or 23kg/m with axleloads ranging from 5 tonnes to 10 tonnes. Sleepers were most commonly of wood. Roadside track might be of standard pattern or, especially in settlements or if laid in the carriageway, of "Broca" tramway-pattern grooved rail, usually of about 36kg/m weight, with the surface made up to rail level. As a general rule one might say track initially was almost always too light and many lines had to upgrade retrospectively. There were experiments with various patent track systems, in particular the Demerbe system in which a heavy bridge rail ("U renverse" or upside down "U" shape) was laid directly in the carriageway with no conventional sleepering, but none were successful.

Engineering works

In contrast to the British Isles where major engineering works were uncommon on minor railways, in France they were important features of many of the larger ones. This was partly because of the difficult terrain encountered in many of the southern and eastern départements especially, partly because of the

133. - Ligne du Tramway électrique de Bellegarde à Chézery
Le Pont du Moulin-des-Pierres sur la Valserine

A typical masonry bridge in mountainous country on the very minor Tramway de Bellegarde à Chezery in Ain. (FACS)

Monumental structures 1: An excellent example of a Gisclard suspension bridge at La Roche Taillade on the Tramways de la Corrèze.

Monumental structures 2: Harel de la Noe's reinforced concrete Viaduc du Souzain at St Brieuc on the CF des Côtes du Nord.

sheer length of départemental systems – if you had a track length of upwards of 300km, there were almost bound to be some natural features in the way and they were quite likely to be deep river valleys! Hence viaducts and imposing bridges were accepted as a normal part of construction while a good deal of extensive cut and fill occurred in negotiating shallower valleys. On the flood plains elsewhere, "estacades", or low trestles to keep tracks above flood level while allowing water to escape, were not uncommon. In mountain areas also, tunnels were frequent, where possible hewn from the rock rather than elaborately lined or portalled. As a result, while many works were unexceptional, the minor railways also claimed some of the most impressive structures of their age. The two big Gisclard suspension bridges on the Tramways de la Corrèze and the Cerdagne; the stupendous Viaducts "dé Sejourné" on the Cerdagne and "de Ste.Marie" on the St.Gervais – Vallorcine are commonly cited but there were others – such as a veritable string on the CF de la Mure – that were almost as impressive. Sometimes they provided very distinctive architectural features such as Harel de la Noë's elaborate reinforced concrete structures for the CF des Côtes du Nord; the towering and complex Viaduc de Souzain at St.Brieuc, (now alas demolished) with its branch junction curving away part-way along it, springs to mind immediately but there were many others...and then what does one make of such curiosities as the cruciform bridge at Le Mans where the town tramways and the metre gauge Tramways de la Sarthe actually crossed each other on the level at mid-bridge. They could have been a lasting heritage but the omnipresent narrow loading gauge has made conversion to road bridges uneconomic in most cases and crumbling stonework is expensive to maintain; tunnels have lasted better, especially as they appear ideal for cultivating mushrooms in!

The other engineering works to make a lasting impression were the long and often continuous gradients of 1 in 40 or less. Even on the main lines in Britain such things were not that common but continental minor railways often had to take them in their stride. 30km or more of almost continuous steep grade with only the odd station as a breathing point were not unknown – the Vivarais men used flippantly to call the climb from Le Cheylard to St.Agrève "la petite colline" (the little hillock) but it was some 24km of 1 in 33 or thereabouts and could make even a compound Mallet roar.

Smallest possible halting place on light railways was where the line crossed a road and a crossing keeper's cottage was needed anyway. (AUTHOR)

MARBOZ (Ain) -- Gare du Tramway

(FACS/DOMENGIE)

Typical steam tramway halt on the Tramways de l'Ain, jut a hut and a weedy loading bank. This one actually has a siding.

Stations and their buildings

As regards station buildings, again there were fairly standard patterns depending on (a) the status of the railway and (b) the importance of the individual locality. Four major categories can be identified:

Passenger halts (very common on roadside tramways). At their simplest these consisted of a nameplaque and gravelled patch of ground. More common was provision of a wood or brick-built shelter, rather like a superior bus shelter, with a central seating space and, often, with closed room(s) at each end which could serve as ticket office or secure store for messageries traffic.

Minor stations, where no provision was made for living accommodation. In this case facilities usually included a small one-storey building containing waiting room, office with ticketing facilities, often a parcels room or space partitioned off by a counter and with a light weighing machine; a single storey goods shed attached to this building and fronting an open loading dock; a separate hut containing toilets and a store cupboard. Again in typical French fashion, male urinals or "pissoirs" open to the sky were usually sited against one wall or in a separate cast-iron enclosure.

"Standard" intermediate stations which were larger versions of the above, usually with a two storey station house having railway facilities below and staff accommodation on the first floor – often with a ground floor kitchen at the back or side. In these cases the goods shed and loading dock might be attached or closely adjacent or they might be widely separated as in British practice. As the station gained in importance, its central block might have one or two single-storey wings, often used as small-goods stores or lamprooms.

Junction and terminal stations. Narrow gauge junctions with the main line were really of three kinds: simplest was the arrangement whereby the minor line just had a loop or siding in the main line station forecourt, together with a spur going off to interchange sidings in a nearby goods yard. In such a case the minor railway usually had its own substantial station some distance away, perhaps on the other side of town, where its servicing facilities were situated. Secondly, it might have a proper terminal of its owm fronting one side of the station square (there were some places like Meyrargues where the secondary stations outnumbered the main line). Lastly, especially if it was of Intérêt Général, the secondary railway might

Substantial intermediate station on a line of Intérêt Général – Rostrenen on the Réseau Breton.

285

A normal minor station without accommodation; Vabre on the CFD du Tarn. Booking office, staffroom, luggage facilities and a small attached goods shed.

(AUTHOR)

Next stage up: railway facilities, simple accommodation, attached goods shed and seperate toilet block. Note the Weighbridge on the loop-siding. Rozoy-en-Brie in Seine-et-Marne.

(FACS)

Regional architecture. Camaret station on the Réseau Breton's western extension. This is basically the same as other stations but with "regional" trimmings on the buildings.   (FACS/Chapuis)

share the main-line facilities, running into either a branch bay or even along one of the main platform lines and using the main line accommodation. Goods transfer between standard and narrow gauge was normally manual, either with sidings each side of a common goods transfer shed and loading dock or different gauges side by side with one track slightly higher than the other; a manually operated yard crane was a common feature and, in later years, a surprising number of transfer points had overhead gantry hoists for loading heavy objects.

Of course a secondary system might not actually connect at all with the main lines at its main station. Big départemental systems such as the Côtes du Nord, Sud-France or Tramways de la Sarthe built their own elaborate terminals on central sites with extensive layouts, multiple rail-level platforms serving several different branches and monumental overall-roofed trainsheds and buildings; often a major depot or Works was an integral part of the scheme.

Station layouts

"Standard" layout for an intermediate station was a running line and siding, serving the goods shed; a typically French feature was that this siding was often extended across the front of the station building to form an apparent loop. This was rarely used as such, passing stations having an additional running loop with a centre platform. Instead it was normally treated for shunting as two dead-end sidings and often included a rail weighbridge with its mechanism recessed into the loading dock. At the expense of some inconvenience to passengers, the arrangement allowed easy placement and collection of wagons from either direction. Another common feature was a separate curved siding along the boundary of the goods yard, used exclusively for handling wagonload traffic.

What did surprise the writer was that, where the line stayed alongside a road through a settlement, the station was often very little different. Smaller town or village halts might consist of at best a shelter or, just as often, an "agence" in a front room or rooms of a roadside house but true stations were common, with all the normal features; the most obvious difference was that the loop and yard trackage were on a narrower site, usually open to the road immediately across the running line(s). It must be said, however, that many

Like Topsy, many Workshops "just growed". This is Caudry, headquarters of the CF du Cambrésis, in its final years.

Others were more substantial – a corner of the Romorantin Works of the CF du Blanc à Argent.

roadside lines deviated from the road around settlements and had their own station somewhere round the back of town.

Depots and workshops

There was no standard format for central depots and workshops. Small lines and systems often had little more than a workshop annexe to the locomotive shed, plus a one-or-two road carriage shed nearby. Larger systems tended to have quite extensive central workshops with a full range of repair facilities including the ability to undertake boiler work, wheel-turning and retyring and general heavy repair. These often possessed an impressive range of buildings, constructed "all of a piece" and covering a substantial site.

The most problematic cases were those of départemental systems with scattered lines or where several concessionaires were involved. In such cases there was often no alternative to setting up what might be called mini-works in more than one place to cope with first line maintenance at least – though again equipment might be conveyed over a main line railway to a central Works for heavy repairs. Most lines and systems of any length in any case had one or more sub-sheds. These were most often at junctions or dead-end termini where it might be desirable to station a locomotive overnight but a long line could well have one at a convenient intermediate point (eg St.Agrève on the Vivarais). This allowed for engine servicing and exchanges en route.

A Note on operation

Operation was normally by train order and telephone, with working timetables being issued to give staff an overall picture. With a common frequency of only two or three trains daily over a given route and low speeds, the urgency involved was not very great in any case; most accidents appear to have been caused by derailments or level-crossing collisions. Active (as opposed to fixed) signalling was generally confined to junctions except on a few electrified lines.

PART 4

Regional Atlas of Minor Railways

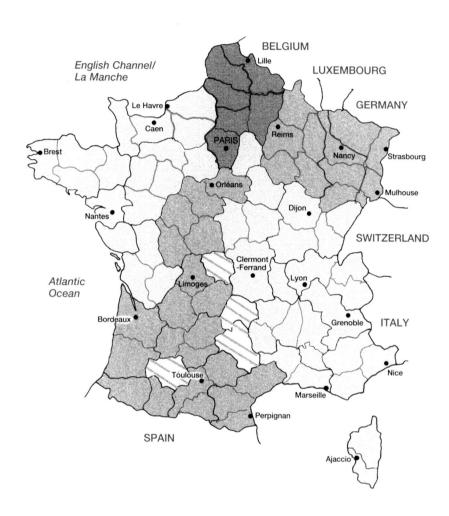

Introduction

The colour maps in this section are intended to give a general overview of the spread of minor railways in France. For quick location they are divided into the regions described in chapters 7-11 and each detail map relates to one or two specific sections within the appropriate chapter; in general the chapter section headings link directly to the appropriate map. The 1914-18 battle zone map is intended to illustrate the extent and strength of devastation.

France in general

Detail regional maps are listed overleaf

ATLAS OF FRENCH MINOR RAILWAYS
and of
SUBURBAN AND RURAL TRAMWAYS

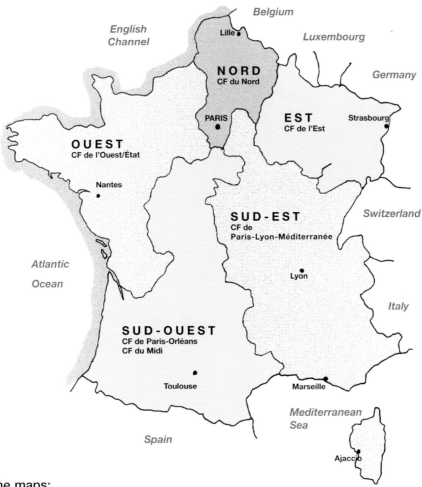

Key to the maps:

Initials on the detail diagrams cross-refer to the lists at the end of the appropriate regional chapter. Note that these are for identification only and are not necessarily those which appeared on companies documentation or stock.

┼─────┼ Standard Gauge	Fauxpas	Junction or Terminal points
━━━━━━━━ Narrow Gauge	Parthenay	Major Workshops
┼┼┼┼┼┼┼ Electrified (all gauges)	LYON	Towns or Cities with urban tramway systems
┼───┴───┼ sg Electric (detail diagrams only)	— · —	Départemental Borders (detail maps only)
━━━━━━━━ Main line railways	— x —	National Borders

FRANCE in its SETTING
showing main relief blocks

English Channel

BELGIUM

Lille

GERMANY

Le Havre

Reims

PARIS

Rennes

Orleans

Dijon

SWITZERLAND

Atlantic Ocean

Clermont -Ferrand

Lyon

Grenoble

ITALY

Bordeaux

Toulouse

Avignon

Pau

Marseilles

SPAIN

Mediterranean Sea

Ajaccio

RÉGION OUEST de la FRANCE
Départements and Préfectures

CHERBOURG

English Channel

Seine-Inférieure

ROUEN

Manche

CAEN

Eure

Calvados

Evreux

Finistere

St Brieuc

Orne

CHARTRES

Côtes-du-Nord

Ille-et-Villaine

Alençon

Quimper

Mayenne

Sarthe

Eure-et-Loir

RENNES

Laval

Le Mans

Morbihan

Vannes

Loire-Inferieure

ANGERS

Maine-et-Loire

Region Sud-Ouest

NANTES

Atlantic Ocean

LA ROCHE-S-YON

Deux-Sevres

Vendee

La Rochelle

Niort

Charente-Inférieure

Charente

Angoulème

Pleubian

St Pol
de Léon

Lannion

Paimpol

Cancale

Brignogan

L'Aber-Wrac'h

Plouescat

Guingamp

ST MALO

Plein
Fougères

Porspoder

Morlaix

Dol

Le Conquet

Landivisiau

Landerneau

St Brieuc

Plancoët

Antrain

BREST

Quintin

Lamballe

Dinan

Fougères

Camaret

Carhaix-Plouguer

Plémy

Rostrenen

La Brohinière

RENNES

Douarnenez

Châteaulin

Gourin

Loudéac

La Trinité-
Porhoët

Bréal

Audierne

Quimper

Pontivy

La Guerche
-de-Bretagne

St-Guénolé

Plouay

Locminé

Ploërmel

Guer

Concarneau

LORIENT

Vannes

Le Grand
Fougeray

La Trinité

Redon

Quiberon

Port-
Navalo

La Roche-Bernard

CM to
St Nazaire

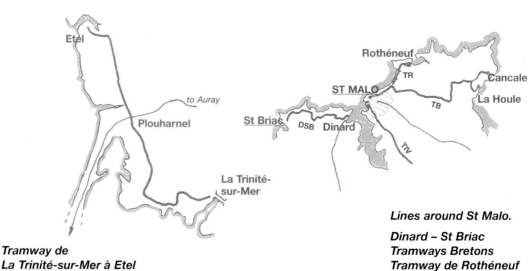

Etel

Rothéneuf

Cancale

TR

ST MALO

La Houle

TB

to Auray

St Briac

DSB

Dinard

Plouharnel

TV

La Trinité-
sur-Mer

Lines around St Malo.

Dinard – St Briac
Tramways Bretons
Tramway de Rothéneuf

Tramway de
La Trinité-sur-Mer à Etel

Lines connected to Morbihan

REGION OUEST: Loire Inférieure; Vendée

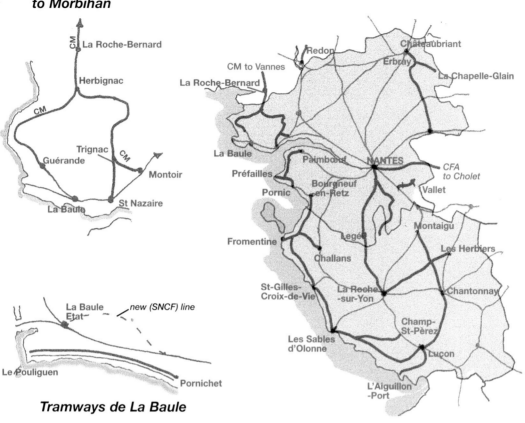

Tramways de La Baule

Lines around Nantes

Tramways des Sables d'Olonne

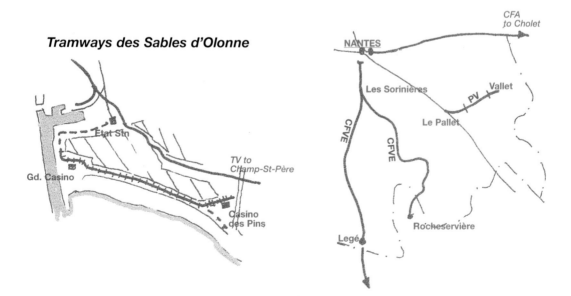

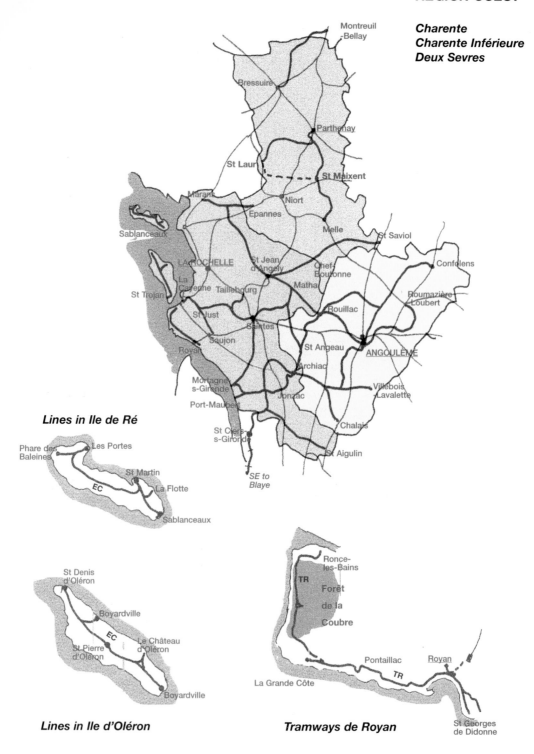

REGION OUEST

Charente
Charente Inférieure
Deux Sevres

Montreuil
-Bellay

Bressuire

Parthenay

St Laur

St Maixent

Marans

Niort

Epannes

Melle

St Saviol

Sablanceaux

LA ROCHELLE

St Jean
d'Angely

Chef-
Bouronne

Confolens

La
Cayenne

Taillebourg

Matha

Bouillac

Roumazière
-Loubert

St Trojan

St Just

Saintes

St Angeau

ANGOULEME

Saujon

Archiac

Villebois
Lavalette

Royan

Mortagne
s-Gironde

Jonzac

Port-Maubert

Chalais

St Ciers
s-Gironde

St Aigulin

Lines in Ile de Ré

Phare des
Baleines

Les Portes

St Martin

EC

La Flotte

Sablanceaux

*SE to
Blaye*

St Denis
d'Oléron

Ronce-
les-Bains

TR

Forêt
de la

Boyardville

EC

St Pierre
d'Oléron

Le Château
d'Oléron

Coubre

Pontaillac

Royan

La Grande Côte

TR

Boyardville

St Georges
de Didonne

Lines in Ile d'Oléron

Tramways de Royan

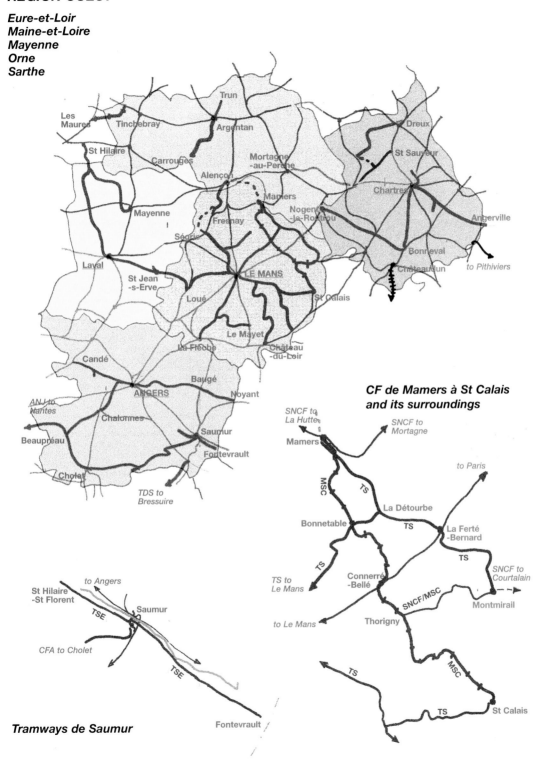

RÉGION OUEST

Eure-et-Loir
Maine-et-Loire
Mayenne
Orne
Sarthe

Trun

Les Maures
Tinchebray
Argentan
Dreux
St Sauveur

St Hilaire
Carrouges
Mortagne -au-Perche
Chartres

Alençon
Mamers
Angerville

Mayenne
Fresnay
Nogent -le-Rotrou

Ségrie
Bonneval

Laval
LE MANS
Châteaudun
to Pithiviers

St Jean -s-Erve
Loué
St Calais

Le Mayet

La Flèche
Château -du-Loir

Candé
Baugé

ANJ to Nantes
ANGERS
Noyant

Chalonnes

Beaupréau
Saumur

Fontevrault

Cholet
TDS to Bressuire

CF de Mamers à St Calais and its surroundings

SNCF to La Hutte
SNCF to Mortagne

Mamers
to Paris

MSC
TS
La Détourbe

Bonnetable
TS
La Ferté -Bernard

TS
TS

TS
SNCF to Courtalain

TS to Le Mans
Connerré -Bellé
SNCF/MSC
Montmirail

Thorigny

to Le Mans

Tramways de Saumur

to Angers
St Hilaire -St Florent
TSE
Saumur

CFA to Cholet
TSE

Fontevrault

TS
MSC
St Calais
TS

RÉGION OUEST

Calvados
Eure
Manche
Seine-Inférieure

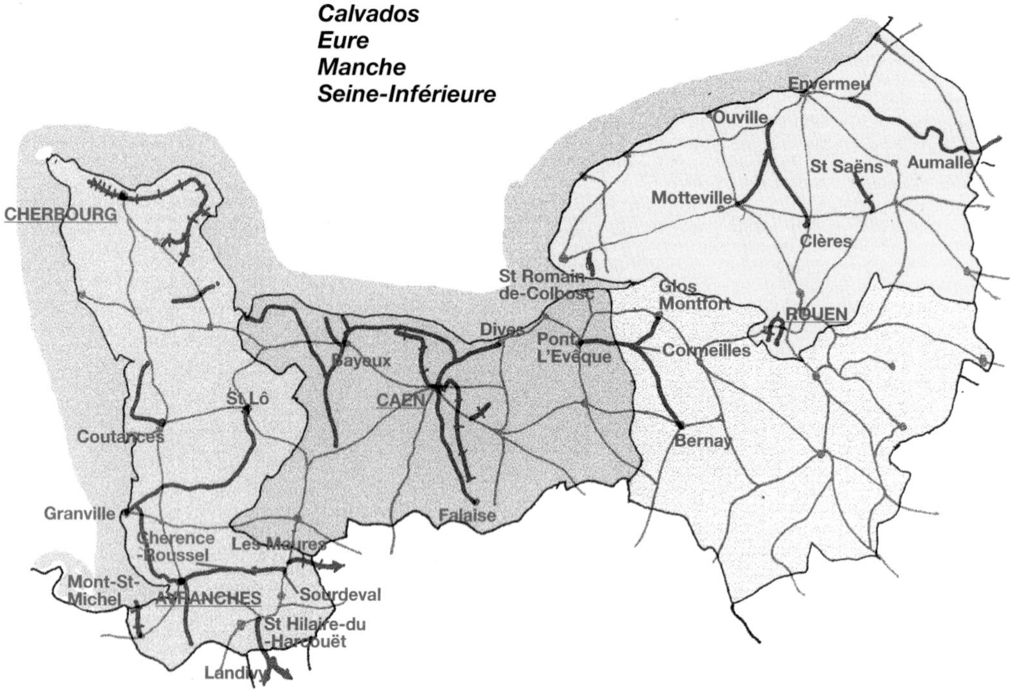

CHERBOURG

Envermeu
Ouville
St Saëns   Aumalle
Motteville
Clères
St Romain-de-Colbosc
Glos Montfort
ROUEN
Dives   Pont L'Evêque
Cormeilles
Bayeux
St Lô
CAEN
Coutances
Bernay
Granville
Falaise
Cherence-Roussel   Les Maures
Mont-St-Michel   AVRANCHES   Sourdeval
St Hilaire-du-Harcouët
Landivy

Lines in the Upper Cotentin

Urville
Barfleur
CHERBOURG   CFM
CFD
Valognes
Montebourg   Ste-Mère-Église
Pont L'Abbé   CFM
CFM   Lessay

Rouen area

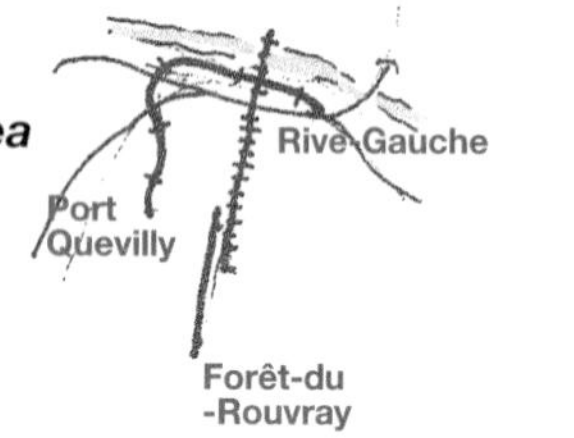

Rive Gauche
Port Quevilly
Forêt-du-Rouvray

Lines in Calvados

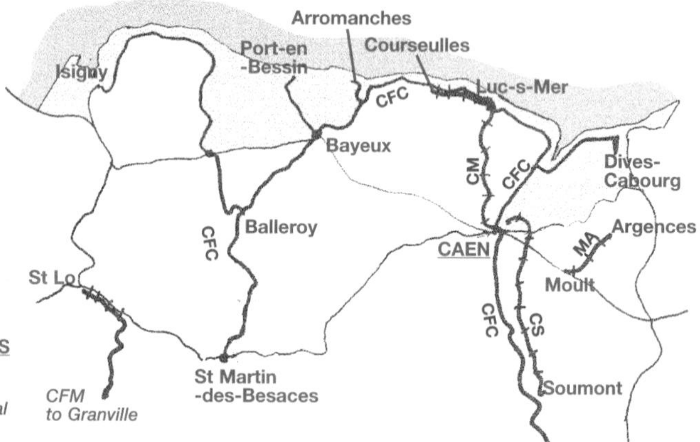

Arromanches
Port-en-Bessin   Courseulles
Isigny   CFC   Luc-s-Mer
Bayeux   CM   CFC   Dives-Cabourg
CFC   Balleroy   CAEN   MA   Argences
St Lô   Moult
St Martin-des-Besaces   CFC   CS   Soumont
CFM to Granville   Falaise

Tramways Normands

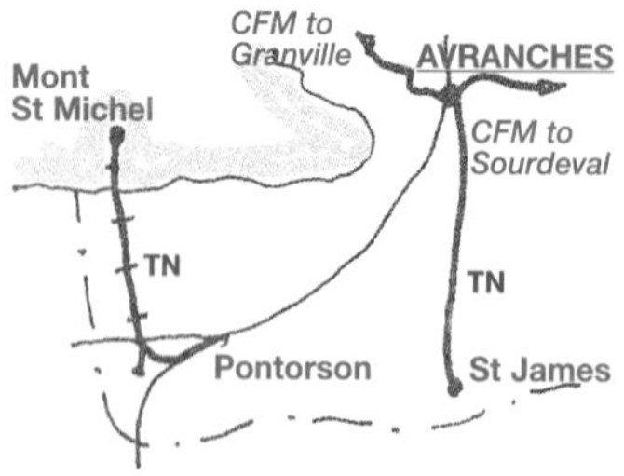

CFM to Granville   AVRANCHES
Mont St Michel   CFM to Sourdeval
CFM to Granville
TN   TN
Pontorson   St James

300

RÉGION NORD de la FRANCE
Départements and Préfectures

England

Belgium

English
Channel

LILLE

Pas-de-Calais

Arras

Nord

AMIENS

Aisne

Somme

Region
Ouest

Beauvais

Laon

Region
Est

Oise

PARIS

VERSAILLES

Seine

Seine-et
-Oise

Region
Sud-Est

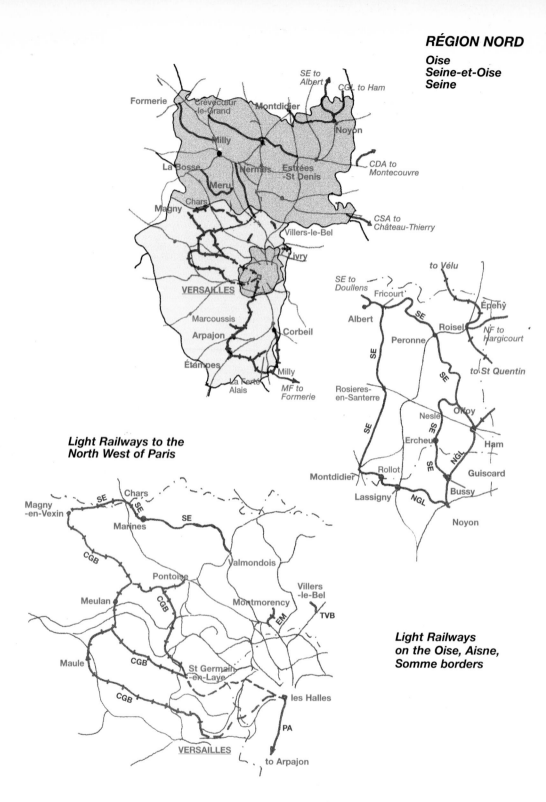

RÉGION NORD

Oise
Seine-et-Oise
Seine

SE to Albert

CGL to Ham

Formerie

Crévecœur-le-Grand

Montdidier

Noyon

Milly

Nermes

Estrées-St Denis

La Bosse

CDA to Montecouvre

Méru

Magny

Chars

CSA to Château-Thierry

Villers-le-Bel

Ivry

VERSAILLES

to Vélu

SE to Doullens

Fricourt

Épehy

Albert

SE

Roisel

NF to Hargicourt

Péronne

Marcoussis

Corbeil

to St Quentin

Arpajon

SE

Étampes

Milly

La Ferte Alais

MF to Formerie

Rosieres-en-Santerre

Olfoy

Nesle

SE

Ercheu

Ham

Light Railways to the North West of Paris

SE

Montdidier

Rollot

SE

NGL

Guiscard

Magny-en-Vexin

Chars

SE

Lassigny

NGL

Bussy

Marines

SE

Noyon

CGB

Valmondois

Pontoise

Meulan

CGB

Montmorency

Villers-le-Bel

EM

TVB

Light Railways on the Oise, Aisne, Somme borders

Maule

CGB

St Germain-en-Laye

CGB

les Halles

PA

VERSAILLES

to Arpajon

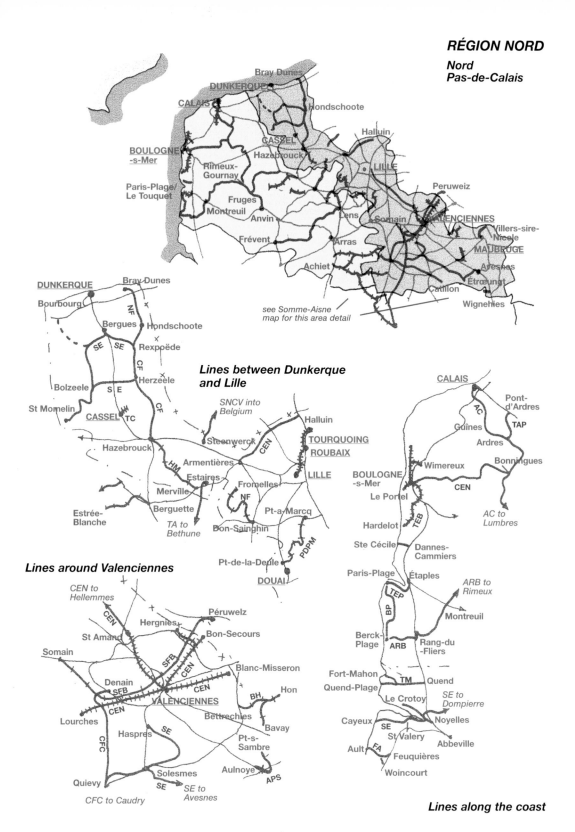

RÉGION NORD

Nord
Pas-de-Calais

Bray Dunes
DUNKERQUE
CALAIS
Hondschoote
Halluin
BOULOGNE -s-Mer
CASSEL
Hazebrouck
LILLE
Peruweiz
Rimeux-Gournay
Paris-Plage/ Le Touquet
Fruges
Montreuil
Anvin
Lens
Somain
VALENCIENNES
Villers-sire-Nicole
Frévent
Arras
MAUBEUGE
Achiet
Avesnes
Étrœungt
Catillon
Wignehies

see Somme-Aisne map for this area detail

DUNKERQUE
Bourbourg
Bray Dunes
NF
Bergues
Hondschoote
SE SE
Rexpoëde
CF
Bolzeele
SE
Herzeele
St Momelin
CASSEL TC
CF

Lines between Dunkerque and Lille

SNCV into Belgium
Halluin
TOURQUOING
ROUBAIX
Steenwerck
CEN
Hazebrouck
HM
Armentières
Estaires
Merville
Fromelles
NF
LILLE
Berguette
Pt-a-Marcq
Estrée-Blanche
TA to Bethune
Bon-Sainghin
PDPM
Pt-de-la-Deûle
DOUAI

Lines around Valenciennes

CEN to Hellemmes
CEN
Hergnies
Péruwelz
St Amand
Bon-Secours
Somain
SFB
CEN
Blanc-Misseron
Denain
SFB
CEN
Hon
CEN
VALENCIENNES
BH
Lourches
CEN
Bettrechies
Bavay
Haspres
SE
Pt-s-Sambre
CFC
Quievy
Solesmes
Aulnoye
APS
SE
SE to Avesnes
CFC to Caudry

CALAIS
Pont-d'Ardres
AC
Guînes
TAP
Ardres
Bonningues
Wimereux
BOULOGNE -s-Mer
CEN
Le Portel
AC to Lumbres
Hardelot
TEB
Ste Cécile
Dannes-Cammiers
Paris-Plage
Étaples
ARB to Rimeux
TEP
Montreuil
BP
Berck-Plage
Rang-du-Fliers
ARB
Fort-Mahon
TM
Quend
Quend-Plage
SE to Dompierre
Le Crotoy
Cayeux
Noyelles
SE
St Valery
Abbeville
Ault
FA
Feuquières
Woincourt

Lines along the coast

303

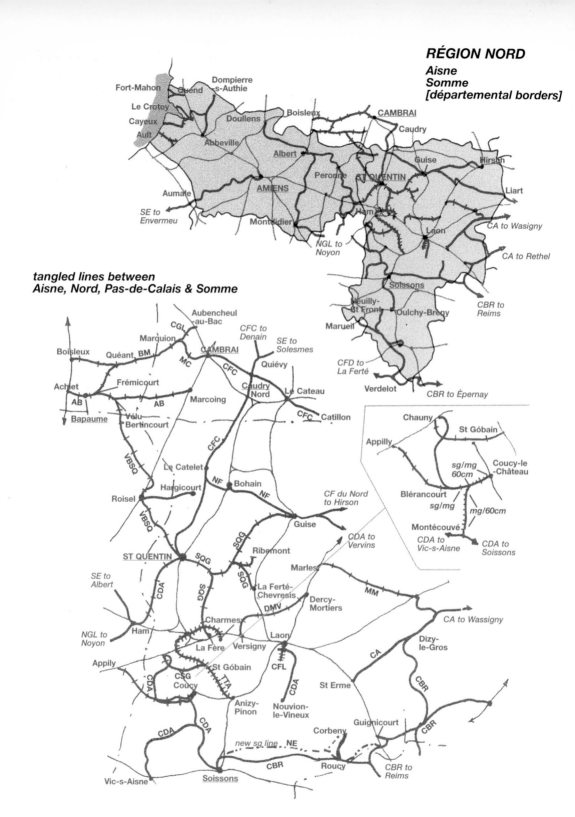

RÉGION NORD
Aisne
Somme
[départemental borders]

Fort-Mahon
Quend
Le Crotoy
Cayeux
Ault
Dompierre-s-Authie
Boisleux
Doullens
Abbeville
Albert
Aumale
AMIENS
Montdidier
Peronne
CAMBRAI
Caudry
Guise
Hirson
ST QUENTIN
Liart
Ham
Laon
Soissons
Neuilly-St Front
Marueil
Oulchy-Breny
SE to Envermeu
NGL to Noyon
CA to Wasigny
CA to Rethel
CBR to Reims

tangled lines between
Aisne, Nord, Pas-de-Calais & Somme

Aubencheul-au-Bac
CGL
Marquion
CFC to Denain
SE to Solesmes
CAMBRAI
Quiévy
Marueil
Boisleux
Quéant
BM
MC
CFC
Caudry Nord
Le Cateau
Verdelot
CFD to La Ferté
CBR to Épernay
Achiet
Frémicourt
Marcoing
AB
AB
CFC
Catillon
Bapaume
Vélu
Bertincourt
CFC
Chauny
St Góbain
VBSQ
Le Catelet
Appilly
Hargicourt
NF
Bohain
CF du Nord to Hirson
sg/mg 60cm
Coucy-le-Château
Roisel
NF
Blérancourt
sg/mg
mg/60cm
VBSQ
Guise
CDA to Vervins
Montécouvé
CDA to Vic-s-Aisne
CDA to Soissons
SQG
Ribemont
ST QUENTIN
SQG
Marles
SE to Albert
CDA
SQG
La Ferté-Chevresis
Dercy-Mortiers
MM
CA to Wassigny
DMV
NGL to Noyon
Ham
Charmes
Laon
Dizy-le-Gros
Appily
La Fère
Versigny
CFL
CA
St Góbain
CDA
CSG Coucy
TTA
St Erme
CBR
Anizy-Pinon
Nouvion-le-Vineux
CDA
CDA
Corbeny
Guignicourt
CBR
new sg line
NE
CBR
Roucy
CBR to Reims
Vic-s-Aisne
Soissons

RÉGION EST de la FRANCE
Départements and Préfectures

Luxembourg

Région
Nord

Belgium

CHARLEVILLE-
MÉZIÈRES

Germany

Ardennes

Meuse

Metz

Châlons
-s-Marne

Moselle

Bas-Rhin

Marne

Bar-le-Duc

NANCY

STRASBOURG

Meurthe-et-Moselle

TROYES

Haute
-Marne

Épinal

COLMAR

Aube

Chaumont

Vosges

Haut-
Rhin

Haute-Saône

BELFORT

Région
Sud-Est

Vesoul

Territoire-
de-Belfort

Switzerland

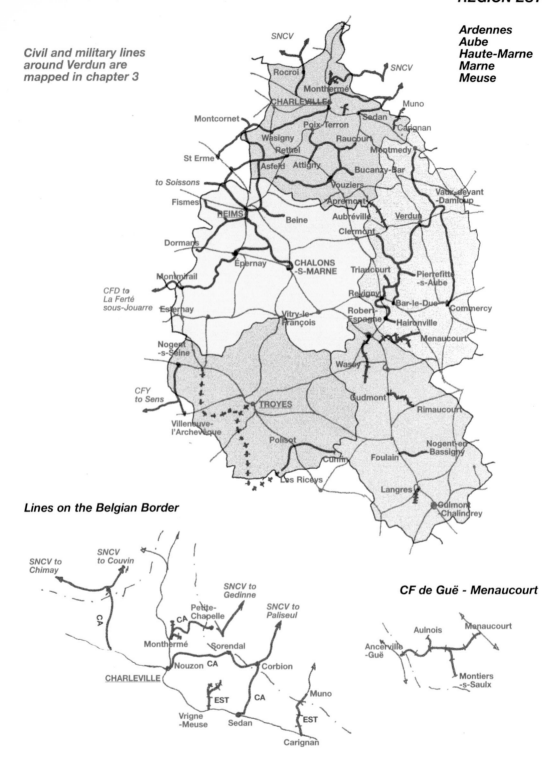

RÉGION EST

Ardennes
Aube
Haute-Marne
Marne
Meuse

Civil and military lines
around Verdun are
mapped in chapter 3

Lines on the Belgian Border

CF de Guë - Menaucourt

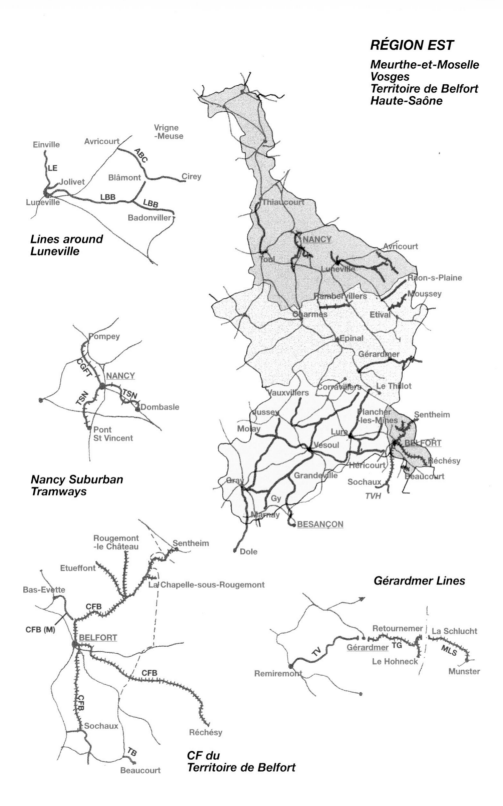

RÉGION EST

Meurthe-et-Moselle
Vosges
Territoire de Belfort
Haute-Saône

Lines around Luneville

Einville
Avricourt
Vrigne -Meuse
ABC
LE
Jolivet
Blâmont
Cirey
Luneville
LBB
LBB
Badonviller

Nancy Suburban Tramways

Pompey
CGFT
NANCY
TSN
TSN
Dombasle
Pont St Vincent

CF du Territoire de Belfort

Rougemont -le Château
Sentheim
Etueffont
La Chapelle-sous-Rougemont
Bas-Evette
CFB
CFB (M)
BELFORT
CFB
CFB
Sochaux
Réchésy
TB
Beaucourt

Gérardmer Lines

Retournemer
La Schlucht
Gérardmer
TG
MLS
Le Hohneck
Munster
TV
Remiremont

Thiaucourt
NANCY
Toul
Avricourt
Luneville
Raon-s-Plaine
Moussey
Ramervillers
Charmes
Etival
Epinal
Gérardmer
Vauxvillers
Cornavillers
Le Thillot
Jussey
Plancher -les-Mines
Sentheim
Molay
Lure
BELFORT
Vesoul
Réchésy
Héricourt
Beaucourt
Gray
Grandeville
Sochaux
Gy
TVH
Marnay
BESANÇON
Dole

307

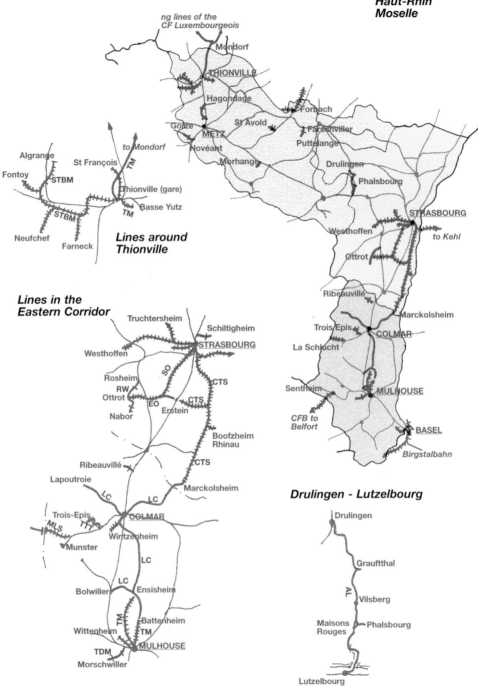

ng lines of the
CF Luxembourgeois

Mondorf

THIONVILLE

Hagondage

Forbach

Gorze

St Avold

Farschviller

METZ

Puttelange

to Mondorf

Novéant

Drulingen

Morhange

Phalsbourg

Algrange

St François

STRASBOURG

Fontoy

STBM

to Kehl

Westhoffen

TM

Thionville (gare)

Ottrot

STBM

TM

Basse Yutz

Neufchef

Farneck

Lines around Thionville

Ribeauvillé

Marckolsheim

Lines in the Eastern Corridor

Truchtersheim

Trois-Epis

COLMAR

Schiltigheim

La Schlucht

Westhoffen

STRASBOURG

SO

Rosheim

RW

CTS

Ottrot

Sentheim

MULHOUSE

EO

CTS

Nabor

Erstein

CFB to Belfort

BASEL

Boofzheim
Rhinau

CTS

Birgstalbahn

Ribeauvillé

Lapoutroie

CTS

Marckolsheim

Drulingen - Lutzelbourg

LC

LC

Trois-Epis

Drulingen

MLS

TTT

COLMAR

Wintzenheim

Munster

Graufthal

LC

AL

Vilsberg

LC

Bolwiller

Ensisheim

Maisons
Rouges

Phalsbourg

TM

Battenheim

Wittenheim

TM

MULHOUSE

TDM

Lutzelbourg

Morschwiller

RÉGION SUD-EST de la FRANCE
Départements and Préfectures

Région Nord

Région Est

Seine et
-Marne
MELUN

Yonne
Auxerre

Haute-Saône

Côte-d'Or
DIJON

Doubs
BESANÇON

Nièvre
Nevers

Jura

BOURGES

Cher

Saône-et
-Loire

Lons-le
-Saulnier

Switzerland

Moulins

Mâcon

Allier

Bourg

Haute-
Savoie

Ain

Annecy

CLERMONT
FERRAND

Rhone
LYON

Loire

Chambéry

Puy-de-Dôme

St ETIENNE

Isère

Savoie

Haute-Loire

GRENOBLE

Le PUY

Valence

Hautes-Alpes

Privas

Haute-
Corse

Mende

Ardèche

Drôme

Gap

Italy

Lozère

Digne

Alpes-
Maritimes

Corse-
du-Sud

Gard

AVIGNON

Alpes de H-Prov

NÎMES

Vaucluse

NICE

Bouches-du-Rhône
MARSEILLE

Var

TOULON

RÉGION SUD-EST

Seine-et-Marne
Yonne

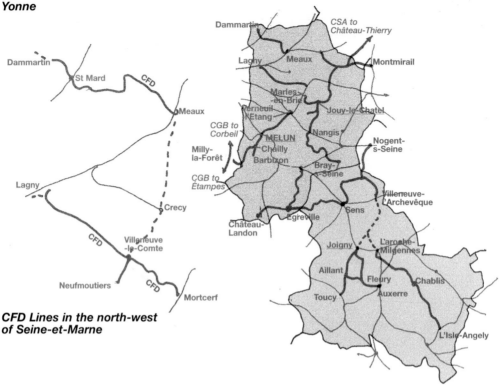

CFD Lines in the north-west of Seine-et-Marne

SE Réseau de Seine-et-Marne

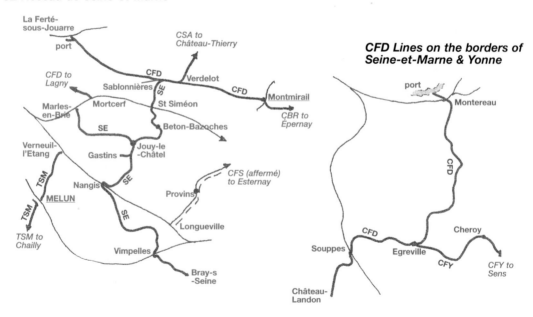

CFD Lines on the borders of Seine-et-Marne & Yonne

RÉGION SUD-EST
Allier
Cher
Loire
Nievre
Puy-de-Dôme

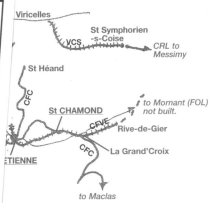

Lines on the borders of Loire & Rhone

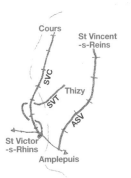

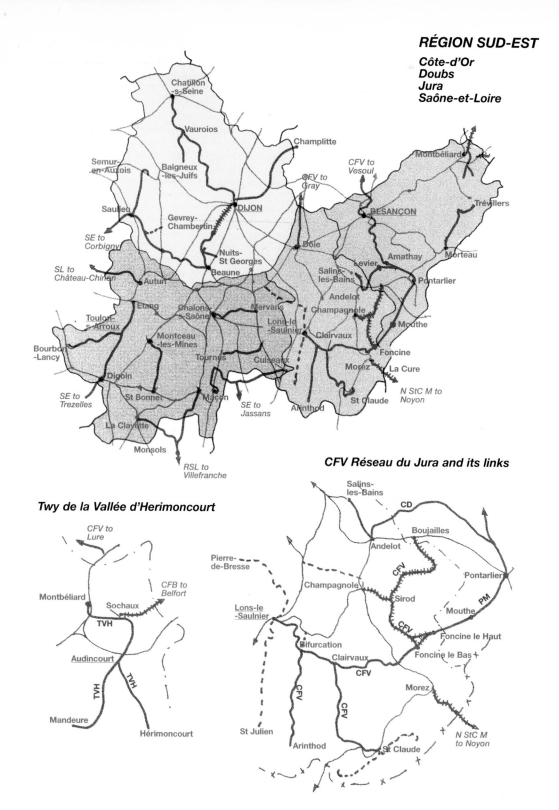

RÉGION SUD-EST

Côte-d'Or
Doubs
Jura
Saône-et-Loire

Chatillon-s-Seine

Vauroios

Champlitte

CFV to Vesoul

Montbéliard

Semur-en-Auxois

Baigneux-les-Juifs

CFV to Gray

Trévillers

Saulieu

BESANÇON

Gevrey-Chambertin

DIJON

SE to Corbigny

Dôle

Levier

Amathay

Morteau

Nuits-St Georges

Beaune

Salins-les-Bains

Pontarlier

SL to Château-Chinon

Autun

Andelot

Champagnole

Mouthe

Etang

Chalons-s-Saône

Mervans

Toulon-s-Arroux

Lons-le-Saulnier

Clairvaux

Foncine

Bourbon-Lancy

Montceau-les-Mines

Tournus

Cuiseaux

Morez

La Cure

Digoin

N StC M to Noyon

SE to Trezelles

St Bonnet

Mâcon

SE to Jassans

Arinthod

St Claude

La Clayette

Monsols

RSL to Villefranche

CFV Réseau du Jura and its links

Salins-les-Bains

CD

Boujailles

Andelot

CFV

Pontarlier

Pierre-de-Bresse

Champagnole

PM

Sirod

Mouthe

Lons-le-Saulnier

CFV

Bifurcation

Clairvaux

Foncine le Haut

Foncine le Bas

CFV

CFV

Morez

St Julien

CFV

CFV

N StC M to Noyon

Arinthod

St Claude

Twy de la Vallée d'Herimoncourt

CFV to Lure

CFB to Belfort

Montbéliard

Sochaux

TVH

Audincourt

TVH

TVH

Mandeure

Hérimoncourt

nt at
nes
rary
050
etails

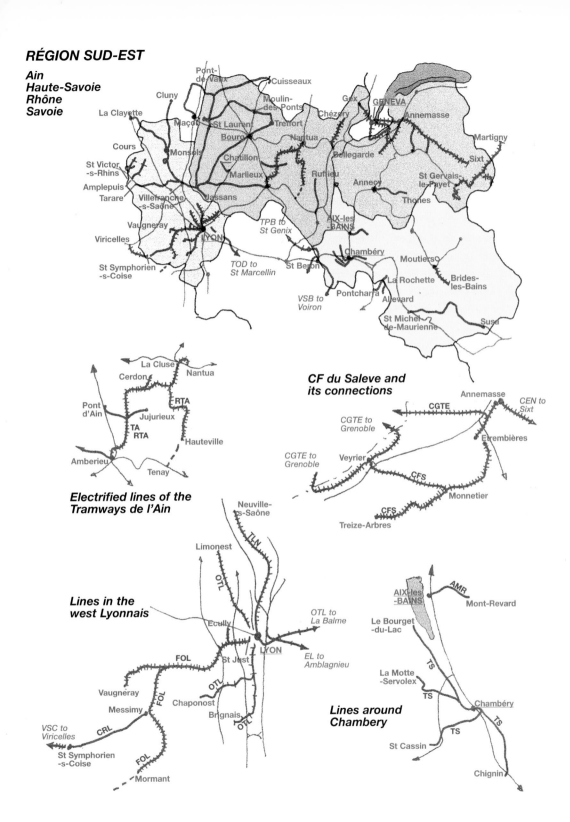

RÉGION SUD-EST

Ain
Haute-Savoie
Rhône
Savoie

Pont-de-Vaux
Cuisseaux
Cluny
Moulin-des-Ponts
Gex
GENEVA
La Clayette
Chézery
Annemasse
Mâcon
St Laurent
Treffort
Bourg
Nantua
Martigny
Cours
Monsols
Chatillon
Bellegarde
Sixt
St Victor-s-Rhins
Marlieux
Ruffieu
St Gervais-le-Payet
Amplepuis
Tarare
Villefranche-s-Saône
Anjou
Thones
Vaugneray
Jassans
TPB to St Genix
AIX-les-BAINS
Viricelles
LYON
Chambéry
Moutiers
St Symphorien-s-Coise
TOD to St Marcellin
St Beron
La Rochette
Brides-les-Bains
VSB to Voiron
Pontcharra
Allevard
St Michel-de-Maurienne
Susa

Electrified lines of the Tramways de l'Ain

La Cluse
Cerdon
Nantua
RTA
Pont d'Ain
Jujurieux
TA
RTA
Hauteville
Amberieu
Tenay

CF du Saleve and its connections

Annemasse
CEN to Sixt
CGTE
CGTE to Grenoble
Etrembières
CGTE to Grenoble
Veyrier
CFS
Monnetier
CFS
Treize-Arbres

Lines in the west Lyonnais

Neuville-s-Saône
Limonest
TLN
OTL
Ecully
OTL to La Balme
FOL
St Just
LYON
EL to Amblagnieu
Vaugneray
OTL
Chaponost
FOL
Messimy
Brignais
OTL
VSC to Viricelles
CRL
St Symphorien-s-Coise
FOL
Mormant

Lines around Chambery

AIX-les-BAINS
AMR
Mont-Revard
Le Bourget-du-Lac
TS
La Motte-Servolex
TS
Chambéry
TS
St Cassin
TS
Chignin

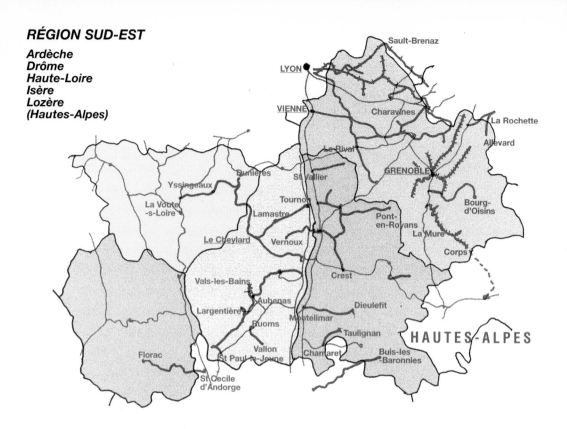

RÉGION SUD-EST

Ardèche
Drôme
Haute-Loire
Isère
Lozère
(Hautes-Alpes)

Sault-Brenaz

LYON

VIENNE

Charavines

La Rochette

Allevard

Le Rival

GRENOBLE

Dunières

St Vallier

Yssingeaux

Tournon

Bourg-d'Oisins

La Voûte-s-Loire

Lamastre

Pont-en-Royans

La Mure

Le Cheylard

Vernoux

Corps

Vals-les-Bains

Crest

Aubenas

Largentière

Dieulefit

Ruoms

Montelimar

Taulignan

Buis-les-Baronnies

H A U T E S - A L P E S

Florac

Vallon

St Paul-le-Jeune

Chamaret

Ste Cecile d'Andorge

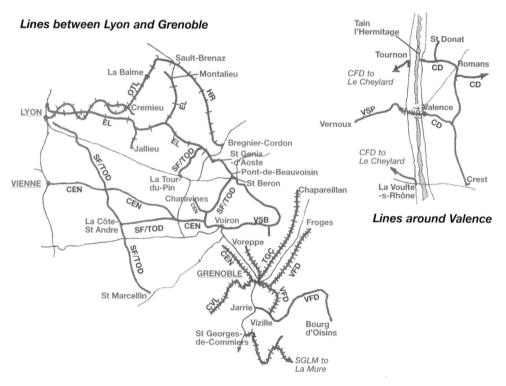

Lines between Lyon and Grenoble

Sault-Brenaz

La Balme

Montalieu

Cremieu

OTL

EL

HR

LYON

EL

Jallieu

EL

SF/TOD

Bregnier-Cordon

St Genix-d'Aoste

Pont-de-Beauvoisin

St Beron

Chapareillan

VIENNE

CEN

CEN

La Tour-du-Pin

CEN

SF/TOD

Charavines

La Côte-St Andre

SF/TOD

CEN

Voiron

VSB

Froges

St Marcellin

SF/TOD

Voreppe

CEN

TGC

VFD

GRENOBLE

VFD

CVL

Jarrie

VFD

VFD

Vizille

Bourg d'Oisins

St Georges-de-Commiers

SGLM to La Mure

Lines around Valence

Tain l'Hermitage

St Donat

Tournon

Romans

CD

CFD to Le Cheylard

CD

VSP

Valence

Vernoux

CD

CFD to Le Cheylard

Crest

La Voûte-s-Rhône

Lines around Valence

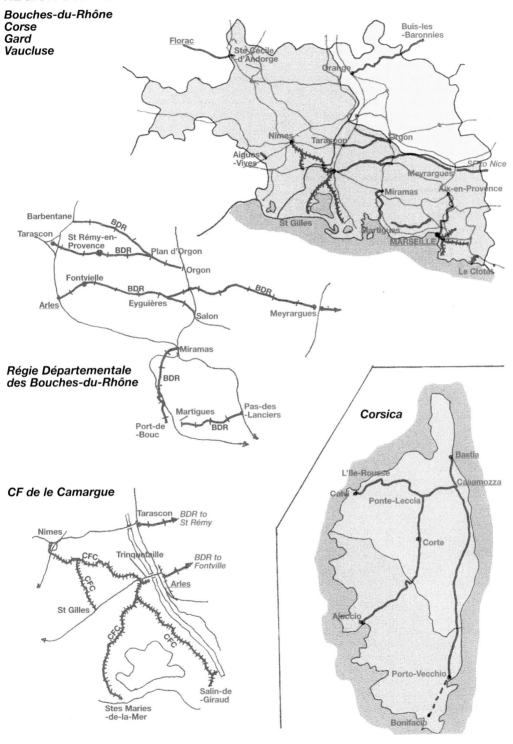

RÉGION SUD-EST

Bouches-du-Rhône
Corse
Gard
Vaucluse

Florac

Buis-les
-Baronnies

Ste Cécile
-d'Andorge

Orange

Nîmes   Tarascon   Orgon

Aigues
-Vives

SP to Nice

Meyrargues

Miramas   Aix-en-Provence

St Gilles

Martigues

MARSEILLE

Le Clotas

Régie Départementale
des Bouches-du-Rhône

Barbentane

BDR

Tarascon

St Rémy-en-
Provence

BDR   Plan d'Orgon

Orgon

Fontvieille

BDR   BDR

Arles

Eyguières   Meyrargues

Salon

Miramas

BDR

Martigues   Pas-des
-Lanciers

Port-de
-Bouc   BDR

Corsica

CF de le Camargue

Tarascon   BDR to
St Rémy

Nîmes

CFC   Tringuetaille   BDR to
Fontville

CFC   Arles

St Gilles

CFC   CFC

Salin-de
-Giraud

Stes Maries
-de-la-Mer

Bastia

L'Ile-Rousse

Casamozza

Calvi   Ponte-Leccia

Corte

Ajaccio

Porto-Vecchio

Bonifacio

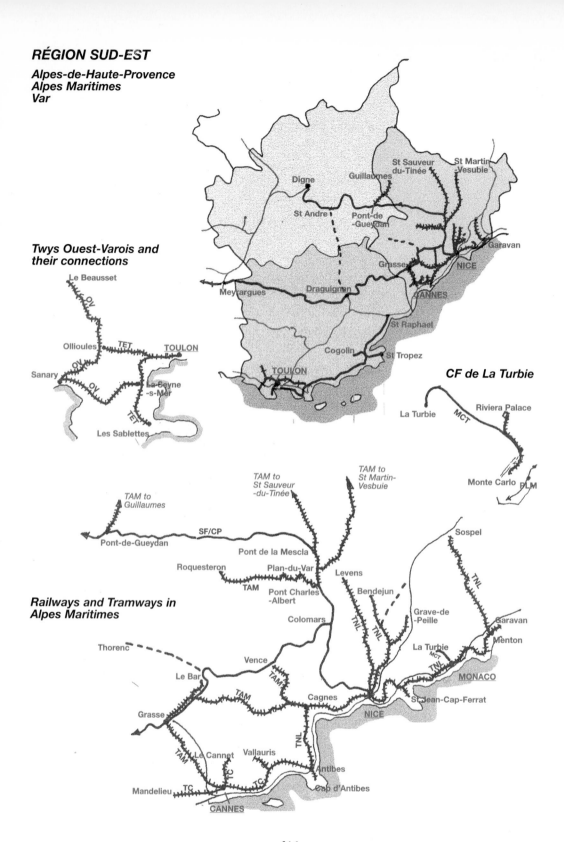

RÉGION SUD-EST

Alpes-de-Haute-Provence
Alpes Maritimes
Var

Twys Ouest-Varois and their connections

Le Beausset

OV

Ollioules
TET
TOULON

OV
Sanary

OV
La-Seyne
-s-Mer

TET
Les Sablettes

Digne

Guillaumes

St Sauveur
du-Tinée

St Martin
-Vesubie

St Andre

Pont-de
-Gueydan

Garavan

Grasse

NICE

Meyrargues

Draguignan

CANNES

St Raphael

Cogolin

St Tropez

TOULON

CF de La Turbie

La Turbie
MCT
Riviera Palace

Monte Carlo
PLM

Railways and Tramways in Alpes Maritimes

TAM to
St Sauveur
-du-Tinée

TAM to
St Martin-
Vesbuie

TAM to
Guillaumes

SF/CP

Sospel

Pont-de-Gueydan

Pont de la Mescla

Roquesteron

Plan-du-Var

Levens

TNL

TAM

Bendejun

Pont Charles
-Albert

Grave-de
-Peille

Garavan

Colomars

TNL

TNL

La Turbie
MCT

Menton

Thorenc

Vence

TNL

MONACO

Le Bar

TAM

Cagnes

NICE

St-Jean-Cap-Ferrat

Grasse

TAM

Le Cannet

Vallauris

TNL

TC

Mandelieu

TAM

TC

TC

Antibes

Cap d'Antibes

CANNES

RÉGION SUD-OUEST de la FRANCE
Départements and Préfectures

Région
Ouest

ORLÉANS

Loir-et
-Cher

Loiret

TOURS

BLOIS

Indre-et
-Loire

Cher

BOURGES

Indre

Châteauroux

Vienne

POITIERS

Creuse

Gueret

Région
Sud-Est

LIMOGES

Haute-Vienne

Corrèze

Perigueux

Tulle

Cantal

Dordogne

Aurillac

BORDEAUX

Lot

Gironde

Cahors

RODEZ

Lot-et
-Garonne

Agen

Aveyron

Landes

Albi

Gers

Tarn

Hérault

Mont-de-Marsan

Auch

TOULOUSE

MONTPELLIER

PAU

Basses-
Pyrénées

Haute-
Garonne

Tarbes

Carcassonne

Hautes-
Pyrénées

Foix

Aude

Ariege

PERPIGNAN

SPAIN

Pyrénées-Orientales

RÉGION SUD-OUEST

Cher
Indre
Indre-et-Loire
Loir-et-Cher
Loiret
Vienne

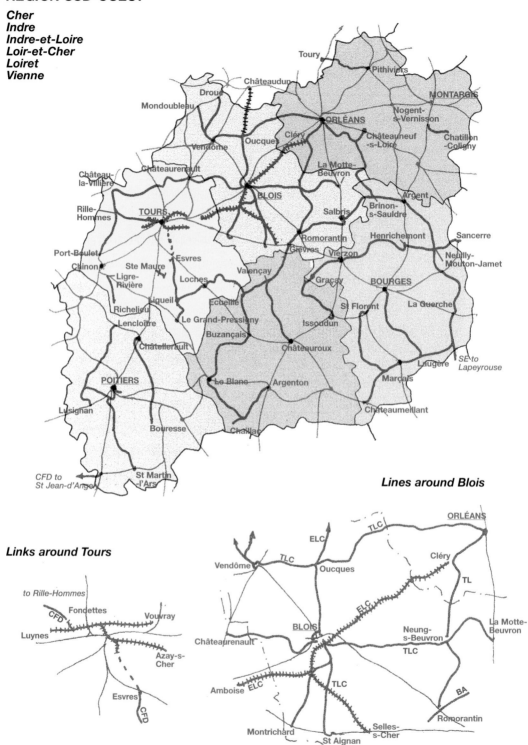

Toury
Pithiviers
Châteaudun
MONTARGIS
Droué
Mondoubleau
Nogent-
s-Vernisson
ORLÉANS
Chatillon-
Coligny
Vendôme
Oucques
Cléry
Châteauneuf
-s-Loire
Château-
la-Villière
Châteaurenault
La Motte-
Beuvron
Rille-
Hommes
BLOIS
Argent
TOURS
Salbris
Brinon-
s-Sauldre
Port-Boulet
Romorantin
Henrichemont
Sancerre
Chinon
Esvres
Grèves
Vierzon
Neuilly-
Mouton-Jamet
Ste Maure
Valençay
Ligre-
Rivière
Loches
Graçay
BOURGES
Liqueil
Echelle
St Florent
La Guerche
Richelieu
Le Grand-Pressigny
Issoudun
Lencloître
Buzançais
Châteauroux
Laugère
SE to
Lapeyrouse
Châtellerault
Marçais
POITIERS
Le Blanc
Argenton
Châteaumeillant
Lusignan
Bouresse
Chaillac
CFD to
St Jean-d'Angel
St Martin
-l'Ars

Lines around Blois

ORLÉANS
TLC
ELC
TLC
Cléry
Vendôme
Oucques
TL
ELC
BLOIS
Neung-
s-Beuvron
La Motte-
Beuvron
Châteaurenault
TLC
TLC
Amboise ELC
BA
Selles-
s-Cher
Romorantin
Montrichard
St Aignan

Links around Tours

to Rille-Hommes
Fondettes
Vouvray
CFD
Luynes
Azay-s-
Cher
Esvres
CFD

318

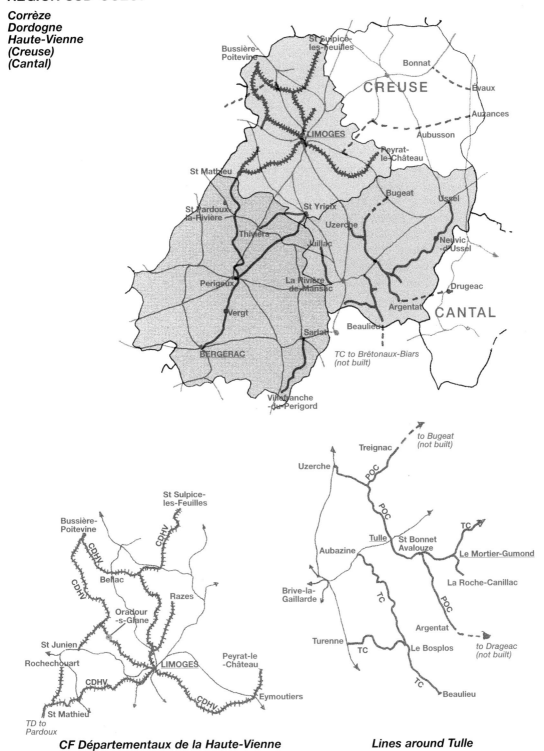

RÉGION SUD-OUEST

Corrèze
Dordogne
Haute-Vienne
(Creuse)
(Cantal)

Bussière-
Poitevine

St Sulpice-
les-Feuilles

Bonnat

Évaux

CREUSE

Auzances

LIMOGES

Aubusson

Peyrat-
le-Château

St Mathieu

Bugeat

Ussel

St Pardoux-
la-Rivière

St Yrieix

Neuvic-
d'Ussel

Thiviers

Uzerche

Vuillac

Périgueux

La Rivière
de-Mansac

Drageac

Argentat

CANTAL

Vergt

Beaulieu

Sarlat

TC to Brêtonaux-Biars
(not built)

BERGERAC

Villefranche
-du-Perigord

CF Départementaux de la Haute-Vienne

St Sulpice-
les-Feuilles

Bussière-
Poitevine

CDHV

CDHV

CDHV

Bellac

Razes

Oradour
-s-Glane

St Junien

Rochechouart

Peyrat-le
-Château

CDHV

LIMOGES

CDHV

CDHV

St Mathieu

Eymoutiers

TD to
Pardoux

Lines around Tulle

Uzerche

Treignac

to Bugeat
(not built)

POC

POC

Aubazine

Tulle

St Bonnet
Avalouze

TC

Le Mortier-Gumond

La Roche-Canillac

Brive-la-
Gaillarde

TC

POC

Turenne

Argentat

to Drageac
(not built)

TC

Le Bosplos

TC

TC

Beaulieu

RÉGION SUD-OUEST

**Aveyron
Lot
Lot-et-Garonne
Tarn-et-Garonne**

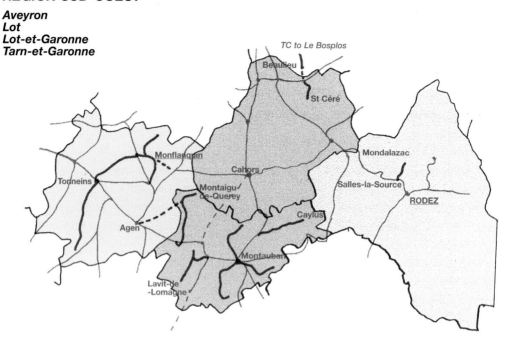

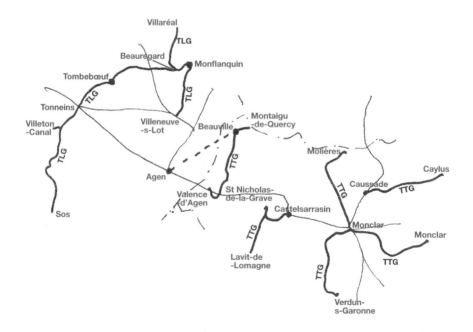

Départemental systems of Lot-et-Garonne & Tarn-et-Garonne

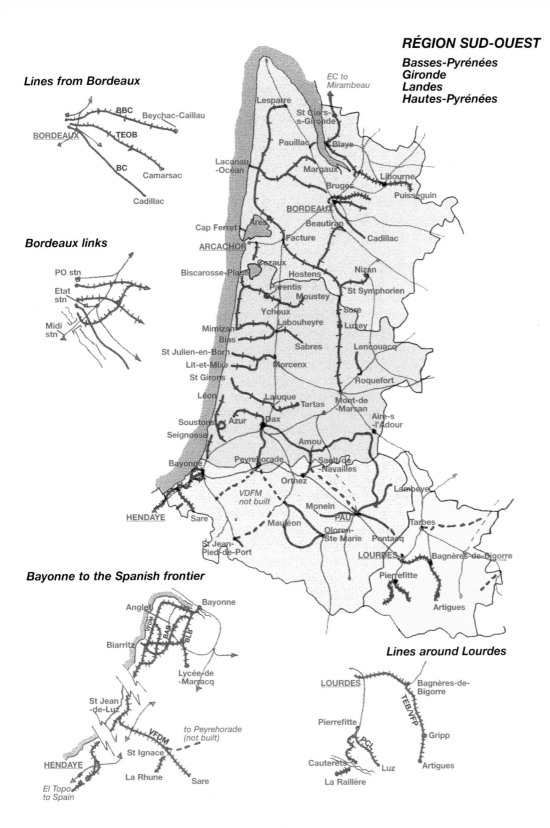

RÉGION SUD-OUEST

Basses-Pyrénées
Gironde
Landes
Hautes-Pyrénées

Lines from Bordeaux

BBC
Beychac-Caillau
BORDEAUX
TEOB
BC
Camarsac
Cadillac

Bordeaux links

PO stn
Etat
stn
Midi
stn

Bayonne to the Spanish frontier

Anglet
Bayonne
VFDM
BAB
BLB
Biarritz
Lycée-de
-Marracq
St Jean
-de-Luz
VFDM
to Peyrehorade
(not built)
HENDAYE
St Ignace
El Topo
to Spain
La Rhune
Sare

Lines around Lourdes

LOURDES
Bagnères-de-
Bigorre
Pierrefitte
TEB/VFP
Gripp
PCL
Cauterets
Luz
Artigues
La Raillère

EC to
Mirambeau
Lesparre
St Ciers-
s-Gironde
Pauillac
Blaye
Lacanau
-Océan
Margaux
Libourne
Bruges
Puisseguin
BORDEAUX
Cap Ferret
Ares
Beautiran
Facture
Cadillac
ARCACHON
Cazaux
Nizan
Biscarosse-Plage
Hostens
Parentis
St Symphorien
Moustey
Ychoux
Sore
Labouheyre
Luxey
Mimizan
Bias
Sabres
Lencouacq
St Julien-en-Born
Lit-et-Mixe
Morcenx
St Girons
Roquefort
Léon
Laluque
Tartas
Mont-de
-Marsan
Soustons
Azur
Dax
Aire-s
-l'Adour
Seignosse
Amou
Bayonne
Peyrehorade
Sault-de
-Navailles
Orthez
Lambeye
VDFM
not built
Monein
HENDAYE
Sare
PAU
Tarbes
Mauléon
Oloron-
Ste Marie
Pontacq
St Jean-
Pied-de-Port
LOURDES
Bagnères-de-Bigorre
Pierrefitte
Artigues

321

RÉGION SUD-OUEST

Ariege
Haute-Garonne
Tarn

(Gers)

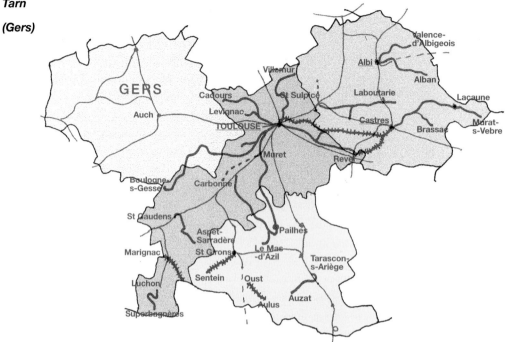

Lines around Toulouse and Castres

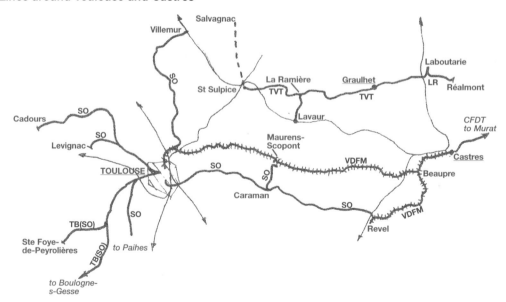

RÉGION SUD-OUEST

Aude
Hérault
Pyrénées-Orientales

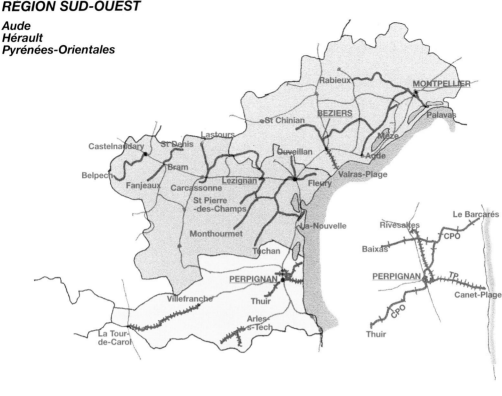

Rabieux
MONTPELLIER
BEZIERS
St Chinian
Lastours
Palavas
Castelnaudary
St Denis
Mèze
Belpech
Bram
Ouveillan
Agde
Fanjeaux
Lezignan
Valras-Plage
Carcassonne
Fleury
St Pierre
-des-Champs
Monthourmet
La-Nouvelle
Rivesaltes
Le Barcarés
CPO
Baixas
Tuchan
PERPIGNAN
PERPIGNAN
TP
Villefranche
Thuir
Canet-Plage
Arles-
-s-Tech
CPO
La Tour-
de-Carol
Thuir

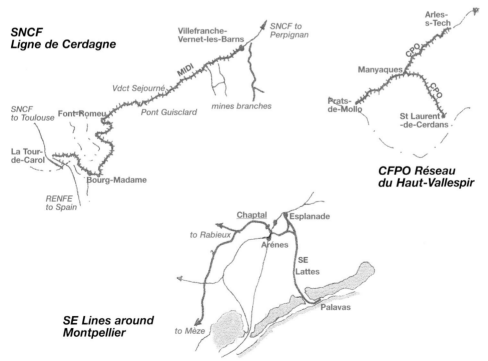

SNCF
Ligne de Cerdagne

Villefranche-
Vernet-les-Barns
SNCF to
Perpignan
MIDI
Vdct Sejourné
mines branches
SNCF
to Toulouse
Font-Romeu
Pont Guisclard
La Tour-
de-Carol
Bourg-Madame
RENFE
to Spain

Arles-
s-Tech
CPO
Manyaques
CPO
Prats-
de-Mollo
St Laurent
-de-Cerdans

CFPO Réseau
du Haut-Vallespir

Chaptal
Esplanade
to Rabieux
Arénes
SE
Lattes
Palavas

SE Lines around
Montpellier

to Mèze

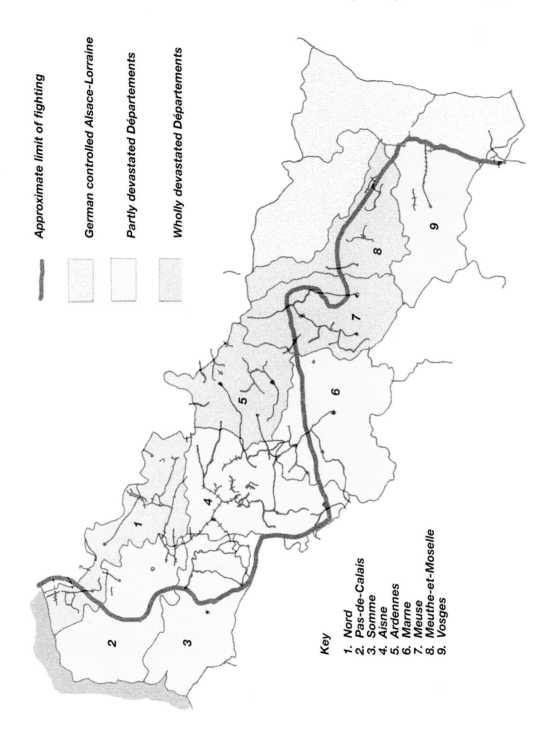

Western Front 1914-18
Secondary railways in the battle zone

Approximate limit of fighting

German controlled Alsace-Lorraine

Partly devastated Départements

Wholly devastated Départements

Key

1. Nord
2. Pas-de-Calais
3. Somme
4. Aisne
5. Ardennes
6. Marne
7. Meuse
8. Meuthe-et-Moselle
9. Vosges

PART 5
Appendices

Gare
du
Tacot.

Prehistory of the French narrow gauge secondary railway

As mentioned briefly in chapter 1, the French, as well as the British, fought the battle of the gauges and at approximately the same time: The main difference was that they had very few citable narrow gauge railways and almost all of those were industrial lines. Three indigenous systems were continually cited in support of the narrow gauge, the mineral railway in Aveyron belonging to the CF de Paris – Orléans (PO) and running from mines at Mondalazac to a standard gauge junction at Salles la Source; The so-called CF de Cessous à Trebiau to coal mines at Cornas in Gard; The CF Minière de Rochebelle a little further south, linking mines to a steelworks at Tamaris, also in Gard. The last two were in the Cevennes coalfield and linked to the PLM Clermont Ferrand – Nimes railway or a branch of it. Otherwise occasional mention was made of experiments in Belgium and fairly detailed studies of three "foreign" mineral railways – the St Leon mines in South Sardinia; the Ergasteria railway in Greece; and the Mokta-el-Hadid line in French Algeria. The two latter were of particular interest in using light railway-pattern 0-6-0Ts by Koechlin or Schneider, together with railway-type wagons properly coupled and braked. The Mokta-el-Hadid company used some passenger vehicles for transport of workers and also owned the Trebiau line.

Rather surprisingly, even writers in the mid-1870s took little notice of the metre gauge railway from Lagny, in Seine-et-Marne, to Villeneuve le Comte which was started as a (rather ineffectual) metre gauge quarry line as early as 1865 but had been conceded to Cornu, Burdin et Cie under Intérêt Général rules in 1871 and opened with steam traction for both public goods and passenger traffic in September 1872. Since it had proper stations, signalling and used six-coupled locomotives this is somewhat surprising; possibly its rather chequered early career, owing to the failure of its bank, had something to do with it. Its outline life is chronicled in chapter 10. Comparative dimensions of equipment are given below, those of the Ergasteria line being included to show why advocates felt they had to look outside France. Although none of the first three railways had any lasting effect, they are of interest and had some features which were advanced for their period. For the record, therefore, they were:

Mondalazac – Salles-la-Source: This railway was established in 1861 to tap iron mines in the hills east of Salles-la-Source and was built as narrow gauge because of the difficult terrain. It was a true 1.10m gauge, running for 7km on its own right of way, and having maximum gradients of 12 mm/m and minimum curve radius of 60m – these tending to occur at the same time. The track was 16.5kg/m Vignoles pattern flat-bottom iron rail on oak sleepers with crushed stone ballast, as might have been expected from a main line company. Traction initially was by horses but steam was introduced in 1864. The locomotives were straightforward industrial 0-4-0 side tank machines by Gouin et Cie and stock originally comprised 55 4-wheeled mine tubs, later increased to 70; they were of interest in having rubber cylindrical springing and in pointing up the need for separate tyres on sharply curved lines for ease of maintenance. In 1865 the PO considered introducing a passenger service, and even went to the extent of designing stock for it, but concluded this would require 0-6-0Ts and a gauge widening to 1.20m (this last was often scorned by proponents of the narrow gauge who argued that going down to metre gauge could be done without any disadvantage). The line was often described and cited but did not last long; it was sold to the Mines & Acieries de France in 1882 and soon replaced by a "proper mineral railway" of 660mm gauge running north west to Decazeville on a PO branch.

CF de Cessous à Trebiau (sometimes known as the CF des Mines de Cornas): This line was built in 1866-68 by the Mokta-el-Hadid company to link mines in the Cornas valley to its works at la Jasse on the never-completed PLM branch from Chamborigaud to Vernarede and on to Besseges. The mineral line was originally horsedrawn and its high and spindly viaduct over the river Oguegne at la Jasse appears never to have been suitable for steam traction. It used 12kg/m Vignoles iron rails (soon changed to steel) on oak sleeprs with local rubble ballast and the gauge was 800mm to the centres of rails, giving a true gauge, according to contemporary data and drawings, of 766mm; this appears to have been later rounded off to

Koechlin metre gauge 0-6-0T of the Ergasteria line in Greece.   (FACS)

770mm, possibly when steel rails were introduced. The initial locomotives were two 0-4-0T by Koechlin (1138-39 of 1868), later supplemented by two similar machines by SACM delivered in 1875 and 1882, makers nos 2363 and 3168. The most interesting feature of these, frequently discussed, was that they had to work underground into the main mine adit - initially for about 1.5km to Shaft 3 but later to the Serre shaft which involved a total underground run of 4.221km out of 5.5km in all, this including three tunnels between the mine entrance and la Jasse. To make this possible, they were fitted with a manually operated condensing circuit that allowed the exhaust to be channelled into the side tanks when required. It is noted that the water became so hot that standard practice was to stop at the adit exit to flush and refill both tanks so that the primitive Giffard injectors could work; a rapid draw-down cock was fitted for this purpose but even so, in later years, auxiliary pumps were fitted to the rear axles. (it must be said that, for drainage purposes, the adit sloped down to its entrance so that the gradient was favourable for loaded trains which could run for much of the way with the main regulator closed). Wagon stock consisted of wooden mines tubs with frame extensions for buffers and having loose wheels on fixed axles. The railway continued in use up to the mid 20th Century. Exact date of closure is not known to the writer but was certainly by 1954 when the standard gauge branch was closed.

CF Minière de Rochebelle: This was built in 1872 by the Forges et Fonderies d'Alais to link mines at Rochebelle village with their works at Tamaris on the PLM Clermont-Ferrand – Nimes line and was developed from steam-worked tramways already in use around the factory and iron-mines complex. These involved a most elaborate bridge over the river Gardon which was initially a low-level road bridge for internal use. The Rochebelle line crossed above it on an iron girder structure with conventional piers at each side and a central iron pier rising from the existing stone pier. The line itself was only 1.861km long, using Vignoles rail with a maximum gradient of 18mm/m and a minimum radius of 60m; gauge was the same as the Cessous line and measured in the same fashion. Original motive power is quoted as being 0-4-0Ts by Schneider Creusot "as supplied to St Léon mines in Sardinia" and dated 1865, so probably ex the internal factory system, though others, including a Koechlin, are recorded as coming later. Wagons had a

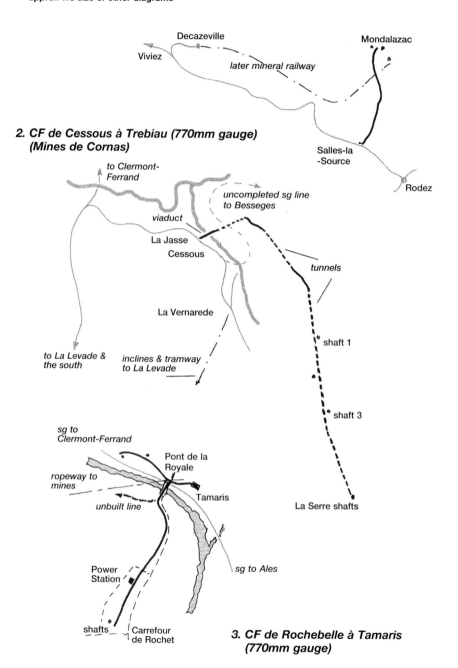

Early French narrow gauge mineral railways

1. PO line from Modalazac (1.10m gauge)
approx 1/3 size of other diagrams

Decazeville

Viviez

later mineral railway

Mondalazac

Salles-la
-Source

Rodez

2. CF de Cessous à Trebiau (770mm gauge)
(Mines de Cornas)

to Clermont-
Ferrand

*uncompleted sg line
to Besseges*

viaduct

La Jasse

Cessous

tunnels

La Vernarede

shaft 1

to La Levade &
the south

*inclines & tramway
to La Levade*

shaft 3

*sg to
Clermont-Ferrand*

Pont de la
Royale

*ropeway to
mines*

Tamaris

La Serre shafts

unbuilt line

Power
Station

sg to Ales

shafts

Carrefour
de Rochet

3. CF de Rochebelle à Tamaris
(770mm gauge)

Early French narrow gauge mineral railways: Mondalazac; Cessous à Trebiau; Rochebelle.

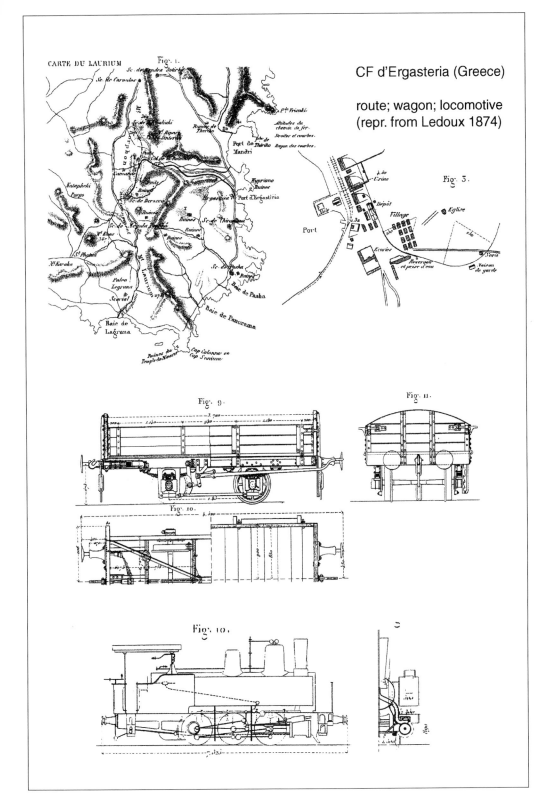

CF d'Ergasteria (Greece)

route; wagon; locomotive
(repr. from Ledoux 1874)

CF d'Ergasteria (Greece): map; wagon drawing; locomotive diagram (side).

useful load of 1000kg and 20 constituted a train. The line remained locomotive-hauled until 1932 when it was changed to cable operation. It closed in 1967.

   CF d'Ergasteria, Greece: As virtually the "beau ideal" of the narrow gauge enthusiasts, perhaps this warrants a short note. It was initially built to convey mineral traffic from valleys inland down to the port of Ergasteria on the eastern coast of the Greek peninsula. Here a plant had been established, initially to process lead and silver from waste tips of old workings but then also to accept freshly mined rock of inferior quality which could be mixed with the former. The quarries were on the inland side of a range of hills and were, in the early 1860s, served by an inadequate mountain road. The railway, of true metre gauge, followed this up from the coast on an average grade of 35mm/m, ran through a tunnel 267.50m long with a summit point of some 155m and then descended to the quarries at 97m above sea level with a maximum adverse gradient (against the load) of 26mm/m. The sharpest curves, down to 60m radius, occurred on the climb up from Ergasteria but otherwise were no sharper than 70m. The main line was 8.5km long and the calculated capacity of the line was some 750 tonnes per day from quarries to coast. As can be seen this was by no means an easy line to work and the equipment was certainly state-of-the art for the time. The locomotives were 23t 0-6-0Ts by Koechlin, with a maximum axleload of approximately 8-tonnes, running on steel flat-bottomed rail of 20.3kg/m weight fixed to squared oak sleepers with local stone ballast. The wagons, of 6-tonnes capacity, although fitted with double buffers and chain-link couplings, were otherwise of railway type with metal underframes and laminated springing to the oil-lubricated axleboxes and having dropsides for easy unloading; some had screw brakes, operated manually, the others having lever parking brakes. By the standards of the 1860s the whole affair was quite efficient and it is easy to see why it should have been cited. If the metre gauge could handle those conditions then it should be capable of providing rural communications in France.

Table A1.1. Main dimensions of locomotives

Line:	Modalazac	Cessou	Tamaris	Ergasteria	Lagny
Maker:	Gouin	Koechlin	Schneider	Koechlin	Fives
type:	0-4-0T	0-4-0T	0-4-0T	0-6-0T	0-6-0T
cyls dia	240mm	220mm	204mm	350mm	250mm
stroke	400mm	300mm	360mm	460mm	360mm
pressure	8atm	9atm	9atm	9atm	8.25atm
weight tare	9500kg	6000kg	5200kg	17500kg	10000kg
weight w/o		8000kg	6790kg	22965kg	13000kg
wheelbase	1400mm	1500mm	1250mm	2200mm	1720mm
wheel dia	950mm	600mm	760mm	900mm	800mm

Table A1.2. main dimensions of wagons

Line:	Modalazac	Cessou	Tamaris	Ergasteria	Lagny
type:			all 4-w		
length o/all	3400mm	2540mm		4520mm	4000mm
body length:	2740mm	2200mm		3620mm	3000mm
" width:	1500mm	640/740mm		1700mm	2100mm
" depth:	450mm	560mm		450mm	700mm
wheelbase:	1500mm	550mm		1450mm	1400mm
wheel dia:	700mm	320mm		925mm	700mm
weight tare:	1400kg	450kg	500kg	2600kg	2500kg
load:	3800kg	925kg	1000kg	6000kg	5000kg

Note: with the excepton of Lagny, wagon body dimensions are internal to indicate useable volume.

Copy of a Report from Stovin Warburton, HM Consul at La Rochelle, France, 1894

Author's note

The report has been reproduced exactly as written except that, to save space, Consul Warburton's very short paragraphs have been combined where possible. He appears somewhat confused as to the French definitions of tramway and light railway but in general his notes paint a very fair picture of a rural département under the 1880 legislation. The "Tramways" referred to were the CF Economiques des Charentes, belonging to the Jeancard group and were indeed classed as tramways since 70% of roadside track was more than two-thirds. It may be noted that, quite naturally for the period, Mr Warburton uses imperial units throughout and anglicises such terms as "départtément".

Report on the Tramways of the Charente Inférieure

During the past year there has been a considerable amount of tramway construction in this district, and as the subject is one which has attracted a good deal of attention in our own country of late, where the advocates of tramway making at the expense of the public have supported their views by quoting the example of this country as an argument in its favour, I think it well to give such information as I have been able to obtain concerning these lines, as well as on the tramway question generally.

The distinction made here between tramways and light railways does not depend upon the mode of construction, but on whether the lines run along the public roads for a certain proportion of their length or not. Any line that runs for more than two-thirds of its whole length on or along the sides of the public roads is a tramway, and one which does so for a lesser distance is a railway. In this Department they are constructed for about 30 per cent of their length on lands purchased for the purpose, and for 70 per cent of it along the roads, and, therefore, not being able to show the proportion necessary to make them tramways, are classed as railways, although commonly described as 'the tramways of the Charente Inférieure'. (*Warburton appears a little confused here, possibly because the company name was CF Economiques des Charentes!*)

The formalities necessary before the construction of the lines is permitted vary also according to the nature of the ground on which they run. If they are made (wherever they follow the roads) on those which belong exclusively to the Department or the communes, the Council-General of the Department can authorize their construction. If, on the other hand, any part of them runs along a road belonging to the State, such as a national road, or the wharf of a maritime port, the Concession can only be obtained from the State, and this last is the case with the tramways of the Charente Inférieure, which have been authorized by a Decree from the President of the Republic. The cost of making the lines is then paid by the State and the Department; here each provides one-half, but the latter has to find the money in the first instance, as the State contribution is not given in cash, but in the form of an annuity spread over a term of fifty years.

This is how the matter was carried out here. The Department is the paymaster, and advertises for a contractor willing to construct the lines, and also to work them during the whole of the Concession, which is for fifty years, engaging to repay him the actual outlay incurred, provided it does not exceed a maximum sum agreed upon, which in this instance is fixed at £2,735 per mile, and includes cost of land purchased, running stock, and everything else. But the contractor does not receive the whole sum in cash, only being paid three-fourths of it; the remaining fourth, being considered as a contribution from him, is deducted from the total sum due, according to his tender, and he is allowed interest on it at the rate of 4 per cent until his Concession expires.

The working of the lines is entirely at his risk, but a calculation is made when giving out the contract as to the probable cost of maintenance and working, as well as of the probable receipts. I am informed that here the estimate agreed upon between the Department and the contractor was that it should be put at £76 per mile, plus two-thirds of the gross receipts.

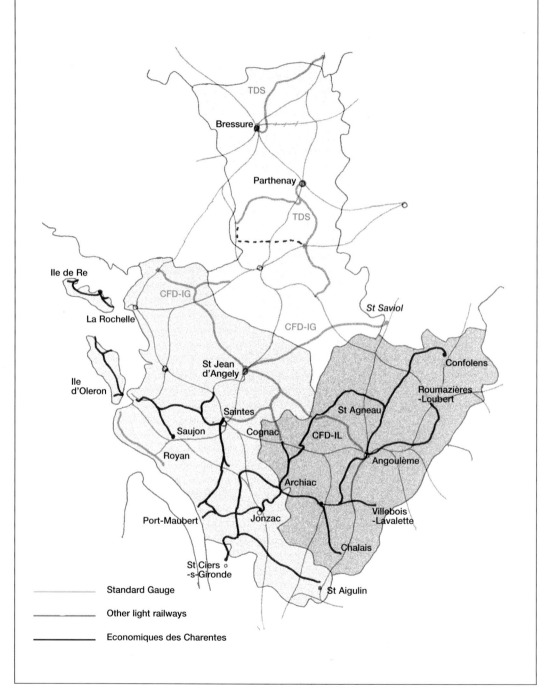

CF Economiques des Charentes in the Charentes & Deux services

TDS

Bressure

Parthenay

TDS

Ile de Re

CFD-IG

La Rochelle

CFD-IG

St Saviol

Ile
d'Oleron

St Jean
d'Angely

Confolens

Saintes

St Agneau

Roumazières
-Loubert

Saujon

Cognac

CFD-IL

Royan

Angoulème

Archiac

Port-Maubert

Jonzac

Villebois
-Lavalette

Chalais

St Ciers
-s-Gironde

St Aigulin

Standard Gauge

Other light railways

Economiques des Charentes

556. Charente-Inf. — SAUJON — Le tramway de Marennes

A pottering tramway train, of the kind which aroused Consul Warburton's disquiet.   (FACS)

The tramways of the Charente Inférieure are intended for the transport of agricultural produce, goods, and passengers; the width of gauge is nearly 40 inches, which has been chosen as likely to be the most useful size; the locomotives weigh 15 tons, and the wagons can carry a load of 10 tons, so that practically they are railways running along the roads for most of their length.

Having described these lines, which are similar to others lately made in different parts of France, the question naturally arises as to the benefit derived from them by the districts into which they have been introduced, and on this subject, having consulted persons competent to form an opinion I have found it to be generally unfavourable. There may be instances in which these lines have been a success, either financially, or by developing the resources of the district to such an extent as to make up for the loss to the public purse which they generally involve, but 1 believe them to be very rare, and I should require very strong evidence that this was so in any case before I could credit it. It is rather soon to pass a judgment on the services which the tramways of this Department may eventually render, but at present I cannot see that they have any chance of doing so to an extent which can ever compensate for the amount of money spent on them.

They run through an agricultural country principally, so that it is to persons engaged in this occupation we should expect the principal benefit to accrue, but I believe that they will be very little used by most of them. The line passes by hundreds of farms of moderate size (say, from 20 to 200 acres), mostly tillage, which necessitates the use of horses and carts, several of which are generally kept on each farm. The farmers have produce to sell, but it is generally sold at the different market towns for 10 or 12 miles round, and delivered at the buyer's house. The tramway only runs from one point to another, and if it passes through a certain number of market towns, it leaves a far greater number equally near to any particular farmer untouched, so that in their case it is of no use to him at all But even when it runs to the exact place to which he wants to send a load, he has first to cart it from his farm to the tramway, then load it m the wagons, and at the end of the journey put it on another cart to get it to the house of the purchaser if sold, while, if not, it has to be sent home in the same way, so that there are very few farms who do not prefer to load their stuff and send it direct to the place of sale than to go through all these operations and the idea of running sidings from the lines up to the farms is entirely illusory in this country, for no one would think of doing it.

The lines can therefore be of very little use to agriculture, and as the district is not a manufacturing one, or sufficiently populous to provide the amount of goods or passenger traffic which would enable them to pay the expenses of working, it is not easy to see what advantage will be derived from them except to a very limited number of persons.

I believe this to be the case in most of the tramway lines which have hitherto been constructed (in a greater or less degree), and it will naturally then be asked why they were ever made at all ?

The answer is, simply because of the great facility which exists for obtaining public money for these and other undertakings, which would never have been attempted if they had to be made with private capital and for commercial reasons.

If the arrangement by which the funds are obtained is looked into, it will be seen how great an inducement is offered for getting up undertakings of doubtful wisdom when this can be done at the public cost. In this case, half the charges are paid by the State in the first place, which would present some difficulty if the money had to be paid down in cash, but the objection to providing so large a sum at once is got over by making it an annual payment extending over fifty years.

The Department naturally wishes to profit by the outlay of this large sum, of which it only pays m infinitesimal part, and in order to do so has to provide the same amount, which it is able to do without inflicting on itself any additional taxation to signify, by borrowing the total sum required at a very moderate rate of interest, which during fifty years will be in a great part paid by the Government annual grant, so that till the end of that period nobody will be much the worse off. This would not be so if they had to make up any great loss on the working of the lines, but this is guarded against by the arrangement made with the contractor to work as well as construct them, by making him subscribe one fourth of the capital, and by paying him the interest of this sum during the period of the Concession. Of course, this increases the cost of the undertaking, as he must consider it in his tender, but if it does, it also increases the half paid by the State and the annual payment in lieu of ready money.

It does not seem to me very surprising that, under the circumstances, every part of the country should wish for tramways without looking very closely into the question of whether they are likely to benefit the

LA BERGERIE (Ch.-Inf.) — Arrivée des trains

Apparent bustle (but few passengers) at the junction station of La Bergerie.   (FACS)

rest of the country at some future time, for there can be no doubt that they benefit some persons at once, and the expenditure of a large sum of money is always popular in a district when the tax-payers are not called on to pay more on account of it.

I have read a great deal of correspondence during the past year as to the desirability of constructing tramways at the cost of the State or county districts in England, and the advantages which would result to the country generally from an expenditure of public money in this way. On this subject I am not competent to form an opinion, but one argument used by the advocates of it appeared to me a very fallacious one. It was, that it had been done in France on a large scale for some years Past, and that as most of the lines did not work at a profit, the direct loss to the State must be counter-balanced by some indirect advantage to the population at large, or they would not be made. This is exactly what ought to be proved before the money of the public is spent on them, but I am afraid that it will be found very difficult, and that if such a proof had been required here many lines would never have been constructed.

Persons who wish us to follow the example of this country should remember that here it has been for many years the practice for the State to contribute liberally towards undertakings of every kind. Tramways form a very small item in the gross sum which is thus granted annually, and they are often the only undertaking on which money can be so spent in a particular district. In these Departments bordering on the sea, millions have been granted by the State for making and improving seaports and for other maritime works of little advantage to the inland population, which expects its share of whatever is going in the shape of Government aid, and will insist on having it.

Then the political question steps in, and these districts have Deputies and Senators like other places, whose first duty is to their constituents, and if they neglected it, and were not able or willing to secure this share for them, their places would be very likely to be taken by others possessed of more energy or more influence. The electors of a district consider that they are the best judges of what is good for them, and it seems a hard case to refuse a grant for a tramway on the ground that it will not pay if they wish to have it, when their neighbours in the same Department have been given sums five or six times as large for other undertakings which pay no better.

I believe that this was the case here, and that some prudent persons in other parts of the Department did at first oppose the tramway scheme as a waste of money, but were met with the answer, 'You have got millions for your district, and you want to prevent us from getting a few hundred thousands for ours.' I think, however, it will be found that, owing to their want of success, tramways are going out of fashion in this country, and that people are not so anxious for them as they were. I am told that many lines which had been projected will not now be carried out and although the mere finishing of the systems already begun, and which cannot be stopped, may amount to a considerable mileage per year until they are completed, I have reason to believe that after this year tramway construction will show a considerable falling off in this country.

An experienced engineer, who supported the tramways of this Department, informs me that since seeing their working he has entirely changed his mind about them, and will never again vote for a steam tramway in rural districts unless it is entirely constructed on land purchased, and does not run anywhere along the public roads. My informant considers that in order to justify the outlay incurred in making tramway lines, every mile of their route should be able to feed them with light or heavy traffic in proportion to their cost of construction and working expenses, and that in order to fulfil this condition they must be made in one of two ways:

1. Cheap to construct and work, and in this case they should be only what used to be known as a tramway, viz., a line running for all its length along the public roads, with light rails, carriages, and wagons, which enables a service to be kept up of carriages running frequently at small cost. This kind of tramway requires to be worked by horses, or by engines of a lighter and more economical build than any at present in use in this country, but except in or near large towns it can scarcely ever pay.

2. By making it (as has been done here and elsewhere) a railway more or less light, worked by ordinary steam locomotives, capable of moving a large amount of tonnage in heavier trains running less often.

A line of this description cannot be run entirely along the public roads in this country for several reasons, one of which is that very few of them are wide enough to allow it to be done with safety, and land must therefore be purchased, which, as I have mentioned already, has been done here on 30 per cent of the whole route, thus enormously increasing the cost, and even this has been insufficient, for where the line does follow the highways, owing to their narrowness many accidents have occurred through horses being frightened, carriages upset in consequence, or from the wheels getting caught in the rails, with the result that a considerable. share of the gross earnings is, I hear, likely to go in damages.

Again, the working expenses are very heavy owing to the rise and fall of the ground on the road parts. In one section of about 16 miles the locomotives have to work the traffic on an incline of as much as 1 in 30, and they are themselves so heavy when fully provisioned with coals and water that they can only draw a load of two and a half times their own weight. This does not matter very much at present, there being so little traffic, but if what is one of the arguments in favour of tramway making proves correct in this instance, and that sufficient traffic is developed to make the line of benefit to the population as a whole, the line will have to be abandoned and a regular railway constructed in its place, entirely on purchased land, so that the steep gradients may be avoided.

I cannot help thinking that it would have, under the circumstances, been wiser to have spent a very small part of the outlay incurred on improving the public roads, which, in this Department, are far from perfect, but then no grant from the State could have been obtained for such a purpose. The general impression now in this country seems to be that the solution of the question of rural traffic does not lie in tramways, but in mechanical traction on the ordinary roads, and that the only difficulty in the way is the want of a locomotive suited to them, and which will not be obliged to carry the great load of coals and water which they do at present; this has not yet been constructed, but the experiments lately carried out in France seem to indicate that the difficulty is most likely to be solved by the use of petroleum as fuel.

If this should turn out to be the case, I feel sure that many country districts will regret having saddled themselves with a costly system of tramways which must be paid for some day, even if the burden is not felt at present, and when we remember the enormous indebtedness of the communes, any addition to it must appear to be a serious matter. This debt, which, in 1862, amounted to £26,000,000, or 15s per head of the population, had risen in 1890 to £129,000,000, equal to £3 4s per head, and must have largely increased since then owing to the liberal expenditure on public works during the last four years, which has been facilitated by the low rate of interest for loans secured by county or municipal guarantee.

There may be (as I have said already) some lines of tramways which are exceptions to the general rule, and have proved a success by benefiting the country generally or paying their way, but I believe this will be found to be owing to exceptional circumstances, such as their supplying a missing link in a railway system, or passing through districts where there are prosperous sugar factories or distilleries. One in particular is always quoted, that between Pithiviers and Toury, but I believe it combines both these advantages to a degree not found elsewhere, and still its earnings have not hitherto been sufficient to prevent loss in the working. As to others, I have never heard anything beyond the general statement that they benefit the district without any facts or figures being given to prove it.

(Signed) R. STOVIN WARBURTON
Consulate of La Rochelle,

16 February 1895.

APPENDIX 3
Notes on the numbering of light railway stock

Locomotives

Methods of numbering locomotives and tractors naturally varied widely between individual companies, and the majority of small companies simply started at '1' and carried on from there; though even so, separated lines under the same management might appear to have their locomotive stock starting mysteriously at, say, '8' or include Nos 51-54; 67; 103 without explanation for the apparent gaps. Other companies had more interesting ways of numbering and some of the more important ones are listed here.

1. The simplest numbering system, other than purely sequential, was that in which each different type or class of locomotive was numbered in its own series, the number being preceded by a cypher, thus: IX, 2X, 3X. (ie: locomotive 34 was the fourth of class 3)

2. A variant of this method was common, in which the initial cypher indicated the number of coupled axles (under continental designations, wheel arrangements are indicated by the number of axles, not by individual wheels). This system normally includes an 'O' after the cypher for the first series in each axlegroup, thus giving the impression of locomotives numbered in the hundreds (e.g. Réseau Breton: IOX-nil, no single-wheelers being employed! 2OX, 21X, 2-4-0Ts of a large class; 3OX, 2-6-0T; 32X, 4-6-0T; 4OX, 0-4-4-0T; 41X – here the sequence breaks down as sometimes happened when new locomotives were brought in at a later date. The 41X class were 0-6-6-0T, probably numbered in the 41s because they were Mallets and the previous Mallets were 40X.)

3. A far more refined version of this method was practised by the SE, which numbered its locomotives thus: cypher indicating axle-number; number indicating class within that axle arrangement (from 1 upwards); number, including zeros if required, giving the individual locomotive in the class. Hence 3.714 was not the 3,714th locomotive owned, but No. 14 in the seventh class of six-coupled locomotives, in this case a cab-first 0-6-2T. This system, incidentally, applied only to locomotives owned by the SE. Machines on systems taken over by the company usually retained their old running numbers.

4. Diesel locomotives were, if rebuilt from steam, usually given the running number of the steam locomotive they replaced in the stock register. New ones might be numbered in the next vacant series or, more often, given a letter prefix such as LT (locotracteur) or DE (diesel-electric) with numbers starting at 1. Later, purpose-built, machines from firms like CFD might use the standard diesel letter prefixes (eg BB for two bogies, all axles driven) and have series numbers allocated by the maker: notable examples were the BB metre gauge machines for Corrèze (401-2): Vivarais (403); Corsica (404); – later confused since 403 eventually went to Corsica which naturally renumbered it 405 and has since added an only vagely related machine as 406.

Railcars

Since railcars now form the main passenger-carrying stock of the surviving railways, their numbering is often interesting, particularly as most retain their old numbers if transferred from one system to another, thus giving a clue to their origins.

1. Letter prefixes: Several of these have been used at various times, the most common ones being A, AR or AT, standing for autorail, and followed by a simple number. The SE (CFTA) prefixed its cars by 'M' for moteur, and the SNCF and some other surviving lines by 'X', this applying also to its narrow-gauge cars and trailers, the latter being prefixed 'XR' - R standing for remorque, or trailer. Other designations have been Z; ZZ (CF de Provence and SNCF); and ZZPE (SNCF); and the initials of the département or company concerned (e.g. P de C – Pas de Calais; CFC – CF du Calvados AB – Achiet – Bapaume).

2. SNCF numbering. SNCF narrow-gauge cars were originally numbered in two series, XI5x and X2xx, different types having their own number groups within the series. The X15x group appears to have been reserved for miscellaneous acquisitions, the X2XX group for new cars or large series of cars. Electric railcars had their own special series, in the Z600s and Z800s.

3. CFD numbering. By far the biggest light-railway user of railcars in France was the CFD and it had a very simple system whereby each line or réseau had a code number followed by individual running numbers, in series starting at 01. The list is given below:

l0x; IIX	Corsica
20x; 21x; 22x	Vivarais-Lozère
30x; 31x	Charentes (Intérêt Général)
40x	Saône et Loire
50x; 51x	Indre-et-Loire (n.g.)
60x; 61x	Dordogne
70x	Vendée
80x	Seine-et-Marne
90x	Indre-et-Loire (s.g.) - later all sg.

The confusions that this system has occasionally given rise to are caused by the transfer or sale of cars which still retain their handsome metal numbers. Buyers have been known to make confusion worse by incorporating the existing numbers into their own series. Thus the CFD du Tarn bought CFD Nos. 511-13, keeping the old numbers; and then promptly numbered their next acquisition 510 to 'fill up' the series. To make things worse, they then acquired two larger cars from a different company numbered 24/5 and promptly added a cypher prefix '5', thus completely obscuring the whole issue!

Other current numberings

Current systems include X301-? on the CF de Provence and X97051-? series for current CF Corses deliveries. Interestingly, while new CFC trailers are scrupulously numbered in an XR 9701-? series, older ones retain their original numbers or the running numbers of the railcars from which they were converted.

Passenger Coaches

Most continental railways included some information about the vehicle in their numbering, normally for stock-register purposes. Some SNCF numbers were so elaborate that one almost suspects it even indicated whether there was a seat in the toilet but most light railways were much simpler.

1. Class distinction (the most common prefix). A indicated 1st class; B is 2nd; C is 3rd; and D could indicate either 4th class (on colonial lines) or a luggage van. Thus AB34 was a Ist/2nd composite; while BCD2 was a 2nd/3rd class composite, with a van portion.

2. Small letter and figure notations. These, rarely found on light railways, indicated;
   (i) various appendages (e.g. f =frein (hand-brake); t = toilet; y = bogie coach);
   (ii) number of compartments in a compartment vehicle (e.g. A1B1).
   They were, and are, obviously mainly for use in the stock register.

3. actual numbering depended on the whim of the company record-keepers and might be strictly sequential, irrespective of class, or in series of one kind or another.

Goods Vehicles

These were normally numbered straightforwardly for each type, the number being preceded by a letter cypher indicating for register purposes the type of vehicle involved (e.g. K van). Identifying letters for particular types could differ between different companies and a few companies used series or groups of numbers.

APPENDIX 4
Funicular Railways in France

Funicular railways – those in which the cars are pulled up and down a steep gradient via a cable – are always a problem for railway historians. In France, at least, they were subject to the normal regulatory procedures, so can be classed as minor railways of Intérêt Local but on the other hand they have not been extensively researched, so information is sparse; all details listed here are, as the French say, offered "sous reserves".

In common with other countries, they comprised both haulage funiculars, with a single car hauled up and lowered via a winding drum, and balanced ones in which two cars were attached, at opposite ends of the line, via a common cable. There was also one short-lived example, at Nancy, which worked on the endless belt system, small 6-seat carriages being clipped on and unclipped as required by density of traffic. Some lines had a central rack for braking purposes and power included all three main systems

* water counterweight where a car tank was filled at the upper station and the car pulled its consort up, releasing water as it proceeded.

* steam stationary engine driving the cable drum

* electric engine driving the cable drum

Eventually electricity triumphed and almost all survivors use this as their motive power; a few use diesel engines.

The main period for the establishment of such lines was around the turn of the 19th - 20th Centuries and a number of those built then are still functioning, albeit usually completely refurbished more than once during their lives. The rise of ski-resorts and mass holidays has also, in recent years seen the construction of a number of specialised and often technologically sophisticated examples, mainly in the Eastern and South Eastern Alps; these have little historical interest but those known at time of printing are listed briefly.

1. Historically important funicular railways in France

name	gauge metres	length metres	rise metres	steepest mm/m	dates	power
Auron (St.Etienne-de-Tinée)	metre	200.00			1938-1976	electric
Aven-Armand	metre (pn)	208.00	62.50	300	1963-?	electric
Bancairon (Tinée)	metre?	790.00	274.00	670	1930-196	1a electric;
Bareges-Ayre	metre	1,850.00	825.00	570	1936-	electric
Belleville (Paris)	metre?	2,000.00		70	1891-1924	steam (1)
Besançon Breguille	metre	423.00	73.00	240	1913-1987	electric
Cannes - Super-Cannes	metre	900.00	300.00	478	1927-1965	electric
Cap Ferrat	600mm	100.00			1927-	electric
Evian	metre	800.00			1907-1969	electric. R1999
Grasse (Gare-Ville)	metre	544.00	112.00	233	1909-1938	electric
La Bourboule Charlannes	metre/SG*	600.00	108.00	500	1901-1955	water
Laon POMA	1.435m	1,500.00			1983-now	
Le Havre Côte Ste.Marie	1.44m	745.00	70.04	98	1895-1902	steam\electric +tram
Le Havre La Côte	1.20m	343.00	78.00	174	1890 now	electric. Abt brake

126. - PARIS
Le Sacré-Cœur de Montmartre
et le Funiculaire
The Sacred Heart of Montmartre
and the Funicular

A straightforward funicular, at Montmartre.

(AUTHOR'S COLLECTION)

LYON — Funiculaire
Saint-Just

The changeling: The Lyon line from St Just to St Jean, in its rack railway incarnation.

(FACS)

1. Historically important funicular railways in France continued...

name	gauge metres	length metres	rise metres	steepest mm/m	dates	power
Le Mont Dore le Capucin	metre	500.00	245.00	570	1898-now	electric
Le Tréport Terrasse	metre	120.00	620		1908-1944	electric
Lourdes (Pic-du-Jer)	metre	1,100.00	470.00	570	1900-now	electric
Luchon-la-Chaumière	metre	270.00	110.00	450	1894-1970	electric
Lyon – Croix-Paquet	1.435m	500.00			1891-1972	electric
Lyon – Rue Terme	1.435m				1862-1967	
Lyon – St.Jean – St.Just	metre		180		1878-1901	electric. rack
Lyon – St.Jean – St.Just (2)	1.3m	440.00	180		1958-now	electric. rack
Lyon – St.Paul-Loyasse	metre				1900-1937	
Lyon St.Jean - Fourvière	metre	830.00	109.00	310	1970r	electric
Marseilles ND de la Garde					1892-1967	
Menton Annonciade	metre	340.00	140.00	450	1914-1944	electric
Meudon Bellevue	metre?	183.00	52.00	300	1893-1934	steam
Montmartre	1.435m	113.00	36.00	350	1899-now*	1935 electric
Nancy Cure d'Air	750mm	229.00	47.80	29	1905-1908	electric
Nice Exposition	600mm?	66.00	21.00	337	1883-1884	hydraulic
Nice Grand Palais	700mm	70.00	17.00	250	1930-1980s	electric
Nice Hermitage	metre	168.00	45.00	300	1906-1944?	electric
Nice Zygofolis	metre	137.00	34.50	252	1987-1991	electric
Pau	metre	120.00	38.95	350	1907-1971	electric
Rives - Thonon-les-Bains	metre	229.00	47.00	220	1888-now	electric r1989
Rouen Bonsecours	1.20m	402.92	131.80	360	1892-1915	hydraulic
St.Hilaire du Touvet	metre	1,480.00	685.00	830	1924-now	electric
St.Martin-Vesubie (EDF)	metre	1,600.00			1958-1971	electric

(1) really a cable tramway on the San Fransisco model.

2. Modern funicular railways and guidedways

name	dates
Arcachon	
Bourg-St.Maurice	1989+
Courchevel	1992+
Deux-Alpes	1989+
Isola 2000	1989+
Mantes Guerville	1987+
Meribel les Allues	1989+
Mine Bleue (Noyant-la-Gravoyère)	1991+
Morzine	1987+
Penly (EDF)	1992+
Rocamadour	1989+
Tignes – La Grande Motte	1993+
Val d'Isère	1988+
Vaujany	1988+

APPENDIX 5
Manufacturers of Equipment for minor railways in France

This lists major French manufacturers of light railway locomotives & rolling stock (under the names by which they were commonly known), plus particularly influential foreign makers.

Motive power:

Alsthom: Sté Générale de Constructions Électriques et Mecaniques Alsthom, Tarbes. Formed by amalgamation of SACM and Thomson.

BDR: Ets. Baudet-Donon et Roussel, Argenteuil.

Battignoles: Originally Gouin et Cie, then the Societé de Constructions Ferroviaires de Battignoles (Anciens Etablissements Gouin et Cie). Paris.

Baume-et-Marpent: Belgium. tramcar manufacturers.

Berliet: Ets Berliet, Venissieux, Lyon.

Billard: Billard et Cie, later les Anciens Etablissements Billard et Cie, of Tours. Specialised in railmotors and light diesel tractors

Blanc Misseron: Les Ateliers du Nord de la France, Blanc Misseron was the French presence of SA La Metallurgique (qv). It sold but did not produce locomotives but appears to have been design leader for rolling stock which it produced in quantity. Most "Blanc Misseron" locomotives were actually built by the company's Ateliers de Tubize in Belgium and were allocated maker's numbers by both concerns.

Brissoneau-et-Lotz: Anciens Etablissemennts Brissoneau et Lotz, Creil.

Buffaud et Robatel: B Buffaud et T Robatel, Lyon.

Cail: E. Cail et Cie. Latterly Sté Française de Constructions Mecaniques (Anciens Etablissements Cail) Denain.

Campagne: Ets. Campagne et Cie., Paris. Specialised in light railcars and draisines

CFD: Compagnie des Chemins de Fer Départementaux, at Montmirail, Seine-et-Marne which became a maker in later years

CGL: see VFIL

COFERNA: Société de Constructions Ferroviaires et Navales, with Works near Sables d'Olonne in Vendée.

Cockerill: SA John Cockerill, Seraing, Belgium

Corpet, or Corpet, Louvet: Firm started by M. Lucien Corpet who later took as partner a M.L Louvet. After M. Corpet's death the firm was continued by his widow and M. Louvet, being known for some years as "Veuve Corpet et L Louvet"; subsquently it again became Corpet, Louvet et Cie.

Couillet: SA des Usines Metallurgiques du Hainaut, Couillet, Marcinelle, Belgium

Crochat: Henri Crochat et Cie, of Paris. This firm designed and produced petrol-electric vehicles until 1924 when it went into liquidation. The rights were bought by Decauville who produced under the name Decauville-Crochat

De Dion Bouton: Sté des Automobiles De Dion Bouton, Puteux. Road vehicle manufacturer which specialised in railmotors initially derived from road buses.

Decauville: Originally Paul Decauville et Cie, this became successively the Nouvelles Etablissements Decauville Ainé and then, in 1895, Les Anciens etablissements Decauville Ainé under which name it traded thenceforth. Works at Petit Bourg and elsewhere.

Fauvet-Girel: SA Fauvet-Girel, Arras. specialised in diesel tractors

Fives Lille: Cie de Fives Lille, with Works at Fives in the département du Nord, was a major manufacturer for the main line companies but also built many machines for secondary railways, in particular the CFD.

Franco-Belge: SA Franco-Belge de Material de Chemins de Fer. Works at Raismes (France) and la Croyère (Belgium)

Gouin: Ernest Gouin et Cie. see Battignoles

Horme-et-Buire:, Ets Horme-et-Buire, Lyon. electric tramcar, rolling stock and small-scale railcar manufacture.

Jeumont: Forges et Ateliers de Constructions Électriques Jeumont, with works at Jeumont.

Koechlin: Andre Koechlin et Cie, later SA Andre Koechlin, of St Etienne was active mainly in the early years of light railways

La Metallurgique: SA la Metallurgique, later SA les Ateliers Metallurgiques, was a large, Belgian based conglomerate with Works at various locations. Major locomotive Works was the Ateliers de Tubize, in Belgium, which sold both under its own name and through the French arm at Ateliers du Nord de la France, Blanc Misseron.

La Meuse: SA des Ateliers de Construction de la Meuse, Liege, Belgium.

le Creusot: Sté des Forges et Ateliers du Creusot (Usines Schneider). Originally Schneider et Cie.

Manage: Cie de Construction, Ateliers de Manage, Belgium. Provider of electric tramcars, especially for interurban lines

Marcinelle et Couillet: see Couillet

Michelin: Sté de Manufacture Française des Pneumatiques Michelin, Clermont Ferrand. Basically a tyre company which became involved in railcar manufacture as an extension of product use!

Moyse: SA Moyse, La Courneuve as successor to SA Locotracteurs Gaston Moyse.

Petolat: SA Boilot-Petolat (formerly A Petolat), Dijon. Constructor of light field railway equipment and draisines.

Pinguely: Sté Pinguely, Lyon, formerly A Pinguely et Cie. built many locomotives for monor railways.

Piguet: Ets. Piguet. Locomotive maufacturer based at Lyon, with works at Lyon-Anzin

Renault: Régie Nationale des Usines Renault, Boulogne-Billancourt. Formerly SA des Usines Renault, then nationalised.

St Leonard: SA des Ateliers Saint Léonard, Liege, Belgium.

SACM: Societé Alsacienne de Constructions Mecaniques with Works at Belfort, Graffenstaden and Mulhouse. French title for Alsace-Lorraine firm building both main-line and minor railway locomotives.

SLM: Schweizerische Locomotive u Maschinenfabrik, alias the Societé Suisse. Major Swiss locomotive manufacturer. Works at Winterthur.

Schneider: Schneider et Cie, le Creusot. See also Le Creusot

Socofer: Sté. Socofer, Tours. successors to Billard.

Soule: railcar maker with works at Bordeaux. Now part of the CFD organisation.

Thomson: Sté Thomson, builder of electrically powered vehicles. Joined with SACM to form Alsthom.

Tubize: see la Metallurgique

VFIL: Cie Générale des Voies Ferrées d'Intérêt Local. This operating company built a fair number of diesel locomotive and railmotors at its Lumbres Works in Pas de Calais.

Verney: Originally Baert et Verney, of le Mans, later removed to the Ardennes as Societé des Constructions Ferroviares (SCF). Sometimes referred to as SCF Verney.

Venissieux: Les Constructions Électriques de France, Venissieux, Lyon. short-lived but influential provider of interurban stock.

Weidknecht: F. Weidkecht, Paris. Firm which produced several series of light 60cm or metre gauge locomotives both for Decauville and under its own name.

Rolling Stock: Where the firm also manufactured motive power, the short name only is given

Blanc Misseron: see la Metallurgique, above

Carel et Fouché: coachbuilders of le Mans. The group also held concessions for a number of light railways.

Decauville

Desouches et David: major rolling stock producer for main line and light railways.

Dyle et Bacalan: International firm with Works at Bordeaux (France) and la Dyle (Belgium).

Lorraine Dietrich: Sté Lorraine des Anciens Etablissements de Dietrich & Cie.

Nivelles: Ateliers de Nivelles – major Belgian Works of SA la Metallurgique (qv).

Working bibliography

This bibliography contains two types of item: Books and periodical articles. In turn these are organised into: general sources, whether or not of recent origin; details of sources relating to specific lins or systems, arranged by region. No claim is made for its completeness since many publications are local and books are being published almost every month.

Part 1: Books

A: General sources

1. Works of reference

Description Raisonnée de Quelques Chemins de Fer à Voie Etroite, Ledoux C; Dunod, Paris 1874

Light Railways, Mackay J C; Crosby Lockwood, London, 1896

Light Railways at Home and Abroad, Cole W H; Griffin & Co, London 1899

Les Chemins de Fer d'Intérêt Local, Tramways et Services Publiques Automobiles, Vasseur L; Baillère et fils, Paris, 1926

Les Chemins de Fer Urbains Parisiens, Biette L; Baillere, Paris, 1928

A Travers les Chemins de Fer, Falaize J & Girod-Ey, Edns Denoel, Paris, 1948

Les Tramways Français, Arrivetz J; author, Lyon, 1957

Chemins de Fer de Montagne Francais 1, Vilain L; Vigot Frères, Paris 1960

Chemins de Fer de Montagne Francais 2, Vilain L; Vigot Frères, Paris 1964

Light Railways, their Rise and Decline, Davies W J K; Ian Allan, London 1964

Railway Holiday in France, Behrend G, David & Charles, 1964

French Minor Railways, Davies WJK, David & Charles, 1965

Evolution du Material Moteur..des CF de l'Etat, Vilain LM, Edns Vincent, Freal, 1967

Histoire des Transports dans les Villes de France, Robert J; Author, 1974

Tourist Railways of France, Haworth R, Rapid Transit Pubns, 1995

Tourist Railways of France 2nd edn, Haworth R, Rapid Transit Pubns, 1996

2. Military light railways in France

Railway Gazette: Special War Transportation Number. RG 1920

Light Railways of the First World War, Davies W J K, David & Charles, 1966

Heeresfeldbahnen, Gottwaldt A B, Motor Buch Verlag 1986

Narrow Gauge to No Mans Land, Dunn R, Benchmark Pubns 1990

Voie de 60 Sur Les Fronts Francais.., Cenac C, author, 1991

Voie de 60 Militaire Vol 1 – 1892-1914, Pradayrol J, Assn ALOIS, 1996

Light Track from Arras, Heritage TR, Plateway Press (repr, 1999)

3. Locomotive & stock manufacturers

Corpet, Louvet et Cie, Klingan K, et al, Industrial Railway Society, 1969

Decauville – ce nom qui fit le tour du monde, Bailly R, Edns Amatteis, 1989

Decauville Steam Locomotives (Works List), Clingan KW & Lanham , Industrial Rly Society, 1993

Decauville: Locomotives Catalogue 130 Pt 4, anon, Confrerie des Amateu, 1990

Decauville: Catalogue 1916.

Locomotives Construites par Pinguely, Piguet, Buffaud-et-Robatel. FACS Cahier No.3 n/d

Petolat (1922 catalogue), anon, Compagnons de la Vapew, 1997

Renault: Le Materiel Ferroviaire, Grannec M, ETAI Boulogne, 1999

4. Industral Railways in France

The Industrial Railway Society publishes regional handbooks listing industrial concerns and their motive power; these are periodically updated and supplements are issued occasionally. Not all appear to be in print at any one time.

B: Book series normally relating to more than one railway

1. Les Petits Trains de Jadis; Domengie H & Banaudo J, Edns du Cabri, dates as below.

An encyclopedaeic series of which five volumes are devoted to minor ralways: This must be regarded as the main current source of reference, providing basic historical details plus outline informaton on routes, locomotive and rolling stock for almost every classified minor railway in France and the result of some 40 years of work by Henri Domengie and his contributors.

Petits Trains de Jadis 6 – Sud Est de la France, 1983
Petits Trains de Jadis 7 – Sud-Ouest de la France, 1985
Petits Trains de Jadis 8 – Ouest de la France, 1989
Petits Trains de Jadis 9 – Nord de la France, 1995
Petits Trains de Jadis 10 – Est de la France, 1995

2. Le Siecle des Petits Trains. Various authors, Edns Cenomane/La Vie du Rail, dates as below.

A continuing series each dealing mainly with a single département or geographical area. It concentrates more on the social and ecomomic history of the lines than on technical details but is very valuable for describing their ambience and effects on their area. Individual titles are also listed under the appropriate region.

Petit Anjou (le siecle des petits trains), 1988
Petits Trains à l'Assault du Jura, 1991
Petits Trains d'Ille-et-Vilaine, 1986
Petits Trains de Savoie et de Haute Savoie, 1996
Petits Trains de Touraine, 1988
Petits trains du Morbihan et de Loire Inférieure, 1993
Vendée des Petits Trains, 1987
Calvados pour les petits trains, 1997
Petits Trains et Tramways Haut-Normands, 1994
Quand Les Petits Trains Faisaient La Manche, 1988
Petit Train Lomgtemps (Ile de la Réunion), 1992

3. Sur les Rails en..... Edns du Cabri, various dates

A continuing series providing general historical information on all public railways within a stated geographical area; individual volumes will include some details of minor railways. but in general the information appears to be taken from already published studies.

C: Books relating to single railways or clusters of lines in a geographical area

1. Region Ouest

Calvados pour les petits trains, De Dieuleveult A, et al, Edns Cenomane, 1997
Petit Anjou (le siecle des petits trains), Harouy M et al, Edns Cenomane, 1988
Petits Trains d'Ille-et-Vilaine, Dieuleveult A et al, Edns Cenomane, 1986
Petits trains du Morbihan et de Loire Inférieure, Hulot R, Edns Cenomane, 1993
Petits Trains et Tramways Haut-Normands, Bertin H, Edns Cenomane, 1994
Quand Les Petits Trains Faisaient La Manche, Dieuleveult A & Haro, Edns Cenomane, 1988
Réseau Breton, Gravett G, Oakwood Press, 1999
Réseau Breton, Laederich P et al, Edns de l'Ormet, 1990
Vendée des Petits Trains, Harouy M, Edns Cenomane, 1987

2. Region Nord

Chemins de Fer de Grande Banlieue, Hulot R, FACS, 1984
Le Chemin de Fer de Paris à Arpajon, Lamand P & Peyrafitte J, FACS, 1987
Petits Trains et Tramways du Val d'Oise, Wagner C, Edns de Valhermeil, 1995
Railways of the Baie de Somme, Pacey P, Oakwood Press, 2000
Les Tramways Parisiens, Robert J, author, 1992.

3. Region Est

Cremaillère de Langres, Gueniot G, author, 1995

4. Region Sud-Est

Annemasse-Sixt, Annecy-Thones, Chapuis J & Renaud J, Edns du Cabri, 1994
Chemin de Fer de l'Est de Lyon, Domengie et al, Edns du Cabri, 1996
Chemin de Fer de la Mure, Bouillin P & Wurmser, authors, Grenoble, 1995
Chemins de Fer du Vivarais, Arrivetz J & Bejui P, Presses et Edns Ferr, 1986
Chemins de Fer Corses, Bejui P, Edns du Cabri 1987
De Nice à Chamonix, Robert J, Author, 1961
Histoire des Transports à Lyon, Arrivetz J, Author,

1966

Petit Train du Buis, Mansip V et al, Edns de l'Ormet, 1993

Petite Histoire du CF..de St Georges de Commiers à la Mure, Reymond R, author, 1978

Petits Trains à l'Assaut du Jura, Boivin M et al, Edns Cenomane, 1991

Petits Trains de Savoie et de Haute Savoie, Messiez P, Edns Cenomane, 1996

Siecle du Train des Pignes,Vol 1: Banaudo J, Edns du Cabri, 1992

Train du Littoral (Vol 2); Banaudo J, Edns du Cabri, 1999

Trains de Mont Blanc Vol 1, Gide J-P & Banaudo J, Edns du Cabri, 1998

Tramways de l'Ain, Domengie H, Edns du Cabri, 1987

Tramways de Nice et de la Côte d'Azur, Robert J, author, 1988

Tramways Valence-Saint Peray, Courant R, Author, 1973

Voies Ferrées du Dauphine, Boyer H & Bouillin R, Author, 1983

Tacot et Galoche en Roannais et Forez, Toublanc F, Edns de l'Ormet, 1994 (light railways in Loire)

Vivarais Narrow Gauge, Organ J, Middleton Press, 1999

Tacots du Bourbonnais, Laederich P, Edns de l'Ormet, 1993

Region Sud-Ouest

50 Ans d'un Tortillard, Gauthier E, Author, 1955

Chemins de Fer d'Intérêt Local de l'Hérault, Maillet M, Edns du Cabri, 1984

Cremaillères Jumelles des Pyrenées, Cenac Dr C, author, 1993

Landes de Gascogne (l'extraordinaire réseau des), Lacombe C & Chanuc L, Edns du Cabri, 1987

le Mata-Burros, (CF des Pyrenées-Orientales), Christol & Guimezanes, Edns du Cabri, 1999

Petit Train de Castres a Murat et a Brassac, Gaches P, Author, 1971

Petit Train Jaune de Cerdagne, Churet J, Edns du Cabri, 1984

Petits Trains de Corrèze, Sorbier M, F.A.C.S., 1990

Petits Trains du Loiret, Various, FACS/AMTP, 1992

Tramways de la Corrèze, Maligne J, la Regordane, 1993

Petits Trains de Touraine, Dieuleveult A & Edom, Edns Cenomane, 1988

Part 2: Select bibliography of major periodical articles (not comprehensive)

Various magazines and societies have been recording French minor railway history for the past 40 years and more. The major commercial ones were La Vie du Rail, then house-organ of SNCF, which over many years published short notes and a number of more detailed articles; and Loco-Revue, in essence a modelling magazine, but which has from time to time included prototype articles: a recent addition, Voie Libre, is promising to continue the theme. The major relevant amateur journals are by:

• Federation des Amis des CF Secondaires (FACS), Gare de l'Est, 75475 PARIS, which publishes a journal originally Chemins de Fer Secondaires (CFS); more recently titled Chemins de Fer Regionaux et Urbains (CFR). This journal has always included high-quality detailed articles on specific aspects (eg railcars) and on individual systems.

• Association Picarde pour la Preservation et l'Entretien des Vehicules Anciens (APPEVA). BP 106, 80 001 AMIENS, publishes Voie Etroite, which has printed very detailed studies of military light railways and more general notes on some of the lesser known public light railways.

• Musee des Transports de la Vallée du Sausseron (MTVS) at time of publication. Published a high-quality journal detailed studies of individual systems and aspects of light railway history under the title Magazine des Tramways à Vapeur et des Secondaires (MTVS). Now ceased publication.

Various more specialist local history societies have from time to time also published useful articles. Those known to the writer but not replicated elsewhere are included but there are undoubtedly others!

Notes: references are to:

• CFS Chemins de Fer Secondaires
• CFR Chemins de Fer Regionaux et Urbains

- HCMF Histoire des Commmunications dans le Midi de la France
- MTVS Magazine des Tramways à Vapeur et des Secondaires
- VE Voie Etroite

In general CFS prior to 1965 are not listed because they were duplicated and ephemeral; in addition most articles were revised and reprinted later.

In the individual railways section, codes indicate:

cfd	cf départemental
CFD	Cie des CF Départementaux
cfe	cf économiques
cfil	cf d'intérêt local
SE	Sté Générale des CF Economiques
td	tramway départemental
te	tramway electrique
vfe	voies ferrées economiques

1. General references

CFD 100 years	MTVS 19
CGTVN (canal haulage lines)	CFS 1967 (81)
French CFIL 1927	MTVS 50
French CFIG 1927	MTVS 51
Harel de la Noë (person)	CFR 1978 (147)
Houillères du Nord/Pas de Calais	CFR 1984 (185)
Monorail Larmanjat	En Aulnoye Jadis 10
locotracteurs	MTVS 38
railcars	MTVS 51

2. Military light railways

Bergerac Powder Works 1914-18	CFR 1975 (127)
General articles: VE. most issues from No.75 onward!	
Regions Liberées (general)	VE 95/98/99
Regions Liberées (60cm)	CFR 1984 (184)
Regions Liberées (Pas de Calais)	VE 122-124
Regions Liberées (Reims & Marne)	VE 131-133

3. Technical articles

Billard mfr	MTVS 24; CFR 1971 (108)
Brissoneau et Lotz mfr	
	MTVS 36; CFR 1998 (269), 1999 (276)
CFD locos & tractors	MTVS 48, 49; CFR 1977 (140)
Cail, locos for Charentes	CFR 1997 (264)
Constns Électriques de France mfr	CFR 1992 (234)
Crochat mfr	MTVS 36
De Dion Bouton mfr	MTVS 21; CFR 1987 (199)
De Dion Bouton railbuses (J series)	VE 167
Hercule mfr	CFR 1997 (263)
Maroc: 60cm gauge mallets	CFR 1973 (115)
Pinguely mfr	CFR 1997 (259)
Purrey mfr	CFR 1991 (223/5/6)
Renault mfr	MTVS 28; CFS 1968 (90)

Serpollet mfr.	CFR 1980 (153)
Tartary mfr	MTVS 21
Tubize/Blanc Misseron mfr	
	CFR 1998 (268), CFR 1999 (272/4/6)

4. Tramways Urbains

Aix les Bains Twys	CFR 1971 (103)
Amiens Twys	CFR 1995 (247)
Aubervillers (Paris) Twys	CFR 1999 (275)
Avignon Twys	CFR 1989 (211)
Belfort Twys	CFR 1994 (245); 1995 (247)
Bergerac Twys	CFR 1975 (127)
Besançon Twys	CFR 1990 (222)
Beziers Twys	CFR 1992 (233)
Blois Twys	CFR 1973 (118)
Bourges Twys	CFS 1966 (75)
Caen Twys	CFR 1983 (180)
Cassel Twys	CFR 1994 (242)
Clermont-Ferrand Twys	CFR 1996 (255-56)
Dieppe Twys	CFR 1993 (240)
Dijon Twys	CFR 1977 (132)
ELRT	CFS 1965 (70), 1967 (80)
ELRT	CFR 1972 (109-114), 1973 (115)
Elbeuf Twys	CFR 1969 (92)
Grenoble Twys	CFR 1987 (201)
le Havre Twys	CFR 1971 (105); 1973 (115)
le Treport Twys	CFR 1976 (135/7)
le Mans Twys	CFR 1988 (206)
Limoges Twys	CFS 1966 (76/8)
Lourdes Twys	CFR 1991 (227)
Lyon Twys	CFR 1983 (177-78)
Marseilles Twys	CFS 1967 (80)
Marseilles Twys	
	CFR 1971 (104), 1975 (127), 1978 (145)
Melun Twys	CFR 1989 (215)
Metz Twys	CFR 1970 (102), 1997 (261)
Monaco Twys	CFR 1990 (220)
Montargis Twys	CFS 1968 (88)
Montpellier Twys	CFR 1985 (191), 1992 (191)
Montpellier Twys	CFR 1992 (229)
Mulhouse Twys	CFS 1961 (46), 1980 (162)
Nantes Twys	CFR 1984 (183)
Orleans Twys	CFR 1976 (138)
Ouest Varois Twys	CFR 1990 (220)
Paris Twys	CFR 1970 (101), 1973 (117),
Paris Twys	CFR 1982 (169/74), 1984 (183/85)
Paris Twys	CFR 1986 (194)
Paris Twys (Nogentais)	CFR 1987 (199)
Pau Twys	MTVS Hors Serie Pau
Rennes Twys	CFR 1972 (110)
Rodez Twys	CFS 1968 (85)
Rouen Twys	CFS 1965/6 (71-74)
Sète Twys	CFR 1987 (201-02)
St Avold Twys	CFR 1983 (175)
St Quentin Twys	CFR 1970 (97)
Strasbourg Twys	CFS 1962 (53), CFR 1980 (157)
Thionville Twys	CFR 1997 (263)

Tours Twys	CFR 1970 (98)
Versailles Twys	CFR 1977 (144)

5. Public light railways

Region Ouest

Anjou cfil railcars	VE 117
Armoricains cfil	VE 65; CFR 1983 (175-76)
Brest-le Conquet td	CFR 1984 (184)
Bretons td	CFR 1972 (110)
Caen à la Mer cf	CFR 1985 (187-88)
Calvados cf	CFR 1983/4 (179-81)
Charentes et Deux Sevres CFD	MTVS 15
Châteaubriant-Erbray cf	CFR 1980 (157)
Cherence le Roussel: see Monsecret	
Cormeilles-Glos Montfort cf	CFS 1967 (83-84)
Côtes du Nord cfil	CFR 1975 (131)
Dinard-St Briac td	CFR 1972 (110)
Deux Sèvres td	CFR 1981 (163)
Eure-et-Loir td	VE 129; CFR 1970 (99); 1997 (262)
Finistère cfd	CFR 1983 (175-76); 1984 (184)
Ille et Vilaine td	CFR 1972 (110)
la Baule, Twy de	CFR 1974 (126)
la Trinité-Etel, Twy de	CFR 1975 (127)
Mamers-St Calais	CFR 1992 (232)
Monsecret-Tinchebray SE	CFR 1970 (97); 1989 (213)
Morbihan cfil	CFR 1975 (127); 1979 (152)
Nantes-Legé-Rochesevière cf	
	MTVS 30; CFR 1968 (88)
Normandie CF de	CFR 1979 (153)
Normands, cf in WW2	VE 135
Normands, Twys	CFR 1999 (271)
Orne vfe	CFR 1989 (212)
Réseau Breton	CFS 1968 (87); CFR 1975 (130)
Rotheneuf	CFR 1972 (110)
Royan	CFR 1977 (139)
St Romain de Colbosc td	CFR 1979 (153)
Sables d'Olonne Twys	CFR 1981 (168)
Sarthe td	CFR 1969 (91)
Sarthe td (La Flèche lines)	VE 118
Seine-Maritime SE (Aumale-Envermeu)	
	CFR 1994 (246)
Vendée td	CFR 1981 (166-68)
Vendée td in WW2	VE 119

Region Nord

Artois cfil	CFS 1966 (77-78)
Berck Plage-Paris Plage	CFS 1965/6 (72; 75)
CF sur Route, ste de	CFR 1997 (261)
Chauny-St Gobain cf	CFS 1965 (68)
Ecully td	CFR 1974 (121)
Feuquières-Ault td	CFR 1995 (249)
Grande Banlieue cf	CFS 1965/6 (72-74/8)
Laon cf de	CFS 1966 (75); CFR 1992 (230)
Meru – Labosse cf	CFR 1999 (274)
Paris-St Germain td	CFR 1974 (122-23)
Quend-Fort Mahon Twy	CFR 1979 (151)
St.Germain – Poissy Twy	CFR 1965 (66)

St Quentin military	CFR 1970 (97)
Somme, SE Réseau de la	CFR 1999 (273)
Somme, SE de (Amiens-Aumale)	VE 133
Sud de l'Aisne cf	CFR 1990 (218)
Tergnier-St Gobain te	CFR 1994 (245)
Versailles à Maule, td	CFR 1965 (66)
Vallée de Celles td	CFR 1992 (232)
Valmondois-Marines SE ligne de	MTVS 31
Valenciennes te	VE 59
Voie de 60, Sté de la (Vis-en-Artois)	VE 123-124
Woincourt-Ault-Onival td	CFR 1995 (249)

Region Est

Aube td	MTVS 23
Bussang-Wesserling	CFR 1984 (184)
Foulain-Nogent en Bassigny cf	CFS 1967 (82)
Gerardmer-la Schlucht td	VE 69; CFR 1990 (217)
Gerardmer - Remirmont td	CFR 1989 (216)
Langres	CFR 1994 (241)
Lunéville-Einville td	MTVS 25
Lunéville-Blamont-Badonviller td	MTVS 27
Lutzelbourg-Drulingen, ligne de	CFR 1991 (226)
Meuse CFIL	CFR 1997 (264)
Meusienne cf	VE 85, 86
Morhange Steam Twys	CFR 1986 (195)
Munster-la Schlucht	VE 69; CFR 1989 (216)
Novéant-Gorze SE	CFS 1965 (70)
Pontarlier à Mouthe cf	CFS 1976 (133)
Ribeauvillé td	CFR 1993 (240)
St.Avold Twy	CFR 1983 (175)
Sud de la Marne td	CFR 1998 (267)
Territoire de Belfort cfil	CFS 1967 (79)
Thionville-Mondorf SE	CFS 1965 (70)
Toul - Thiaucourt SE	VE 79
Vallée de Celles Twy	CFS 1991 (231)
Vosges, td (Remiremont-Gerardmer)	see Gerardmer
Woëvre, SE réseau de la	VE 90-91

Region Sud-Est

Ain td	CFS 1965 (68)+ 56/62
Ain td (Tenay – Hauteville)	VE 143
Alpes Maritimes td	MTVS 46; CFR 1978 (150)
Ardèche td	HCMF3; MTVS 22
Beaujolais cfil	MTVS 52; CFR 1980 (159-60)
Camargue	CFR 1977 (143)
Centre, CF du (Vichy-Cusset-Malavaux)	VE 121
Chamonix - Montenvers cf	CFR 1981 (165)
Cornas Mines Rlys	CFR 1986 (196)
Centre, SE réseau du	VE 76
Corsica CFD	MTVS 32; CFS 1967 (79)
Corsica CFD	CFR 1973 (119); 1998 (270)
Corses cf	see Corsica
Côte d'Or cfd	CFR 1979 (155)

Dauphiné (TOD)	see Ouest du..
Dijon - Gevrey-Chambertin, Twy de	CFR 1979 (155)
Doubs cfd	MTVS 42; 43
Est de Lyon	CFR 1973 (119)
Feurs-Panissières (monorail)	CFR 1981 (164)
Haute-Rhône cf	CFR 1989 (214)
Jura cf vicinaux	MTVS 10
la Mure cf	CFR 1988 (205)
Lagny-Mortcerf CFD	MTVS 44
le Revard	CFR 1971 (103); 1995 (252)
Lozere CFD	VE 138; CFR 1974 (125)
Meaux-Dammartin td	MTVS 45
Mont Blanc, Twy du	CFR 1985 (192)
Montenvers CF du	CFR 1981 (165)
Montereau - Château-Landon CFD	CFR 1988 (206)
Nice et du Littoral te	CFS 1968 (88)
Nievre, SE de la	CFR 1998 (269)
Orange-Buis les Baronnies SE	MTVS 35
Ouest du Dauphiné td	
	CFS 1966 (78); CFR 1987 (202-03)
Ouest-Varois Twy	CFR 1990 (220)
Pontarlier-Mouthe Ed	CFR 1976 (133)
Provence cf	CFR 1971 (104); CFR 1972
	(109/11-114); CFR 1998 (266)
Provence cf (mineral traffic)	VE 104
Puy-de-Dôme cf du	VE 61; CFR 1996 (255)
Revard cf du	CFR 1995 (252)
Rhône-Saône et Loire cfd	CFR 1986 (194)
Rhône-et-Loire cfil	CFR 1982 (173-74)
Riom-Volvic cf	CFS 1968 (87)
Rochebelle, CF Minière	CFR 1979 (154)
Saône-et-Loire cfil	VE 109
Salins de Giraud, (ind)	CFR 1996 (258)
Savoie td (Chambery)	CFR 1971 (103/8)
St Gervais-Vallorcine	
	CFR 1977 (141); 1994 (246); 1997 (263)
Seine et Marne CFD	MTVS 16
Seine-et-Marne SE	MTVS 37
Sud-France cf	CFR 1978 (146/50); CFR 1998 (265)
Sud-France (military uses)	VE 113-115
Valence-St Peray td	CFR 1974 (122)
Vertaizon-Billom cf	CFS 1965 (68)
Vichy-Cusset td	CFR 1974 (126)
Viricelles-St Symphorien te	CFR 1982 (172)
Vivarais CFD	CFR 1974 (125)
Vivarais CFD	CFR 1993 (237)
Yonne cfil	CFR 1988 (209)
Yonne cfil (réseau de Sens)	CFR 1990 (221)

Bayonne-Lycée-Biarritz	HCMF2; CFR 1975 (132)
Bordeaux-Cadillac td	MTVS 34
Bordeaux-Camarsac td	HCMF8
Cap Ferret Twy de	CFR 1994 (244)
Castres-Toulouse VFDM	CFR 1978 (149)
Cerdagne SNCF	CFR 1982 (170/74)
Chalosse et du Bearn tv	MTVS 33
Chinon-Richelieu CFD	CFR 1969 (92)
Corrèze PO	CFR 1969 (93)
Corrèze td	CFS 1965 (67)
Dordogne td	HCMF9/13; MTVS 39; CFR 1996 (257)
Haute Vienne cfd	MTVS 41; CFS 1965 (69); 1966 (73)
Indre et Loire CFD	MTVS 18; CFR 1969 (94-95)
La Bigorre, td	CFR 1969 (96)
La Rhune cf	CFR 1973 (120)
La Testé-Cazaux cfil	CFR 1995 (249)
le Blanc-Argent cf	MTVS 8; CFR 1983 (176)
Ligre Rivière - Richelieu CFD	CFR 1969 (92)
Loir et Cher Électriques te	CFR 1973 (118)
Loir et Cher Vapeur td	CFR 1973 (116)
Loiret td	CFR 1975 (128)
Lot et Garonne td	MTVS 47
Luchon-Superbagnères	CFR 1996 (253)
Marignac au Val d'Aran te	CFR 1999 (276)
Pau-Oloron-Mauleon cf	MTVS HS Pau
Perigord cfil	HCMF9
Pierrefitte-Cauterets-Luz te	
	HCMF4; CFR 1995 (250-51)
Pithiviers-Toury td	CFR 1976 (134)
Pyrénées Orientales cf	CFS 1968 (89)
Pyrénées Orientales (Haut-Vallespir)	VE 81
Réalmont-Labouterié td	HCMF5; CFR 1985 (190)
Réseau Basque VFDM	CFR 1973 (120)
St Céré-Bretonoux Biars td	HCMF3/6
Ste.Maure (stn-town)	CFR 1969 (92)
St Trojan Twy (Ile d'Oleron)	VE 165
Sud Ouest cfil	HCMF7; 10; 12
Tarn cfd	CFS 1965 (70) + 56
Tarn Twys à vapeur du	
	VE 106; CFR 1972 (113); 1985 (190)
Tarn & Garonne td	HCMF2

Addenda

St Gervais-Vallorcine	
Mont Blanc, Twy	} le Train Special 20.
Chamonix-Montenvers cf	

Region Sud-Ouest

Aude td	CFR 1982 (171)
Bayonne-Anglet-Biarritz	HCMF2; CFR 1975 (132)

INDEX OF HISTORICAL REFERENCES

To provide a complete index to a book of this nature would require almost the length of a chapter, so compromises have to be made. If you are, for example, trying to trace reference to a particular line or system you presumably have some idea at least as to where it is situated. At the end of each of the regional gazetteer chapters (7-11) are lists of the light railways and urban tramways in that region. If you then scan through the chapter until you see the appropriate departement in a sub-heading, you will be very close. If you are wondering what there is in a given area you can do exactly the same! This skeleton index therefore simply references the main historical events and any major descriptions of individual lines or technical matters in a historical context (mainly chapters 1-6). Highlighted page references are to route maps.